A
ROSS MACDONALD
COMPANION

A
ROSS MACDONALD
COMPANION

Robert L. Gale

GREENWOOD PRESS
Westport, Connecticut • London

Library of Congress Cataloging-in-Publication Data

Gale, Robert L., 1919–
    A Ross Macdonald companion / Robert L. Gale.
        p.   cm.
    Includes bibliographical references and index.
    ISBN 0–313–32057–8 (alk. paper)
    1. Macdonald, Ross, 1915—Encyclopedias.   2. Detective and mystery stories,
American—Encyclopedias.   3. Archer, Lew (Fictitious character)—Encyclopedias.   I.
Title.
PS3525.I486Z67   2002
813'.52—dc21   2001058645

British Library Cataloguing in Publication Data is available.

Library of Congress Catalog Card Number: 2001058645
ISBN: 0–313–32057–8

First published in 2002

Greenwood Press, 88 Post Road West, Westport, CT 06881
An imprint of Greenwood Publishing Group, Inc.
www.greenwood.com

Printed in the United States of America

The paper used in this book complies with the
Permanent Paper Standard issued by the National
Information Standards Organization (Z39.48–1984).

10 9 8 7 6 5 4 3 2 1

For three dear granddaughters
DIANA, CAROLINE, and STEPHANIE

Contents

Preface

Kenneth Millar, better known as Ross Macdonald, was unique in the annals of literary history. Most writers, I suppose, are. But Ross Macdonald (as I will call him from this page forward) was most unusual. He was born in California to Canadian-born parents who were unstable, especially his father, who abandoned his wife and their only child. Macdonald's mother was left so impoverished that she soon took her little boy to an orphanage in Canada, only to be dissuaded by his tears from leaving him there. After much anguish and trouble in early adolescence, Macdonald married Margaret Ellis Sturm, whom he had first seen years earlier in their Canadian high school. They separately published their first fiction in a 1931 issue of the magazine in the collegiate and vocational school they attended in Kitchener, Ontario. They were married in 1938.

Their one child, bright, attractive, but unstable, twice ran afoul of the law, married, and died in her late twenties. Her one child died of a drug overdose in his mid-twenties. Before, during, and after all this, Macdonald and his wife published fifty or so novels, as well as other works. Her eyesight gradually deteriorated until she was declared legally blind, but she continued writing. Macdonald, a vigorous man, developed Alzheimer's disease but continued swimming with his faithful dog. Macdonald died some three years after the onset of his dreadful disease. His wife survived him by eleven years, stoical to the end.

Macdonald's first story, "The South Sea Soup Co.," parodies detective fiction à la Sir Arthur Conan Doyle. Soon Macdonald began to grace that still undervalued subgenre with what several discerning critics have called the best crime and mystery novels ever written. W.H. Auden, whom Macdonald knew personally, helped dignify detective fiction by confessing in print his addiction to it. Macdonald's nearest American rivals for accolades are Dashiell Hammett, Raymond Chandler (and—may I add?—

Mickey Spillane, whom Macdonald despised). Macdonald admired and made use of techniques developed by Hammett and Chandler. One adept reviewer put it this way: "Without in the least abating my admiration for Dashiell Hammett and Raymond Chandler, I should like to venture the heretical suggestion that Ross Macdonald is a better novelist than either of them" (Anthony Boucher, *New York Times Book Review*, January 24, 1965). *The Maltese Falcon* by Hammett remains a tradition-motivating classic; some of his other fictional pieces, however, especially his Continental Op short stories, border on the crudely gory. Chandler's delineation of his hero Philip Marlowe is complex, beginning with *The Big Sleep*, while his style in general has a durable veneer of sophistication. Macdonald was aware of his early debt to these predecessors but later justifiably asserted that he outranked them both. Eudora Welty put the matter nicely: "He [Macdonald] had always acknowledged and respected his early teachers and influences, but he found his own voice and became a more serious and complex writer than Chandler and Hammett ever were. He pressed his work toward an end far different from what either of them had tried for" ("Finding the Connections," *Inward Journey: Ross Macdonald)*.

A *Ross Macdonald Companion* may help all sorts of readers—young, middle-aged, getting on, scholarly, and feverish in rising degrees for crime-fiction addiction—to develop renewed respect for Macdonald. But, please, read Macdonald first and only afterward consult my *Companion*, which is designed never prematurely to reveal who-done-it but instead to remind his readers and refresh their memories, so that, perhaps, they will approach him with a little better understanding and return to re-reading him more pleasurably and profitably. I have written about the plots and the characters in his twenty-four novels and twelve short stories, and also about the major nonfictional aspects of his life, including his family members, and his most significant personal and professional acquaintances. Exigencies of space have required me to be terse occasionally, which I regret.

Macdonald is a joy to read, for many reasons. His handling of background and foreground scenes is spectacular. Surely no writer has used the California setting to better effect. His characterizations are subtle, not only when his attention is devoted to Lew Archer, his nonpareil private detective, but also when he portrays thoughtless commercial types, worried parents, their footloose offspring, and minorities. His dialogue is on target—quick, revealing, and as dramatic as any breakneck film script. Humor often lightens his violence, which is almost never gratuitous. Given his background, Macdonald understandably often concentrates on dysfunctional families at university locations. His plots, many times with connected if tangential subplots, are intriguing, challenging, and replete with pitfalls for the slipshod reader. The moral of most of Macdonald's writings is that greed damages the environment, corrupts legitimate commercial enterprises, and—worst of all—wrecks loving human relationships, most wrenchingly through whole generations of families.

It is a pleasure to express my thanks to my colleagues in the Department of English at the University of Pittsburgh, especially H. David Brumble III, and to innumerable friends at Hillman Library, at Pitt, especially those working at the interlibrary loan desks, notably Patricia Duff. Finally, my love, always, to my wife Maureen, and to John, Jim, Christine, and Bill.

Chronology

1915   Kenneth Millar (1915–1983) born December 13 in Los Gatos (near San José), California, the son of John Macdonald Millar* (1873–1932) and Anna Moyer Millar* (c. 1875–1935).

1919   Kenneth moves to Vancouver, British Columbia; parents separate (but never get divorced); Kenneth lives with Canadian relatives (to 1928).

1928   Attends St. John's School, Winnipeg, Manitoba.

1930   Attends Kitchener-Waterloo Collegiate and Vocational School, Ontario (to 1932).

1933   Enrolls at the University of Western Ontario, London, Ontario (earns B.A. with honors, 1938).

1936   Travels in Europe, biking in England, Ireland, France, and Germany (to 1937).

1938   Marries Margaret Ellis Sturm (1915–1994) (*see* Millar, Margaret); takes graduate courses at Ontario College of Education, University of Toronto (to 1939).

1939   Daughter, Linda Jane Millar Pagnusat,* born (1939–1970); Millar teaches English and history, Kitchener Collegiate Institute (to 1941).

1941   Enrolls at the University of Michigan (M.A., 1942; Ph.D., 1952).

1942   Is teaching fellow, University of Michigan (1942–1944, 1948–1949).

1944   Publishes first novel, *The Dark Tunnel* (by Kenneth Millar), serves in U.S. Naval Reserve in Pacific, as communications officer, from ensign to lieutenant junior grade, aboard escort carrier *Shipley Bay* (to 1946).

1946   *Trouble Follows Me* (Kenneth Millar); moves to Santa Barbara, California.

1947   *Blue City* (Kenneth Millar)

1948   *The Three Roads* (Kenneth Millar)

1949   *The Moving Target* (by John Macdonald)

1950   *The Drowning Pool* (by John Ross Macdonald)

1951   *The Way Some People Die* (John Ross Macdonald)

1952   *The Ivory Grin* (John Ross Macdonald)

1953   *Meet Me At the Morgue*

1954   *Find a Victim* (John Ross Macdonald, with statement that he is Kenneth Millar)

1955   *The Name Is Archer* (John Ross Macdonald)

1956   *The Barbarous Coast* (by Ross Macdonald, as are all later works); daughter charged with vehicular homicide; Millar treated by psychotherapist in Menlo Park, California (to 1957).

1957   Reviews books for *San Francisco Chronicle* (to 1960).

1958   *The Doomsters*

1959   *The Galton Case*; daughter's eleven-day disappearance causes Millar to be hospitalized and treated for hypertension.

1960   *The Ferguson Affair*

1961   *The Wycherly Woman*

1962   *The Zebra-Striped Hearse*

1964   *The Chill*

1965   *The Far Side of the Dollar*; elected president of Mystery Writers of America; wins Crime Writers Association Golden Dagger award in England.

1966   *Black Money*

1968   *The Instant Enemy*

1969   *The Goodbye Look*

1971   *The Underground Man*; Book-of-the-Month Club alternate selection.

1973   *Sleeping Beauty*; *On Crime Writing*; wins Mystery Writers of America Grand Master Award and Popular Culture Association Award of Excellence.

1974   Receives Mystery Writers of America Grand Master Award.

1976   *The Blue Hammer*

1977   *Lew Archer, Private Detective*

1980   Begins to suffer from Alzheimer's disease.

1981   *Self-Portrait: Ceaselessly into the Past*; wins Private Eye Writers of America Life Achievement Award.

1982   Given Robert Kirsch Award for distinguished writing (in absentia).

1983   Dies July 11 in Santa Barbara.

Abbreviations

Bruccoli   Matthew J. Bruccoli. *Ross Macdonald* (New York: Harcourt Brace Jovanovich, 1984).

IJ   *Inward Journey: Ross Macdonald*, ed. Ralph B. Sipper (New York: Mysterious Press, 1984).

Nolan   Tom Nolan. *Ross Macdonald: A Biography* (New York: Scribner, 1999).

Schopen   Bernard A. Schopen. *Ross Macdonald* (Boston: Twayne, 1990).

Speir   Jerry Speir. *Ross Macdonald* (New York: Frederick Ungar, 1978).

"WG"   "Writing the Galton Case," pp. 25–45, in Ross Macdonald, *On Crime Writing* (Santa Barbara, Calif.: Capra Press, 1963).

Wolfe   Peter Wolfe. *Dreamers Who Live Their Dreams: The World of Ross Macdonald's Novels* (Bowling Green, Ohio: Bowling Green University Popular Press, 1976).

A

ABERNATHY. In *The Ferguson Affair*, he participates in a suicide pact.

ADA. In *The Zebra-Striped Hearse*, she is Harriet Blackwell's deceased aunt and left her $500,000, available when she turns twenty-five.

AL. In *Blue City*, he was a wrestler who signed his photograph and addressed it to Charlie, a poolroom owner.

AL. In *The Drowning Pool*, he is a Hollywood studio guard who allowed Archer to see Mildred Fleming.

ALBERTSON. In *The Far Side of the Dollar*, he is the bus driver, about forty, who drove Thomas Hillman to Santa Monica to meet Stella Carlson.

ALEC. In *Blue City*, he is one of the policemen under Dave Moffatt. Alec slugs John Weather in the police station but later apologizes.

ALEC. In *Blue City*, he is a kid in Floraine Weather's neighborhood, shouted at to get ready for school.

ALFIE. In "Gone Girl," he auditioned Ella Salanda.

ALGREN, NELSON (1909–1981). Writer. Nelson Algren Abraham, born in Detroit, grew up in Chicago, and graduated from the University of Chicago (1931) with a degree in journalism. He became an underemployed outsider during the Depression. He published a short story in 1933, his first novel two years later, and worked with the WPA Federal Writers' Project in Chicago, where he met the novelist Richard Wright.

Algren published *Never Come Morning* (1942, a naturalistic novel), served in the U.S. Army (1942–1945), and was in combat in France and Germany. Success followed with *The Neon Wilderness* (short stories, 1947), *The Man with the Golden Arm* (1950), *Chicago: City on the Make* (prose poem, 1951), and *A Walk on the Wild Side* (1956, his best, grittiest novel). He traveled widely, taught at the University of Iowa (1965–1966), and lived in Paterson, New Jersey, and Sag Harbor, Long Island. He married (1937), divorced (1939), married again (1965), and divorced again (1966). He had a relationship (1947–1964) with Simone de Beauvoir, the French feminist. She dubbed him "Division Street [Chicago] Dostoevsky." Though elected to the American Academy of Arts and Letters (1981), Algren died in misery in Sag Harbor. *The Devil's Stocking*, his fictional account of the boxer Rubin "Hurricane" Carter, appeared posthumously (1983).

Algren praised Macdonald's *Blue City* for originality and lean language (*Philadelphia Inquirer*, August 17, 1947). Algren's *The Man with the Golden Arm* influenced Macdonald's *The Ivory Grin*. Macdonald once said that Algren was the living writer he most admired (*New York Times Book Review*, December 4, 1977).

Bibliography: Bruccoli; Nolan.

ALICE, AUNT. In *The Three Roads*, she was the older sister of Bret Taylor's father, George Taylor. When George's wife left, Alice cared for Bret, five, spanked him for asking about his mother, and died a year later.

ALLISON, FREEMAN. In *Blue City*, he was a lawyer in the D.A.'s office, ran on a reform ticket for mayor, and was elected. In his thirties, he is married, loves Francesca Sontag, and is blackmailed by Roger Kerch into condoning municipal corruption. He aids John Weather but, when caught, is shot by Francesca.

ALLISON, MRS. FREEMAN. In *Blue City*, her husband calls her a "harridan out of hell."

ALVAREZ, MRS. CONCHITA. In *The Blue Hammer*, she is the Copper City Southwestern Savings bank clerk.

ANDERSON. In *Trouble Follows Me*, he is a criminal oilman, long associated with Mary Thompson and involved in transmitting information on U.S. Navy ship movements. He boards the Chicago–Los Angeles train, kills Private Rodney Hatcher, tries to kill Sam Drake, but is cornered in Tijuana, where he is killed by Hector Land. (Anderson's real name: Lorenz Jensen.)

ANDREWS. In *The Moving Target*, he is the fingerprint expert under Humphreys, the D.A.

ANGELO. In *The Galton Case*, he is Archer's friend who made olive oil and whose father was killed by the "Maffia."

ANNE. In "Wild Goose Chase," Roy Harvey's wife caught him with Anne and said she would kill the next woman he ever got intimate with.

ANTON. In *The Barbarous Coast*, he runs a Los Angeles ballet school. Five times married, he gives Archer information about Clarence Bassett and Hester Wall.

ANTONIO ("TONY"). In *The Drowning Pool*, he is the reliable owner of a Quinto bar where Archer and Pat Reavis drink, and where Archer hides the $10,000 he took from Pat Reavis.

AQUISTA, TONY. In *Find a Victim*, Archer finds him on the highway mortally shot. He was a Mexican truck driver for Meyer, liked Meyer's daughter, conspired in a hijacking, and was killed by Anne's sister, Hilda Church.

ARBUTHNOT. In *The Drowning Pool*, he and his family live in the fashionable Staffordshire Estates.

ARCHER. In *The Drowning Pool*, he is Lew Archer's father, whom the son remembers as having taken him to San Francisco and meeting his Uncle Jake.

ARCHER, LEW (full name: Lewis A. Archer). In *The Moving Target*, he makes his first appearance. Now thirty-five, he was born June 2. (On June 2, 1938, Macdonald and Margaret Millar* were married.) Archer was a World War II army intelligence officer, worked for the Long Beach police until dismissed for criticizing corruption, and has been a private detective since. Hired for $65 a day by Elaine Sampson to spy on her rich, irresponsible husband Ralph Sampson, Archer is entangled in kidnapping and murder, and discovers a ring bringing Mexican workers across the border. He meets Ralph's daughter Miranda Sampson; Albert Graves, who likes her; Alan Taggert, Ralph's pilot; and shady entertainers, including the actress Fay Estabrook (with her associate Dwight Troy) and musician Betty Fraley. Archer is an adept swimmer and is knowledgeable about jazz. Lew Archer is called Lew Arless in the British edition (London: Cassell & Company, 1951).

In *The Drowning Pool*, Archer mentions that he spent five years with the Los Angeles police force, has been a private detective "doing divorce work" ten years, and was divorced last year. Maude Slocum, of Quinto, hires him to find out who wrote a letter she received calling her an adulteress. Archer investigates her family members, including her mother-in-law, Olivia Slocum, who drowns, and Maude's friends, and solves several murders that occur.

In *The Way Some People Die*, Archer reveals that he attended Oakland grade school (1920), was in the army on a "West Pacific" island, and knew a shark-hunting general in Colo'n. Now thirty-seven, he weighs 185 pounds and has a five-room bungalow between Hollywood and Los Angeles. Hired at $50 a day plus expenses to find Mrs. Samuel Lawrence's missing daughter, Galley, Archer soon finds her, but in the process encounters a tourist named Marjorie Fellows, who is seeking her husband. Galley has married Mario Tarantine's crooked brother, Joseph Tarantine, who is missing. Archer solves three murders and so pressures the man who cheated Herman Speed that he commits suicide.

In *The Ivory Grin*, Archer says that he was a Long Beach detective sergeant before the war. Una Durano hires him at $50 a day plus expenses to find Lucy Champion. He finds her, but she is soon murdered. Archer's adventures lead him to connect Lucy with Dr. Samuel Benning, for whom she worked, and with the missing Charles A. Singleton, Jr., whose family has posted a reward for information about him. When Archer helps to identify a burned corpse thought to be Singleton, he goes back to Benning. When Benning's wife asks Archer his name, he says it is Horace Larkin.

In *Find a Victim*, Archer mentions that as a teenager he ran with Los Angeles thugs and hijacked cars, but was persuaded by a kind policeman to reform. He twice mentions having fought on Okinawa. Finding Tony Aquista dying, Archer involves himself in solving a truck hijacking and three murders. He is brass-knuckled and has a fistfight with a sheriff, and grows emotionally attached to two women.

In *The Barbarous Coast*, Archer says that seeing Raymond Campbell as the honorable Inspector Fate in old movie serials inspired him not only to become a cop but also, when the Long Beach police force "went sour," to quit. Archer's most famous line is this: "The problem was to love people, try to serve them, without wanting anything from them. I was a long way from solving that one." Asked to be a man's bodyguard, Archer instead seeks to find a missing wife, Hester Wall, a task involving him in five murders.

The Doomsters presents Archer most subjectively, and he reasons provocatively about "good" and "evil." Hired to help an escaped mental patient, he solves three murders and also unearths evidence concerning the earlier death of a woman thought to be a suicide. Archer recalls that he was "a street boy . . . , gang-fighter, thief, poolroom lawyer." He remembers that while in an "alcoholic haze," unable to save his marriage to Sue, and rushing for a date with "a younger blonde" with social pull, he ignored a man in need, and directly caused that man's return to drugs and indirectly may have caused the three murders.

In *The Galton Case*, Archer says he played high school football, is about 6 feet tall, 190 pounds, and has a West Hollywood office. He is hired to find Anthony Galton and his son; they are the long-missing son and grandson of Maria Galton. Anthony is dead, however. In taking up the trail of Anthony's son, christened John Brown (Jr.), Archer becomes involved in a mysterious murder, and the seeming impersonation of John by the supposed son of Fred Nelson, who killed Anthony, married Anthony's wife, and went with his wife and "son" to Canada. Archer exposes the machinations of Maria's lawyer. Archer is battered in Reno by thugs employed by a gambler. In handling the Galton assignment, Archer is uncharacteristically mistaken in many of his initial conclusions.

In *The Wycherly Woman*, Archer mentions Okinawa, says he has been a detective for twenty years, and feels "pity and shame" working among "lost, battered souls who lived in hell." Hired by Homer Wycherly to find his missing daughter, Phoebe, Archer pursues the following: Phoebe's unannounced fiancé; her adulterous mother, Catherine Wycherly; that woman's real-estate agent and blackmailer, soon murdered; his sexy, outmaneuvered widow; her would-be blackmailing brother, soon murdered; and Carl Trevor, Homer's sister's evil husband. Archer saved the business card of a man named William C. Wheeling, Jr., a Santa Monica insurance salesman, presents it to Sally Merriman as his, and calls himself Bill when talking with her.

In *The Zebra-Striped Hearse*, Archer recalls being a youthful Long Beach movie patron, San Pedro dock trouble, the army, and "memories" of women. He is now over forty and has a Sunset Boulevard office. When Colonel Mark Blackwell hires Archer to find his missing daughter, Harriet, Archer goes to Los Angeles, San Francisco, and Mexico. He investigates two murders and Harriet's supposed murder. Archer finds both Isobel Blackwell, Blackwell's young second wife, and a woman in Mexico who is disturbingly attractive.

In *The Chill*, which takes place in late September 1960, Archer says his grandmother had a house in Martinez, and he spent an "uneasy youth" in Long Beach. When Alex Kincaid hires Archer to find his bride, Dolly, he is challenged to solve a murder in 1940; the murder of Dolly's mother in 1952; and the murder of Helen Haggerty, shot on September 26, 1960. Archer proceeds from California to Illinois and back, making essential connections among victims and killers.

In *The Far Side of the Dollar*, Archer says he had a summer job at seventeen in the Sierra foothills and had a Model-A Ford in Long Beach. Graying, he says his net worth is about $3,500. Hired to find Thomas Hillman, Archer becomes involved in following the lad's efforts to locate his true parents and to solve their murders.

In *Black Money*, he is hired by young Peter Jamieson to find Virginia Fablon. In the process, he solves the murders of her parents and another killing as well.

In *The Instant Enemy*, Archer recalls his father holding his hand while he waded in the waters of Long Beach, where he was born and raised. He comments on his counter-punching prowess. Hired to find Alexandria Sebastian, Archer must first solve four murders. In addition, a fatal shooting occurs before his very eyes.

In *The Goodbye Look*, Archer remembers his grandmother who lived in Contra Costa County and is buried in Martinez, remembers surfing at San Onofre in the 1930s, says he was divorced in the 1940s, drives a car not yet paid for, and prefers rare mercy to frequent "justice." Archer's being hired to find a missing gold box opens a Pandora's box. He sorts out the tangle generated by sex, name changing, and habitual lying. He finally solves four murders.

In *The Underground Man*, Archer is aging, speaks of his divorce, and says he no longer envies people with children. Hired by Jean Broadhurst to find her husband, Stanley, and their son, Ronny, Archer discovers the connection between the murder of Stanley's father in 1955 and the 1970 murders of Stanley and an ex-con. The best thing Archer does is rescue Ronny.

In *Sleeping Beauty*, Archer works hard to solve three murders against a backdrop of environmental pollution occasioned by an ugly oil spill.

In *The Blue Hammer*, Archer, by now in his sixties but claiming to be younger, says he has "worked on several dozen murder cases." Hired to find a missing portrait, he is challenged to solve a murder in 1943, another in 1950, and two in October 1975. One of his useful mottoes is never to tell a person more than he needs to know, because he will repeat it. Archer, mellow here, is ready for a love affair with a young reporter who permits him to think his "life might have a new beginning after all."

Lew Archer figures in nine short stories. In "Find the Woman," Archer determines that a woman drowned when her husband purposely flew low over a raft when she was committing adultery on it. In "Gone Girl," Archer solves a murder, sees the weak-minded killer killed, and kills his killer. In "The Bearded Lady," Archer says he served during World War II in the Philippines. He finds a stolen painting and solves the murders of the artist and the thief. In "The Suicide," Archer helps a girl find her missing sister, who then commits suicide. In "Guilt-Edged Blonde," Archer can't be Nick Nemo's bodyguard because Nick's sister-in-law kills

Nick before Archer meets him. In "The Sinister Habit," Archer seeks J. Reginald Harlan's dangerously married sister, only to get involved in two deaths, one being Harlan's. Archer says he can translate *Ora pro nobis* (pray for us) because his mother was Catholic. In "Wild Goose Chase," Archer is hired by Janet Kilpatrick to observe a murder trial but gains details too late to prevent her murder. In "Midnight Blue," Archer stumbles on an oversexed, teenaged murder victim outside Los Angeles, rules out three suspects, and identifies the killer as a scorned woman. In "Sleeping Dog," Archer identifies the killers of two dogs and two men. Macdonald undoubtedly derived the name Archer from that of Miles Archer, Sam Spade's partner in *The Maltese Falcon* by Dashiell Hammett, whose works Macdonald admired.

Bibliography: Daniel R. Barnes, " 'I'm the Eye': Archer as Narrator of the Novels of Ross Macdonald," *Mystery & Detection Annual* (1972): 178–190; David Fine, *Imagining Los Angeles* (Albuquerque: University of New Mexico Press, 2000); Jeffrey H. Mahan, "Investigations of Lew Archer," *Clues* 8 (Fall-Winter 1987): 1–39; Speir; Wolfe.

ARCHER, MRS. In *The Drowning Pool*, she is mentioned as Lew Archer's mother, who was ashamed of Uncle Jake, her husband's brother.

ARCHER, SUE. In *The Moving Target*, she is mentioned as Lew Archer's wife. They are now divorced. "She didn't like the company I kept," Archer tells a friend. In *The Drowning Pool*, she is mentioned as Archer's ex-wife, living in Nevada. In *Find a Victim*, Archer says his wife left him because he "gave too much to other people and not enough to her." In *The Barbarous Coast*, Archer says he lost his wife "in . . . silences" into which she retreated to express annoyance; he is "pushing forty, with no chick, no child." In *The Doomsters*, Archer remembers her face and ash-blonde hair, and "wondered where she was." In *The Zebra-Striped Hearse*, Archer mentions that she left him, married elsewhere, has children, and is happy. In *Sleeping Beauty*, she is mentioned as Archer's deceased wife. In *Harper*, the movie based on *The Moving Target*, Sue, the detective's unhappy wife, who does not appear in any of Macdonald's Archer fictions, is played by Janet Leigh.

Bibliography: Nolan.

ARLESS, LEW. *See* Archer, Lew.

ARMISTEAD, FRAN. In *The Underground Man*, she is the wealthy wife, married before, of Roger Armistead, who owns the sloop *Ariadne*. They moved four years earlier from Newport to Santa Teresa. Elizabeth Broadhurst disparagingly calls them *nouveaux riches*. The Armisteads are childless.

ARMISTEAD, ROGER. In *The Underground Man*, he is the young husband of Fran Armistead, whose first husband he crewed for. Roger likes his sloop, the *Ariadne*, and let Jerry Kilpatrick crew for him.

ARMSTRONG. In *The Barbarous Coast*, he was a boxer who defeated Tony Torres.

ASPINWALL, COLONEL. In *The Blue Hammer*, he is an "elderly" guest, with an English accent, at Francine Chantry's cocktail party.

ASPINWALL, MRS. In *The Blue Hammer*, she is the colonel's young English wife and a guest at Francine Chantry's cocktail party. Archer says she finds him "socially unacceptable."

AUBREY. In *The Instant Enemy*, she is the daughter, sixteen, of Captain Robert Aubrey, who worries about her.

AUBREY, CAPTAIN ROBERT. In *The Instant Enemy*, he is a Malibu police officer who cooperates with Archer, even though Archer withholds some evidence from him. Aubrey bursts into the home of Stephen Hackett to arrest him and his mother.

AUDEN, W.H. (1907–1973). Versatile man of letters. Wystan Hugh Auden was born in York, England; attended Christ Church, Oxford; and traveled widely, to Germany, Iceland, China, and Spain. The Spanish Civil War made him anti-fascist and pessimistic. Beginning in 1939, Auden lived out the war years in the United States, then became a naturalized American citizen (1946). Influenced by Karl Marx, Sigmund Freud, and Carl Gustav Jung, Auden gradually returned to a Christian faith tinged by existentialism. His phenomenal literary production—political, travel, religious, and domestic poetry; literary criticism; drama and operatic libretti—is too extensive to permit detailed comment. Representative are "Spain" (1937), "The Sea and the Mirror" (1945), *The Age of Anxiety: A Baroque Eclogue* (1948), *The Dyer's Hand and Other Essays* (1948), *The Enchafèd Flood: The Romantic Iconography of the Sea* (1951), and collections of his poetry (1945, 1959, 1966, 1969).

Auden was an influential visiting professor at several American universities. In 1941 he taught at the University of Michigan; Macdonald, with a few friends, including Donald Pearce,* enrolled in "Fate and the Individual in European Literature," a formidable class, with a thirty-two-book reading list, taught by Auden. Auden was impressed with Macdonald, invited him to dinner, and was entertained in turn at the home of Macdonald and Margaret Millar.* Macdonald was intrigued by, while disagreeing with parts of, "The Guilty Vicarage: Notes on the Detective Story, by an Addict," Auden's influential 1948 essay in which he confesses his incurable devotion to detective fiction. Auden delighted Margaret when he said he admired her mystery novels. Macdonald's career was boosted by Auden's view of detective fiction as a legitimate subgenre.

Bibliography: John Fuller, *A Reader's Guide to W.H. Auden* (New York: Farrar, Straus & Giroux, 1970); Elmer R. Pry Jr., "Lew Archer's 'Moral Landscape,' "*Armchair Detective* 8 (February 1975): 104–107.

B

BAGLEY, NELSON. In *Sleeping Beauty*, he is a survivor of the *Canaan Sound* explosion off Okinawa in 1945.

BAGSHAW, MAJOR GENERAL HIRAM. In *Black Money*, he is a deceased army officer, whose widow lives in Montevista.

BAGSHAW, MRS. In *Black Money*, she is Major General Hiram Bagshaw's widow, about seventy. She evidently got Francis Martel into the Montevista Tennis Club and leases her Montevista home to him.

BAILEY. In *The Dark Tunnel*, he is the English Department head at Midwestern University and serves as the campus air-raid warden.

BAILEY, JOSEPHINE ("JAMAICA JO"). In "The South Sea Soup Co.," she is so unattractive that when Black Bleerstone, her lover, called her beautiful, he aroused Herlock Sholmes's suspicions.

BAKER. In *Trouble Follows Me*, he is a Shore Patrol sailor on duty in Honolulu. He is summoned when Sue Sholto was murdered.

***THE BARBAROUS COAST* (1956).** Novel. (Characters: Anton, Lew Archer, Sue Archer, Armstrong, Clarence Bassett, Clarence ("Clare") Bassett, William Bassett, Mrs. Bean, Mrs. Carol Busch, Raymond Campbell, Rina Campbell, Teeny Campbell, Peter Colton, Jeremy Crane, Padraic Dane, Desideria, Finney, Flake, Dr. Frey, Leroy Frost, Isobel Graff, Simon Graff, Gregory, Miss Hamblin, Peter Heliopoulos, Beatrice M. Jackson, Mrs. Sarah Lamb, Lashman, Lance Leonard, Theodore Marfeld, Martha Matthews, Mercero, Charles Meyer, Mona, Musso, Myrin, Dr. Anthony Reeves,

Jr., Colonel Risko, Rudy, Miss Seeley, Joshua Severn, Captain Spero, Stefan, Carl Stern, Sammy Swift, Joseph Tobias, Toko, Gabrielle Torres, Tony Torres, Vera, George Wall, Hester Wall, George Wallingford, Carl Walther, Dr. Wolfson.)

December 27. Archer goes to the Channel Club near Malibu, is admitted by Tony Torres, the ex-boxer watchman, and sees Joseph Tobias, the pool lifeguard. Clarence Bassett, manager and secretary, wants Archer to protect him from George Wall, who thinks Bassett is after Hester Wall, George's estranged wife. Bassett befriended Hester Campbell when she was a teenage novice diver at the club pool. Years later, failing as an aquacade performer, she married George, a sportswriter, in Toronto, left him within a year, and returned to California last September. Bassett loaned her money, which she used for lessons at Anton's Los Angeles School of Ballet. George appears. Bassett tells Archer and George what information he has. George says Hester, who got religion in Canada and confessed sins involving Gabrielle Torres, phoned George from Anton's two nights ago, in danger. When the line went dead, he flew from Toronto to help.

Archer lets a coin flip decide whether he will let Bassett or George hire him. George wins. Archer drives him to some seedy Malibu apartments Mrs. Sarah Lamb runs. According to Bassett, she was Hester's landlady. Sarah tells Archer this: Sarah worked at the club snack bar; she knew Hester, Hester's mother, and Hester's sister, Rina Campbell; Hester had dangerous boyfriends, including Lance Torres, Tony's nephew, and his gunman companion; Tony's daughter, Gabrielle Torres, was shot to death on the beach almost two years ago. Archer and George return to Tony, who now dislikes Lance. He was a club lifeguard; Tony trained Lance to box; the punk threw fights, was jailed, ran around with Hester last summer, and consorts with Carl Stern, a wealthy criminal. From Anton, Archer learns that Hester was a cynical guest at his Christmas party. Anton's secretary, Miss Seeley, adds that Lance, now the actor Lance Leonard, was also there and told Hester to cooperate "with the operation" or Carl would fix her.

Archer phones Peter Colton, the D.A.'s retired investigator, and learns that Simon Graff, a movie producer and club member (as is his wife, Isobel Graff), is building a Las Vegas hotel-casino financed by Stern. Archer phones the Hollywood writer Sammy Swift, learns that Graff and Lance plan a movie venture in Italy, and gets Lance's address. Archer drives George there. Lance and Hester are home. When Archer asks to talk with her, Lance knocks him down. Seeing Hester, George intervenes but is also pummeled. Hester drives Lance's car away, leaving her sun hat behind. Archer takes George, suffering a concussion, to his doctor and goes home to rest.

Hester's sun hat came from the Taos Shop on the Coast Highway. When Archer asks about Hester Wall there, a salesgirl says a Hester Campbell just quit working with her because her daughter inherited a fortune. Archer gets Mrs. Campbell's address and goes there. The woman boasts of her pretty daughter Hester's success: Hester married George Wallingford, a rich Canadian whose death left her wealthy; Hester has just taken over the Beverly Hills mansion the Campbell family once owned and is redecorating it; Hester, a movie star, is going to Italy; Hester's equally pretty older sister, Rina, is, sadly, nothing but a psychiatric nurse. Archer warns Mrs. Campbell: Hester's husband, George Wall, is alive, poor, and looking for her.

Given the Campbells' mansion address, Archer drives up, sees a man park his car and enter, and sees Lance leave. Archer notes that the car is registered to Theodore Marfeld, enters the house through the open door, only to encounter Marfeld and get decked with a brass poker. He falls, dimly sees a bleeding blonde on the floor, and passes out. When he comes to, he is being driven in Marfeld's car to Graff's movie studio. Marfeld marches Archer to Leroy Frost, head of the private police for Graff's film company. Frost is smooth, friendly, and threatening. He complains that Archer bothered Lance, entered the Beverly Hills mansion, and is disturbing a multimillion-dollar company. He wonders whether Archer's client is "schizzy" Isobel Graff. Archer says no. Lashman, a studio guard, is outside pursuing George, who, he says, threatened Graff. George is caught and pistol-whipped. Archer rushes to his aid but is knocked unconscious.

Sunset. Archer awakens near a swimming pool by Stern's house, guarded by Frost, Lance, and a fellow named Flake. Mentioning that he must pick up Stern at the airport, Lance leaves with Frost. Flake starts watching television, and Archer knocks him out, takes his gun, hides as Lance drives past with Stern, hitchhikes to a Westwood hospital for scalp stitches, and takes a taxi to his car near Hester's empty house. He breaks in, hides when Frost enters with the obsequious Marfeld, watches while they inspect the bloodstain the blonde left, and sees them replace the poker used on Archer with a property-warehouse duplicate.

The two leave. Archer drives to Lance's house, finds Lance shot dead, rummages around, and returns to his car. He sees Stern enter, hears a scream, and when Stern drives off follows him to Hester's mansion. Stern walks in, soon walks out, and drives off. Seeing the shadow of a dancing woman, Archer sneaks into Hester's bedroom and finds a pretty girl packing. When she hints that she is expecting Lance, he tells her Lance has been murdered and she is being set up as a patsy in Gabrielle's murder. Archer pities her, doubts his suspicions of her, warns her when she says Stern is to take her somewhere, and leaves.

Graff is hosting a club party when Archer arrives. He talks to a woman diver, who says she knew Hester. Sammy Swift, another guest, tells Archer he hates writing and rewriting for Graff, then freezes at the mention of

Hester's name. Now 1:30 A.M., Tobias, the lifeguard, takes Archer to Tony, who has a basement room at the club. He says that the night his daughter Gabrielle was murdered, she had been with Hester, while Lance was in jail. Tony produces a lurid magazine article about that fatal night: Gabrielle had sex, then was shot twice with a .22, and the sheriff's plainclothesman, Theodore Marfeld, investigated. Tony shows Archer his heavy .45 and vows to use it on Gabrielle's killer.

The woman diver tells Archer that last summer Hester stole from her and from Bassett, then snubbed her. Archer overhears Isobel Graff tell her husband she knows he gave Hester that house. Isobel argues with Stern. When he slaps her, Archer decks him and takes a knife away from him. Bassett enters, develops real courage, and orders Stern out. Inviting Archer to her cabana for a drink, Isobel reveals this: Peter Heliopoulos, Graff's deceased film-company partner, was her father; Stern is a drug-dealing homosexual; Stern wrongly accused her of meddling with Lance, his lover. Graff enters, threatens to have Dr. Frey recommit her, tries to snub Archer, but gets insulted. Bassett enters and snubs Graff.

Archer and Bassett go drinking in Bassett's office. Bassett reveals this: Bassett loved Isobel, the daughter of Heliopoulos, who disapproved of him; Bassett introduced Graff to Heliopoulos; soon Graff was producing movies with Heliopoulos and married Isobel; Hester, to whom Bassett was merely "avuncular" and whose family he and his mother knew from the 1920s, never stole from him. Archer wonders if Graff or, more likely, his wife killed Gabrielle. Dead drunk, Bassett collapses.

After looking in on Tobias, who is reading in his room, Archer puts Bassett to bed and falls asleep. At about 3:45 A.M., Tobias returns, makes coffee and fried eggs, and reveals this: Tobias, a Korean War veteran, liked but had no chance with sexy Gabrielle; lazy Lance corrupted her, wanted to pimp for her in Los Angeles; Tobias told Tony, who broke with Lance but couldn't save her; Gabrielle and Graff went to a cabana for an occasional intimate hour; Gabrielle, in the morgue, was wearing one earring; Tobias found the other by a cabana; Hester was a temporary lifeguard that morning. Dawn is breaking. Tobias drives off. Archer walks toward the beach, sees a corpse floating ashore, and determines that it is Stern's, with his throat slit. Three miles north, by the water, he finds Stern's blood-spattered car. Archer goes home to bed.

His answering service awakens Archer at 7:30 A.M. A Las Vegas doctor phoned: George was picked up dazed and is hospitalized. Archer flies to him, is told that he may have a fractured skull, but learns this from him: George was flown from Los Angeles by private plane, was told that Hester needed him, was turned loose on the street to seek her at the Dry Martini Hotel—only to be found by the police. Archer goes to the Martini, locates a taxi driver who drove Hester to a street with sleazy motels, and finds her at the Dewdrop Inn. She turns out to be Rina, Hester's sister. The frightened girl, closely resembling Hester, explains that she was flown from Malibu to Las Vegas so as to be seen alive as Hester's alibi. The crooked taxi driver leads Marfeld, Lashman, and Frost to the Dewdrop. Archer slugs the first two viciously, dodges Frost's gunfire, and shoots him in the arm.

Archer forces Frost to talk. The two men, with Rina driving Frost's car, go to a house outside town. Frost, sick and scared, tells all he knows: Isobel shot Gabrielle; Hester got the gun and with it was, with Stern, blackmailing the Graffs; with his money and for profit, Stern made Graff build the Las Vegas hotel-casino. With Marfeld and Lashman in custody, Archer and Rina fly back to Los Angeles that evening. En route, Rina reveals much: Isobel was a patient in Dr. Frey's private sanitarium at Santa Monica; Rina was her nurse; weeks before, Rina, with Stern, double-dated with Hester and Lance; Rina discovered that Stern and Lance were homosexually inclined, voiced suspicions that the three were blackmailing Graff, and departed; Isobel discovered that Graff and Gabrielle were lovers, left Frey's sanitarium the night Gabrielle was killed, and probably shot her.

At the Los Angeles airport, Archer gets his car, drops Rina at her mother's, drives to Frey's hospital, and interrupts his dinner. Frey says Isobel, just recommitted, escaped this morning; he theorizes that Bassett, who visited her weekly, might have been a better husband for her than Graff. Archer rushes to the club, breaks into the Graff cabana, and discovers how Isobel could have spied through louvers on her husband and Gabrielle making love there. Tony enters, says Bassett will vacation in Mexico, and leaves. Archer finds Isobel, now wan, on the beach. She reveals that she loved Bassett and shot Gabrielle with Graff's .22. Graff enters with the weapon, says he just bought it from Bassett for $100,000, and suggests Archer steal that money and shut up. Instead, Archer takes the .22. They rush to Bassett's office. The following emerges: Bassett brained Hester with a poker, shot Lance, killed Stern, and retrieved the .22; Isobel went to Hester's house to kill her as Graff's paid girlfriend but found her already dead; Bassett suggested that she shoot Graff abed in the cabana with Gabrielle, after which Isobel and Bassett could wed; she caught Graff with Gabrielle, fired at him, but shot her once; she crawled away; while Isobel washed off the blood, Bassett took the gun and killed Gabrielle. Bassett gets the $100,000 from his safe. Tony enters, says Graff just told him Bassett killed Gabrielle, and kills Bassett. Archer phones the police. This outcome initially delights Graff, who offers Archer the $100,000 for the .22. Archer declines, says he'll tell the authorities Graff seduced Gabrielle, puts the .22 near dead Bassett's hand, and will say Tony fired in self-defense.

Enthusiastically reviewed as Macdonald's best Archer novel to its date, *The Barbarous Coast* was condensed as "The Dying Animal" by *Cosmo-*

politan (March 1956), for $4,500, and issued in London (Cassell, 1957). Social historians value its ruthless depiction of southern California's ability to degrade. Peter Heliopoulos and Simon Graff use Greek energy to make tinsel films. Sammy Swift is overpaid to turn *Salammbô*, the tragic novel by his "worship[ped]" Gustave Flaubert, into a movie script with a happy ending. Hollywood types waste time, energy, and money by drinking and talking at the Channel Club (based on Santa Barbara's Coral Casino), often making racist comments. Action is crowded into roughly forty hours. Archer solves four murders and witnesses a fifth—all the while being sucker-punched, decked, conked, kicked, pistol-whipped, choked, gashed, and shot at. Partly unifying the plot is a photograph. In it are three young divers—Gabrielle, Hester, and Lance—in midair, "[c]aught in unchanging flight," forever young. Macdonald was delighted when *The Barbarous Coast* was published in Romania in 1968.

Bibliography: Bruccoli; David Geherin, "Archer in Hollywood: The Barbarous Coast of Ross Macdonald," *Armchair Detective* 9 (November 1975): 55–58; Nolan; Schopen; Speir.

BARKER, ASA. In *The Ferguson Affair*, he was presumably Ella Barker's deceased father.

BARKER, ELLA. In *The Ferguson Affair*, she is a young, pretty nurse in the Buenavista hospital. She is charged as participating in a burglary ring. William Gunnarson, who is assigned to defend her, clears her.

BARNEY. In *The Galton Case*, he is a policeman at the scene of the burned Jaguar near Gordon Sable's home.

BARONESS, THE. In *Trouble Follows Me*, she is the Japanese mastermind spy in Tijuana. She is Anderson's boss, uses Miss Green's brothel, and commits suicide.

BARRON, GEORGE. In *The Way Some People Die*, he is Marjorie Barron's divorced husband. He is the golf-playing, boring secretary-treasurer of the Simplex Ball Bearing Company. He flies from Toledo to Palm Springs to be reunited with Marjorie.

BARRON, MARJORIE. In *The Way Some People Die*, she is George Barron's heavy, pseudo-dainty ex-wife. Herman Speed, posing as Colonel Henry Fellows, marries her, honeymoons with her near Palm Springs, takes her money and car, and disappears. Majorie happily welcomes George upon his reappearance.

BARTOLEMEO ("BART"). In "Gone Girl," he was a criminal killed by Donny.

"THE BASILISK LOOK." *See The Wycherly Woman.*

BASSETT, CLARENCE. In *The Barbarous Coast*, he wrote *The Bassett Family*, chronicling the family's story from its 1634 arrival in Massachusetts to the year 1914. His son, also named Clarence Bassett, proudly shows Archer the book.

BASSETT, CLARENCE ("CLARE"). In *The Barbarous Coast*, he is the manager and secretary of the Channel Club at Malibu. He went to Harvard, was a stretcher bearer in World War I, and is about sixty. He revered his mother and drinks too much. He loved but lost Isobel Heliopoulos, then introduced her to Simon Graff (*see* Graff, Isobel). Bassett wants Archer to be his bodyguard so he can locate Hester Wall. Archer ascertains that Bassett killed Gabrielle Torres, to gain dominance over Isobel, and later kills Hester and Carl Stern to get a .22 to blackmail Simon. Gabrielle's father, Tony Torres, kills Bassett.

BASSETT, WILLIAM. In *The Barbarous Coast*, he landed in Massachusetts in 1634 and is Clarence Bassett's original American ancestor.

BASTIAN, LIEUTENANT. In *The Far Side of the Dollar*, he is the honest El Rancho sheriff's aide. He helps Archer, who partly cooperates with him. Bastian traces Dick Leandro's car and identifies the owner of the knife used to murder Carol Harley and Mike Harley.

BEAN, MRS. In *The Barbarous Coast*, she was the religious neighbor when George Wall and Hester Wall, much troubled, lived in Toronto.

"THE BEARDED LADY" (1948, 1955, 1959). Short story. (Characters: Lew Archer, Devlin, Mrs. Harris, Walter Hendryx, Shaw, Dr. Silliman, Hilary Todd, Admiral Johnston Turner, Alice Turner, Mrs. Turner, Sarah Turner, Hugh Western, Mary Western.) Lew Archer visits his artist friend, Hugh Western, in San Marcos, north of Los Angeles, and finds his detective ability challenged when a 1744 Jean Baptiste Siméon Chardin painting is stolen, resulting in the murder of Hugh and that of art-dealer Hilary Todd by Alice Turner, fiancée of Hugh, whose nude charcoal of Sarah Turner, Alice's stepmother, so outraged Alice that she drew a beard on it. When Macdonald rewrote "The Bearded Lady," he changed the name and occupation of its hero-narrator—originally Sam Drake, an experienced newspaperman. Its 1959 reprint was titled "Murder Is a Public Matter."

"THE BEAT-UP SISTER." *See* "The Suicide."

BECKER, LAWRENCE. In *The Moving Target. See* Lassiter, Eddie.

BEGLEY, CHUCK. In *The Chill. See* McGee, Thomas.

BEGLEY, MARY. In *The Chill. See* Kincaid, Dolly.

BELSIZE, JACOB ("JAKE"). In *The Instant Enemy*, he is Davy Spanner's Los Angeles probation officer. Archer respects him and calls him conscientious in a difficult job.

BENDIX, ARNOLD. In *The Instant Enemy*, he is a Van Nuys lawyer. Keith Sebastian retains him after Keith's daughter, Alexandria Sebastian, injured Lupe Rivera. Was Macdonald expressing his dislike of lawyers by reworking the name Benedict Arnold?

BENNETT, JUDGE. In *The Ferguson Affair*, he is a Buenavista judge, in his sixties, who denies William Gunnarson's request to reduce Ella Barker's bail.

BENNING, DR. SAMUEL ("SAM"). In *The Ivory Grin*, he graduated from medical school (1933), married Bess Wionowski in Indiana (1943), served in the U.S. Navy, and practiced medicine, badly, in Bella City. His receptionist is Florida Gutierrez. When his wife's lover, Charles A. Singleton, Jr., was wounded, Benning could not or would not save him, converted his corpse into an anatomical skeleton with an "ivory grin" for office display, and killed Lucy Champion, his black nurse. His father was a respected Bella City high school principal.

Bibliography: Nolan.

BENNING, ELIZABETH ("BESS"). In *The Ivory Grin*, she is Dr. Samuel Benning's wife (formerly Bess Wionowski), with a long criminal record, mainly in Detroit. Leo Durano abused her, then bribed her way out of jail. She married Benning (1943), and worked with him in Bella City after the war. Her downfall came when she fell in love with Charles A. Singleton, Jr., and permitted sick Leo and his sister, Una Durano, to reside near Bella City. She seeks a reward from Charles's mother after Charles's disappearance, meets Archer in his office, and is killed by Una.

BERGLUND. In *Black Money*, he and his family were guests at the Montevista Tennis Club in September 1959.

BERKER, ELLIE. In *The Three Roads*, she is Lorraine Taylor's sister.

BERKER, JOE. In *The Three Roads*, he is Lorraine Taylor's alcoholic father. Part of his right forefinger was severed by a corn cutter in Michigan back in 1915.

BERKER, LORRAINE. In *The Three Roads*. *See* Taylor, Lorraine.

BERKER, MRS. JOE. In *The Three Roads*, she is Lorraine Taylor's mother, a "gross and aging hag." Paula West arranged for her and her husband to move into dead Lorraine's Los Angeles house.

BARNARD. In *The Goodbye Look*, Nicholas Chalmers's vomit is analyzed at Bernard's laboratory.

BERRY, JOHN. In *The Underground Man*, his name appears on an 1866 map owned by Elizabeth Broadhurst. Berry was evidently a land-commission worker.

BESS, DR. In *Blue City*, he is the coroner who examined Floraine Weather's body.

BIDWELL, ARTHUR. In *The Ferguson Affair*, he is the manager of the Foothill Club. He gives William Gunnarson information.

BIEMEYER, DORIS. In *The Blue Hammer*, she is the daughter, twenty, of Jack and Ruth Biemeyer. Drug-addicted, Doris knows Fred Johnson, accompanies him to the Copper City commune, and is rescued by Archer.

BIEMEYER, JACK. In *The Blue Hammer*, he is Ruth Biemeyer's husband, Doris Biemeyer's father, Mildred Mead's ex-lover, and William Mead's father. A millionaire who made his money in copper by working for Felix Chantry, Mildred's husband, Jack tolerates Ruth's hiring Archer to find a missing painting she bought. Jack is humiliated by Archer's discoveries and encounters William, his long-lost son, weeping in prison.

BIEMEYER, MRS. In *The Blue Hammer*, she was Jack Biemeyer's mother and Felix Chantry's cousin.

BIEMEYER, RUTH. In *The Blue Hammer*, she is Jack Biemeyer's wife and Doris Biemeyer's mother. Ruth buys a Chantry portrait of a woman resembling Jack's former mistress. When it disappears, she hires Archer to find it.

BILL. In *The Drowning Pool*, he owns a Quinto bar that Archer and Pat Reavis avoid.

"THE BLACK HOLE OF CALCUTTA." *See The Far Side of the Dollar.*

BLACK MONEY **(1966).** Novel. (Characters: Lew Archer, Major General Hiram Bagshaw, Mrs. Bagshaw, Berglund, Allan Bosch, Ralph Christman, Davis, de Houvenel, Domingo, Marietta Fablon, Roy Fablon, Virginia Fablon, Grantham, [Miss] Grantham, Mrs. Grantham, Harry Hendricks, Kitty Hendricks, Mrs. Peter Jamieson, Peter Jamieson [Jr.], Peter Jamieson, Kayo Ketchel, Mrs. Loftin, Eric Malkovsky, Marco, Martel, Francis Martel, Martin, McMinn, Inspector Harold Olsen, Dr. Charles Park, Captain Perlberg, Colonel Plimsoll, Rasmussen, Ward Rasmussen, Ricardo Rosales, Secundina Rosales, Sanderson, Sekjar, Maria Sekjar, Smythe, Stanley, Reto Stoll, Strome, Mrs. Ella Strome, Audrey Sylvester, Dr. George Sylvester, Tappinger, Bess Tappinger, [Miss] Tappinger, Taps Tappinger, Teddy Tappinger, Vera, Dr. Wills.)

At the Montevista Tennis Club, Archer meets fat young Peter Jamieson, who hires him to rescue Virginia ("Ginny") Fablon, his ex-fiancée, from Francis Martel, an adventurer said to be French. On his way to the Bagshaw house, where Martel is staying, Archer stops Harry Hendricks, who was posing as a detective and was hired by a woman to follow Jamieson. While getting information from Harry, Archer is interrupted by Martel and Ginny in his Bentley. Martel pulls a gun, warns Harry, and breaks his camera. Archer visits Ginny's widowed mother, Marietta Fablon, whose friend, Dr. George Sylvester, suddenly rushes off and who boasts that her daughter never liked Jamieson much and prefers Martel. Next door to Mrs. Fablon is the Jamieson house. Archer meets Peter's father, old Peter Jamieson, and learns that Ginny's father drowned himself—his body was ravaged by sharks—and that Martel deposited $100,000 in the Montevista bank. At the club pool, a lifeguard tells Archer that Martel is leaving immediately. Archer goes to Mrs. Bagshaw's club cottage and learns that she sponsored Martel as a club member with insufficient recommendations and suspects him of being an impostor. Peter takes Archer to the home of Taps Tappinger, a professor of French at the local college. He agrees to write difficult questions regarding French culture, to expose Martel if his background is inauthentic. Archer flirts with Bess, Taps's sexually frustrated wife. Peter takes Archer to Mrs. Bagshaw's mansion. Ginny screams; Archer queries her outside; Martel says he killed a bloody rat, adding that he and Ginny are married. He answers Archer's French-quiz questions correctly but too glibly. Seeing Harry's car, Archer queries Mrs. Bagshaw, who says she called Martel's Georgetown reference, who denies knowing him. Archer learns from the polylingual club manager that Martel once threatened him with a sword and is not Parisian. Ella Strome, club secretary, says Mrs. Fablon has lost money and will locate a photograph of Martel. At dinner, Peter, overeating repulsively, tells Archer that Roy Fablon lost much of his wife's fortune. At the bar, Dr. Sylvester, for whom Ginny worked, tells Archer he has washed his hands of her. The bartender hints to Archer that Roy may have been murdered. Eric Malkovsky, the club photographer, says a beautiful redhead sought Martel's photograph. Archer drives off, sees Harry's empty car, finds Kitty, Harry's wife, at the cheap Breakwater Hotel, and learns that she asked Harry to photograph Martel, whom she calls South American, for someone Martel stole from. She and Archer seek Harry, who is missing. Eric produces a photograph of Kitty and a hairy man; the pair are identified by Audrey Sylvester, George's wife, as Mr. and Mrs. Ketchel. Sylvester drives Marietta, who is quite ill, home. Returning, Sylvester talks to Archer about the manner of Roy's death. Audrey reminds Sylvester that she put him through medical school and paid his gambling debts, and accuses him of sleeping with Marietta, who wants to borrow money from them. Visiting Marietta's home, Archer listens while she rambles: Ketchel, a gambler, got Roy into debt; Roy was Audrey's lover; he didn't kill himself. Archer stops at the Jamiesons' residence nearby. Old Jamieson just learned that Martel withdrew his $100,000, the source being a Panama bank. While Archer is lecturing Peter, who is alternately devouring goose and vomiting, Marietta crawls in from next door, mortally shot, by—she mutters— "lover-boy." In the Fablon house, Archer finds evidence that Marietta exhausted her Panama bank holdings and wonders if she "sold" Ginny to Martel. Inspector Harold Olsen arrives and criticizes Archer's theory that this murder and Roy's death may be connected. Conferring with old Jamieson, Archer learns this: Roy gambled with Ketchel and lost; Marietta worried; Jamiesen gave her the adjacent house. On his drive to the Breakwater for a room, Archer sees Harry's stolen car, smashed, with him in the trunk, battered. Ward Rasmussen, an able policeman, takes Harry to the hospital.

After sleeping briefly, Archer has breakfast, and tells Rasmussen about Ginny and Martel, and about funds Martel and Marietta had in the Panama bank. Eric brings an enlarged photograph, taken seven years earlier. It features Kitty, Ketchel, and Martel—the last as a club bar-boy. Rasmussen remembers knowing Kitty in school. Archer shows the photograph to the club manager, who recognizes Martel and says that he went briefly to the local college. Archer goes to its administration office and determines that Martel (calling himself Feliz Cervantes) transferred from Los Angeles State College and studied French at the local college under Tappinger. Archer locates Taps and goes home to lunch with him and Bess. Archer takes champagne along, and when Taps returns to class, Archer listens to Bess's boozy complaints about her husband—an academic "talking machine." Bess says Taps brought Martel home once; Bess ad-

mired Martel's macho manner, but Martel preferred another student—
namely, Ginny. Archer tells Bess that Martel just married Ginny, then
drives her to go shopping. Archer visits Mrs. Grantham, who rented Martel a room. She says he was a cocky, ambitious Mexican and soon drove
off with Ketchel and Kitty. When Archer visits Harry, now hospitalized,
and tells him about Ginny and Martel, Harry says Ketchel, who is really
Leo Spillman, a former boxer and presently a Las Vegas gambler, is after
Martel for an enormous robbery. Harry offers to cut Archer in. No. On
to Sylvester's clinic. Archer worms from him the fact that he lost $20,000
seven years ago to Ketchel, who came to Montevista with Kitty; Sylvester
repaid half the debt and, in lieu of the remainder, treated him for high
blood pressure. Ginny phones Sylvester: Martel has been shot. Archer
drives Sylvester to a Los Angeles address she names. Martel, her husband,
driving after the gunman, is dead in his car; the $100,000 has been taken
by the gunman. Captain Perlberg, a police officer, assumes command.
While returning to Montevista, Archer briefs Ginny and shows her the
photograph of Ketchel, Kitty, and young Martel. She says Ketchel, with
Kitty, each of whom she saw only once, was in Montevista the day her
father died. Archer takes Ginny to her mother's home, tells her that her
mother has just been shot by "lover-boy," and gets Peter to protect her.

Archer queries Dr. Wills, the deputy coroner, who says Roy drowned
in salt water. By telephone, Archer learns that while at Los Angeles State
College, Martel called himself Pedro Domingo and that he became a Central American diplomat. Archer finds Kitty's mother, Maria Sekjar, who
laments that Ketchel lured Kitty away from Harry, tried to bribe Maria,
and is wanted for income-tax evasion. Though angry at Kitty, she won't
reveal Kitty's whereabouts. Archer flies to Las Vegas, gets to the Scorpion
Club, where Ketchel hung out, and seeks its manager, Davis. Their talk
reveals that Ketchel is Davis's partner and that Martel was Ketchel's "boy,"
whom Ketchel probably killed for keeping "black money"—sums rou-
tinely skimmed and hidden from the IRS. Davis fails to bribe Archer to
locate Ketchel, who stole millions. Archer flies home to sleep.

Archer tells Perlberg that Ketchel and Martel evaded taxes and Ketchel
probably killed him and also Roy, which Marietta knew about. Archer
checks with Taps, who is sorry Martel is dead and persuades Archer to
quit seeing Bess. Archer phones Washington and learns that Martel was
a well-placed Panamian diplomat. On to Sylvester. He tells Archer the
Jamiesons are caring for Ginny, asks Archer to conceal his financial relationships with Ketchel and Marietta, and reveals that he just located
Ketchel's address, in nearby Santa Teresa. Archer goes there, finds Kitty,
and finally sees Ketchel, paralyzed and unable to communicate. Hoping
Archer can locate the missing millions, Kitty reveals all: Seven years ago,
Ketchel wanted Ginny, argued with Roy, slugged him, and he fell into
the salt-water club pool and drowned. Ketchel and Martel transferred his

body to the ocean. Ketchel sent Martel to a school in Paris. Martel returned and when Ketchel got sick sent money stolen from him to Panama.
Marietta knew about the murder and blackmailed Ketchel. Kitty is hiding
Ketchel from Davis only to find the money. In Los Angeles and after
dinner, Archer goes to the Jamiesons', and asks Ginny if Martel helped
dispose of Roy's body. She says Taps visited her this afternoon and adds
that she got pregnant while in college and that her father took her to
Tijuana for an abortion.

Next morning, Perlberg telephones Archer: Martel's mother, Secundina
Rosales, has flown in from Panama for his body. Archer confers with Allan
Bosch, Taps's student at the University of Illinois, now a professor at "Cal
State L.A.," and Martel's teacher briefly. Saying Martel was registered as
Pedro Domingo, Bosch details the Domingo family history and theorizes
that Martel saw himself as the ruined, poetic product of Caucasian, Indian, and Negro forebears. He stole to impress a girl studying French
when Taps brought her to an arts festival seven years earlier. Archer identifies her as Ginny, now Martel's widow. Bosch says that twelve years ago
Taps, teaching in Illinois, impregnated Bess, then a student, and married
her. Archer takes Bosch as translator to meet Martel's mother. She says
she married Ricardo Rosales, her son's friend and an important banker,
two months ago. She blames some woman, not gangsters, for her son's
murder. When Archer says she cannot see Ginny, Secundina storms out.
Archer surprises Bosch into admitting Taps and Ginny might have been
lovers. Bess thought so. Bosch admits Taps canceled classes to visit him
the afternoon Martel was shot. Archer visits Bess. She reveals this: She
saw Ginny fondle Taps at the festival and concealed their love affair; Taps
fathered her aborted baby; Bess told Ginny's father about it once Ginny
took classes at Montevista with Taps again. Wondering if Taps killed
Ginny's parents, she says that the night she was killed Marietta telephoned Taps, who said he would always love Ginny. Archer searches
Taps's room for a gun Bess says he owns, goes to Ginny's home, and
finds her with Taps. She reveals that Taps got her pregnant but blamed
Peter, and planned to marry and divorce him for a lucrative settlement,
and go to France with Martel to study. Taps got jealous, drowned injured
Roy and shot suspicious Marietta, then shot Martel, who identified Taps
to her as his killer. When Ginny rebukes Taps as a weakling, he shoots
himself. Ginny coolly awaits the police Archer summons.

A condensation of *Black Money*, titled "The Demon Lover," was published in *Cosmopolitan* (December 1965). Rejected titles for the novel
were "The Darkness at the Window" and "The Scrambling Shadow." The
novel, favorably reviewed, sold almost 10,000 hardbound copies within
two months. Macdonald was pleased at its acceptable "tone." The five
days of breakneck action oblige Macdonald, for clarity, to identify many
dates, days, times, and places. Domingo/Cervantes/Martel resembles Gatz/

Gatsby in F. Scott Fitzgerald's *The Great Gatsby*, which Macdonald said he read annually. Martel, a poor lad with a partly faked past, fatally pursues a materialistic lover, as Gatsby did. Taps resembles Macdonald, but with this difference: Macdonald abandoned the academic life and stopped trying to publish his dissertation on Samuel Taylor Coleridge, whereas Taps rationalized that, if unburdened by teaching demands, he could write a book showing the French influence on Stephen Crane. Macdonald parodies academe by presenting Taps's ludicrous introduction to the subject. Of symbolic significance in *Black Money* is Jean-Paul Sartre's *Huis-Clos* (1944; *No Exit*, 1947), which Tappinger, Bess, Ginny, Bosch, and Martel saw at Los Angeles State College's festival. The play concerns a collaborationist, a lesbian, and a nymphomaniac trapped in a room that is an imaginary contemporary hell, and destroying each other psychologically—behold Taps, Ginny, and Martel. Sartre's play was in Macdonald's mind earlier when, in *The Ferguson Affair* (1960), William Gunnarson listens to a pair of mutual double-crossers and observes, "It resembled a conversation on a lower floor of merry hell, where two dead souls re-enacted a meaningless scene forever. It was the meaninglessness that made it hell."

Bibliography: Bruccoli; Nolan; Schopen; Speir.

"THE BLACK YARN." *See The Far Side of the Dollar*.

BLACKWELL, COLONEL MARK. In *The Zebra-Striped Hearse*, he is Pauline Hatchen's ex-husband and Isobel Blackwell's present husband. He has retired after a so-so military career, pursued only because his father was a colonel. Mark Blackwell is Harriet Blackwell's father (by Pauline) and Dolly Campion's infant son. When Harriet is missing, Blackwell hires Archer to find her. Archer gets close to exposing family secrets; so Blackwell fires him, but Isobel hires him. A missing button from Blackwell's tweed coat leads Archer to Harriet, whose supposed suicide Blackwell stages, after which he kills himself. Macdonald blames much of Blackwell's familial blunders on his mother's smothering-loving behavior.

Bibliography: Speir.

BLACKWELL, HARRIET. In *The Zebra-Striped Hearse*, she is Colonel Mark Blackwell's tall, unattractive daughter, twenty-four, by his former wife, now Pauline Hatchen. Harriet was raised amiss by her father. Wanting a son, he called her Harry. She loves Bruce Campion and is jealous of Dolly Campion, Bruce's wife and Mark's infant son's mother. When Quincy Ralph Simpson uses Blackwell's coat to incriminate Blackwell in Dolly's death, Harriet kills him and buries his body to throw suspicion on her father's second wife, Isobel Blackwell. Archer traces Harriet to Mexico and persuades her to return to face charges.

BLACKWELL, ISOBEL. In *The Zebra-Striped Hearse*, she is Colonel Mark Blackwell's attractive second wife, just over forty. Her first husband was Ronald Jaimet, Blackwell's cousin. While Isobel and Ronald lived in Citrus Junction, their neighbors were Elizabeth Stone and Jack Stone, whose daughter, Dolly (*see* Campion, Dolly), Isobel tried to refine. Dolly called Isobel Aunt Izzie. Ronald died while hiking with Blackwell. Once married to Blackwell, Isobel tried unsuccessfully to get along with Harriet Blackwell, his daughter by a previous marriage. When Blackwell, who hired Archer to find Harriet, discharges him, Isobel hires him. She is a reluctant source of information for Archer, who finds her attractive.

BLACKWELL, MRS. In *The Zebra-Striped Hearse*, she is Colonel Mark Blackwell's deceased mother. Her raising him amiss contributes to his damaged personality.

Bibliography: Speir.

"THE BLACKWELL IMBROGLIO." *See The Zebra-Striped Hearse.*

"THE BLACKWELL TRAGEDY." *See The Zebra-Striped Hearse.*

BLANCHE. In *Sleeping Beauty*, she runs the seaside seafood restaurant and gives Archer useful information.

BLANEY. In *The Way Some People Die*, he is a skinny, loyal gunman, about forty, employed by Danny Dowser. He takes Archer, and later Galley Lawrence, to Dowser. He is arrested by Lieutenant Gary.

BLEERSTONE, BLACK. In "The South Sea Soup Co.," he calls ugly Josephine Bailey, his lover, beautiful, thus arousing Herlock Sholmes's suspicions.

BLEVINS, ALBERT D. In *The Instant Enemy*, he married, at twenty, Henrietta R. Krug (*see* Marburg, Ruth), seventeen, in San Francisco (March 3, 1927). Their son is Jasper Blevins. When they separated, Albert sent Jasper to Henrietta's parents, Joseph L. Krug and Alma R. Krug, in Santa Monica. Albert became a wandering worker. Forty years later, Archer finds Albert in a seedy San Francisco hotel and buys vital documents from him.

BLEVINS, DAVID. In *The Instant Enemy*. *See* Spanner, David.

BLEVINS, HENRIETTA R. KRUG. In *The Instant Enemy*. *See* Marburg, Ruth.

BLEVINS, JASPER. In *The Instant Enemy*, he is the son, about forty, of Albert D. Blevins and Henrietta R. Krug Blevins (*see* Marburg, Ruth). When his parents separated, he went to Henrietta's parents, Joseph L. Krug and Alma R. Krug, in Santa Monica. Jasper married Laurel Dudney (*see* Smith, Mrs. Laurel) (May 1948); their son is David Blevins (*see* Spanner, David). Henrietta, calling herself Ruth, married Mark Hackett; their son is Stephen Hackett. When Mark, disgusted with his faithless wife, rewrote his will to favor Stephen, she and Jasper conspired and Jasper murdered Mark (May 28, 1952). Jasper arranged to have the corpse, battered unidentifiably, beheaded on railroad tracks, and assumed Stephen's identity. For the next fifteen years, Jasper flourished financially as Stephen, studied art, and married Gerda abroad. Jasper is Keith Sebastian's boss. Jasper and Ruth provided money to Alma R. Krug and Mrs. Laurel Smith, to buy their silence. When Laurel finds David, Jasper kills her. Archer exposes these machinations and turns Jasper and his mother over to Captain Robert Aubrey, a Malibu police officer.

BLEVINS, LAUREL. In *The Instant Enemy*. *See* Smith, Mrs. Laurel.

BLUE CITY (1947). Novel. (Characters: Al, Alec, Alec, Freeman Allison, Mrs. Freeman Allison, Dr. Bess, Bobby, Dr. Brush, Archie Calamus, Charlie, Dundee, F. Garland, Gert, Inspector Ralph Hanson, Mrs. Ralph Hanson, Henry, Hirschman, Willie Hoppe, Rusty Jahnke, Kaufman, Carla Kaufman, Mrs. Selby Kerch, Roger Kerch, Selby Kerch, Mabel, Malteoni, McGinis, Dave Moffatt, Pete, Peter Piscator, Ron, Rose, Rourke, Flicka Runymede, Professor Salamander, Alonzo P. Sanford, Joseph Sault, Sid, Sim, Judge Ernest Simeon, Mrs. Francesca Sontag, Stan, Swainie, Ronald Swift, Teagarden, Terry Terhune, Frederick Wales, Mrs. Frederick Wales, Floraine Weather, Jerry D. Weather, John Weather, Mrs. J.D. Weather, Weber, Mrs. Sonia Weil, Whitey, Mrs. Dorothy Williams.)

John Weather, twenty-two and a U.S. Army veteran, hitchhikes early in 1946 to his hometown after being away ten years, to seek employment. His mother tired of his philandering father, J.D. ("Jerry") Weather, left him, and poisoned John's mind against him. She died five years ago. Jerry remarried and was shot to death (April 1944). John, stationed in England then, never knew. Jerry's beautiful second wife, Floraine, about thirty-five, inherited his substantial property, and sold his hotel, the Weather House, to Alonzo Sanford, who converted it into the Palace Hotel. She kept the Cathay Club, now a radio station located in the Palace and featuring Professor Salamander, a disreputable ex-physician.

John gains background information by calling on the self-assured Sanford, the owner of a polluting, anti-union rubber factory, Inspector Ralph Hanson of the police, John's stepmother, Floraine Weather, and Kaufman, an anarchistic secondhand dealer. Jerry, John's murdered father, controlled the town's slot machines and was a force behind city corruption, now managed by Sanford, who controls Freeman Allison, the powerless mayor. The gun used to kill Jerry was stolen from Kaufman by Joseph ("Joey") Sault, who sold it but feared to say to whom. Kaufman tells John his granddaughter, Carla Kaufman, knew Joey but he abandoned her. Kaufman directs John to the apartment of Joey's sister, Mrs. Francesca ("Francie") Sontag. Asked where Joey is, Francie directs him to Charlie's poolroom, where Whitey sends him to F. Garland's place. There he finds slick, tough Joey, says he wants a gun like one used two years ago, identifies himself as Jerry's son, and when Joey pulls a knife disarms and slugs him. Joey, and also Garland, a vicious homosexual, warn John that they work for the dangerous Roger Kerch.

John takes a taxi to the Cathay Club, owned by Floraine. He chances to meet Carla there, where she has become a prostitute. Over drinks, she says she works for but dislikes Kerch, hopes to leave town soon, says Kerch must have something on the second Mrs. Weather, and leads John upstairs. Admitting he talked with her grandfather, he criticizes her self-deluding cynicism and identifies himself as Jerry's son. After she weeps, they make love with hungry sincerity. John goes to Kerch's office in the club, asks for any old job, spars with Rusty Jahnke, Kerch's huge, stupid bodyguard, to prove his feistiness, and is hired. But Garland turns up and identifies him as Jerry's son. John is grabbed by Moffatt, a crooked policeman beckoned by Kerch, and is driven out of town, slugged, and dumped.

John gets a bus into town and makes his way to Mayor Allison's home. After identifying himself and explaining his desire to cleanse the town, he persuades Allison to get him a gun, hears him negotiate for one by telephone, and remembers the phone number. He intends to kill Kerch. John grabs some food at an all-night restaurant, sees and follows Joey, and watches him enter Floraine's house. Climbing up a familiar drainpipe and through a window, he eavesdrops as Floraine and Joey reveal their longstanding intimacy. She asks Joey to kill Kerch, retrieve some damaging papers from his safe, and share Kerch's dishonest setup with her. But Kerch and Garland enter, grab the pair, and announce plans to cart them to Wildwood, a deserted inn. John finds Floraine's car keys and drives in pursuit. He spies helplessly as Kerch tortures and kills Joey and knifes Floraine's face horribly. John drives to a gas station, phones the number Allison used, and leaves a message with a woman who answers, begging for honest police action at the murder site.

John returns to Wildwood, slugs Rusty as he is digging a grave for Joey, but is caught by Garland. Salamander, brought by Kerch, ministers to Floraine but only delays her death. Kerch takes a button and some hair from John to implicate him in her murder. John is ordered to dump Joey's body in the grave and stow Floraine's body in Kerch's car. Leaving John guarded by Garland, Kerch departs to consult with Sanford. John disarms the dainty Garland, breaks his wrists, and drives Floraine's car to Sanford's home. John learns from an obliging maid that Kerch was there but just left. Upstairs, Sanford serenely tells John that Kerch, with Floraine's power of attorney, plans to buy her house and club. John distresses Sanford by revealing that Floraine is dead.

John drives to Floraine's house, retrieves his button and hair, but is spotted by a screaming servant, and flees through the streets and hops into a delivery truck. It drops him near Carla's apartment. He tells her Joey and Floraine are dead, accepts breakfast but declines another lovemaking session, and suddenly sees Allison. It seems that, though married, Allison supports and secretly visits Francie, who is Carla's next-door neighbor. Allison agrees to aid John and departs. Carla phones Kerch for a rendezvous at his club office and drives John there ahead of him. When Kerch arrives, John tortures him until he opens his safe. Inside are proofs that Kerch and Floraine are married, her power of attorney in his favor, and a letter from Allison to Francie that would ruin his career. Moffatt bursts in with a machine gun and arrests John.

Moffatt gets John to the police station, fails to beat a confession out of him, and is stopped when Hanson, having examined the scene at Wildwood with Allison, enters and orders Moffatt and his crooked cops out. Sanford enters, hears John's report, posts his bail, and leaves as Allison enters. John urges Allison to reveal his affair with Francie, arm himself, and grab Kerch and the contents of his safe, the combination of which John remembers and tells Allison. Hanson brings in Rusty, grills him, and makes him confess that he saw Garland kill Jerry. Salamander, brought in, confesses that he treated Floraine.

John accompanies Hanson to Kerch's office. They find Kerch shot dead and Carla wounded. John drives Carla's car to Francie's, finds Allison trying to mollify her, and worms a confession out of him: Allison killed Jerry two years ago, was blackmailed by Kerch, rushed just now to Wildwood and killed Garland, and with the combination rushed to Kerch's safe for evidence against him. He found Kerch there, killed him, and wounded Carla. While John tells Hanson these facts over the phone, Francie shoots and kills Allison. John intends to marry Carla, who is reported to be recovering, and plans to remain and try to clean up the city.

Macdonald dedicated *Blue City* to Robert Ford (*see* Ford, R.A.D.). *Blue City*, Macdonald's most violent novel, shows the influence of *Red Harvest* by Dashiell Hammett, whose work Macdonald admired. It has been suggested that Weather's unnamed hometown is a combination of Kitchener, Ontario, and Jacksonville, Florida. Dodd, Mead, which published Macdonald's first two novels, rejected *Blue City*, as did Simon & Schuster. So Macdonald sought and gladly accepted a contract from Alfred A. Knopf* and happily remained with Knopf for the rest of his career. For $500, Macdonald sold "Blue City," a condensation of the novel, to *Esquire* (August September 1950). Saul David,* senior editor of Bantam Books, liked the condensation so much that he pursued Macdonald for reprint rights. In 1972, *Blue City* was translated into Russian, serialized in *Znamya*, a Russian literary review, and provided with an introduction stressing Macdonald's dramatization of the connection in America between corrupt capitalistic politicians and criminal syndicates. The novel was the basis for a dull movie (*Blue City* [Paramount, 1986], starring David Caruso, Ally Sheedy, and Paul Winfield).

The pace of *Blue City* is slowed by the didacticism of John Weather. Through teeth broken by Moffatt, Weather debates political theory with Sanford, who, ironically, enjoys reading *The Theory of the Leisure Class* by Thorstein Veblen. Notable are Macdonald's early stress on characters' eyes, mentioned more than sixty times, and his frequent comments on their smiles.

Bibliography: Bruccoli; Nolan; Schopen; Speir.

THE BLUE HAMMER (1976). Novel. (Characters: Mrs. Conchita Alvarez, Lew Archer, Colonel Aspinwall, Mrs. Aspinwall, Doris Biemeyer, Jack Biemeyer, Mrs. Biemeyer, Ruth Biemeyer, Brailsford, Mrs. Fay Brighton, Brotherton, Mrs. Brotherton, Sheriff Brotherton, Deputy Cameron, Carlos, Felix Chantry, Francine Chantry, Richard Chantry, Larry Fallon, Jessie Gable, Juanita Grimes, Paola Grimes, Paul Grimes, Holman, Mrs. Holman, Dr. Ian Innes, Mrs. Ian Innes, Joe, Fred Johnson, Gerard Johnson, Sarah Johnson, Delbert Knapp, Roy Lackner, District Attorney Lansing, Simon Lashman, Sergeant Leverett, Captain Mackendrick, Mrs. Mackendrick, Mead Mildred Mead, William Mead, Stanley Meyer, Arthur Planter, Jackie Pratt, Puddler Henry Purvis, Jeremy Rader, Molly Rader, Ralph, Rico, Ralph Sandman, Siddon, Betty Jo Siddon, Jacob Whitmore, Mrs. Jacob Whitmore.)

One October morning in 1975, Archer drives to Santa Teresa to see Jack Biemeyer and his wife, Ruth Biemeyer. A Richard Chantry painting Ruth bought from Paul Grimes, a local art dealer, was stolen from the Biemeyers's mansion yesterday. It conventionally portrays a yellow-haired young woman in an Indian serape. Archer must find it. Jack, rich from copper mines in Arizona, and Ruth have retired here. Jack relishes a photograph of the great wound his mine pierced in the earth. Ruth knew Chantry in Arizona but hasn't seen him in twenty-five years. Jack, ridiculing both Chantry and Ruth, exits. Ruth shows Archer a souvenir copy of a farewell letter Chantry wrote to his wife, Francine Chantry (July 4, 1950), before disappearing. Ruth knows Francine. Between their houses is a barranca. Ruth tells Archer their daughter, Doris Biemeyer, twenty, is a sophomore at the local university. Doris's friend, Fred Johnson, about thirty, is a perennial student and a docent at the local art museum; when he visited the Biemeyers, he saw and admired the picture.

Archer seeks Francine at her home. She is out. He checks into a harbor motel and seeks Grimes at his office; but Paola, his Indian secretary, says he is away. Archer bribes a black clerk at a liquor store next door to tell him about Grimes, described as gray and goateed. Archer goes to the museum, finds Francine, and professes interest in its Chantrys. When he explains his assignment, she blanches and calls the Biemeyers "ignorant" and the painting bought from Grimes "a fake" possibly painted by Grimes, who taught Chantry during his Arizona period.

Archer drives to the Johnson house, where Fred lives with his parents. His father, Gerard Johnson, is a wounded, alcoholic veteran. Archer tells Fred's mother, Sarah Johnson, a full-time nurse, he is a journalist working on a story about Richard Chantry. She boasts about Fred, who is soon to graduate; but when Fred drives up in an old Ford, she signals him away. Archer follows, loses him in traffic, and drives to Academia Village, where Doris rooms. Opening her door to him, she half-faints from taking downers. He seats her and listens: Doris's mother wants to institutionalize her and get her a shrink; her parents have argued with each other for years, sometimes about someone named Mildred; Doris feels lost; Fred's mother dislikes Doris; Fred asked Doris to lend him the Chantry picture to authenticate it. Archer leaves, consumes a "natureburger" on campus, spots Fred's car, and intercepts Fred near Doris's room. Fred admits he took the picture yesterday to his room at home but insists it was stolen after that. Archer takes a burger to Doris, checks with the liquor-store clerk, buys some whisky, and is told Paola packed her car as if she were planning to leave.

Archer seeks Fred at the museum. It is closed. He returns to the Johnson house. Sarah is at the nearby hospital. Archer bribes Gerard with whisky to let him see Fred's room. The missing picture is not there, and Gerard knows nothing about it. Archer cannot get into a locked attic.

On his way to the hospital to see Sarah, Archer finds Grimes in the street, horribly beaten. Grimes calls Archer "Chantry" and asks to be left alone. Hospital attendants come, then the police, headed by Captain Mackendrick. Grimes dies. Archer finds Grimes's parked car. In it is an invitation to Francine's cocktail party this evening, together with several canvases. Putting one painting in his car, Archer drives to the party, uninvited but welcomed. Francine introduces him to Betty Jo Siddon, a local reporter, who introduces him to numerous guests and asks Rico, Francine's handsome, devoted servant, to get Archer a sandwich and some beer. Betty, quick and attractive, agrees to trade information with Archer. He tells her about Grimes's death. She leaves to cover the story. When Francine returns, Archer tells her Grimes has been murdered. She admits that Grimes was invited to her party. Archer asks her if Richard Chantry, her missing husband, is alive. She doesn't know. Archer tells her that as he was dying Grimes confused him with Chantry. Rico enters. Rico and Francine are locked in conversation. Archer walks to another room. He sees Arthur Planter, an art critic he met earlier. When shown the painting in Archer's car, Planter says it is not a Chantry but a poor seascape by Jacob Whitmore, a local painter who died of a heart attack yesterday while swimming. Whitmore lived with his girlfriend north of the campus, at Sycamore Point. Archer goes there, finds the impoverished girl there, and learns this: Grimes bought two paintings from Whitmore; one, of a beautiful blonde, was not by him; the girl suspects Grimes of dishonesty; Paola is Grimes's daughter. When the woman says she needs money for Whitmore's coffin, Archer buys five Whitmore paintings for $40 and proceeds to the hospital morgue. To the deputy coroner, Henry Purvis, he says Whitmore may have been murdered. Purvis says that Grimes has old drug-needle marks and that a dark woman, who mourned over his body, is now in the hospital chapel. She is Paola, who says this: Grimes, her father, was a heroin addict in Arizona, was cured in prison, was briefly a university teacher, turned homosexual; the stolen picture, probably a Chantry, Grimes bought on the beach and sold to the Biemeyers; Purvis found the photograph of it in Grimes's pocket; she won't continue her father's risky business. Purvis tells Archer that Mackendrick let Betty Jo take the photo for office use.

Archer learns at the hospital that Sarah was released for stealing drugs and now works at La Paloma, a nearby convalescent home. Finding the defensive woman there, Archer learns Fred drove by with Doris this evening and got money from her. Sarah insists that Fred only borrowed the painting to analyze it and that it was stolen from him at the museum. Calling Sarah a liar, Archer asks if Fred sold it for drugs. When Archer says Grimes has been murdered, Sarah faints. He proceeds to Betty's newspaper office, acquaints her with his facts and theories, and naps while she gets him a copy of the photograph of the missing picture. They decide, although it is past midnight, to revisit Francine. Rico, with lipstick on his mouth, admits them. While waiting for Francine, Betty tells Archer that her father took her to meet Chantry twenty-five years ago when she was about four years old. Emerging freshened, Francine looks at the photograph and admits the woman in it may possibly resemble a beauty she met in Santa Fe in 1940. When Archer theorizes that Chantry may be alive and may have recently painted from memory the picture now missing, Francine grows threatening and vows to protect her husband's reputation. Archer drives with Betty to his motel, and the two sleep together.

When "cool" dawn comes, Betty has departed but soon phones. They agree to meet at the museum, where a worker says the subject of the missing painting, the photo of which he has seen, resembles that in *Penelope* by Simon Lashman, a Tucson artist. It was displayed for a show Fred might have seen. Suspecting Fred has headed for Tucson, Archer phones Lashman, tells him the stolen picture is also of his model, whom Lashman names as Mildred Mead, and is invited to visit Lashman. Archer revisits the Biemeyers, antagonizes Jack, but is paid $500 by Ruth to go to Tucson and find Doris. Ruth tells Archer this: Felix Chantry, Richard's father, was an engineer, developed the copper mine, built a fine house, died; Jack, whose mother was Felix's cousin, operated the mine; Jack and Lashman both loved Mildred; Jack won, bought and gave the house to Mildred, not Ruth; Ruth bought the so-called Chantry painting of Mildred because she was interested in Chantry. Archer returns to Betty, who warns him about Fred's imbalance. Archer asks Betty, while he is in Arizona, to check on Francine, whom he tells Betty he just saw from the Biemeyer house cutting weeds in her greenhouse with Rico.

Archer flies from Santa Teresa to Los Angeles and Tucson, rents a car, and interviews Lashman by afternoon. The crotchety old painter has started another memory portrait of Mildred. He tells Archer this: Fred and Doris came by; Lashman told Fred he thinks Chantry is dead; Mildred loved Felix, Richard's father, bore him a son who called himself William Mead; Mildred's house is in Chantry Canyon, near New Mexico; William on army leave was beaten to death in the desert; Sheriff Brotherton of Copper City "mishandled" the investigation; Mildred, whom he hasn't seen in twenty years, sent him a Christmas card last year; the photo is probably of a Chantry painting.

Archer finds Brotherton's substation in Copper City, has cheese and beer, and asks directions to Chantry Canyon. Brotherton tells Archer this: Mildred sold her house three months ago to the Society of Mutual Love for $100,000, moved to "her folks in California"; Fred and Doris drove on toward Mildred's former place. Archer soon gets there, sees Fred's junky car, hears music at the commune, and sees Fred. He got his nose battered in a fight with a religious zealot. When Archer, more intimidating, demands to see Doris, a black-robed leader brings her out. She says she is being helped here to overcome her drug habit, is unwanted at home, is "spiritually unwell," and needs her new commune friends' prayers. Feeling powerless, Archer leaves, pockets Fred's car keys, and takes Fred with him.

While they are driving to Copper City, Fred admits taking the painting but insists it was then stolen from the museum. His purpose in coming to Arizona was to "trace" it. Brotherton meets them, has someone repair Fred's nose, learns about the picture from Archer, and reveals this: Brotherton slept with Mildred when he was a youth; Richard and Francine Chantry lived in Arizona; Brotherton knew Grimes, who lived with the Chantrys and was Richard's art teacher; Grimes taught high school here, lost his job, "married a half-breed"; Felix died (1942), and Biemeyer took over the mine; after William was murdered (1943), his body was shipped to his wife in California; an army buddy of William's, named "Wilson or Jackson," mentioned William to Brotherton and sent Brotherton a postcard from a California "vets' hospital" after the war. Brotherton bridles when Archer tardily reveals he is working for Biemeyer and the girl at the commune is Biemeyer's daughter, Doris.

Brotherton drives Archer back to the commune. Doris agrees to go home. The religious leader, half-zealot, half-practical, tells Archer they send mortgage payments for Mildred's house to the Copper City Southwestern Savings. Archer gives him Fred's car keys for safety. Back in the city, Brotherton phones Biemeyer, who alerts a company jet to return Doris, Fred, and Archer to Santa Teresa. Doris spends the night with Brotherton and his wife. Archer gets a motel room for himself and Fred, who speaks maturely about his vain hope of making a name for himself by autheticating the Chantry painting, which he calls genuine though stylistically recent and with recent paint. He defends his quarrelsome parents. Archer admires Fred.

With Fred held by a deputy, Archer enjoys a shave and breakfast, and locates Grimes's ex-wife Juanita Grimes's art-supply shop. This fine-looking woman, whose daughter Paola phoned about Grimes's murder, tells Archer this: Grimes and Richard Chantry, Grimes's art student in Copper City, were bisexual; William, Richard's half-brother, and Francine, Richard's wife, were in love with each other; William got a girl pregnant, married her, was drafted (1942), and on leave back home was murdered (summer 1943); Francine considered a divorce then but persuaded Richard to move instead to Santa Teresa; Paul moved to Santa Teresa this year; Juanita wonders if Richard, alive and hiding in Santa Teresa, murdered Grimes; Juanita received a postcard from Mildred, living in Santa Teresa; Mildred wrote about planning to move into a nursing home. Juanita gives Archer $50 for her impoverished daughter, Paola, living at Santa Teresa's sleazy Monte Cristo Hotel. From a bank clerk Archer gets Mildred's address and post office box number.

Archer, Doris, and Fred fly home. The Biemeyers are waiting. Jack rebukes Fred, enjoys seeing the police arrest Fred, and takes Doris home without Ruth. Archer locates his car at the airport and drives Ruth to her young lawyer, Roy Lackner, whom she just consulted about a possible divorce. Archer proceeds to Paola's hotel, to give her the $50 from her mother. The girl is out. He visits Betty, frustrated in trying to write her

Chantry story. Archer tells her Mildred is in a local nursing home and suggests that Betty interview her. Archer visits police headquarters. He and Mackendrick exchange facts and theories. In 1945, fresh out of the army, Mackendrick as a patrolman met Richard Chantry but has no notion concerning his present whereabouts. Purvis tells Archer that Whitmore was drowned in fresh water and dumped in the ocean to look like an accident. Archer visits Whitmore's disconsolate girlfriend. Calling herself Jessie Gable, she reveals this: Jessie stole Jacob from his wife; Jacob attended art shows and sales at the waterfront; Jessie identifies the missing painting, from the photo, as one Jacob bought from an old woman for $50 and sold to Grimes for a large, undisclosed sum. Archer gives Jessie $20, promises more, and asks her to go to the next art show to look for Mildred.

Betty is not at the newspaper building, but Archer meets Mrs. Fay Brighton, the newspaper librarian. Fay says Betty found Mildred's nursing home and left two hours ago, close-mouthed like the news hen Fay once was. She gives him Betty's address and phone number. They seek Betty at a nearby restaurant, without success. Archer tells Fay he is worried about Betty and mentions the Biemeyers's painting and Whitmore's murder; Fay says she worked fruitlessly on Chantry's disappearance twenty years ago and thinks he was murdered.

Leaving Fay to phone nursing homes in pursuit of Betty, Archer drives to the Biemeyers's house. He asks Jack to help him locate Betty, who, he says, was looking for Mildred. Jack tries to deny ever knowing Mildred, until Archer squeezes this from him: Jack loved sexy Mildred, set her up in Santa Teresa a few months ago, asks Archer not to tell Ruth, who is "insanely jealous." Ruth, listening at the door, blasts him for preferring a motherly "old hag" to a straight wife and says the whole town knows he visited Mildred at her beach apartment. Jack replies that he dumped Mildred when she demanded money for better accommodations and that she is with relatives. When Jack will not do more to find Betty, Archer threatens him and in Ruth's kitchen phones Fay. She has no news, says she is scared, and sobs. Ruth tells him Fred has been released to his parents and Doris has run out. Archer observes lights in Francine's greenhouse, checks with binoculars, tells Ruth that Francine and Rico are pressing dirt into a hole, runs down for a closer look, and finds Doris also spying as well. Archer and Doris return to the house. Archer phones Mackendrick, tells him about the digging, and asks him to put an alert out for Betty. Archer sees Rico toss a sack into his car and drive off. Archer pursues him, stops at a pier, overpowers Rico, and retrieves the sack. Archer takes both man and sack to Mackendrick, at his office. Rico confesses the following: Rico was working for the Chantrys twenty-five years ago; a brown-suited stranger visited Richard, returned a few days later with a brunette, about thirty, and a boy, seven or eight; the stranger died;

Francine said if Rico would bury him in the greenhouse "she would be nice to me"; Richard, leaving his farewell letter, "walked away." Archer, admitting he is Betty's "boyfriend," persuades Mackendrick to scour the nursing homes for her.

Archer goes to the Johnson house. Lackner is there. Sarah and Fred are grateful to both men; but Gerard, drunk, orders them to leave. In the post-midnight moonlit night, Archer and Lackner are discussing alcoholism and dysfunctional families when Gerard reappears, clicks an empty gun at Archer, and quickly gets disarmed. Sarah apologizes, and Archer drives her to her La Paloma night shift. Mackendrick is there.

On to Francine's. When Archer says Rico is singing to the police about the bones, Francine blusters, offers a bribe, and half-offers sexual favors. Failing, she says this: Richard, far from being bisexual, was excited almost exclusively by his art; Richard named the brown-suited man, but she cannot remember his name; he was a wounded veteran who spent time in a veterans' hospital; his death was accidental; Rico buried the body; Richard wrote that letter and disappeared; she has been buying Rico's silence with sex ever since; just now, she got Rico to dig up and destroy the bones through fear of an imminent police search; she doesn't know where Betty is; a strange woman phoned Francine last night for hush money to be delivered tomorrow. Francine professes shock when Archer says Richard had a half-brother named William, and she denies knowing him.

Back at his motel, Archer finds a message from Paola, goes to her, and gives her Juanita's welcome $50. Paola thinks Richard may be alive, believes he painted the missing portrait recently, killed her father, and may be gunning for her. She says her father took her a few days ago to see Mildred, at the Magnolia Court. The woman was bitter and said little. Archer gets Paola some food and a room in his motel.

At the Magnolia, Archer finds Mildred. An alcoholic with remnants of beauty, Mildred admits Betty visited her this evening, learned little, and left for Sycamore Point. While telling Mildred about Whitmore's murder and Rico's bone digging, Archer learns this: Mildred's son William's body is buried in California, but she does not know where; his widow married another man, who changed her son's name to his; she still likes Lashman. Archer theorizes thus: Biemeyer bought her the Chantry house to silence her about her son's murder; the mangled body thought to be William's might not have been his; the dug-up bones might be William's.

At Sycamore Point Archer finds Jessie. For $100 Jessie tells him that a hospital orderly told her Sarah sold the Chantry picture to Whitmore. Jessie adds that Betty visited Jessie, who told Betty all that. Archer rushes to La Paloma, where the black nurse, Mrs. Holman, reveals that Sarah and Mildred are related and that the two argued when Mildred left La Paloma.

Archer gets to Mackendrick's office about 7:00 A.M., shaves there, and at breakfast with him reveals that he talked with Francine, who said the brown-suited man might have been a wounded veteran from a veterans' hospital. Mackendrick leaves, irate at having been kept in the dark. Archer sleeps four hours at his motel, then phones Brotherton, who reports this: Jerry Jackson, or Jerry Johnson, might be the name of the man asking about Chantry; he was in a Los Angeles veterans' hospital; the Chantry half-brothers were rivals for "the same girl." Archer raps on Paola's door. She says that her parents knew Richard, "an s.o.b.," and that Copper City rumors suggested William was the better painter and when William was drafted Richard stole his drawings, his paintings, and Francine. When Archer tells Mackendrick over the phone that William stole Richard's work and that a Jerry Johnson went to Arizona to check into William's death, Mackendrick replies that Purvis, the coroner, found expertly treated shrapnel wounds in those old bones.

Archer learns through Fay at the newspaper office that a well-spoken black woman phoned last night about Betty. He guesses the woman is Mrs. Holman, obtains her address from the liquor-store clerk, and gets her to admit she was worried about Betty, who "huddle[d]" with Sarah at La Paloma yesterday evening. Mrs. Holman said nothing earlier because Sarah told her to deny that either Mildred or Sarah was ever there, if the cops should ask.

At the Johnson house, he finds Fred, dropped there by Lackner, who will summon the police. Archer entices Gerard with whisky to open the attic, where he finds Betty, naked and trussed. She says Gerard painted her picture. He did the recent Chantry too, in that very room. Archer finds and puts it in his car. Mackendrick seizes Gerard, Sarah, and Fred for questioning. After Archer and Betty have lunch, she returns to her office. Mackendrick says the bones are those of a veteran named Gerard Johnson, a former veterans' hospital patient. So the whole Johnson family is a fake. Francine has fled. Brotherton just reported to Purvis that William was buried in Santa Teresa, where his wife lives or lived. A neighbor at her address says she married a drunk named Johnson and is a nurse. Archer and Purvis talk to Sarah, who is preparing to leave. Archer parks outside and watches. Betty takes a cab to her car. She says her editor is squeamish about printing her Chantry scoop. Her car battery being stolen, Betty accepts Archer's offer to drive her to Long Beach. This because Francine just phoned Betty from a waterfront bar there; she had a car accident and is stranded. They arrive in two hours and return Francine to Santa Teresa to freshen up and face interrogation. On the way she reveals this: She never knew Richard began posing as Gerard Johnson; Sarah was the woman who phoned demanding money. Archer and Betty bed down in his motel.

At dawn, this fifth day, Archer awakens alone, has a bite, seeks Mildred at the Magnolia, and learns that she took a cab to the courthouse. Pursuing, he learns she was refused permission to see Chantry. He spots her at the railing of the courthouse observation platform. Archer rushes up, prevents her from jumping to her death, and releases her to Lansing, the glory-seeking district attorney. He shares with Archer this confidential information: Mackendrick says Chantry (formerly Gerard) murdered Mildred's son thirty years ago in Arizona; they just found a stiletto on Mildred, intended for Chantry or perhaps herself.

Not permitted to talk with Chantry, Archer returns the painting to Ruth, accuses her of knowing Mildred was in town, of knowing Jack was revisiting her, and of buying the picture as a warning to Jack. To both Jack and Ruth, Archer summarizes: William killed Richard in the desert, put his own uniform on the corpse; Francine accepted William as her husband thereafter; Mildred identified the dead Richard as William; Jack got Brotherton to quash the murder inquiry. Hopeless now, Jack gloats to Ruth that William is his son by Mildred. While Archer is driving Jack to the courthouse, Jack amplifies: Felix and Mildred threw a party; Jack attended; he was seventeen when William was conceived; Mildred told Felix he was the father; Mildred helped Jack through college and then got Felix to hire him; Felix stopped support money for Mildred when she turned to Lashman. Jack sees his weeping son in jail.

The title *The Blue Hammer*, a phrase from an obscure poem by Macdonald's friend Henri Anthony Coulette,* concerns arterial blood. When Betty is sleeping, Archer sees her temple pulse beating like a blue hammer and hopes it "would never stop." Other titles considered were "Guilty Knowledge," "The Noon of Night," "Portrait of the Artist," "Portrait of the Artist as a Dead Man," "The Silent Hammer," and "The Tarantula Hawk." *The Blue Hammer* sold well; quick press runs totaled 48,000 copies. It was reprinted in London (Collins, 1976; and others), and in paperback (Bantam, 1977; Fontana/Collins, 1978). It was widely reviewed, often favorably, despite its repetition of old thematic and plot patterns. *The Blue Hammer*, Macdonald's longest novel, was also his last. Archer is uniquely mellow and introspective in it, perhaps as a hint that it is his swan song.

Bibliography: Bruccoli; Nolan; Gilbert Sorrentino, "Ross Macdonald: Some Remarks on the Limitation of Form," in *IJ*, pp. 148–153; Speir.

BOB. In *Trouble Follows Me*, he is a black bartender at Detroit's Paris Bar and Grill. He is reluctant to serve Bessie Land more liquor.

BOB. In *Trouble Follows Me*, he is mentioned in Private Rodney Hatcher's letter to Laura Eaton. Bob, evidently a soldier, knows her.

BOBBY. In *Blue City*, he is the brother of the waiter at the restaurant where John Weather grabs a meal. The waiter says strike breakers at Alonzo P. Sanford's factory broke Bobby's elbow and threw him out of town.

"THE BOGEY MAN." *See The Underground Man*.

BOLLING, CHAD. In *The Galton Case*, he edited *Chisel*, the San Francisco magazine in which Anthony Galton published his poem "Luna." Archer finds him at the Listening Ear, chanting his idiotic poetry to a jazz accompaniment. Bolling helps him substantially. Macdonald satirically paraphrases Bolling's beatnik verse, accompanied by jazz. Bolling owes something to the personality of the Santa Barbara poet Kenneth Rexroth, whose performance of chanting his poetry cum recorded jazz Macdonald once attended and disliked. Macdonald has said he regarded Bolling as "an object of parody and my spokesman for the possibilities of California life."

Bibliography: Nolan; Schopen; "WG."

BOSCH, ALLAN. In *Black Money*, he was one of Taps Tappinger's students at the University of Illinois. Bosch teaches at Los Angeles State College. His best student was Francis Martel, then known as Pedro Domingo. Bosch, in his mid-thirties and a splendid teacher, gives Archer useful information.

BOTKIN, JOSEPH. In *The Far Side of the Dollar*, he is the owner of an El Rancho sporting-goods store. He is middle-aged, not successful, but cheerful. He directs Archer to The Barroom Floor and to Ringo's auto yard. He sold Ralph Hillman the knife used to kill Carol Harley and Mike Harley.

BOUCHER, ANTHONY (1911–1968). (Real name: William Anthony Parker White.) Writer and editor. He was born in Oakland, California, and attended Pasadena Junior College, the University of Southern California (B.A., 1932), and the University of California, Berkeley (M.A., 1934). He published his first novel in 1937, married (1938), and had two children. Boucher cofounded and edited the *Magazine of Fantasy and Science Fiction* (1949–1958), edited *True Crime Detective* (1952–1953), "Mercury Mysteries" (1952–1955), "Dell Great Mystery Library" (1957–1960), and "Collier Mystery Classics" (1962–1968); wrote "Criminals at Large," a weekly column, for the *New York Times Book Review* (1951–1968); wrote reviews for *Ellery Queen's Mystery Magazine* (1948–1950, 1957–1968), the *San Francisco Chronicle* (1942–1947), and other outlets; wrote and edited many mystery, science-fiction, and fantasy books; reviewed science-fiction books and opera; and wrote radio programs. Boucher was an invaluable member of various organizations associated with mystery and crime writers, notably Mystery Writers of America, of which he was founding director, and Baker Street Irregulars. A Roman Catholic, a linguist, and a translator, he was interested in spectator sports, poker, good food, silent movies, and music.

Macdonald and Margaret Millar* met Boucher in October 1945, when Macdonald's naval vessel, the *Shipley Bay*, docked in San Francisco. Boucher had favorably reviewed her 1945 novel *The Iron Gates* and Macdonald's *The Dark Tunnel*. Encouraged by Boucher, Macdonald wrote a short story titled "Find the Woman" while at sea, entered it in an *Ellery Queen's Mystery Magazine* contest, and won the $300 fourth prize (1946). Macdonald and Boucher enjoyed a fruitful relationship, underpinned by correspondence and Boucher's helpful reviews of Macdonald. Boucher admired the similes and metaphors in *The Drowning Pool* (dedicated to Boucher), praised the style of *The Way Some People Die* and its three-dimensional characters, and called *Find a Victim* "strange and haunting," with a "powerful and personal" plot. *The Galton Case* disappointed Boucher, who raved about *The Ferguson Affair*. By the time *The Far Side of the Dollar* appeared, Boucher had elevated Macdonald to a rank superior to Dashiell Hammett and Raymond Chandler.

Bibliography: Bruccoli; Nolan.

BOURKE. In *Meet Me at the Morgue*, he runs the Acme Investigative Agency in Los Angeles. He needs money to avoid losing his wife, Carol. He is in trouble when he and Molly Fawn conspire to grab ransom money paid by Abel Johnson for the return of his son. Macdonald sought to sketch Bourke as a non-narrator private-eye resembling Archer—this, partly at the request of Hugh Kenner,* Macdonald's friend.

Bibliography: Hugh Kenner, "Learning," in *IJ*, pp. 55–58; Schopen.

BOURKE, CAROL. In *Meet Me at the Morgue*, she is Bourke's estranged wife.

BOZEY. In *Find a Victim*, he is a tough criminal, twenty-one. He devised a hijacking with Don Kerrigan, planned a getaway with Jo Summer, outfights Archer, but is double-crossed by Brandon Church, sheriff of Las Cruses. Although Archer apprehends Bozey, Archer's kindness persuades Bozey to turn state's evidence to get a lighter sentence. At a Los Angeles hotel, he registered himself and Jo as Mr. and Mrs. John Brown. When asked by the Las Cruses D.A., Bozey says his first name is Leonard.

BRADSHAW. In *The Chill. See* Osborne, Senator.

BRADSHAW, DEAN ROY. (Full name: George Roy Bradshaw). In *The Chill*, he was a poverty-stricken student at Bridgeton City College. Then known as George, he ran an elevator in Luke Deloney's apartment building. He married Letitia O. Macready, Deloney's sister-in-law and murderess. Twenty-five years his elder, she sent Roy to Harvard for his Ph.D. and pretended to be Mrs. Bradshaw, his mother, when he became dean of Pacific Point College. Roy, in his forties, loved Constance McGee, and when tired of Mrs. Bradshaw fell for and married Laura Sutherland. To throw off suspicion, Roy professed to be in love with Helen Haggerty, whom Mrs. Bradshaw therefore murdered. Roy is killed when Mrs. Bradshaw smashes into his car with her Rolls. Macdonald's prejudice against Ivy League academics manifests itself when he has Dean Bradshaw lose his Harvard accent at a stressful moment. Donald Ross Pearce,* Macdonald's California professor friend, so objected to hints in *The Chill* linking him and Bradshaw that he threw the book in the trash.

Bibliography: Nolan.

BRADSHAW, MRS. In *The Chill*, she was born Letitia ("Tish") Osborne, and is Mrs. Luke Deloney's younger sister. They are Senator Osborne's daughters, in Bridgeton, Illinois. Tish married and divorced Val Macready. When Luke, her brother-in-law, found Tish and her lover, Roy Bradshaw, in bed, an argument resulted in her killing Luke. Tish married Roy. He became dean of Pacific Point College, and the two pretended to be mother and son with an age difference of twenty-five years. When Roy became Constance McGee's lover, Mrs. Bradshaw killed her. Archer meets Mrs. Bradshaw, in her sixties and with a "lumpy body." After he uncovers the truth, she kills Roy in a car accident.

BRAGA, SAL. In *Find a Victim*, he is a deputy under Brandon Church, the Las Cruses sheriff. Braga is furious when his cousin Tony Aquista is murdered. His interference with Archer causes Jo Summer to escape temporarily.

BRAILSFORD. In *The Blue Hammer*, he owns the Santa Teresa newspaper Betty Jo Siddon works for. Francine Chantry is so important that she partly controls what Brailsford can print.

BRAKE, LIEUTENANT. In *The Ivory Grin*, he is the Bella City police officer, in his fifties, with whom Archer works to investigate Lucy Champion's and Maxfield Heiss's deaths.

BRANCH, ROBERT ("BOB"). In *The Dark Tunnel*, he is the hero-narrator, twenty-nine. He teaches English literature at Midwestern University. When his friend, Dr. Alec Judd, is murdered, Branch investigates. He suspects Dr. Herman Schneider until he is murdered. With the aid of Chester Gordon, FBI agent, Branch goes to Canada, rescues Ruth Esch, whom he loves, and fingers Schneider's son, Peter Schneider.

Bibliography: Schopen.

"THE BRASS BED." *See The Far Side of the Dollar*.

BREWER, JOE. In "The Sky Hook," he was Frederick's partner in their gold-rush days.

BRIGHTON, MRS. FAY. In *The Blue Hammer*, she is the widowed Santa Teresa newspaper librarian. She knows Betty Jo Siddon. Once a news hen, Fay failed twenty years ago to locate Richard Chantry. She knew Jacob Whitmore and gives Archer information.

"BRING THE KILLER TO JUSTICE." *See The Doomsters*.

BROADHURST, CAPTAIN LEO. In *The Underground Man*, he was Elizabeth Broadhurst's unfaithful husband and Stanley Broadhurst's father. He evidently participated in nine or ten Pacific landings, then did a lot of boating and tennis playing. He seemingly made plans in 1955 to meet Ellen Kilpatrick in Reno but was murdered and buried in his red Porsche sports car. When he planned his getaway (with Ellen?), he bought steamship tickets for Mr. and Mrs. Ralph Smith.

BROADHURST, ELIZABETH ("NELL"). In *The Underground Man*, she was Captain Leo Broadhurst's frigid wife and is Stanley Broadhurst's mother, Jean Broadhurst's mother-in-law, and Ronny Broadhurst's grandmother, about fifty. She discovered Leo's affair with Ellen Kilkpatrick in 1955, shot Leo in the head, but did not kill him. Mrs. Edna Snow was then Mrs. Broadhurst's housekeeper. Mrs. Broadhurst, whose maiden name was Falconer, is being cheated by Brian Kilpatrick.

BROADHURST, JEAN. In *The Underground Man*, she is Stanley Broadhurst's wife and Ronald Broadhurst's mother. She hires Archer to find Ronny when Stanley disappears with him. Archer is attracted to her but bothered by her histrionics.

BROADHURST, RONALD ("RONNY"). In *The Underground Man*, he is Stanley and Jean Broadhurst's charming son, five or six. When Stanley takes Ronald away, Jean hires Archer to find him. Eudora Welty, in her review of *The Underground Man* (*New York Times Book Review*, February 14, 1971), says Ronny is "the real kernel of the book, its heart and soul." Ronny is closely based on James Pagnusat,* Macdonald's grandson.

BROADHURST, STANLEY ("STAN"). In *The Underground Man*, he is the son, twenty-seven, of Captain Leo Broadhurst and Elizabeth Broadhurst. He is Jean Broadhurst's husband and Ronald Broadhurst's father. Stanley's life was ruined when as a child he heard the shot fired by Elizabeth at Leo; he never sees his father again and, in denial, spends time and energy seeking him. While digging for his father's car, he starts the Santa Teresa forest fire with his cigarillo and is murdered.

BROADMAN, HECTOR. In *The Ferguson Affair*, he is a widowered pawnbroker. Ella Barker nursed him in the hospital. He proposed to her. When she rejected him, he introduced her to Larry Gaines. Broadman worked with the burglary gang and is murdered.

BROCCO, AL. In "Midnight Blue," he is Green's cook. Al killed his adulterous wife. Years later, his daughter, Anita, kills Franklin Connor, who spurned her.

BROCCO, ALICE. In "Midnight Blue," she is Al Brocco's younger daughter.

BROCCO, ANITA. In "Midnight Blue," she is Al Brocco's older daughter. She is a police radio dispatcher and one of Franklin Connor's earlier sexual conquests. She sees him making love with Virginia Green and kills her.

BROCCO, MRS. AL. In "Midnight Blue," she was the wife of a cook. When he caught her with another man, he killed her and got off with manslaughter because her lover was "a Mex."

BROCH, DR. In *The Wycherly Woman*, he is an alcoholic physician, available to stitch Archer's temple wound.

BROCKLEY, DR. In *The Doomsters*, he works at the state hospital and tells Archer about Carl Hallman and Thomas Rica.

BROKAW, DR. LAWRENCE. In *Sleeping Beauty*, he is Harold Sherry's physician, in his thirties.

BRONSON. In *The Far Side of the Dollar*, he is a Laguna Perdida School student.

BROTHERTON. In *The Blue Hammer*, she is Sheriff Brotherton's grown daughter. Sheriff Brotherton tells Archer that Doris Biemeyer can sleep in his daughter's old room.

BROTHERTON, MRS. In *The Blue Hammer*, she is Sheriff Brotherton's wife. She is expected to welcome Doris Biemeyer to their home overnight.

BROTHERTON, SHERIFF. In *The Blue Hammer*, he is the leading police authority, fifty-nine, in Copper City, Arizona. He boasts to Archer that forty years before he slept with Mildred Mead. He deliberately mishandled the investigation of William Mead's 1943 murder. Sheriff Brotherton cooperates somewhat with Archer, who regards him as a fine man if artificially folksy.

BROWN. In *The Far Side of the Dollar*, he is mentioned as Robert Brown's father, who died at eighty.

BROWN, JOHN. In *Find a Victim. See* Bozey.

BROWN, JOHN. (Full name: John Brown, Sr.) In *The Galton Case. See* Galton, Anthony.

BROWN, JOHN. (Full name: John Brown, Jr.) In *The Galton Case*, he is the son, born December 2, 1936 in Luna Bay, of Anthony Galton, who calls himself John Brown, and Theodora Gavin Brown. Fred Nelson murdered Anthony, married Theodora, escaped with John and her to Canada. While there Brown was called Theodore Fredericks to agree with his parents' assumed names, Nelson and Theodora Fredericks. Brown, when sixteen, crossed to Michigan with Peter Culligan, who was in league with Gordon Sable and who told him about his parents and Nelson. Brown got to Ann Arbor, was befriended by Gabriel R. Lindsay, graduated from the University of Michigan, and impersonated Anthony Galton's son— which he truly was—to collect Anthony's mother Maria Galton's fortune. Archer wrongly accuses Brown of fakery. Brown falls in love with Sheila Howell and will inherit. Brown said that in childhood fantasies he called himself Percival Fitzroy, son of an English lord; in college, he registered as John Lindsay. Macdonald saw in John Brown, Jr., an Oedipus-like son angry at his parents for exiling him. In two aborted versions of *The Galton Case*, John Brown (Jr.) was named Tom and Willie.

Bibliography: Nolan; Schopen; "WG."

BROWN, MRS. ROBERT. In *The Far Side of the Dollar*, she is Carol Harley's once-beautiful mother, about fifty-five. Mrs. Brown and her husband bicker about their earlier, different treatment of their murdered daughter. Mrs. Brown gives Archer a lead enabling him to locate Otto Sipe.

BROWN, MRS. ROBT. In *The Far Side of the Dollar. See* Harley, Carol.

BROWN, ROBERT ("ROB"). In *The Far Side of the Dollar*, he was a Pocatello, Idaho, high school coach and counselor. His befriending Mike Harley led to Mike's corrupting Brown's daughter, Carol (*see* Harley, Carol). When Archer meets Brown, he is about fifty-eight.

BROWN, ROBT. In *The Far Side of the Dollar. See* Harley, Mike.

BROWN, THEODORA ("TEDDY"). (Full name: Theodora Gavin Brown.) In *The Galton Case*, she is the mother of John Brown (Jr.). Beginning life as Theodora Gavin, Teddy had a rough background, and was Fred Nelson's lover. She married Anthony Galton (who called himself John Brown) in Benecia, California, in September 1936. She gave birth to his son, John Brown (Jr.), in December 1936. Fred murdered John's father, married Theodora, and escaped to Canada with her and her son. The couple changed their names to Mr. and Mrs. Nelson Fredericks. Archer finds them all. She is never truly reconciled with her son.

BRUCCOLI, MATTHEW J. (1931–). Biographer, editor, and educator. Matthew Joseph Bruccoli was born in New York City; studied at Yale (B.A., 1953) and at the University of Virginia (M.A., 1956; Ph.D., 1961); and taught at Ohio State University (1961–1969) and the University of South Carolina (1969–). He married Arlyn Firkins in 1957; they have four children. In the 1970s Bruccoli cofounded and became president of Bruccoli Clark Layman, a prolific publishing firm. Bruccoli has written, edited, and coedited biographies, bibliographies, and collections of critical essays; his subjects include Nelson Algren,* Raymond Chandler, James Gould Cozzens, James Dickey, F. Scott Fitzgerald, Ernest Hemingway, Ring Lardner, John O'Hara, and Ross Macdonald.

Work on a Chandler bibliographical checklist (1968) led Bruccoli to consider preparing one on Macdonald. Bruccoli visited Macdonald in Santa Barbara (1970). Thus began a correspondence that flourished between Bruccoli's 1971 *Kenneth Millar/Ross Macdonald: A Checklist* and his 1983 *Ross Macdonald/Kenneth Millar: A Descriptive Bibliography* (1983). Macdonald dedicated *The Underground Man* (1971) to Bruccoli. Bruccoli's *Ross Macdonald* (1984) is a short biocritical study. The Macdonald-Bruccoli correspondence is deposited at the University of California, Irvine.

BRUSH, DR. In *Blue City*, he is a physician who will examine Rusty Jahnke after Rusty was roughed up in jail.

BUCHANAN-DINEEN, GRACE. On August 24, 1943, Grace Buchanan-Dineen, thirty-four, was arrested in Detroit, Michigan, charged with conspiracy to violate the Wartime Espionage Act. Also arrested were Dr. Fred Thomas, an obstetrician, and Theresa Behrens. In New York City, Bertrand Hoffman, a merchant marine stationed near Detroit, and two German women were arrested. Buchanan-Dineen was accused of trying to give German government agents information concerning Ford Motor Company war production and plans for ferrying military aircraft abroad. Thomas was charged with gathering information about Western Electric Company war production in Ohio. Behrens was accused of gathering data about war-materiel transportation. Hoffman, a Canadian-born American citizen who worked at the Ford Motor Company (1942), was accused of giving Buchanan-Dineen production and shipping data. Buchanan-Dineen was said to be of noble French extraction, well educated, and from Canada. She had been recruited for espionage work (1941) by the Nazis, through Sari de Hajek, a Hungarian exchange student at Vassar College. Hajek gathered information on America's defenses while lecturing in the United States (1938) on Hungarian folklore. Her husband, Gyula Rozinek, a German spy, accompanied her, was arrested in San Francisco for kiting checks, and was deported. Buchanan-Dineen entered the United States (1941) and lived near a naval armory in Detroit. Behrens, born in Yugoslavia to German parents, moved to Detroit (1913), was naturalized (1929), and often visited Germany. Thomas, born in Ohio, studied in Germany and practiced in Detroit (from 1930). Hoffman, born in Canada, knew a restaurateur serving a life sentence for helping a Nazi aviator escape from a Canadian prison. Behrens pleaded guilty (October 3, 1943). Countess Marianna von Moltke, wife of a suspended Wayne State University professor of languages, pleaded guilty in Detroit (Ocober 8, 1943) to charges of espionage and collaborating with Buchanan-Dineen. Her sentence was delayed (March 1944) because she offered the authorities information. Buchanan-Dineen pleaded guilty (October 27, 1943). Thomas, mentally incompetent, was convicted (February 25, 1944), but his sixteen-year prison sentence (March 17, 1944) was dismissed. Sentences of the others varied from five to twenty years.

Elements in the Buchanan-Dineen case, which made national headlines (1943–1944), parallel characters and their activities in Macdonald's *The Dark Tunnel*. The action of the novel occurs September 22–25, 1943, in Detroit and Canada. Macdonald wrote *The Dark Tunnel* in Ann Arbor, Michigan (fall 1943). It was published on September 12, 1944.

Bibliography: New York Times, August 25 and 26, 1943; September 18 and 29, 1943; October 3, 8, and 27, 1943; March 17 and 26, 1944.

"THE BURIAL PARTY." *See The Underground Man.*

BURKE. In *The Chill*, he is Sally Burke's ex-husband. From her description, Archer concludes that Burke must be "a combination of Dracula, Hitler, and Uriah Heep."

BURKE, SALLY. In *The Chill*, she is Judson Foley's sister, whose car he drove to Pacific Point to see Helen Haggerty. Archer drinks with her to gain information about Judson.

BURNS, JOHN. In *The Wycherly Woman*, he is Captain Theodore Mandeville's dependable lawyer.

BUSCH, MRS. CAROL. In *The Barbarous Coast*, she runs the Dewdrop Inn in Las Vegas. She leads Archer to Rina Campbell in a room there. When Leroy Frost, Theodore Marfeld, and Lashman enter, Mrs. Busch tackles Marfeld until she is pistol-whipped. Though depicted as "a blend of gin and fermenting womanhood," she is admirably brave.

BUZZELL, MRS. SLOAN. In *The Zebra-Striped Hearse*, she is the alcoholic mother of Ray Buzzell, owner of the zebra-striped hearse. She lives in Malibu and tells Archer where Ray is.

BUZZELL, RAY ("RAYBUZZ"). In *The Zebra-Striped Hearse*, he is the owner of the zebra-striped hearse, lives in a canyon above Malibu, and has several cronies, notably Mona Sutherland. Through them, Archer locates Colonel Mark Blackwell's tweed coat.

C

C., R. In *The Galton Case*, he is Deputy Mungan's colleague and works in Sacramento. R. C. gives Mungan information about Fred Nelson over the phone.

CAINE, THE REVEREND CARY. In *The Ferguson Affair*. *See* Gaines, Larry.

CALAMUS, ARCHIE. In *Blue City*, he is an entertainer at the Cathay Club whose gig John Weather just missed, doubtless fortunately.

CALLAHAN. In *The Way Some People Die*, he is a deputy at the waterfront bar where Archer and Mario Tarantine happen to stop. Callahan is at the courthouse with Galley Lawrence and at Joseph Tarantine's autopsy. Through Callahan, Archer learns that Mario Tarantine and Galley have fled to Oasis.

CAMBERWELL. In *The Ivory Grin*, this is filed as the name of one of Dr. Samuel Benning's patients.

CAMERON, DEPUTY. In *The Blue Hammer*, he is Sheriff Brotherton's assistant. Campbell treats Fred Johnson's injured nose.

CAMPBELL, BILL. In *The Zebra-Striped Hearse*, this is the fictitious person who, Harriet Blackwell tells Archer, owns the shaving kit marked "B.C." Bruce Campion, Harriet's companion, owns it.

CAMPBELL, DR. In *Meet Me at the Morgue*, he is Helen Johnson's physician.

CAMPBELL, HESTER. In *The Barbarous Coast. See* Wall, Hester.

CAMPBELL, RAYMOND. In *The Barbarous Coast*, he was a silent-movie actor whose portrayal of Inspector Fate inspired Archer. Campbell was a failure as a family man, providing inadequately for his wife, Teeny Campbell, and their daughters, Helen Wall and Rina Campbell.

CAMPBELL, RINA. In *The Barbarous Coast*, she is the older daughter of Raymond and Teeny Campbell, and Hester Wall's less-favored sister. As Dr. Frey's psychiatric nurse, Rina tended to Isobel Graff. Leroy Frost and others persuade Rina to go to Las Vegas and double as Hester, to provide an alibi. Rescued by Archer from mortal danger, she reveals much about Isobel. Rina did postgraduate work at Camarillo, California. Macdonald's daughter, Linda Millar,* was committed to the State Hospital at Camarillo after being charged with vehicular homicide (February 23, 1956).

Bibliography: Nolan.

CAMPBELL, TEENY. In *The Barbarous Coast*, she is the mother, about fifty, of Rina Campbell and Hester Wall. Her husband was the movie actor Raymond Campbell. She worked in the Taos Shop until she thought Hester had struck it rich in Hollywood. Teeny, an airhead, says "absotively," "indeedy," and "very mooch."

CAMPION. In *The Zebra-Striped Hearse*, he is the father of Bruce Campion, who calls him "a lousy Chicago cop, with both front feet in the trough." He is also Evelyn Jurgensen's father.

CAMPION, BRUCE. In *The Zebra-Striped Hearse*, he is a struggling artist, about thirty. He is a Korean War veteran, Quincy Ralph Simpson's friend, Dolly Campion's husband, and Harriet Blackwell's companion mainly in order to use her money. Campion so admires Dr. Edmund Burke Damis, an art teacher and painter, that he calls himself Burke Damis when he and Harriet go to Mexico. Campion calls himself "a moral typhoid carrier." He is arrested for Dolly's murder. When his sister, Evelyn Jurgensen, tardily offers moral support, he rebukes her. Archer proves Campion's innocence, breaks down his antisocial defenses, and sees goodness in him.

CAMPION, DOLLY. (Original name: Delores Stone.) In *The Zebra-Striped Hearse*, she was the daughter of Elizabeth and Jack Stone, of Citrus Junction. Isobel Jaimet (*see* Blackwell, Isobel) tried to refine Dolly; but, oversexed, she married Bruce Campion (September 1960) and gave birth to Jack Campion (March 1961). Jack's father was Isobel's second husband, Colonel Mark Blackwell, whose daughter, Harriet Blackwell, by his first marriage, was jealous of Dolly and murdered Dolly, twenty-one (May 5, 1961).

CAMPION, JACK. In *The Zebra-Striped Hearse*, he is the son, four months old, of Dolly Campion and Colonel Mark Blackwell. After Harriet Blackwell, the colonel's jealous daughter, murdered Dolly, she placed Jack in a nearby car. Dolly's mother, Elizabeth Stone, began to care for Jack.

CARLOS. In *The Blue Hammer*, he is a black worker in the Santa Teresa newspaper building. He makes a photograph of the Chantry painting for Betty Jo Siddon. Archer uses it effectively.

CARLOS. In *The Underground Man*, he is "a sawed-off middle-aged Chicano" who works for Roger and Fran Armistead.

CARLSON, JAY. In *The Far Side of the Dollar*, he is Rhea Carlson's husband, Stella Carlson's father, and the neighbor of Ralph and Elaine Hillman. He treats Stella harshly until Archer rebukes him.

CARLSON, MRS. In "Sleeping Dog," she is Sheriff Carlson's wife. She was a member of the hunting party in Canada that included her husband, Allan Hooper, and Fay Hooper.

CARLSON, RHEA. In *The Far Side of the Dollar*, red-headed and "handsome," she is Jay Carlson's wife, Stella Carlson's mother, and the Hillmans' neighbor. She discouraged Stella from seeing Thomas Hillman until Archer persuaded her to lighten up.

CARLSON, SHERIFF. In "Sleeping Dog," he is the official near Malibu. In 1945 Carlson (not yet sheriff), his wife, Allan Hooper, and Fay Hooper were hunting in Canada. Carlson killed George Rambeau when George was about to kill Allan, who had just killed George's dog. Allan soon financed Carlson's campaign for sheriff. Twenty years later, Carlson kills Allan to prevent his squealing.

CARLSON, STELLA ("STELL"). In *The Far Side of the Dollar*, she is the lovely daughter, sixteen, of Jay and Rhea Carlson. She loves Thomas Hillman, her neighbor. When Thomas disappears, Stella helps Archer search for him. Stella twice evades her parents; Archer houses her with his friend, Susanna Drew, then drives her back home.

CARLYLE, COLONEL ISAAC. In *The Ivory Grin*, he was Charles A. Singleton, Jr.'s maternal grandfather. His wife was Maria Valdes Carlyle.

CARLYLE, MARIA VALDES. In *The Ivory Grin*, she was Charles A. Singleton, Jr.'s maternal grandmother. Her father founded the huge Valdes land-grant estates.

CARMICHAEL. In *The Doomsters*, he is a gun-happy deputy under Duane Ostervelt. He seems too eager to track and shoot Carl Hallman.

CARMODY. In *The Drowning Pool*, he is a Quinto policeman whose wife is having a baby.

CARMODY, MRS. In *The Drowning Pool*, she is the pregnant wife of a Quinto policeman.

CARSON. In *The Ivory Grin*, this is the name of one of Dr. Samuel Benning's patients, according to his files.

CARSTAIRS, DEPUTY. In *The Wycherly Woman*, he asks Jack Gayley and Sam Gayley where they saw Phoebe Wycherly's Volkswagen.

CASSETTARI, LIEUTENANT. In *Trouble Follows Me*, he is a police officer who investigates Bessie Land's death. Sam Drake treats him contemptuously.

CASSIDY, ELAINE RYAN. In *The Drowning Pool. See* Schneider, Mrs. Elaine.

CASTLE, ANNE ("ANNIE"). In *The Zebra-Striped Hearse*, she owns an arts and crafts shop in Ajijic, Mexico. She befriended and slept with Bruce Campion. Archer, impressed by her beauty and seriousness, gains information from her. She left Vassar to marry a poet—briefly. Anne reads of Campion's arrest for murdering his wife, rushes to California to stand by him, and is relieved when Archer tells her Campion is innocent.

"THE CASTLE AND THE POORHOUSE." *See The Galton Case*.

CASTOLA, ARTURO ("ARTIE"). In "Guilt-Edged Blonde," he is a gangster not involved in Nick Nemo's murder.

CAVE, GLENWAY ("GLEN"). In "Wild Goose Chase," he is wrongly tried for the murder of his wife, Ruth Glenway. Acquitted, he inherits her money, buys a Ferrari, and crashes and dies in it.

CAVE, RUTH. In "Wild Goose Chase," she is murdered by Rhea Harvey, who discovered her husband, Rod Harvey, was having an affair with her.

CERVANTES, FELIZ. In *Black Money*. *See* Martel, Francis.

CHADWICK, HELENE. In *The Moving Traget*, she is an actress mentioned by Fay Estabrook as "gone and forgotten."

CHALMERS. In *The Goodbye Look*, he is mentioned as Lawrence Chalmers's grandfather, who, after fighting in the Civil War, went to California and married a Spanish land-grant heiress.

CHALMERS, ESTELLE. In *The Goodbye Look*, she was Judge Harold Chalmers's wife and Lawrence Chalmers's mother. Widowed early, she treasured Lawrence's war-time letters to her, was friendly with her neighbors, John Truttwell and his wife, contracted glaucoma, and died (July 1945). Rumor has it she was intimate with Samuel Rawlinson.

CHALMERS, IRENE. In *The Goodbye Look*, she is Lawrence Chalmers's attractive wife and Nicholas Chalmers's mother. She was born in 1929 as Rita Shepherd, the daughter of Randolph Shepherd and his wife. Shepherd encouraged her to conspire with a Pasadena bank robber named Eldon Swain, Nicholas's natural father. She and Lawrence robbed Swain of his loot, drove in a stolen car to Pacific Point, hid the money in Lawrence's mother Estelle Chalmers's home safe, ran over and killed John Truttwell's wife, and escaped (July 3, 1945). Irene sinfully permitted guilt to fester in Nicholas's mind for years, after Nicholas shot Swain.

CHALMERS, JUDGE HAROLD. In *The Goodbye Look*, he was Estelle Chalmers's husband and Lawrence Chalmers's father, and a California Superior Court judge. Nicholas Chalmers, his grandson, calls him "the hanging judge."

CHALMERS, LAWRENCE ("LARRY," "SONNY"). In *The Goodbye Look*, he is the son of Judge Harold Chalmers and Estelle Chalmers; Irene Chambers's vapid husband; and supposedly the father of her son, Nicholas Chalmers. At eighteen, Lawrence joined the U.S. Navy (1943), washed out, but got a job in the La Jolla post office (1943–1945); sent letters, with passages plagiarized from Dr. Ralph Smitheram's letters, to his mother presenting himself as an idealistic, brave, and fatigued pilot; lived with Moira Smitheram, who called him "Sonny" (1943–1945); married Rita (who became Irene) Shepherd (July 1945) and treated her son, Nicholas, as theirs; became Smitheram's patient and established the Smitheram Clinic as a reward (1967); and read to Nicholas his fake letters as proof of his manliness. When exposed for killing Sidney Harrow and Jean Trask, and trying to kill Nicholas, Lawrence puts on his naval uniform and slits his throat.

CHALMERS, NICHOLAS ("NICK"). In *The Goodbye Look*, he is the son of Irene Chalmers and Eldon Swain, born December 14, 1945. Lawrence Chalmers, Irene's husband, pretends to be Nick's father. At the age of eight, Nick was fondled by Swain, shot him, and has been treated for depression by Dr. Ralph Smitheram for years. When the truth is revealed to Nick, it is possible that he may find happiness with Betty Truttwell, his faithful fiancée.

CHAMPION, LUCY. In *The Ivory Grin*, she is a black registered nurse, in her early or mid-twenties. She nursed Leo Durano in Detroit, and moved with him and his sister, Una Durano, to the Arroyo Beach area. Lucy witnessed Charles A. Singleton, Jr.'s murder by Leo, moved to Bella City, and lived near Anna Norris. She fell in love with Alex Norris, Anna's son. When ill, Lucy consulted Dr. Samuel Benning. She thought of asking Mrs. Charles A. Singleton, Charles's mother, for reward money, tried instead to escape with Alex, and was murdered by Benning.

CHANTRY, FELIX. In *The Blue Hammer*, he was a mining engineer who developed the copper mine near Copper City. He married Mildred Mead, whose son, William Mead, by Jack Biemeyer, Mildred told Felix was Felix's. Felix hired Jack; when Felix died (1942), Jack took control of the mine.

CHANTRY, FRANCINE. In *The Blue Hammer*, she is the still-attractive, gray-haired Santa Teresa socialite, allegedly Richard Chantry's wife or widow. In reality, she married Richard in Copper City, Arizona; when he was murdered (1943), she consorted with William Mead; they said he was Richard; when he disappeared (1950), Rico became her live-in companion. When William killed Gerard Johnson, she and William had Rico bury him in their greenhouse. For years Francine has been a neighbor of Jack and Ruth Biemeyer. Employed by the Biemeyers, Archer attends Francine's cocktail party. When Archer begins to expose her villainy, she drives to Long Beach but has a car accident. Archer returns her to Santa Teresa.

CHANTRY, MRS. FELIX. In *The Blue Hammer*, *See* Mead, Mildred.

CHANTRY, RICHARD. In *The Blue Hammer*, he was a painter, the son of Felix Chantry and his wife, known as Mildred Mead. Richard's wife was

Francine Chantry. William Mead, Richard's half-brother and a better painter, killed Richard (1943) and assumed Richard's identity.

CHANTRY, WILLIAM. In *The Blue Hammer. See* Mead, William.

CHARLENE. In *Sleeping Beauty*, she is the the cashier at the Cup of Tea cafeteria. She knows Harold Sherry.

CHARLIE. In *Blue City*, he owns a poolroom where John Weather goes to look for Joseph Sault.

CHARLIE. In *The Three Roads*, his name appeared in a personals column Theodora Swanscutt read. Charlie was telling Jack and Sim the deal is still on.

CHAS. In *Find a Victim*, his name figures in graffiti near Jo Summer's apartment.

CHASEN. In *The Moving Target*, his is the place where Timothy says he can get au gratin potatoes.

CHICO. In *The Moving Target*, he is the boss of The Corners, where Lew Archer seeks information on Eddie Lassiter. Chico's waitress helps Archer.

THE CHILL **(1964).** Novel. (Characters: Lew Archer, Bradshaw, Dean Roy Bradshaw, Mrs. Bradshaw, Burke, Mrs. Sally Burke, Sheriff Herman Crane, Dr. de Falla, Deloney, Luke Deloney, Mrs. Luke Deloney, Mrs. Simmy Fargo, Simmy Fargo, Dr. Farrand, Judson Foley, Judge Gahagan, Dr. Geisman, Gerhardi, Madge Gerhardi, Dr. James Godwin, Mrs. James Godwin, Bert Haggerty, Helen Haggerty, Heidi, Earl Hoffman, Mrs. Earl Hoffman, Jenks, Miss Alice Jenks, Alex Kincaid, Dolly Kincaid, Frederick Kincaid, Mrs. Frederick Kincaid, Val Macready, Maria, Mario, Jerry Marks, Constance McGee, Thomas McGee, Nell, Ogilvy, Osborne, Bridget Perrine, Commissioner Robertson, Rosie, Dr. Otto Schrenk, Uncle Scott, Stella, Gil Stevens, Dean Laura Sutherland, Theo, Thompson, Miss Wadley, Arnie Walters, Phyllis Walters, Whitmore.)

At soon as Archer finishes giving testimony one Friday morning in September concerning Bridget Perrine at court in Pacific Point, fifty miles south of Los Angeles, Alex Kincaid hires him to find his missing bride, Dolly Kincaid. Six weeks earlier, Alex and Dolly met each other while taking courses at Pacific Point College (PPC), planned to stay at the nearby Surf House over Labor Day weekend, and were married in Long Beach by a judge that Saturday. They waited to consummate their union until Sunday. But on that day Dolly talked to a mysterious, gray-bearded

man and disappeared. Alex shows Archer a photograph of himself and
Dolly, published in a local newspaper when they first arrived. His father,
Frederick Kincaid, a Long Beach oil-company manager for whom Alex
works, opposed Alex's marriage.

Archer and Alex drive to the Surf House, obtain a clear copy of the
picture from the hotel photographer, Simmy Fargo, who says the gray-
bearded man is Chuck Begley, a nearby liquor store employee. Archer
and Alex go there, learn Begley was fired and lives with Madge Gerhardi
at a Shearwater Beach address, drive there, and find them both home.
Begley tells Archer this: Dolly's picture reminded him of his daughter,
Mary, who is in her early twenties and whom he has not seen for a dec-
ade, ever since he began working at a New Caledonia chrome mine, recently closed; his wife is dead; he talked briefly with Dolly, who explained
she was from Los Angeles and her parents were dead. Madge tells Alex
that while she was at a garage she saw Dolly drive off in an old Rolls,
with an old woman in the passenger seat.

At the garage, a mechanic says Mrs. Bradshaw owns the Rolls. They find
her Pacific Point mansion, drive past its gatehouse, and see her out gar-
dening. She identifies Dolly from the photograph; says the girl is enrolled
at PPC, works in the library, and lives in her gatehouse; and adds that
her son is PPC's Dean Roy Bradshaw. Alex rushes to the gatehouse and
finds Dolly's clothes there. When he becomes obstreperous, Archer tells
him to get them rooms at the nearby Mariner's Rest Motel.

Archer goes to PPC, hears that Roy is in conference, but learns from
Laura Sutherland, dean of women, that Dolly falsely registered as Dorothy
Smith. Laura finds Dolly and takes her to Roy's office. While waiting,
Archer and Helen Haggerty, a feisty faculty member, engage in banter.
Dolly emerges and tells Archer she won't return to Alex; he should get
an annulment and feel relieved, since her specialty is "[s]preading ruin."
She leaves. Laura says Dolly revealed hideous things about Alex, and Roy
adds that Dolly, with two years of undergraduate study elsewhere, can
remain, is majoring in psychology, and, according to Helen, Dolly's academic counselor, has a flair for the subject.

Waiting in the parking lot, Helen invites Archer to her rented "eyrie"
for drinks and promises to discuss Dolly. Once there, however, Helen
says she read about his detective work for Mrs. Perrine, gets seductive,
and begs him to remain and protect her from recent phone threats—
concerning her past in Bridgeton, Illinois. She mentions her father, a
crooked policeman, and something about a murder and a witness. Archer
declines, asserting that Alex is his client now.

At the motel, Archer finds Alex out but Fargo there. After gossiping
about how influential the Bradshaws are at Pacific Point and how Roy, in
his forties, is a mamma's boy, Fargo reports that Begley is really Thomas
McGee, recently released after serving a ten-year sentence for murdering

his wife in Indian Springs. Alex rushes to find "Begley," but Madge between drinks reveals that he hastily packed and decamped. When Archer tries to connect McGee to murder, prison, and visiting a daughter, Madge denies everything but adds that he appeared only two weeks ago, the two planned to get married, and he mentioned catching a bus to Los Angeles.

Archer returns to Mrs. Bradshaw's gatehouse. Inside, Alex and Dolly are arguing. While Alex tries to embrace her, Dolly, her hands bloody, rambles about murders present and past in ways linking her father and Helen's father. When Archer asks, Dolly agrees that McGee is her father and says the monster shot a woman and now has shot Helen. Prompted, Dolly names Dr. James Godwin as her longstanding psychiatrist. Archer phones him. Roy drives up, mollifies his querulous mamma, and, when filled in, accompanies Archer to Helen's place. A stranger rushes past them, into a car, and away. Archer gets his Nevada license-plate number. Roy and Archer enter Helen's place. Roy finds her shot dead and phones Sheriff Herman Crane. Archer discovers a sad letter from Helen's mother about Helen's argument with her father and Helen's recent divorce. Archer tells Roy that Helen felt threatened. Roy explains that Helen was hired at the last minute when a modern-language professor had a coronary, and that Dolly chose Helen to be her adviser. Sheriff Crane blusters in, criticizes Archer, wants to talk to Dolly, and is rebuked by Roy, who tells him Godwin forbids it for now. Big, forceful Godwin enters and says he will hospitalize Dolly immediately. Alex accompanies them to the Whitmore Nursing Home in Pacific Point.

Back at the motel, Archer phones Arnie Walters, a detective he knows in Reno, Nevada, and asks him to check on the owner of the car whose license plate he noted. Alex appears, brave and loyal to his Dolly. Archer advises him to get her a lawyer. Alex decides not to phone his father. Instead, he phones Miss Alice Jenks, the older sister of Constance McGee, Dolly's murdered mother, and alerts Alice to Dolly's predicament. Alice lives in Indian Springs, seventy miles away. Archer makes a date to see her at 11:00 the next morning.

Saturday. Archer leaves Alex asleep, has breakfast, and visits Godwin at 8:00. The conscientous physician reveals this: Dolly was a troubled child under his care, at her mother's request; later Dolly, twelve, saw her father fleeing in the yard with a gun, then found her mother's body; Alice persuaded Dolly to testify in court; Dolly now insists her father did not kill her mother, fantasizes that she is responsible for her mother's and Helen's deaths. Godwin believes, however, that McGee killed Constance. Alex wonders aloud whether Helen's father, a Bridgeton policeman, is connected with Constance's murder. Crane bursts in, seeking to question the "fugitive" Dolly; but Godwin rebuffs him for the time being—thus earning Archer's "unfeigned admiration."

Archer drives to Indian Springs and interviews Alice, a rigidly righteous welfare worker under Crane's supervision. She explains this: McGee, indeed all McGees, are disreputable; McGee was the only man in Constance's life; Dolly saw him with the gun; McGee's expensive lawyer, that "old fox" Gil Stevens, got him a light sentence; Godwin treated Constance as well as Dolly but now wrongly coddles her. Archer, allowed to inspect Dolly's old room, tells Alice the girl couldn't have seen McGee with a gun at night in the yard and adds that Dolly now says she didn't.

Archer phones Stevens's office, but he is gone this afternoon. Archer finds Jerry Marks, Mrs. Perrine's defense attorney, tells him about Dolly, and persuades him to represent Dolly if asked. Back at his motel, Archer phones Arnie's office. His wife, Phyllis, an ex-Pinkerton, says Mrs. Sally Burke owns the Nevada car in question but claims it was stolen. Phyllis says she will cozy up to Sally for information. Alex returns to the motel with Frederick Kincaid, his father. That domineering businessman heard about Alex on the radio, phoned Crane, and learned "the murder weapon"—a revolver with a curious handle—was found in Dolly's gatehouse room. Kincaid rushed to Pacific Point, now orders Alex home to his sick mother, and fires Archer.

Archer looks for Roy, but he is gone. So Archer confers with Mrs. Bradshaw, who, apologizing for her previous aloofness, turns friendly. She says Roy, whom she calls "a mother's boy" but praises for his academic ambition, is attending a previously scheduled meeting of small-college deans at the University of Nevada in Reno. She says she and Roy wondered this morning how they could help Dolly. Archer replies that Mrs. Bradshaw could hire him since the Kincaids just fired him. He feels Dolly is innocent despite what Crane has told Mrs. Bradshaw about Dolly's alleged gun. Archer adds that he has a promising lead in Reno. Mrs. Bradshaw will ask Roy, when he phones, about hiring Archer.

The police will not allow Archer to inspect Helen's place. So he goes in search of Laura, but she is out of town. He finds Dr. Geisman, chairman of modern languages, in his office. He is about to interview a possible replacement for Helen. He is annoyed that both deans, Roy and Laura, are currently away. Archer chats with Geisman about Helen, whose mother, Mrs. Hoffman, Geisman says he is to meet at the Los Angeles airport. She is flying in from Bridgeton. Archer volunteers to meet her and does so, at 6:30 P.M. On their drive to Pacific Point, Mrs. Hoffman ramblingly reveals the following: Earl Hoffman, Helen's father, was in the Navy in San Diego and is now a veteran Bridgeton detective; he drinks too much; the Hoffmans live in an apartment building once owned by wealthy Luke Deloney, who married the daughter of Osborne, a U.S. senator; Helen often argued with her father, had "a crush" on Deloney when she was nineteen; Deloney, when forty, accidentally killed himself while cleaning a gun; Hoffman investigated the tragedy, said Deloney was alone; Helen was mistaken in calling it murder and in mentioning a witness; Helen left home at nineteen, went to Chicago, and met Bert Haggerty, then a newspaperman; they married a few years later; Bert is now a "failure," teaches journalism and English in Maple Park, near Bridgeton, and is kind to Hoffman.

Archer drives Mrs. Hoffman to a Pacific Point hotel, where Geisman takes over. Archer goes to the hotel bar; sees his former client, Mrs. Perrine, drunk and ineffectively seductive; phones Mrs. Bradshaw and learns that she cannot authorize family money for Archer's fee and that her son and Laura are in Reno. Archer finds Dr. Godwin's home, goes there, meets his wife, and learns he is attending Dolly—perhaps too conscientiously. Mrs. Godwin says she and her husband were in France last summer.

Archer gets to the hospital. Godwin tells him Alex has returned to stand by Dolly. She is better, still blames herself for the turn of events, but says the gun as described might be her Aunt Alice's. Archer tells about conferring with Helen's mother, theorizes that her murder and that of Dolly's mother may be connected, and describes Deloney's death in Bridgeton. Godwin agrees to finance Archer's continuation on the case; but when Alex appears, he assumes that responsibility. Suddenly Alice barges in. Archer gets her to discuss the revolver, which she says was hers but was stolen before Constance's murder. Alex introduces himself to Alice, who gives him the cold shoulder. When Godwin will not let Alice see Dolly, Alice accuses him of formerly encouraging Constance's attentions. Getting Alice into another room, Godwin admits to Archer that Constance, as his informal patient, fell in love with him and he responded merely with friendly feelings. Alex gives money to Archer to fly to Illinois.

Sunday morning. Archer flies to Chicago, rents a car, and drives to Bridgeton, where he locates Helen's father and her ex-husband, together. Hoffman, thoroughly drunk, his moods swinging from amiable to belligerent, responds to whisky-sipping Archer's prompting and reveals this: Deloney, separated from his aging wife, was a womanizer, never pursued "young stuff" such as Helen; Helen was fond of George, Deloney's young elevator operator; Deloney knew an unnamed married woman in town, shot himself accidentally (June 1940) with no one present; Bert followed Helen to Reno last spring but was unable to preventing her from divorcing him. Hoffman breaks down, says he is sorry he "clobbered" Helen, smacks his own face, and falls asleep. Bert tells Archer this: Bert introduced Helen to sex; she became "a tramp" with men, for money; in Reno, Helen and Bert socialized ineffectively with Sally Burke and her brother, Jud; Bert, conscience-stricken and confused, is not sure that the overly dramatic Helen had evidence her father knew of a cover-up concerning Deloney's death.

Archer phones to reserve space for a flight to Reno and manages to get an appointment, before flight time, to see Deloney's widow. That imperious old woman admits Archer and says this: Senator Osborne, her father, died on December 14, 1936; Mrs. Deloney's remaining family, tired of Deloney's philandering and gambling, stopped financing Deloney; for revenge, Deloney shot himself, leaving a critical note she burned; the authorities agreed to call the death accidental; Helen, whose death Mrs. Deloney assuredly deplores, lied. Archer also has time to see Hoffman again, finds him wandering into the Deloney apartment building, and follows him up to Deloney's former penthouse. On the roof a couple are sunbathing. Hoffman, drunk and raving, confuses the girl with Helen and when her boyfriend objects fires a gun near him. Rushing up, Archer tells Hoffman he had solved Deloney's murder and should summon reinforcements. Hoffman agrees, goes to the penthouse, and telephones quite irrationally for a squad with a concrete drill. Then he babbles on: A woman's body is under the basement floor; someone surely wouldn't hurt a friend's clean little girl; "Never found out who put the chill on Deloney." The police arrive and take charge.

On to Reno. Phyllis, Arnie's wife, greets Archer, says she got Sally Burke drunk and talkative, and now Sally wants to date Archer this evening at 8:30. Phyllis drops him at Sally's door. The two go off for drinks, and she talks about her brother, Judson Foley, a handsome failure now mooching off her. Archer gets her home, meets Foley, watches him put sleepy Sally on a couch, and confronts him. Foley reveals this: Helen was awaiting her divorce in Reno in August; Bert, Sally, Helen, and Foley socialized; Roy met Helen then; Foley, fired from cashiering at the Solitaire Club, sought work in Los Angeles; Helen phoned him last Friday asking him to protect her; he drove to her Pacific Point place, saw her corpse, panicked, and ran past Archer and Roy; Roy queried Foley today and is at the Lakeview Inn in Reno. Foley suddenly lunges at Archer, who subdues him until the police arrive.

Arnie drives Archer to the Lakeview Inn. He finds Roy with Laura. They have been married for some time, Roy explains, but hope to conceal the fact both because college rules prohibiting nepotism might cost Laura her PPC teaching position and because Roy's mother would disapprove. Roy adds this: He was not sure he recognized Foley leaving Helen's murder scene; Foley, though a petty criminal, was innocent of her death; Roy fears Foley knows that Roy knew and liked Helen. Arnie takes Archer to his Reno home; they drink into the wee hours; Archer reads poetry from the undergraduate magazine in which Helen published.

Monday. Arnie gets Archer to the airport, and he flies to Los Angeles. He talks with Marks, whom Alex, now smiling, has hired to defend Dolly. Marks hopes Stevens, McGee's lawyer ten years ago, will be informative. Archer happens to see Mrs. Hoffman and Mrs. Deloney on the street together. He follows the latter to Stevens's office. When she departs, Archer goes in to talk with Stevens, who says McGee wouldn't let Stevens cross-examine little Dolly, and therefore her testimony convicted McGee of killing Constance. Archer tells Stevens he thinks the murders of Deloney, Constance, and Helen are related. Stevens admits McGee was probably innocent, says Constance had a lover, but won't identify him or reveal what Mrs. Deloney wanted of Stevens.

Archer seeks Mrs. Hoffman but is told she checked out. By phone Arnie reports this: Foley was fired from the Solitaire Club for running an unwarranted credit check on Roy, who had thousands in the bank; last August, Roy got a Reno divorce from a woman named Letitia O. Macready. Archer proceeds to Mrs. Bradshaw. She says Roy was in Europe last summer and shows Archer his correspondence from there. Archer convinces her it could have been faked, and says Roy just divorced Letitia Macready. Crushed, Mrs. Bradshaw confesses that Roy, while attending Harvard twenty years ago, married Letitia, a red-headed floozie who demanded $2,000 from Mrs. Bradshaw for a divorce—evidently never then obtained.

By phone, Arnie reports that Helen knew Roy from way back and that Foley got Bradshaw's credit report for Helen, who surely was blackmailing him thereafter. Archer sees Marks, who has studied McGee's trial transcripts. Marks doubts McGee's guilt and will question Dolly at 8:00 P.M. Madge raps on Archer's motel door and tells him McGee is hiding on Stevens's yacht and wants to see Archer. Going there, Archer learns this from McGee: McGee did not kill Constance; Alice coached Dolly to lie in court; Roy, one of Godwin's patients, was Constance's lover, with Alice's connivance; McGee saw Dolly's premarriage photo, found her "that Sunday," asked why she lied in court and whether she killed Constance. Archer distresses McGee by implying that either Alice or Madge might have been "Letitia" in Boston. The police storm in, arrest McGee, and detain Archer. Crane gloats that ballistics tests have just proved the same revolver killed Constance and Helen. Archer calls Marks, who brings Stevens to aid McGee. Archer and Marks rush to Godwin's office. Under sodium pentothal Dolly, comforted by Alex, reveals this: Alice wrongly thought Dolly stole Constance's revolver; Alice made Dolly lie in court; at their front door, Alice argued with a lady she called Tish; Tish shot Constance; Dolly blames herself for everything, especially for thinking Helen was Tish, for telling her everything, and thus for causing her murder. Alex takes Dolly to her room. Archer criticizes Godwin for concealing Bradshaw's and Constance's affair and embarrasses him by linking Tish and Letitia.

Retrieving his car at dockside, Archer looks for Madge, but she has "evaporated." From his motel, he phones Mrs. Bradshaw, who is worried about Roy and describes his Letitia from Harvard days: big, red-haired, lush figure, overdressed. Marks phones that McGee says he discussed Roy's and Constance's affair only with Roy. Archer tells Marks to describe

Tish to Crane. Archer proceeds to Laura's campus residence and is told by the newlywed the following: Laura never knew any Tish; Roy gave Laura a poetry book with "Tish" written in the margin; Roy wrote Laura from Europe last July and August; Godwin was in Europe then; she and Roy were married September 10 in Reno; Roy is with Mrs. Deloney at the Surf House now. Archer tells Laura that Tish is connected with the murders of Deloney, Constance, and Helen. When shown Roy's letters to Laura from Europe, Archer finds them identical to what Roy sent his mother.

Rushing to the Surf House, Archer finds Mrs. Hoffman. Over cocoa, she reveals this: Roy, called George, was an impoverished, fibbing student in Bridgeton and worked in Deloney's apartment building; when Deloney was separated from his wife, his sister-in-law, Tish Osborne Macready, acted as hostess for him in his penthouse; rumor had it Tish shot Deloney; Hoffman took to drink after politicians pressured him into calling Deloney's death accidental; Tish died in Nazi-occupied France; Mrs. Deloney flew to Pacific Point to tell Mrs. Hoffman, whom she scarcely knew, to clam up.

Archer finds the Surf House cottage Mrs. Deloney has rented. She is there with Roy. Tired of it all and despite her threats to cut him off financially, Roy confesses that Deloney caught him in bed with Tish and beat both of them with a gun. Letitia shot Deloney with it, had facial surgery in Boston, married Roy there, and honeymooned with him in France. Roy's mother forced him to come home and leave Tish. She died abroad. Mrs. Deloney shows Archer her sister Tish's French death certificate, dated July 16, 1940. Archer counters that Tish is surely alive. Otherwise, why would Roy divorce her in Reno? Roy says that last Saturday he put Tish on a plane for Brazil, to avoid extradition. Tish told him she killed Helen, who learned of his divorce and was blackmailing him. Roy says he met Constance in Godwin's office and fell in love with her. He didn't learn until Saturday that Tish also shot Constance. Roy's words bother Mrs. Deloney, who reminds him that his mother's finances support him. Roy warns her to shut up, gets her out of the room, and tells Archer that Constance stole the revolver from Alice and gave it to Roy, then distraught, to use on Tish. Tish found it in his mother's house, must have heard Roy and McGee discussing Constance, and killed her when she could. Archer counters by telling Roy he suspects Tish is still in California.

The phone rings. Archer hears Laura warn Roy that "she" just phoned, knows (of their marriage), and is "coming over." Roy hits Archer on the head from behind with a poker and drives off. Mrs. Deloney revives Archer. Archer sees a picture of her father in Mrs. Deloney's adjoining room; it matches a portrait supposedly of Mrs. Bradshaw's father, which Archer saw in her mansion. Archer drives off in pursuit of Roy. Roy suddenly blocks the road—not against Archer but against his mother's oncoming Rolls. It crashes into Roy, killing him. Mrs. Bradshaw gets out and hugs "the child of my womb." But Archer confronts her with the truth: Mrs. Bradshaw, you are Tish; you bought your fake French death certificate; you killed Deloney; you married Roy in Boston; he loved Constance and so you killed her; you and Roy lived ten years in a secret marriage; he loved Laura but told you he loved Helen and so you killed her. Tish takes umbrage at Archer's criticism, offers to bribe him, fails, and tries to get her "new revolver"—intended for Roy's "new wife"—from her Rolls. Archer takes it.

Macdonald condensed *The Chill* for *Cosmopolitan* (August 1963). The novel was reprinted in London (Collins, 1964), and became a popular Bantam paperback (from 1965), for which Macdonald was paid $4,500, and a Collins/Fontana paperback (1966). The working title of *The Chill* was "A Mess of Shadows." The novel has been lavishly praised but occasionally criticized for its convoluted plot. Simmy Fargo reveals the first day of the action to be a Friday. Three days later, Laura tells Archer she married Roy "[t]wo weeks ago last Saturday, September the tenth." September 10 fell on Saturday in 1960. So *The Chill* takes place September 23–26, 1960. Its surprising climax remains one of the most startling in all of detective fiction. *The Chill* includes the most literary references and allusions of any Macdonald novel—to Heraclitus, Zeno of Elea and Parmenides, Samuel Taylor Coleridge, Paul Verlaine, William Butler Yeats, Samuel Beckett and his *Waiting for Godot*, and J.D. Salinger and his *The Catcher in the Rye*. In 1964 producers from Twentieth Century-Fox expressed an interest in buying movie rights to *The Chill* for $15,000 but soon complained they lacked funding. In 1966 Warner Brothers contracted to pay $50,000 for movie rights. Macdonald was paid, but in 1967 Paul Newman voiced objections to the complicated screenplay version (he purposely never read the novels on which movies he starred in were based) and also feared being typecast after appearing, as Lew Harper, in *Harper* and *The Drowning Pool*. In 1969 Sam Peckinpah planned to film *The Chill*, but lack of money doomed the project.

Bibliography: Williams W. Combs, "The Detective as Both Tortoise and Achilles: Archer Gets the Feel of the Chase in *The Chill*," *Clues* 2 (Spring–Summer 1981): 98–105; Nolan; Thomas J. Roberts, *An Aesthetics of Junk Fiction* (Athens and London: University of Georgia Press, 1990); Speir; Wolfe.

CHRIS. In *The Ferguson Affair*, William Gunnarson finds among Ella Barker's possessions a Valentine that Chris sent her.

CHRISTMAN, RALPH. In *Black Money*, he is a friend of Archer's, lives in Washington, D.C., and provides him with information about Francis Martel.

CHURCH, BRANDON ("BRAND"). In *Find a Victim*, he is the college-educated Las Cruses sheriff; Hilda Church's husband for nearly ten years; and former lover of Anne Meyer, Hilda's younger sister. When Meyer's truck is hijacked, Church tangles with Archer, tries to warn him off the case, fights him twice, but confesses he let Bozey through his roadblock with hijacked whisky, hoping Bozey would be arrested later and charged with murders he did not commit. Archer concludes that Church "was an honest man, according to his lights."

Bibliography: Schopen.

CHURCH, HILDA. In *Find a Victim*, she is the daughter, thirty-two, of Meyer, the trucker, whom she dislikes and who calls her Peaches; the older sister of Anne Meyer, of whose beauty she is jealous; and the wife of Brandon Church, who has slept with Anne. Hilda is a compulsive cleaner. Archer tries to help and even comfort her, but ultimately uncovers the truth that she killed not only Anne but also Tony Aquista, a trucker, and his conspirator, Don Kerrigan.

CIRO. In *The Way Some People Die*, he is the owner of the establishment where Irene, Danny Dowser's girlfriend, wants to shop.

CLARK, DR. In *The Three Roads*, he is Burton Garth's Glendale physician. He tells Bret Taylor he removed Dr. Homer L. Ralston's stitches from Garth's eyelid.

CLAUDE. In *The Moving Target*, he is a fraudulent cult leader, tall, bearded, and disreputable, to whom Ralph Sampson gave the mountain where Claude runs "The Temple in the Clouds." The location is a transfer point for illegal Mexican workers.

CLEAT, LIEUTENANT. In *Meet Me at the Morgue*, he is the Pacific Point police officer Howard Cross cooperates with.

CLEMENT. In *The Wycherly Woman*, he was the *President Jackson* purser during Homer Wycherly's cruise.

CLEMENT, MRS. In *The Ferguson Affair*, she is the Buenavista jail matron. She watches over Ella Barker.

CLINCHER. In *Find a Victim*, Bozey names him as one of the three Albuquerque thugs who beat him up. Mike Faustino is another. The third is not named.

CLINE. In *The Ferguson Affair*, he was the husband, deceased, of Mrs. Cline, Ella Barker's landlady. Cline was a Portland, Oregon, accountant.

CLINE, MRS. In *The Ferguson Affair*, she is Ella Barker's widowed landlady. William Gunnarson detects "frustrated decency" in her. She provides Ella's bail money.

COLLINS, SERGEANT NORRIS E. In *The Dark Tunnel*, he is a Canadian policeman who theorizes that escaped German prisoners of war attacked Ruth Esch outside Kirkland Lake.

COLTON, PETER. In *The Moving Target*, he was an army intelligence colonel under whom Archer worked during World War II. He is the senior investigator in the office of Humphreys, the Los Angeles D.A. Archer relies on Colton for information and cooperation. In *The Way Some People Die*, Peter Colton, in his fifties, commends Archer to Lieutenant Gary and asks Gary to go easy on Archer. In *The Barbarous Coast*, Colton tells Archer about Carl Stern's criminal activities, including money laundering in Las Vegas by financing Simon Graff's hotel-casino there. In *The Wycherly Woman*, Archer mentions Colton to Captain Lamar Royal as a character reference. In *The Zebra-Striped Hearse*, Colonel Mark Blackwell tells Archer that Colton recommended Archer to him. In *The Far Side of the Dollar*, Archer asks Colton to seek information from Sacramento concerning Harold Harley and Mike Harley.

CONCHITA. In *The Goodbye Look*, she was the owner of the Conchita Cabins, in Imperial Beach, sold thirty years ago to Mrs. Florence Williams.

CONEY. In *The Galton Case*, he is a bellhop at the Salisbury, a San Francisco hotel where Archer stays while looking for Chad Bolling.

CONGER. In *The Galton Case*, he is a policeman at the site of the wrecked, burning Jaguar. When Archer sasses him for alleged incompetence, Conger handcuffs him. Sheriff Trask tells Conger to provide police protection for Maria Galton. No mention is made later of this assignment.

CONNOR, FRANKLIN ("FRANK"). In "Midnight Blue," he is a philandering high school counselor whose wife, Stella Connor, deserts him briefly. He makes love with Virginia Green. They are spied on by Anita Brocco, who kills Virginia.

CONNOR, STELLA. In "Midnight Blue," she is Franklin Connor's wife. His philandering causes her to leave him briefly. When she returns, the two will probably stick together.

CONSUELA. In *The Wycherly Woman*, she was bothered by spirits, according to her sister Tonia, a Champion Hotel cleaning lady. Tonia tells Archer a spell cast on Consuela was lifted by a *curandero*.

"THE CONVENIENT CORPSE." *See Meet Me at the Morgue.*

CONVERSE, DR. In *The Instant Enemy*, he is the youthful-looking physician who treated Alexandria Sebastian. He is reluctant to provide Archer with information.

COOLEY. In *The Ivory Grin*, this name is on file as that of one of Dr. Samuel Benning's patients.

COOPER, CAROL. In *The Far Side of the Dollar. See* Harley, Carol.

COPLEY, VELMA. In *The Ferguson Affair*, she is Belle Weinstein's answering-service friend.

COULETTE, HENRI ANTHONY (1927–1988). He was a poet, educator, and editor. Born in Los Angeles, he married Jacqueline Meredith (1950), served in the U.S. Army (1945–1946), and attended Los Angeles State College (now Los Angeles State University; B.A., 1952) and the University of Iowa (M.F.A., 1954; Ph.D., 1959). Coulette taught at the University of Iowa writer's workshop (1957–1959) and at California State University, Los Angeles (1959–1988). Coulette's books of poetry include *The War of the Secret Agents* (1966) and *The Family Goldschmitt* (1971).

In 1965 Hank Coulette invited Macdonald to be a visiting writer-professor. He declined, but the two discussed Macdonald's use of "Cal State" in *Black Money*. Each admired the other's distinctive flair with words. Macdonald also liked Jacqueline Coulette, who, however, found him too quiet. Macdonald dedicated *The Goodbye Look* to Coulette. The title *The Blue Hammer*, meaning the human pulse-vein, comes from a line in an obscure Coulette poem. The name of Culotti in *The Galton Case* may have been suggested to Macdonald by Hank Coulette's last name. Coulette's line, "prime rib of unicorn, or breast of phoenix," in his "The Blue-Eyed Precinct Worker" (in *The War of the Secret Agents*) has as its acknowledged source a passage from Macdonald's *The Ferguson Affair*.

Bibliography: Nolan; Obituary, *Los Angeles Times* (April 14, 1988).

COWAN, MISS. In *The Goodbye Look*, she is a Los Angeles General Hospital nurse who treats Archer's shoulder wound.

COX, WILBUR. In *Sleeping Beauty*, he is a local reporter who questions Archer at the scene of the oil spill.

CRAIG, JUDGE. In *Find a Victim*, he was Kate Kerrigan's father, deceased. Brandon Church's father knew him. Craig helped Church through college. Craig donated land and founded Las Cruses College on it.

CRAM, DETECTIVE. In *Trouble Follows Me*, he is a Honolulu police officer. He investigates Sue Sholto's death after an inquest rules it suicide.

CRAM, FRED. In *The Instant Enemy*, he works at the Power Plus gas station near Santa Teresa. Three years older than David Spanner, Cram, who limps and is honest, knew Spanner in high school. He tells Archer that Spanner and Alexandria stopped at the station and later lets Archer use his phone.

CRAMM, HILDA. In *The Moving Target*, she is Morris Cramm's wife. She is "a fat and fading blonde," and is hospitable to Archer when he visits her husband. In *The Drowning Pool*, she is Morris Cramm's happy Jewish wife. She likes Archer in a motherly way.

CRAMM, MORRIS. In *The Moving Target*, he is a Los Angeles night legman. His name suggests his crammed "card-index brain," by which Archer learns about Fay Estabrook and her associates. In *The Drowning Pool*, Cramm is a Glendale newspaper columnist's legman. Cramm gives Archer information on Walter J. Kilbourne.

CRANDALL, LESTER ("LES"). In *The Underground Man*, he is Martha Crandall's husband and acts as the father of Susan Crandall, Martha's child born out of wedlock. Crandall, fifty, owns a chain of coastal motels, including the Yucca Tree Inn. He treats Susan in an uncomprehending and unsympathetic manner until Archer steps in.

CRANDALL, MARTHA. In *The Underground Man*, she is the sensuous mother of Susan Crandall, whose father, Martha says, was probably Captain Leo Broadhurst. As Marty Nickerson, when fifteen, she consorted with Al Sweetner and Frederick Snow, and went with them in a car stolen from Lester Crandall to Hollywood intending to make it in the movies. Crandall married Martha and assumed responsibility for Susan. Crandall calls Martha "Mother." To Archer, who finds her "complex," she vows she will tell Susan the truth.

CRANDALL, SUSAN ("SUE," SUSIE"). In *The Underground Man*, she is Martha Crandall's daughter, probably by Captain Leo Broadhurst. When three, she saw Leo shot while he and Martha were making love. Lester Crandall married Martha and raised Susan as his overprotected child. She became friendly with Jerry Kilpatrick, did drugs with him, drove out of Santa Teresa with Stanley Broadhurst, saw Stanley murdered, and was raped by Al Sweetner. Susan and Jerry take Ronald Broadhurst on the *Ariadne*, the sloop owned by Roger Kilpatrick, Jerry's father. Archer persuades her not to commit suicide and returns her to her mother.

CRANE, JEREMY. In *The Barbarous Coast*, he is the orchestra leader of his "joy boys" at Simon Graff's post-Christmas Channel Club party.

CRANE, SHERIFF HERMAN. In *The Chill*, he is Pacific Point's main law-enforcement officer. His investigation of Helen Haggerty's murder is ineffective.

CROSS, HOWARD ("HOWIE"). In *Meet Me at the Morgue*, he, the narrator, is a county probation officer working in Pacific Point. A war veteran, single at thirty-seven, he supervises the case of Fred Miner, accused of a DUI homicide. Suspicion that Fred kidnapped his employer Abel Johnson's son leads Cross to investigate. His work with Sam Dressen, an aging police officer, enables them to pin the crimes on Amy Miner. Cross and Helen fall in love. Macdonald gratuitously has Cross mention his parents' unhappy marriage. Cross is identical in plot function to Lew Archer, except that the latter, as a series hero, must not fall in love and marry.

CROSS, LIEUTENANT. In *The Dark Tunnel*, he is a police officer called to the scene of Dr. Alec Judd's murder. He is at the police station when Detective-Sergeant Haggerty brings Robert Branch to town after Peter Schneider tried to hang Branch.

CRUTTWORTH. In *The Zebra-Striped Hearse*, he is a Toronto coat retailer from whose firm Colonel Mark Blackwell bought the tweed coat.

CUDDY, RALPH. In *The Instant Enemy*, he manages the Santa Monica apartment building where Alma R. Krug once lived. Cuddy tells Archer where she presently resides. Archer is surprised to find Cuddy as a security guard at the Hackett family's Long Beach oil-company building. When Archer questions Cuddy about Mark Hackett's murder, Cuddy pulls his gun and orders Archer out.

CULLEN, MISS. In *The Doomsters*, she is Dr. J. Charles Grantland's receptionist. Grantland rebukes her for talking too much with Archer.

CULLIGAN, MARIAN. In *The Galton Case*. *See* Matheson, Marian.

CULLIGAN, PETER ("HAPPY," "PETE"). In *The Galton Case*, he was a criminal with a long record. He was hospitalized after a San Francisco dock fight (1936), was attended by a nurse's aide named Marian (*see* Matheson, Marian), married her, was a marine cook (1941), was divorced after fifteen years, and associated with Fred Nelson and Otto Schwartz. Culligan was arrested in Detroit on an outstanding larceny charge five or so years before the action of the novel. Culligan, Gordon Sable, and John Brown, Jr., who was then a University of Michigan student, schemed to have Brown impersonate Maria Galton's grandson. Culligan got intimate with Sable's wife, Alice, in Reno. Culligan became Sable's "houseman" in Santa Teresa. Schwartz sends Tommy Lemberg to the Sables to scare them into paying Alice's gambling debt. Culligan intervened, shot Tommy, was knocked out by Tommy, and then was stabbed to death by Sable, who by that time feared Culligan and Brown planned to eliminate him from their scheme. Macdonald said that aspects of Culligan's seafaring past echo memories of his father, John Macdonald Millar.*

Bibliography: "WG."

CULOTTI, GENEROUS JOE. In *The Galton Case*, he is the Reno car dealer to whom Archer is lured, to be beaten up. In the struggle, Generous Joe's glass eye drops out. The name Culotti may have been suggested to Macdonald by the last name of his friend Henri Anthony Coulette.*

CUMMINGS, SERGEANT. In *The Dark Tunnel*, he is a Canadian policeman at the Kirkland Lake hospital.

CURTIS. In *The Dark Tunnel*, he helps examine Dr. Alec Judd at the Naval Procurement Office in Detroit.

D

DACK. In *The Far Side of the Dollar*, he was the former owner of Dack's Auto Court, which Stanislaus bought years earlier.

DAHL, LIEUTENANT. In *The Way Some People Die*. *See* Dalling, Keith.

DALLING, KEITH. *The Way Some People Die*, he is a handsome, alcoholic radio actor. Jane Starr Hammond was in love with him. Galley Lawrence persuaded Keith to get her mother, Mrs. Samuel Lawrence, to hire Archer to look for her. Galley uses Keith for criminal purposes, has him kill Joseph Tarantine, then kills Keith. While interviewing Mrs. Lawrence, Keith poses as a detective calling himself Lieutenant Dahl.

DALY. In *The Far Side of the Dollar*, he is Ben Daly's son. Young Daly tells Archer his father won't look at Dick Leandro's photograph.

DALY, BEN. In *The Far Side of the Dollar*, he is a World War II veteran who fought at Guadalcanal. Since 1945, he has owned and still operates a gas station near the Barcelona Hotel. He goes with Archer to the hotel grounds. They find Otto Sipe trying to bury Mike Harley's body. When Sipe attacks Daly, Daly shoots Sipe with Archer's gun. Daly identifies Dick Leandro as the driver of a blue Chevrolet seen at the hotel.

DALY, MRS. BEN. In *The Far Side of the Dollar*, she and her husband were photographed by Harold Harley when he was the Barcelona Hotel photographer.

DAMIS, BURKE. In *The Zebra-Striped Hearse*. *See* Campion, Bruce.

DAMIS, DR. EDMUND BURKE. In *The Zebra-Striped Hearse*, he is a painter and art professor at the University of California at Berkeley. While on sabbatical, he lends his cabin near Citrus Junction to Bruce Campion and is distressed when Campion later demands the use of his car. Macdonald gratuitously makes Damis a hawk trainer (*see* Michelangelo).

DAMIS, MRS. In *The Zebra-Striped Hearse*, she is Dr. Edmund Burke Damis's mother and lives with him. She met Bruce Campion, never liked him, and said he possessed "a dark aura."

DAMMAN. In *The Dark Tunnel*, his name is on a faculty file in the cabinet in which Robert Branch searches for Ruth Esch's record.

DANE, PADRAIC ("PADDY"). In *The Barbarous Coast*, he was a Toronto dance teacher whom Hester Wall liked.

DANELAW, CAPTAIN. In *Find a Victim*, he is the identification expert working under Brandon Church, the Los Cruses sheriff. Danelaw determines that the same .38 killed Anne Meyer, Tony Aquista, and Don Kerrigan. Danelaw arrests Meyer, the gun owner.

THE DARK TUNNEL **(1944).** Novel. (Characters: Bailey, Dr. Robert Branch, Sergeant Norris E. Collins, Lieutenant Cross, Sergeant Cummings, Curtis, Damman, Eisberg, Erskine, Ruth Gerda Esch, Fenton, Rudolf Fisher, Florrie, Franz, Dr. Galloway, Garvin, Chester Gordon, Detective-Sergeant Haggerty, Hunter, Dr. Jackson, Joe, Johnnie, Dr. Alec Judd, Captain Killoran, Hilda Kramm, Colonel Leverett, Helen Madden, John Maldon, Dr. Bill Meisinger, Moran, O'Neill, Dr. Rasmussen, Raym, Officer Sale, Dr. R. A. Sandiman, Dr. Herman Schneider, Peter Schneider, Mrs. Shantz, Shiny, Max Simon, Robert Louis Stevenson, Sylvie, Thomas, the Tube, Vallon, Captain Carl von Esch, Frau Wanger, Dr. Wiener.)

In 1937, Robert Branch, the narrator, was traveling in Germany, intervened when a Jew was clubbed, was hit by a Nazi officer, and suffered a permanently damaged left eye. Branch got engaged to Ruth Esch, a student and an actress, who remained in Germany. The war separated them. It is now September 22, 1943. With a Ph.D. in English, Branch, twenty-nine, and his friend, Dr. Alec Judd, thirty-nine and co-editor of a Middle English dictionary, teach at Midwestern University, at Arbana, south of Detroit. They are also members of the War Board there, as are Hunter, Dr. Jackson, Colonel Leverett, Dr. Herman Schneider, and Vallon. Alec suspects that war secrets are being leaked to Nazi agents and wants to investigate before joining the U.S. Navy. Through Schneider, a refugee from Germany since 1935 and head of the German Department, Alec learns that Ruth, formerly Schneider's student in Germany, is coming to campus as an instructor in German.

Branch tells Hunter how he met Ruth, a red-headed bilingual anti-Nazi, during a parade in Munich, where he was studying the influence of British romanticism on Continental gardens, for his dissertation. He asked her to marry him and join him back home, but she insisted on remaining in Germany. One day they witnessed a Jewish physician being slugged by some Nazis. Ruth's brother, Captain Carl von Esch, was there, saw her, and called her a whore. She hit him. He roughed her up. Branch hit him and was clubbed in the eye. The Jew was killed. Branch was deported.

Alec's secretary and fiancée, Helen Madden, tells Branch she is worried, since Alec seems nervous. Branch goes to dinner at Schneider's house. The two plan to meet Ruth, coming in by train from Canada. Branch meets Peter, Schneider's nimble, albino-like son, formerly left behind in Germany. Peter superciliously presents his pro-Nazi stand. Afterwards, he duels Branch, who fenced well in college. At first they use foils harmlessly. They turn to sabres, with which Branch never competed. Peter is ferocious. Branch, his glasses broken, quits, so exhausted that he thinks he sees Ruth. Schneider drives Branch toward the station, veers near a cliff, and leaps out. Branch escapes, pushes the car on over so as to require a police report, and snarls at Schneider for trying to kill him.

Branch takes a taxi to the station, but Ruth never arrives. He goes to McKinley Hall, the main faculty building, breaks into Schneider's offices, and from his files learns details of Ruth's academic past in Germany and her contract at Midwestern. Alec finds Branch, and they discuss their suspicions. Alec gave Schneider valuable data concerning students being prepared for military and postwar work in Europe; further, Schneider has a German-born student named Rudolf Fisher in a Detroit extension class. Branch and Alec drive to Schneider's home. Branch sees Peter practicing sabre maneuvers with Ruth, then kissing her passionately, then insulting his father when the angry man confronts them. Alec and Branch enter, and Peter introduces Ruth as his fiancée.

Back in his apartment, Branch gets a phone call from Alec, who says he has something on Schneider, says "taillour," and nothing more. "Taillour" in Middle English means "tailor," as does "schneider" in German. In Branch's mail is a letter from Ruth, postmarked September 20. She writes that she was held captive by her Nazi father, escaped through Vichy France to Algiers, was jailed, is now through Schneider's influence with his son Peter in Kirkland Lake, Ontario, and will teach at Midwestern. Branch knows that a day ago some German prisoners of war escaped from Kirkland. At midnight, he goes to McKinley Hall to find Alec but sees him fall to his death, evidently pushed from his fifth-floor office window. Branch observes a woman break into Alec's faculty office and fall back. He rushes upstairs, sees Helen in a faint, checks Alec's editorial office a floor below, and calls the police. While they investigate, Branch phones Dr. Galloway, president of the university, who rushes over. Summoned by Galloway, a former student named Chester Gordon, now a Detroit FBI agent, joins the War Board members, the police, and Helen, in a postmidnight meeting to discuss the evidence. The conclusion is that Alec committed suicide. Branch disagrees and accuses Schneider of killing Alec.

Since Schneider told the police Ruth was staying at a downtown hotel, Branch phones around and learns that Ruth registered at the Palace Hotel. He asks Detective-Sergeant Haggerty, just leaving McKinley Hall, if he will check on Ruth, is refused, and drives to the hotel, where he encounters the hotel detective. He saw Ruth. Branch bribes him into nosing around, is told about Ruth's night movements and phone calls, and is upset when the detective says Ruth is a lesbian.

Branch gets coffee, chats with Shiny, a taxi driver he knows, and re-enters McKinley Hall from the rear, to avoid Officer Sale out front. Branch checks an editorial file labeled "taillour," finds an envelope with a copy of military data Alec said he lent Schneider, but is interrupted when Schneider enters with a Luger. He says he'll kill Branch to protect his honor, isn't a spy, but demands the evidence. Branch pretends to faint through fear, trips Schneider, and Schneider falls and knocks himself out. Branch grabs a horseshoe paperweight as a weapon, stoops over him, ascertains he is not dead, and goes downstairs for Sale. Rushing up, Sale determines that Schneider is dead of a crushed skull, with the horseshoe paperweight as the weapon. Sale detains Branch for possible murder, but Branch sees that the envelope and Luger are gone, throws the horseshoe at Sale, takes his gun, locks him in the office, and escapes down the stairs. He sees Gordon, armed and searching, and rushes into a tunnel with a maze of steam pipes for heating university buildings.

Branch finds the Natural History Museum door, in the dark sees Peter and Ruth, exchanges gunfire with them, and dashes to the furnace room and out over a coal pile, past railroad tracks, and to Helen's apartment. He has lost Sale's gun. He tells Helen his story. She agrees to retrieve his car, parked on campus, and to meet him near a roadhouse called the Slipper outside town. But when he gets there, he sees two cops with her. Observing a taxi driven out of town by Shiny, Branch proceeds down the road and finds a noisy brothel. Shiny, who delivered a customer there, is inside with some other men. While discussing Schneider's murder, Branch describes a redhead. Shiny, startled, says he drove such a woman from McKinley Hall downtown at 11:45 P.M. Everything clicks, and Branch starts back to the police. But a car bringing Ruth and Peter approaches.

Branch runs into the woods, unsuccessfully tries to buy a gun at a rural square dance and when looking for a telephone in the next farmhouse is captured by Peter, escapes, buys a shotgun from two deaf-mute rabbit hunters, fires at Peter, but is outwitted, lassoed, and rendered unconscious by Peter with a hypodermic needle.

Gordon rescues Branch from Peter's ingenious effort to have Branch hang himself by a weight restraining a rope only until he would come to and move, by which time Peter would be seen first elsewhere, for an alibi. Gordon and Branch explain their actions to each other. They drive in Gordon's car toward the brothel, see two drunks who say Ruth stole their car and clothes, and find Haggerty at the house.

Branch mentions Rudolf Fisher's name to Gordon, who is heading for a bomber plant near Detroit. Haggerty drives Branch to the police station for questioning, then deposits him at the hospital for food, a bath, and rest. Treated as a mental case, Branch experiments with a heavy tip-up window like the one Judd was pushed from and then greets Galloway. They talk. A doctor whom Branch knows sees the bruise on his arm from Peter's needle and states his opinion that the injection was sodium pentothal. He releases Branch, and a janitor sneaks him fresh clothes. Galloway drives him to McKinley Hall, where he meets Gordon, who has learned Alec was drugged. Branch explains the murder: Alec was sedated and laid out on the window; when he woke up and moved, he plunged screaming to his death, an apparent suicide.

Branch gets a coat from his office, cashes a check, and sees Helen. She apologizes for alerting the police and says she has just joined the Red Cross. After reporting to Galloway, Gordon drives, taking Branch along, to the bomber plant, to which Peter has been traced. In Peter's abandoned car is a Canadian newspaper, dated September 22, with a news item cut out. Plant records indicate Peter, as Ludwig Vlathek, worked at the plant with machine tools. His Detroit address is identical to Rudoph Fisher's. Gordon, assisted by Fenton, another FBI agent, and Branch, call on Fisher, a homosexual eager to talk. Fenton says that when the government "cracked the Buchanan-Dineen circle, Peter dropped his Vlathek alias and cleared out for Canada," dumping dear Rudy. It seems that Peter's decent father had spirited Peter out of Germany, only to discover that he had become a vicious Nazi; beginning summer 1941, Peter worked in several U.S. war plants. (*See* Buchanan-Dineen, Grace.) Intelligence sources report that Ruth is at Kirkland Lake, injured, and that Captain Carl von Esch is in Chicago. Gordon takes Branch to the Chicago airport to fly to Toronto.

Branch lands at twilight and in his hotel reads in a copy of the newspaper which Peter mutilated that an unidentified redheaded woman with amnesia is in the hospital at Kirkland Lake. By taking a night train, Branch arrives there the next morning. Phoning Gordon, he learns that Carl, now arrested, and Peter knocked Ruth down a mine shaft on September 20 and left her for dead. Carl took Ruth's passport, dressed like her, and accompanied Peter to the United States. Peter, calling himself Vlathek and

Ruth's brother, returned to Canada, and visited her in the hospital. Branch finds and kisses Ruth, who recognizes him; he persuades the hospital physician to let him replace her until Peter returns, supposedly for her release When Peter sneaks in, dressed as a nurse, Branch chases him and knocks him out. As a Canadian sergeant comes up, Branch, resting, dreams of Ruth's sunlit hair.

Dodd, Mead accepted *The Dark Tunnel* after it had been rejected by Random House because Margaret Millar* was already publishing there. Well reviewed, *The Dark Tunnel* capitalized on the arrest and confession (August, October 1943) of Grace Buchanan-Dineen and her associates for giving German agents information about war production in Detroit. The novel, retitled *I Die Slowly*, was reprinted as a paperback (Lion, 1950; 1955). Since tunnels and darkness are frequently mentioned in the novel, the original title is better.

Midwestern University, near Detroit, is based on the University of Michigan, at Ann Arbor. Arbana echoes Urbana, the locale of the University of Illinois. Macdonald patterned Robert Branch's run through the steam tunnels after Macdonald's own illegal wartime exploration of identical tunnels connecting buildings at Ann Arbor. The autobiographical flashback to Germany in 1937 is awkward. Branch, whose dissertation topic Macdonald spoofs, paraphrases poetry—mainly from John Donne, T. S. Eliot, and William Shakespeare—even as he survives physical challenges. No need to mention Macdonald's politically incorrect handling of homosexuality and transvestism; one must no longer write, for example, "pansy drag."

Bibliography: Bruccoli; Nolan; Speir.

DAVID, SAUL (1921–1996). Publishing executive, movie producer, and author. Davis was born in New York City, attended the Rhode Island School of Design (1937–1940); worked for a radio station in York, Pennsylvania, and a newspaper in Port Huron, Michigan; and during World War II wrote for *Stars and Stripes* and *Yank* in Europe and North Africa (1942–1945). Hired in 1950 by Bantam Books, David was a reader and then an editorial director (to 1960). He left the East for Hollywood, where he held executive positions with Columbia, Warner Brothers, and Twentieth Century Fox (in the 1960s), and Universal, Rastar, and MGM (in the 1970s). David retired, wrote his frank and funny autobiography (*The Industry: Life in the Hollywood Fast Lane*, 1981), was an instructor at the Peter Stark Producing Program (University of Southern California), and was a screenplay adviser for Touchstone and Interscope. David was married twice and divorced twice, and had two children. The most memorable of the seven movies he produced are *Von Ryan's Express* (1965) and *Fantastic Voyage* (1966), both for Twentieth Century-Fox.

David read the 1950 *Esquire* condensation of Macdonald's *Blue City*, sought to woo him from Pocket Books to Bantam for more money, succeeded in 1953, and became what David called Macdonald's "reprinter," beginning with *Find a Victim*. In it David persuaded Macdonald to have Don Kerrigan beaten up before he was shot. David got him to revise seven short stories for *The Name Is Archer*, Bantam's popular 1995 assembly, the title of which David chose from Macdonald's list of suggestions. In 1958, David visited Macdonald at Santa Barbara and delighted him by reporting that Macdonald was Bantam's most popular mystery writer. Once in Hollywood, David evidently lost contact with or interest in Macdonald. David's autobiography does not mention him.

Bibliography: Nolan.

DAVIE, DONALD (1922–), Critic, poet, and editor. Davie was born in Barnsley, Yorkshire, England, to Baptist parents, earned three degrees at Cambridge University (ending 1951), served in the British navy, married Doreen John, and had three children with her. He taught in the 1950s and 1960s at Trinity College, Dublin, and published ultraconservative literary criticism and antimodern verse, as a member of The Movement, a group of poets believing that poems had to be moral to be of value. Davie's *Purity of Diction in English Verse* (1952; 2nd ed., 1967) and *A Winter Talent and Other Poems* (1957) provide precept and example. While Davie was visiting professor at the University of California at Santa Barbara (1957–1958), he enjoyed many new friendships, notably with the conservative critic Ivor Winters. In *The Forests of Lithuania* (1959), which reworks parts of *Pan Tadeusz*, Adam Mickiewicz's 1834 epic, Davie shows the influence of Ezra Pound, on whom he wrote a controversial book (1964). Davie lectured at the University of Cincinnati (1963), became busy in Europe, and translated and wrote about Russian literature. Davie returned to California (1968) to teach at Stanford University. An expatriate's homesickness is evident in his *Thomas Hardy and British Poetry* (1972). Of interest are Davie's late-career studies of English church verse, his editing, and his reviews.

Macdonald and Davie met in Santa Barbara (1957). Although Margaret Millar* resented the Davies' too-frequent visits and bad-mouthed Macdonald in their presence, the two men found much common ground. Macdonald wrote a short article in praise of Davie's poetry ("A Vein of North Country Iron Runs Through Davie's Poems," *San Francisco Chronicle—This World*, June 1, 1958). *The Forests of Lithuania*, which Davie was working on, concerns the lost-father search, a subject that had long obsessed Macdonald. Davie encouraged Macdonald's fruitless efforts to publish his dissertation on Samuel Taylor Coleridge, a revision of which Davie helped him with (1960). Macdonald dedicated *On Crime Writing*

(1973) to Donald Davie. In his *Collected Poems* (1990), Davie included two elegies for Macdonald: "Alzheimer's Disease: for Kenneth Millar (Ross Macdonald)" and "A Measured Tread/for Kenneth Millar dead." Davie pronounced *The Galton Case* Macdonald's finest novel, undoubtedly because of its lost-father theme.

Bibliography: Bruccoli; Donald Davie, "On Hearing About Ross Macdonald," in *IJ*, p. 95; Nolan.

DAVIS. In *Black Money*, he owns the Las Vegas Scorpion Club. He and Kayo Ketchel skimmed "black money" from their profits, hid it from the IRS, but were robbed by Francis Martel.

DAVIS, MISS. In *The Three Roads*, she is Dr. Ralston's nurse and verifies the time Burton Garth went to the physician's office after Larry Miles slugged him.

DAWSON, DR. In *The Galton Case. See* Sable, Gordon.

DEARBORN, LEFTY. In *The Galton Case*, he is a member of Lempi's gang.

"DEATH MASK." *See The Ferguson Affair*.

"THE DECAPITATED MAN." *See The Galton Case*.

DEE. In *Trouble Follows Me*, Private Rodney Hatcher mentions him in a letter to Laura Eaton. Hatcher says Dee sends his regards.

"THE DEEP DARK NIGHT." *See The Far Side of the Dollar*.

DEERING. In *The Far Side of the Dollar*, he is a ping-pong–playing student at Laguna Perdida School.

DE FALLA. In *The Chill*, he applies for the teaching position made available when Helen Haggerty is murdered.

DE HOUVENEL. In *Black Money*, he and his family were guests at the Montevista Tennis Club, September 1959.

DELONEY. In *The Chill*, he was Luke Deloney's father, who started the family on the road to success by being an energetic cement worker in Bridgeton, Illinois.

DELONEY, LUKE. In *The Chill*, he was a successful businessman in Bridgeton, Illinois. His sister-in-law was Letitia O. Macready (*see* Bradshaw, Mrs.). His discovery of her love affair with George Bradshaw resulted in Letitia's killing him in June 1940. He was then forty. Earl Hoffman concealed circumstances and called the shooting accidental.

DELONEY, MRS. LUKE. In *The Chill*, she is Senator Osborne's daughter and the sister, ten years older, of Letitia O. Macready (*see* Bradshaw, Mrs.). Archer interviews the widowed Mrs. Deloney in her home in Bridgeton, Illinois, learning little. When she suddenly flies to Pacific Point after Helen Haggerty's murder, Archer finds her again and determines that Letitia, far from being Dean Roy Bradshaw's mother, is his wife.

DELONEY, SCOTT. In *The Chill*. *See* Scott, Uncle.

DELONG, MRS. In *The Goodbye Look*, she is a clerk at the Sunset Motor Motel in Pacific Point. She provides Archer with information about Sidney Harrow.

"THE DEMON LOVER." *See Black Money*.

DENNIS. In *The Drowning Pool*, he owns the Hunt Club, where Archer meets Mavis Kilbourne and her husband, Walter J. Kilbourne.

DENTON, MRS. In *The Ferguson Affair*, she was the owner of the watch Larry Gaines stole and gave to Ella Barker.

DERMOTT, MISS JEANETTE. In *The Drowning Pool*, she is a young blonde cast as Clara in Francis Marvell's play, *The Ironist*.

DESIDERIA. In *The Barbarous Coast*, she is Tony Torres's sister. Desideria blamed Tony for his nephew Lance Torres's slide into corruption. (*See* Leonard, Lance.)

DESMOND, JULIAN. In *The Ivory Grin*. *See* Heiss, Maxfield.

DEVLIN. In "The Bearded Lady," he is one of Walter Hendryx's thugs.

DEVON, ANN ("ANNIE"). In *Meet Me at the Morgue*, she is Howard Cross's pretty assistant, twenty-four, in the probation office. She loves Larry Seifel, is jealous of his relationship with Helen Johnson, but finally will marry Larry and move from Pacific Point to Seattle with him.

DEVORE. In *Find a Victim*, he is mentioned as Sally Devore's husband, a former constable who left her. He is or was Ralph Devore's father.

DEVORE, SALLY. In *Find a Victim*, she is the gossipy gas-station operator near Lake Perdida. She gives Archer information.

DEVORE, RALPH. In *Find a Victim*, he is Sally Devore's son, a college student, who forced Tony Aquista to leave when he bothered Sally.

DEWAR, OWEN. In "The Suicide," he was a Las Vegas poker dealer and the second husband of Ethel Larrabee, who, after he beats her up, shoots him dead.

DEWEY. In *The Ivory Grin*, he is a salty old Arroyo Beach parking attendant who helps Archer try to locate the Buick belonging to Charles A. Singleton, Jr.

DICKSON, MRS. RUTH. In *The Moving Target*, her renting of a limousine in Los Angeles, as reported by Peter Colton to Archer, proves to be a false lead.

"DIGGER." *See The Underground Man*. ("Digger" is a rural term for death.)

DINEEN, DR. GEORGE T. In *The Galton Case*, he is a Luna Bay physician, graduated from "the University of Ohio Medical School" (1914), and knew Anthony Galton (as John Brown) and his wife, Theodora Brown. Dr. Dineen delivered their son, John Brown (Jr.). insists that that son, now grown up, is Maria Galton's grandson, and introduces him to Archer.

DINEEN, MRS. In *The Galton Case*, she is Dr. George T. Dineen's wife, about sixty, with "blue-white hair" and a contented look.

DINGMAN, JERRY. In *The Wycherly Woman*, he is the Champion Hotel bellhop. Archer bribes him for information. When Archer is injured, Dingman summons Dr. Broch.

"THE DISSOLVING MAN." *See The Underground Man*.

DITMAR, MISS. In *The Zebra-Striped Hearse*, she runs a modeling agency next door to Archer's Sunset Boulevard office.

DOLAN, CAPTAIN. In *Sleeping Beauty*, he is a police officer who appears after Harold Sherry and Jack Lennox exchanged shots. Lew Archer sees him there and at the hospital.

DOLPHINE, JACK. In "The Sinister Habit," he strangles his wife, Stella Dolphine, because she prefers Leonard Lister to him. When Jack shoots J. Reginald Harlan, Archer shoots Jack.

DOLPHINE, STELLA. In "The Sinister Habit," she prefers Leonard Lister to her husband, Jack Dolphine, who kills her.

DOMINGO. In *Black Money*, this is Francis Martel's maternal grandmother's name.

DOMINGO, PEDRO. In *Black Money*, this was Francis Martel's real name. He used it when he was a student at Los Angeles State College, where he studied under Allan Bosch. *See* Martel, Francis.

DOMINGO, SECUNDINA. In *Black Money*. *See* Rosales, Secundina.

DONAGUE, FINGERS. In *The Galton Case*, he is the pianist at San Francisco's Listening Ear. When Archer goes there seeking Chad Bolling, he sees Fingers introduce Chad.

DONALD. In *The Ivory Grin*, he takes care of Leo Durano, is fat, stupid, but loyal. Leo's vicious sister, Una Durano, demeans him.

DONATO, AUGUSTINE ("GUS"). In *The Ferguson Affair*, he is Manuel Donato's younger brother and Secundina Manuel's husband. When released from prison, he joins the gang led by Hector Broadman and Larry Gaines, and is shot dead by Sergeant Pike Granada.

DONATO, MANUEL. In *The Ferguson Affair*, he is Augustine Donato's older brother and is disgusted by Augustine's criminal activities. Manuel owns a tamale shop, next door to Hector Broadman's pawnshop, and first found Broadman when he was slugged.

DONATO, SECUNDINA ("CUTEY"). In *The Ferguson Affair*, she is Arcadia Torres's sister, Augustine Donato's wife, and Manuel Donato's sister-in-law. Sergeant Pike Granada and Tony Padilla have long loved her to no avail. William Gunnarson observes Secundina's "licorice hair." Secundina regards her family as cursed because Augustine is a criminal. She is horribly depressed when he is murdered. She takes a dangerous number of sleeping pills but dies of asphyxiation.

DONCASTER. In *The Wycherly Woman*, he was the husband of Phoebe Wycherly's landlady. Doncaster, deceased, was a Church of Christ minister. His dour portrait gives Archer the willies.

DONCASTER, MRS. In *The Wycherly Woman*, she was Phoebe Wycherly's Boulder Beach landlady. She mollycoddles her son, Robert Doncaster, who is in love with Phoebe. This pious widow speaks of "the wrath of gosh."

DONCASTER, ROBERT ("BOBBY"). In *The Wycherly Woman*, he is the handsome son, twenty-one, of Phoebe Wycherly's overly protective Boulder Beach landlady. At nearby Medicine Stone last August, Bobby and Phoebe fell in love, and she got pregnant. Archer gradually gets the truth out of him: Bobby went with Phoebe to San Francisco intending to marry her, drove Catherine Wycherly's body back to the cliff near Medicine Stone, and registers with Phoebe as Mr. and Mrs. Smith at the Siesta Motel, before she reports to Dr. Sherrill of Palo Alto. Bobby helps Archer locate Phoebe.

DONNY. In "Gone Girl," he is Ella Salanda's weak-minded friend, thirty-eight. When Bartolemeo threatened her, Donny killed him.

***THE DOOMSTERS* (1958).** Novel. (Characters: Lew Archer, Sue Archer, Dr. Brockley, Carmichael, Miss Cullen, Durkin, Dutch, Gley, Mrs. Gley, Dr. J. Charles Grantland, Gwen, Haines, Alicia Hallman, Carl Hallman, Jerry Hallman, Martha Hallman, Mildred Hallman, Senator Jeremiah Hallman, Zinnie Hallman, Hutchinson, Mrs. Hutchinson, Juan, Lawson, Dr. Levin, Marie, Maude, Sheriff Duane Ostervelt, Rose Parish, Thomas Rica, Belle Scott, Glenn Scott, Eugene Slovekin, Spaulding, Sam Yogan.)

One September morn, Carl Hallman, twenty-four, knocks on the door of Archer's Los Angeles house. Over breakfast, Archer learns this: Jerry Hallman, Carl's brother, thirty-four, got Carl's wife, Mildred, to help commit him to a nearby hospital; Carl escaped last night, with Thomas Rica, now vanished. Persuading Carl to return to the hospital while he investigates, Archer learns this on the drive there: Carl's father, Jeremiah Hallman, was a state senator from Purissima, owned an orange ranch, exploited illegal Mexican workers, and snapped up land from Japanese hounded away when World War II began. Carl studied philosophy at Berkeley, married Mildred, had a breakdown, returned to the ranch, and hoped to treat workers and dispossessed Japanese honorably. After a "ruction" with materialistic Jerry and his domineering wife, Zinnie, against Carl, Mildred being in the middle, Jeremiah died, evidently of a heart attack in his bathtub. Carl will be blamed unless Archer proves otherwise. Carl says there is evidence against Dr. J. Charles Grantland, doubts Archer's assurance that he will help, knocks Archer unconscious, and steals his car.

Archer walks to the hospital and learns from Dr. Brockley that Rica, Carl's fellow escapee, was a heroin-addicted patient. Archer remembers Rica. Ten years ago, Archer helped Rica but later failed him. Brockley asks Archer to delay reporting his car theft, says he has notified Carl's family and Duane Ostervelt, Purissima's sheriff, and says Carl blames himself both for his father's death and for his mother Alicia Hallman's earlier suicide. Archer leaves his phone number with Miss Rose Parish, a lovely psychiatric social worker, who bad-mouths Rica but likes Carl.

Archer takes a cab to the home of Carl's whining, alcoholic mother-in-law, Mrs. Gley, who says she fears Carl. Mildred, living with her and notified about Carl, returns from work for lunch. Mildred says Carl is the harmless victim of a controlling family. Zinnie phones: Carl has been seen at the ranch, and Ostervelt and deputies are there. Driving out with Archer, Mildred tells him Jerry controls the family's holdings as long as Carl is institutionalized. Before letting Archer and Mildred through, Ostervelt kids her that Archer is her new boyfriend. Zinnie, overtly sexy, admits them. Her daughter, Martha, three, is there and displays affection for Mildred. Archer asks to talk with Sam Yogan, the Japanese gardener who first spotted Carl. Carmichael, a deputy, struts about. Handsome, flashy Dr. Grantland drives up and walks into the house. Archer overhears him kissing Zinnie and discussing their wanting her to get divorced. Jerry drives up, yells at Grantland to leave, and threatens him with garden shears. Archer urges Jerry to wise up.

Carl is suddenly seen again. Carmichael runs into the orange grove in search of him. Archer follows, cannot keep up, and returns to the house. He learns that Jerry has been shot twice in the back and is dead in the greenhouse. Ostervelt produces the weapon, an ornamented .25. He lets Grantland return to Purissima, with Martha and a gray-haired servant named Mrs. Hutchinson. Ostervelt roughly questions Sam, who says he heard two shots, saw nothing, and identifies the .25 as Alicia's.

Zinnie invites Archer in and offers her sinuous self for silence about Grantland's intimate talk with her. She says this: She does not love Grantland, is sure Carl killed his father and now Jerry; Grantland and Ostervelt called the death a heart attack so Carl could be hospitalized not arrrested. Archer asks if perhaps Grantland killed Jerry. When Archer rejects Zinnie, she explodes. Mildred, napping, enters, is accused of conspiring with Archer, and exits with him.

The police have brought Archer's car. Archer tells Mildred he doubts Carl's guilt and will work for her. She reveals that Ostervelt, who doubles as coroner, told her Carl killed his father but, for sex with her, would call it a heart attack. Her equivocating since then has angered Ostervelt, whom she fears. Lawson, Ostervelt's deputy coroner, tells Archer this: Ostervelt may carelessly handle the bullets that killed Jerry; Alicia drowned herself but also was bruised; Glenn Scott, a Los Angeles detective whom Archer knows, investigated her death; Grantland, whom Lawson dislikes, was her physician; Carl's father had a heart attack in his bath, died, and was cremated. Ostervelt appears, rebukes Lawson, and becomes so angry at Archer's sarcasm that he gun-butts Archer and tears his ear. Eugene Slovekin, a reporter on the scene, intervenes with his notebook. Archer arranges to talk with him later.

Archer gets a hotel room in Purissima, phones and drives out to see Scott, now retired just outside Malibu. Scott tells Archer his beliefs: When Alicia threatened suicide in Grantland's office, Grantland took her .25, promising to say nothing; Carl could have killed both of his parents. Having phoned for a 5:30 appointment, Archer reports to Grantland's office. While waiting, he reads Slovekin's newspaper account of the murder, then learns from Miss Cullen, Grantland's gossipy receptionist, that Mildred is a sinus patient and Carl visited the office this morning. Grantland comes in, rebukes Miss Cullen, attends to Archer's ear, and, when questioned, explains: Alicia was on barbiturates, when denied more threatened to shoot herself; Grantland kept her gun in his office; Carl did visit this morning, must have taken the gun; only when Grantland saw it beside Jerry's body did he remember it; he returned here, looked in vain for the gun, and phoned Ostervelt about it. Doubting Grantland's integrity, Archer departs.

Waiting until Grantland drives off, Archer follows him out of town. Grantland stops beside a car driven by Rica, who speeds away erratically. Archer follows to the Buenavista Inn, a brothel. Maude, in charge, playfully orders Tom Rica inside. She tells Archer she picked up Carl and Rica after their escape, dumped Carl, and intends to aid Rica, who is still on heroin. Rica boasts of having a sure-fire "racket" now and proceeds to an inner room. Maude orders her bouncer Dutch to eject Archer, who decks him instead, goes after Rica, and stops him from shooting up. Rica says that he is blackmailing Grantland and, further, Carl did not shoot Jerry. When Maude, with a .32, and Dutch burst in, Archer decks him again and takes her gun, whereupon Maude warns that she and "the top law of the county" are in cahoots.

Hoping to spot Carl, Archer drives toward Purissima, sees a crowd along the beach, and hears the rumor that Carl has been spotted foraging for food there. Mildred, having heard this news on her radio, drives up. Distraught, she walks onto the highway and narrowly avoids being hit by a truck. She drives home. Archer follows. They find Mrs. Gley drunk, then asleep. Mildred tells Archer that when Carl was committed, Ostervelt tried to establish her at the Buenavista as his mistress. She escaped his advances. Ostervelt phones that he and Rose Parish, with whom he has worked, want to come over. Although she does not want them, they soon arrive. After some blustering, Ostervelt is persuaded by Rose to leave while she talks with Archer. Meanwhile, Mildred is upstairs changing her clothes. Rose believes Carl, whom she counseled, is innocent and reveals her affection for him. She says Carl irrationally confessed his responsibility for both parents' deaths but later recanted.

Mildred reappears, spiffily dressed, and snipes verbally at Rose until interrupted by Carmichael, leading some vigilantes. He reports that Carl may have been spotted near the Red Barn, an eatery near a dry creekbed and a culvert. Wondering if Carl might be looking for Martha, Archer and Rose visit Mrs. Hutchinson. She says Grantland supplied Alicia with drugs, describes Alicia's gun, is surprised to learn that it was used to kill Jerry, and calls the Hallman house "bad-luck." Martha enters and goes to Rose's embrace.

A manhunt is on. Archer walks to the Red Barn, where he spots Slovekin with a girl carhop who reported seeing "a bum," perhaps Carl. Munching a hamburger, Archer tells Slovekin that he believes Carl is innocent and learns from Slovekin that Senator Hallman died a week after suddenly hearing that Ostervelt was probably taking payoffs. Archer returns to Mrs. Hutchinson's place, finds dead Jerry's station wagon suddenly there, and in it Zinnie's stabbed corpse, still warm. Archer vomits. Without mentioning this murder, Archer quizzes now conscience-stricken Mrs. Hutchinson, who reveals this: Jerry first met Zinnie in a Los Angeles nightclub; after they married, they often argued; she wanted a divorce; she probably lusted for Grantland; Grantland told Mrs. Hutchinson not to mention Alicia's gun; Alicia felt controlled by "Doomsters[,] . . . evil fates like"; and Sam drove Alicia to the wharf the night she died. Rose, entering the room, happily reports she got Martha to fall asleep, shortly after 11:00 P.M.

Archer drives Rose to Zinnie's car, observes Sam being dropped off there by a fellow servant, and shows him Zinnie's corpse. After admitting he drove Alicia to a street near the wharf that fatal night, he wants to inform the police about Zinnie. Archer and Rose proceed to Grantland's office and find Rica crawling outside, bloody from trying to get drugs there and saying he saw Grantland butcher "the old lady." Archer goes to a gas station, calls an ambulance for Rica, and learns that Grantland just bought cleaning gas there.

Archer drives to Grantland's home, arms himself with Maude's .32, finds Grantland scrubbing blood off the carpet, sees an electric blanket nearby, and accuses him of killing Zinnie and trying to blame Sam. Grantland maunders about Alicia's accidental death in his office, sees his plans collapse, asks Archer to give him time to get to Mexico, and when Archer orders him to summon the police kicks the gas can over him, decks him with the telephone, and sets his house afire. Archer comes to, crawls to safety, and sees Grantland driving away.

Archer follows Grantland to Mildred's house. Carl emerges with a knife. Grantland shoots him three times, aims at Mildred, but runs out of bullets. Ostervelt appears, orders Grantland to stop, and when he runs shoots him dead. Ostervelt and Archer theorize about the hour of Zinnie's death. Cradling Carl's head, Mildred says he entered the house from the rear while Archer and Rose were talking. An ambulance takes Carl to the hospital. Archer cannot find the knife Carl was wielding.

Drunk, Mrs. Gley tells Archer that Mildred followed Carl to Berkeley, got pregnant by him before their marriage, lost the baby, and was tended to by Grantland. Archer eavesdrops on Mildred and Ostervelt in the front room. She kept Carl in her mother's house throughout the day. She lets Ostervelt fondle her. He promises multiple cover-ups, including her brief affair with Grantland. He tells her he got Carl to kill Jerry. She agrees to share the Hallman estate with Ostervelt, who leaves.

Archer tells Mildred she stabbed Zinnie, whose body Grantland kept warm with the electric blanket. Mildred produces the knife, which Archer keeps her from using on herself. Mrs. Gley snores away. Mildred confesses: Carl loved her; Alicia disapproved; Alicia took Mildred to Grantland, who performed an abortion; Mildred slugged Alicia; Grantland drowned her and slept briefly with Mildred; when Mildred married Carl, he became idealistic and celibate; after the two moved to the Hallman ranch, Grantland starting blackmailing her; when Jerry got his father to argue with Carl and threatened to disinherit him, Mildred banged his head and drowned him in his bathtub; she would have killed her own father for abandoning her and her mother. Dawn breaks. Mildred continues: Jerry blamed Carl for their father's death, had him committed with Mildred's agreement, took over the ranch; yesterday, when she saw Carl with Alicia's gun, given him by Grantland, she took it, told Carl to hide at her mother's house, shot Jerry, and later finding Zinnie in Grantland's bed stabbed her. Archer holds quaking Mildred in his arms for some time.

Archer breakfasts with Rose at the hospital. Rose loves Carl, will await his recovery, hopes Mildred can be nurtured, and warns that Rica, under restraint in the hospital, has worrisome thoughts. Archer remembers: Rica entered his office three years ago needing help but was dismissed then. Archer now talks with Rica, who confesses he helped Grantland get Alicia to the wharf and toss her in, let her flounder and sink, went at that juncture to Archer for advice but was brushed off, turned to blackmailing Grantland for drugs, agrees to make an official statement, praises Maude for trying to cure him, and wishes Carl well. Rica sent Carl yesterday to Archer hoping Archer would help Carl and Rica, too, somehow. Archer and Rica apologize to each other.

An earlier title for *The Doomsters* was "The Enormous Detour." Mac-

donald, proud of *The Doomsters*, was disappointed by inadequate adver-
tising, slow sales, and some negative reviews. He prepared a
condensation titled "Bring the Killer to Justice" for *Ellery Queen's Mystery
Magazine* (February 1962). The original title came from lines in Thomas
Hardy's "To an Unborn Pauper Child": "The Doomsters heap / Travails
. . . around us here." Archer feels that we may be our "own doomsters,"
especially when mishandling family relationships.

Bibliography: Bruccoli; Nolan; Clifford A. Ridley, "Yes, Most of My Chronicles
Are Chronicles of Misfortune," *National Observer* (July 31, 1976); Schopen.

DOSS, JOE. In *Trouble Follows Me*, he is a sailor on Lieutenant Eric
Swann's ship in San Diego harbor. Chester Gordon grills him.

DOTERY, FRANK. In *The Ferguson Affair*, he was James and Kate Dotery's son. Kate tells William Gunnarson that Frank was killed in an accident involving a car Ralph Spindle drove.

DOTERY, HILDA ("DOTTY"). In *The Ferguson Affair*, she is the daughter
of Colonel Ian Ferguson and Katie Mulloy (*see* Dotery, Kate). Posing as
Ferguson's wife (*see* Ferguson, June), she conspires with her lover, Larry
Gaines, in her own fake kidnapping to get money from Ferguson. She
distrusts Gaines, shoots him, incinerates him, but is accidentally killed by
Michael Speare.

DOTERY, JACK. In *The Ferguson Affair*, he is James and Kate Dotery's
son. Long ago, Jack permanently left them.

DOTERY, JAMES ("JIM"). In *The Ferguson Affair*, he is Kate Doherty's
alcoholic, abusive husband, and the father of Frank, Jack, June, and Renee
Dotery. James always hated Hilda Dotery, his stepdaughter. He runs a
store in Mountain Grove.

DOTERY, JUNE. In *The Ferguson Affair*. *See* Ferguson, June.

DOTERY, KATE. In *The Ferguson Affair*, she is Hilda Dotery's mother,
by Colonel Ian Ferguson, when she was Katie Mulloy of Boston. She
married James Ferguson and with him had Frank, Jack, June, and Renee
Doherty. Kate, forty-three, and James Dotery live in Mountain Grove. Her
revelations to William Gunnarson help him solve the kidnapping of Ferguson's supposed wife.

DOTERY, RENEE. In *The Ferguson Affair*, she is James and Kate Dotery's
daughter, long gone.

DOWSER, DANNY. In *The Way Some People Die*, he is a mob boss for whom Herman Speed and Joseph Tarantine, among others, worked. When Joe Tarantine rips him off, he asks Archer to find both Joe and Galley Lawrence, who is with Joe. Archer causes Dowser and his cohorts to be arrested. Dowser has been likened to Mickey Cohen, the notorious, self-aggrandizing criminal. Both were boxers, fight promoters, West Coast racketeers with Hollywood connections and well-guarded mansions; and both were imprisoned. Born in Brooklyn, Cohen died in Los Angeles.

Bibliography: Robert J. Kelly, *Encyclopedia of Organized Crime in the United States* (Westport, Conn.: Greenwood Press, 2000); Nolan.

DRAKE. In *The Zebra-Striped Hearse*, he owns the Citrus Junction hardware store where Elizabeth Stone bought the silver icepick and corkscrew she sent to Isobel Jaimet as a present when she married Colonel Mark Blackwell.

DRAKE, JESSIE. In *The Wycherly Woman*, she was an actress, lived in Nevada, and was charged with drug possession and prostitution. She knew Sally Quillan before Sally married Ben Merriman. Twenty-four, calling herself Jezebel Drake, and writing her memoirs, Jessie lives with Stanley Quillan, Sally's brother, in an apartment near San Mateo. By pretending to want to rent next door, Archer gains information from this airhead.

DRAKE, SAM. In *Trouble Follows Me*, he is the hero-narrator, formerly a Detroit reporter, now a U.S. Navy ensign on leave after combat action in the Pacific. In Honolulu, he finds the hanged body of Sue Sholto, likes Mary Thompson, looks up Bessie Land in Detroit, finds her body, and takes a train to Los Angeles with Mary to pursue his investigation. On board the train, Drake meets an oilman named Anderson and drinks with Private Rodney Hatcher, who soon dies. In Santa Barbara, Drake interviews Laura Eaton, a friend of Hatcher's, and cooperates with Chester Gordon, an FBI agent on the case. Drake pursues Anderson through his companion, Miss Green, to Tijuana, is attacked by Anderson, immobilizes him, and sees him killed by Bessie's husband, Hector Land, who then commits suicide. Throughout, Drake vacillates between cockiness and self-doubt. In the 1948 version of "The Bearded Lady," Sam Drake is the hero, an experienced newspaperman; in the 1955 revision, he becomes Lew Archer. Sam Drake, Macdonald's second detective (Robert Branch of *The Dark Tunnel* came first) may owe his first name to that of Sam Spade, hero of several works, notably *The Maltese Falcon*, by Dashiell Hammett, whose pioneering detective fiction Macdonald admired.

DREEN, MRS. MILLICENT. In "Find the Woman," this Hollywood script reader hires Archer to find her missing daughter, Una Sand.

DRENNAN, DOROTHY. In *The Ferguson Affair*, her name appears in the clipping in Larry Gaines's wallet.

DRESSEN, MRS. SAM. In *Meet Me at the Morgue*, she is the identification expert's wife.

DRESSEN, SAM. In *Meet Me at the Morgue*, he is an identification expert, gray and near retirement after eighteen years with the police. He and Howard Cross work together to apprehend Amy Miner. Dressen and his wife care for Molly Fawn overnight. Dressen is portrayed as being a friend of Ray Pinker, a real-life Los Angeles forensic chemist.

Bibliography: Nolan.

DREW, CAPTAIN ANGUS. In *Meet Me at the Morgue*, he was a naval officer aboard the *Eureka Bay*, 1944–1946. He commended Fred Miner.

DREW, CLYDE. In *The Moving Target*, he was Millicent Drew's husband, arty, perhaps homosexual, according to Elaine Sampson. Archer investigated matters when Clyde's wife sought a divorce.

DREW, MILLICENT. In *The Moving Target*, Elaine Sampson tells Archer that her friend Millicent Clyde called his work "helpful" when she was divorcing her husband, Clyde Drew.

DREW, SUSANNA. In *The Far Side of the Dollar*, she was a Hollywood script girl, twenty in 1945. She befriended Carol Brown (*see* Harley, Carol) and was seduced by Ralph Hillman after he had impregnated Carol. Susanna and Archer were once close friends. Now "fortyish," she is approached by Archer to learn about Carol. Susanna helps Archer by letting Stella Carlson stay overnight with her. Susanna also tells him about Hillman. In an unpublished last chapter of *The Far Side of the Dollar*, Macdonald planned to have Susanna and Archer renew their intimacy.

Bibliography: Bruccoli.

THE DROWNING POOL **(1950).** Novel. (Characters: Al, Antonio, Arbuthnot, Archer, Lewis A. Archer, Mrs. Archer, Sue Archer, Bill, Carmody, Mrs. Carmody, Hilda Cramm, Morris Cramm, Dennis, Miss Jeanette Dermott, Eddie, Don Fargeon, Farrington, Mildred Fleming, Felicia France, Detective-Sergeant Simeon J. Franks, Mrs. Leigh Galloway, Goldfarb, Helen, Henry, Uncle Jake, Jane, Gretchen Keck, Kenny, Mavis Kilbourne, Walter J. Kilbourne, Chief Ralph Knudson, Eleanor Knudson, Lewisohn,

Leonald Lyons, Miss Macon, Charles Mariano, Francis Marvell, Dr. Melliotes, Enrico Murratti, Bud Musselman, Musso, Pat Reavis, Romanovsky,
Dr. Sanders, Oscar Ferdinand Schmidt, Mrs. Elaine Schneider, Simmie,
Slocum, Cathy Slocum, James Slocum, Maude Slocum, Mrs. Olivia Slocum, Mrs. Strang, Tappingham, Rita Treadwith, Valmy, Von Esch, Winowsky, Wood.)

Maude Slocum of Quinto, California, thirty-five, has been married for
sixteen years to James Slocum, a so-so actor, and is the mother of Cathy,
fifteen. Maude asks Archer to discover who sent her husband a letter she
intercepted calling her an adulteress. Getting a motel room near Santa
Monica, Archer proceeds to the Quinto Theatre, where Maude said James
was rehearsing in a play. The play is *The Ironist*, by Francis Marvell, a
Britisher and a Quinto resident also present. Miss Jeanette Dermott, Mrs.
Leigh Galloway, and James are on stage. Pat Reavis, the Slocums' handsome young chauffeur, is sitting in the theater with Cathy. She objects
loudly when he tries to kiss her. James fires Reavis and rebukes Cathy.

Archer telephones Maude; they agree that he will pose as a Hollywood
literary agent at a cocktail party this afternoon at the Slocums' big place
in Nopal Valley. Arriving, Archer chats with Cathy, James, and affected,
hard-drinking Marvell. He overhears James saying Cathy is precious and
must be protected from Reavis. Maude warns James to shut up. Maude
privately tells Archer she feels trapped since James's widowed mother,
Olivia Slocum, controls the family wealth and is domineering. In the garden, Archer meets Olivia. She boasts of her unemployed son's talents and
of oil-rich land she won't let be exploited. Chief Ralph Knudson, head of
Quinto's police force, drives up, joins the noisy drinkers, and insults
James's singing to Marvell's piano accompaniment.

Archer starts to drive away but finds the feline Cathy sitting in his car.
He orders her out, hits the road, picks up the hitchhiking Reavis, and
pumps the macho braggart for gossip about the Slocums. They drive to
Antonio's bar in Quinto. Detective-Sergeant Simeon J. Franks enters.
While Reavis sneaks away, Franks hauls Archer back to Knudson at the
Slocums' place, since Olivia has suspiciously drowned in the family's out-
door pool. Marvell mincingly tells how he found the body. Archer and
Knudson get along all right until Archer says he gave a ride to Reavis,
who likes Cathy. Eavesdropping on an argument between Maude and
James, Archer learns this: Maude wants Cathy and half the estate immediately; Maude visited Chicago and returned "that spring" changed; James
is bisexual and likes Marvell; Maude despises James. He slaps her, but
they quickly make up. Knudson asks Archer to locate Reavis and gets him
transportation to Quinto. He goes to Helen's bar, where Reavis said he
had a girlfriend named Gretchen Keck. Gretchen, a teenage prostitute,
gives Archer Reavis's Los Angeles address.

Archer drives to Reavis's place, then follows in a taxi when a limousine chauffeured by a man named Mell drives Reavis to a nightclub. Archer flirts with Mavis Kilbourne, a movie-style blonde there, until her husband, fat, rude Walter J. Kilbourne, leaves with her and Reavis. Kilbourne and Mavis stop by another club. Archer taxis after the limo but loses it. Archer sneaks into Reavis's room, where he finds correspondence from his sister, Mrs. Elaine Schneider of Las Vegas, and dishonorable U.S. Marine discharge papers for Reavis (real name: Patrick Murphy Ryan). Archer is suddenly slugged and taken away by two of Kilbourne's thugs—Mell (later called Dr. Melliotes) and Enrico Murratti, to be grilled by the latter at his place. Already there is Mavis, who lost out in Hollywood and was pressured into marrying Kilbourne because he gave Murratti, for safekeeping, a cylinder containing nude movies of her. She talks seductively to Murratti and helps Archer disarm him. Archer keeps the film to silence Murratti, whom they release. Archer takes a cab with Mavis, who snuggles close, leaves her at her club, gets his car near Reavis's place, goes home, and sleeps in his clothes.

Next morning, Archer discovers that Mavis took the film cylinder from his pocket. From a newspaper friend he learns this: Kilbourne was in the black market during the war, laundered his money by investing in the Pacific Refining Company in California, lives at the lush Staffordshire Estates nearby, and covets Olivia's oil. Archer seeks Kilbourne there, finds he is away, encounters a thick-headed chauffeur, and warns him. Archer drives to Las Vegas, finds Reavis's sister Elaine at a bar, and shows her an illustrated newspaper account of Olivia Slocum's murder, with Reavis named as a suspect. Archer drives after Elaine as she speeds to a hideaway, finds her brother, and rebukes him. She leaves when Archer approaches and pulls a gun on him. Archer finds $10,000 on Reavis. With Reavis in tow, Archer returns to the bar, hires a lad named Bud Musselman to be his driver, and heads for home with Reavis. On the way, he phones Knudson's office, tells an operator there he is bringing in Reavis, and continues. Suddenly a truck blocks the road. Gunmen emerge, saying they want the "prisoner"; Archer shoots one in the arm; Reavis thinks he is being rescued and fights Archer, who is slugged unconscious. When Archer wakes up, Bud tells him they shot and torched Reavis.

At the Quinto police station, Archer learns that Franks took his call, drives with Bud to the Slocums, and confronts the obdurate Knudson with the facts. Knudson announces that he will take care of Reavis's body, with the help of the local sheriff at the site. Archer tells him to care for Bud and stays to grill Maude. She says she knows Kilbourne and had dinner with him and Cathy earlier this evening. Kilbourne holds first refusal for oil rights on Slocum land, which they may now grant him. Telling Cathy he thinks Reavis did not kill her grandmother, Archer finds Franks's address, takes a cab there, and watches as the man Archer wounded in the ambush walks in. When he leaves, Archer detains him briefly and learns that he is Oscar Ferdinand Schmidt, given $500 by Kilbourne for information from Franks leading to the killing of Reavis, whose $10,000 Archer hands to Antonio for safekeeping.

Mrs. Strang lets Archer break into Maude's locked room, where he finds her dead. Evidence includes a suicide note to "Dear Heart," from the same typewriter used for the original letter calling Maude an adulteress, also a recent letter from Mildred Fleming, a Hollywood friend, and an old clipping about Knudson's heroic duty as a Chicago cop. Knudson enters, seizes the paper evidence, says he loved Maude, and after exchanging information warns Archer to bug out or be charged for transporting Reavis across state lines. Before Archer can leave, Mavis calls him to meet her at the Quinto pier, which he does at 4:00 A.M. She says that aboard their yacht she overheard Kilbourne order Schmidt to kill Reavis. She has just escaped them. Kilbourne recorded on film her making love with Reavis; instead of minding, Kilbourne planted Reavis as the Slocums' chauffeur and was blackmailing Mavis with the film. She has secretly burned it but still fears him. Some of his thugs, including Dr. Melliotes, arrive, capture Archer and Mavis, and take them to Kilbourne, on his yacht. Kilbourne boasts: He planted Reavis; Reavis killed Olivia Slocum and demanded $10,000 from Kilbourne for silence; Schmidt told him Reavis was on the highway from Las Vegas with Archer; Kilbourne ordered Reavis killed. He offers Archer his life, the $10,000—make it $20,000—and a job, if he will sign a letter confessing that he delivered Reavis to Kilbourne to be killed. No. So Melliotes slugs Archer.

Archer awakens in Melliotes's nursing home ashore, in a water-treatment room. When he struggles, he is tortured with fierce water jets by Melliotes and his half-demented nurse, Miss Macon. They leave him in a water-tight room, from which he escapes by flooding the place until tons of water burst a door open and sweep his assailants off their feet. He knocks Melliotes out, seizes Miss Macon's gun, finds his own gun and clothes, and unlocks Mavis from an adjoining room. Kilbourne suddenly enters. Archer fires at him, gives a gun to Mavis to hold on Kilbourne, and awaits Kilbourne's chauffeur, whom he flattens. Mavis shoots Kilbourne dead, claiming self-defense. He rejects her invitation to share Kilbourne's millions and her gorgeous self, tells her instead to call the police, and promises to send her to friends in Mexico later.

Leaving Mavis at the Hall of Justice, Archer finds Maude's old friend, Mildred Fleming, at a Hollywood studio. She reveals this: In 1932 she and Maude were sophomores at Berkeley and rented rooms in the home of Knudson, then a policeman there, and his self-righteous wife, Eleanor; Maude got pregnant by Knudson, who couldn't get a divorce and left for Chicago; Maude quickly married the mother-spoiled James Slocum, who with "a faggot tendency" wanted Maude to "save him"; Cathy believes James is her father. Archer finds Gretchen and gives her the $10,000 he persuades her to believe that Reavis, now dead, got from his boss for a murder he never committed. At the Slocum home, Archer finds foolish James, who is playing chess with simpering Marvell. James says he accused Maude of killing his mother with Archer's aid and therefore Maude's suicide was proper. Archer gets Cathy to confess this: Cathy killed her grandmother when she saw Maude, whom she always "hated," and Knudson together; Cathy typed the damaging letter hoping they would disappear together and leave her with sweet daddy. Archer finds Knudson there; he acknowledges Cathy as his daughter, says he has resigned from the Quinto police, and will take Cathy to Chicago for treatment.

Alfred A. Knopf* liked the manuscript of *The Drowning Pool* so much that he gave Macdonald a $1,000 advance. The novel, dedicated "To Tony" (i.e., Anthony Boucher*), was well reviewed but sold poorly in hardcover. (The Bantam paperback edition, from 1970, enjoyed numerous printings.) *The Drowning Pool* was made into a 1975 movie, of the same name, starring Paul Newman, Joanne Woodward, and Tony Franciosa. The title has two meanings. It is the place where Olivia Slocum drowned, and Archer says falling under Mavis Kilbourne's sexual sway would be like entering a "whirling vortex . . . , the drowning pool." Archer says the action begins on Wednesday, July 20; therefore the year is 1949. The big theme is stated succinctly: "Sex and money: the forked root of evil." Margaret Millar* disliked two parts in the novel, the brief intimacy between Mavis Kilbourne and Archer, and Archer's unlikely fistfight with Knudson. Also, even though Archer's being tortured in Dr. Melliotes's hydrotherapy chamber was based on an actual event in Santa Barbara, the event seems forced here.

Bibliography: Nolan; Speir.

DRUMMOND, DR. LARRY. In *Sleeping Beauty*, he is Lew Archer's physician and prescribed the sleeping pills that Laurel Russo stole.

DUKE THE DUDE. In *The Goodbye Look*, he scribbled his name on a wall in the Pacific Point police building and identified himself as from Dallas and here on a bum rap.

DUNDEE. In *Blue City*, he is the Palace Hotel room clerk. Dundee tells John Weather that Alonzo P. Sanford owns the hotel.

DURANO, LEO. In *The Ivory Grin*, he is Una Durano's demented brother. He has a long criminal record, starting when he was twenty in 1925 and including Michigan and Chicago prison terms. He became a feared numbers racketeer. Una hires Lucy Champion and Donald as Leo's attendants, moves him to a mansion near Arroyo Beach, and tries to cover up when he kills Charles A. Singleton, Jr., his rival for Elizabeth Benning's love.

DURANO, UNA. In *The Ivory Grin*, posing as flashy Una Larkin, she hires Archer to find Lucy Champion, her brother Leo's nurse. Una wants to silence Lucy since she saw Leo kill Charles A. Singleton, Jr. Una follows Elizabeth Benning, the wife of a Bella City physician Lucy worked for, when Elizabeth goes to Archer in West Hollywood to claim the reward offered by Singleton's family for information about him. Una shoots Elizabeth dead, and Archer kills Una. Archer describes androgynous Una as "a sexless imp who had grown old in hell."

Bibliography: Schopen.

DURKIN. In *The Doomsters*, he is a ballistics technician working under Duane Ostervelt.

DUTCH. In *The Doomsters*, he is Maude's bouncer at her Buenavista Inn. She asks Dutch to "take out" Archer, who takes him out instead, twice.

"THE DYING ANIMAL." *See The Barbarous Coast* and *The Underground Man*.

E

EASTON, ROBERT (1915–). Author and environmentalist. Easton attended Stanford University (1933–1934) and Harvard University (B.S., 1938), and did graduate work at Stanford (1938–1939). In 1940 he married Joan Faust, the daughter of Frederick Faust, better known as Max Brand, the prolific writer of westerns. Easton and his wife had four daughters. Easton served in the U.S. Army in the artillery and infantry (1942–1946). He became the copublisher and editor of the *Dispatch* at Lampasas, Texas (1946–1950), taught English at Santa Barbara City College (1959–1965), attended the University of California, Santa Barbara (M.A., 1960), and was a writer and consultant at the U.S. Naval Civil Engineering Laboratory at Port Hueneme, California (1961–1969). His novels are *The Happy Man: A Novel of California Ranch Life* (1943) and *This Promised Land* (1982). His other books are *California Condor: Vanishing American* (with Dick Smith, 1964) *Black Tide: The Santa Barbara Oil Spill and Its Consequences* (1972), *Max Brand: "The Big Westerner"* (1970), and the autobiographical *Life and Work* (1990) and *Love and War: Pearl Harbor Through V-J Day* (1991).

Macdonald met Easton in Santa Barbara in 1957, and the two became close friends. They joined forces in 1964 to protect the endangered California condor. Macdonald privately edited Easton's *California Condor* and persuaded Brooks Atkinson to write an introduction. Easton and Macdonald founded the Santa Barbara Citizens for Environmental Defense and numbered themselves among the fifteen coplaintiffs in a class-action lawsuit against the companies responsible for the January 1969 oil spill off Santa Barbara. (*See Sleeping Beauty*.) Macdonald asked Dorothy Olding,* one of his agents, to read Easton's *Black Tide*; she sold it to Delacorte, and Macdonald wrote the introduction. When asked to read the manuscript of *The Blue Hammer*, Easton suggested useful word and structural changes. When in 1980 or so Easton asked Macdonald to critique on some writing of his, Macdonald confided that he was losing his memory and therefore could not do so.

Bibliography: Bruccoli; Dolan; Robert Easton, "A Quiet Man," in *IJ*, pp. 45–54; Ross Macdonald, "A Death Road for the Condor," *Sports Illustrated* (April 6, 1964): 86–89; Nolan.

EATON, LAURA. In *Trouble Follows Me*, she is Private Rodney Hatcher's friend. Living with her father, William Eaton, in Santa Barbara, she gets a letter from Hatcher, who is later murdered, which causes Sam Drake and Chester Gordon to interview her.

EATON, WILLIAM. In *Trouble Follows Me*, he is Laura Eaton's father. They live together in Santa Barbara. He is absent when Sam Drake and Chester Gordon see her.

ED. In "Find the Woman," he is Terry Neville's agent.

EDDIE. In *The Drowning Pool*, he is a police stenographer who takes notes during Chief Ralph Knudson's investigation of Olivia Slocum's death.

EDDIE. In *Meet Me at the Morgue*, he is the assistant of Forest, the FBI agent. The two are present when Fred Miner's body is returned to Abel Johnson's desert cabin.

EDIE. In *The Three Roads*, in a personals column Theodora Swanscutt read, Edie's mother appeals to him to return home, forgiven.

EDWARDS. In *Trouble Follows Me*, he is an intelligent black Pullman porter. He and Sam Drake courteously discuss Black Israel, the radical black political movement. Edwards hopes Drake won't reveal him as a source of information.

EISBERG. In *The Dark Tunnel*, he is a faculty member among others whose files Robert Branch looks past in seeking Ruth Esch's file.

ELAINE. In *The Instant Enemy*, she is the babysitter employed by Henry and Kate Langston.

ELEGANT. In *The Underground Man*, she is Al Sweetner's girlfriend. Archer finds her in a motel near Topanga Canyon, gains information about

Al, and tells her Al has been murdered. She was hoping Al would collect money from Stanley Broadhurst and take her to Mexico.

ELLIS, LEROY. In *Sleeping Beauty*, he was a shipmate of Captain Benjamin Somerville, who let him take the blame for the *Canaan Sound* explosion and rewarded him with employment thereafter. In the hospital morgue, Ellis, who drinks, identifies Nelson Bagley's body.

ELLIS, MRS. In *Sleeping Beauty*, she tries to comfort Ellis but is domineering in the process.

EMILIO. In *The Goodbye Look* he is a loyal servant employed by Lawrence and Irene Chalmers. With them more than twenty years, he chauffeurs them in their Rolls.

"THE ENORMOUS DETOUR." *See The Doomsters and The Galton Case.*

ERSKINE. In *The Dark Tunnel*, when Robert Branch is looking for Ruth Esch's file among the faculty records, he moves past Erskine's.

ESCH, RUTH. (Original name: Ruth Gerda von Esch.) In *The Dark Tunnel*, she was an actress-student in Munich when Robert Branch met her. They fell in love. She was held in Nazi Germany for a while, escaped, and was brought to Canada by Dr. Herman Schneider, to teach at Midwestern University. She was injured by her Nazi brother, Captain Carl von Esch, and by Peter Schneider. Branch rescues her when she is hospitalized at Kirkland Lake. Carl, a transvestite, misleads Branch by posing as Ruth.

ESTABROOK, FAY. In *The Moving Target* she is a fading, alcoholic actress, about fifty. Her photograph, signed "Fay" and found in Ralph Sampson's cottage, leads Archer to find her, get her drunk, and case her residence. She associates with Dwight Troy, evidently her husband.

EVELYN. In "Shock Treatment," she is a wealthy young diabetic whose greedy husband, Tom, kills her by substituting insulin of the wrong dosage that she innocently takes.

"EXPERIENCE WITH EVIL." *See Meet Me at the Morgue.*

F

FABLON, MARIETTA. In *Black Money*, a former Proctor, she is Roy Fablon's husband, Virginia Fablon's mother, and a neighbor of old Peter Jamieson and his son. Her murder provides one of Archer's challenges.

FABLON, ROY. In *Black Money*, he was Marietta Fablon's husband and Virginia Fablon's evil, gambling father. He and their neighbor, old Peter Jamieson, were Princeton roommates. Owing money to Kayo Ketchel of Las Vegas prompted him to offer Ginny in lieu of payment. Roy's apparent suicide by drowning provides one of Lew Archer's challenges.

FABLON, VIRGINIA ("GINNY"). In *Black Money*, she is the daughter of Roy and Marietta Fablon. She fell in love with Taps Tappinger, then Francis Martel, and then became engaged to young Peter Jamieson. Roy's forcing her to have an abortion caused her to hate him. Now twenty-four, Ginny disappears. Peter hires Archer to find her.

FALCONER, ROBERT, JR. In *The Underground Man*, he was Elizabeth Broadhurst's father. Falconer, who attended Harvard, gave land to the Forest Service for a trail. Ludicrously devoted to her father's memory, Elizabeth writes he "was a god come down to earth in human guise."

FALCONER, ROBERT DRISCOLL. In *The Underground Man*, he was Elizabeth Broadhurst's grandfather. According to Elizabeth, he was in the Union Army during the Civil War, was wounded at Chancellorsville, came to California, and married a woman enriched by a Mexican land grant.

FALK, GRETCHEN. In "The Suicide," she is Clare Larrabee's hospitable, fat friend with whom Clare stays overnight in San Diego.

FALK, JAKE. In "The Suicide," he is Gretchen Falk's hard-working husband.

FALLON, LARRY. In *The Blue Hammer*, he is a guest at Francine Chantry's cocktail party. His close friend is Ralph Sandman.

THE FAR SIDE OF THE DOLLAR (1965). Novel. (Characters: Albertson, Lew Archer, Lieutenant Bastian, Joseph Botkin, Bronson, Brown, Mrs. Robert Brown, Robert Brown, Jay Carlson, Rhea Carlson, Stella Carlson, Peter Colton, Dack, Daly, Ben Daly, Mrs. Ben Daly, Deering, Susanna Drew, Jack Fletcher, Harley, Carol Harley, Harold Harley, Lila Harley, Martha Harley, Mike Harley, Hillman, Elaine Hillman, Ralph Hillman, Thomas Hillman, Mrs. Sam Jackman, Sam Jackman, Dick Leandro, Lion, Mrs. Mallow, Dr. Murphy, Katie Ogilvie, Mr. Patch, Perez, Mrs. Perez, Rachel, Ringo, Dr. Shanley, Otto Sipe, Dr. Sponti, Squerry, Stanislaus, Joe Sylvester, Tony, Tyndal, Frederick Tyndal III, Vernon, Arnie Walters, Phyllis Walters, Dr. Elijah Weintraub.)

One rainy Monday morning in August, Archer drives south to Laguna Perdida School (LPS), a reform school halfway between Los Angeles and San Diego, hired by Dr. Sponti, LPS's administrator, to find Thomas Hillman, a runaway student. Sponti explains: Tom, a big, high-strung seventeen-year-old, was admitted without proper review because of his rich businessman father Ralph Hillman's money. Tom agitated for students' civil rights and escaped Saturday, after less than a week. Archer chats with some boys in the East Hall lounge and with Mr. Patch, the school supervisor. Archer hears that Tom stole a car back home in El Rancho, tried to start a riot, and Patch had to knock him down. Patch blames Sponti for being too soft. Mrs. Mallow, the alcoholic hall house mother, taunts Patch. Each knows secrets about the other that Sponti needn't know. Alone with Archer, Mrs. Mallow reveals that Sponti has a worthless diploma-mill doctorate and says Tom's father wanted the boy "out of his sight."

Walking toward Sponti's office to get Hillman's address, Archer is almost hit by a taxi, delivering Ralph Hillman, too agitated to drive, to LPS. When Archer reveals his mission, Hillman, big and rich, tells him kidnappers have phoned demanding $25,000 for Tom's safe return. They will phone instructions this afternoon. Hillman hints at an inside job to Sponti, who has LPS's comptroller refund Hillman's first payment of $2,000 by check, which Hillman spurns but Archer retrieves. Archer drives Hillman to his home in El Rancho, near Pacific Point, where Hillman's company is. On the way Hillman explains that a week ago last Saturday Tom merely borrowed a car from Rhea Carlson, their neighbor, whose daughter, Stella, Tom likes. Tom wrecked it but refused to provide details of his activities. Hillman shows Archer the crash site. Rhea dislikes Tom more than her husband, Jay, does; she and Elaine, Hillman's ill wife, disapproved of his friendship with Stella.

Archer meets Elaine. Hillman brings drinks and boasts of his M.I.T. degree, successful engineering business, and early retirement, and Boston-born Elaine's having attended Radcliffe. He hints about Tom's foolish ambition to play the piano professionally. Elaine, knitting nervously, gives Archer a photograph of Tom. The phone rings. Archer listens in. A wheezy voice needles Hillman thus: Alerting the police means "goodbye Tom," who is here voluntarily; the caller knows much about Hillman; sweat a while; wait with the money for instructions.

Walking to the Carlsons, Archer tells Rhea he is an insurance agent investigating Tom's car crash. Rhea says Tom formerly spent time with them but this summer starting teaching their daughter, Stella, "bad habits." Stella, eavesdropping, shouts her defiance. When Archer leaves, Stella, sixteen and on the verge of lovely womanhood, sneaks after him. They go to a treehouse she and Tom rendezvoused in. Stella reveals this: She and Tom love each other, had planned to marry later; she gave Tom her family car keys; her parents knew this, lied about it to implicate Tom, are covering up to the police; Tom neither drinks nor does drugs; he was offered a job with a musical combo at The Barroom Floor; leaving last Saturday for "something secret," he hinted he might not return. Archer tells Stella that Tom was sent to LPS, escaped two nights ago, and is being held somewhere for ransom—perhaps by friends. Stella can name only one, Sam Jackman, a trombonist.

Archer drives into El Rancho. He learns from a sporting-goods storekeeper named Joseph Botkin that Hillman filed a complaint about The Barroom. At an auto yard Archer is allowed to look at the Carlsons' wrecked car. In it he finds and takes a key to Number 7, Dack's Auto Court. The Barroom bartender gives him Jackman's address. Aware of Tom's predicament, Jackman, a former drug addict, explains: Hillman, whom Jackman fears, had him fired from a beach-club job for associating with Tom and encouraging his piano playing; Jackman knows Sponti through a relative who once worked for Sponti; Jackman saw Tom three times—sixteen days ago, ten days ago, and yesterday—with a Mrs. Brown, blonde, in her thirties, and looking like an actress; she drank and needed money, to get away from her husband; Tom seemed to be in love. At Dack's, Archer learns this from Stanislaus, the owner: Mr. and Mrs. Robert Brown are in Number 7; Brown is abusive; Mrs. Brown was also seen with a "teen-ager." Shown Tom's photograph, Stanislaus identifies him as the lad.

When Archer revisits the Hillmans, Dick Leandro, their friend, is there with $25,000. Archer tells them Tom was seen yesterday at The Barroom with a flashy Mrs. Brown. Archer warns that Tom may be in on the extortion. A phone call from the same "kidnapper" orders Hillman to drop off the money at a specified place by the Ocean View beach—alone or else.

Archer returns to Dack's, lets himself into Number 7; locks the door; finds Mrs. Brown, beaten to death, and in her purse crooked dice and a business card of Harold Harley, photographer. A stranger, evidently Brown, drives up, cannot get in, and shouts further warnings and a threat to abandon her. Archer rushes the departing fellow, but his head is creased by a bullet. He awakens in the hospital. He phones Hillman, who dropped off the money, but—no Tom. Archer tells Hillman about the Browns and says Brown may be the extortionist. Lieutenant Bastian of the El Rancho police examined Archer's wallet, found his detective's license and a check from LPS, questions him, learns about the Browns but not the Hillmans, and tells Archer that Brown's car is from Idaho.

Tuesday morning. Archer is still in the hospital. Sponti storms in. He was alerted by Bastian, says he told Bastian everything about Tom's case, and gloats that Hillman has ordered Sponti to fire Archer. Deciding to help Tom anyway, Archer phones Arnie Walters, a Reno detective, to unearth something about Brown of Idaho and perhaps Reno, since Mrs. Brown had crooked dice. When Bastian provides a photograph of Mrs. Brown, Archer reveals details of his investigation, is commended for staying on the case, and is asked to help identify the murder victim. Rushing to meet with Bastian, Hillman declines to cooperate with Archer.

Archer checks with Joe Sylvester, a Hollywood agent, who identifies the photograph as that of Carol, an actress whose friend was Susanna Drew, now a Television City producer. Archer calls on Susanna, once a flame of his, and she explains this: Carol Harley was here in 1945; in Tijuana she married Mike Harley, a violent sailor; he promised her a movie career, was picked up AWOL by the Shore Patrol in the Barcelona Hotel near Santa Monica, and abandoned Carol, who was pregnant; Carol, afraid to return to her father in Pocatello, had the baby—whereabouts unknown— and returned to Mike upon his discharge. After reporting this to Bastian, Archer drives Susanna home. She stops reminiscing with him when her phone rings. She answers and turns cryptic. Archer broods in his office until she phones and says her messenger will deliver a 1945 photo of Carol she found. Its back is stamped Harold Harley, Barcelona Hotel.

Archer drives to the Barcelona, but it has gone out of business and is guarded by Otto Sipe, wielding a gun. Archer pursues leads provided by Ben Daly, a gas-station attendant across the road from the Barcelona, to Harold's Van Nuys address. In his garage just before midnight Archer spots the Idaho Ford, registered to Robert Brown. Harold, a timid man, comes out. Pretending to be a policeman, Archer learns this: Mike Harley, Harold's no-good older brother and nice Carol's husband, got Harold into trouble and intimidated him for years, and last night at about 10:30 drove in; he repaid Harold, for old loans, $500 (which Archer retrieves), left his car, and took Harold's 1958 blue Plymouth. That morning Harold read about a kidnapping and a murder, and guessed his brother was involved and Carol was the victim. Archer searches Mike's car but finds only a strand from Tom's knit sweater, as described by Jackman. Harold describes Mike and says Mike worked at the Jet near Tahoe. Archer phones Arnie about Mike and about Harold's car, and asks him to check the Jet. Archer phones Bastian a full report. While Archer is driving Harold to El Rancho, he learns this: Mike's and Harold's father was an abusive farmer on Rural Route 7, near Pocatello; Mike ran away, lived with Robert Brown, a Pocatello high school teacher, joined the navy, and married Carol, Brown's daughter; Harold became a photographer; Harold accidentally "set . . . up" the kidnap plot for Mike but won't give details. Archer delivers Harold and the $500 to Bastian and finds the nearest hotel.

Wednesday. After coffee, Archer reports to Bastian, who says Carol was stabbed, not beaten, to death. Archer delivers the yarn. The two men go to the Hillmans' house. Elaine identifies the yarn as from a sweater she knitted for Tom. Hillman takes Archer into his study, replete with old navy pictures, including one of his jeep carrier, the *Perry Bay*. It comes out that Mike Harley served aboard the ship but was discharged for stealing an expensive government camera. When Archer gives Hillman a report, he gratefully rehires Archer by endorsing over to him Sponti's check for $2,000. Archer encounters Stella Carlson on the street. She says someone, probably Tom, phoned this morning but hung up when her mother answered. Stella is shocked about Archer's suspicion that Tom has been consorting with Carol. When Rhea storms up, Archer suggests that she treat Stella with more love and respect. On a hunch, Archer drives back to Harold's house, encounters his wife, Lila, who recently left Harold in disgust but is back. She says Mike phoned at 3:00 A.M., begging her to wire him $500 to Las Vegas. She refused.

Archer phones Arnie's Reno office and learns that the car Mike took from Harold was spotted at a Las Vegas motel. Archer flies there. With Arnie, he finds the car's new owner. He is Jack Fletcher, a flashy Texas poker player who boasts that he won over $20,000 from Mike—"a born loser"—bought his useless car for $500 as a good-will gesture, and gave him $100 to get home. Mike said he was returning to Idaho.

Archer flies to Pocatello, rents a car, and arrives at the Harley farm by mid-afternoon. Mrs. Harley, the mother of Mike and Harold, blames Carol for seducing and corrupting Mike. When Archer says Carol was murdered, perhaps by Mike, Mrs. Harley counters that she did her best and that her husband sought to drive the Devil out of Mike by permissible severity. His father, after milking some cows, answers Archer's queries by threatening to pitchfork him and "call down the judgment on you." Mrs. Harley laments that she won't ever see her grandson now. Archer drives off to confront Brown. He and his still-beautiful wife, Carol's grieving parents, admit him. Mrs. Brown rebukes her husband by saying he wanted a son and therefore half-adopted Mike, who was no good and ruined Carol. Last June Carol visited home, and she and her mother argued because Carol's son had been adopted and was hence lost. Mrs. Brown takes Archer to Carol's room. In her old suitcase he finds a letter from Harold to Mike, mentioning both Sipe and Hillman as job prospects for Mike. Mrs. Brown says Sipe was a crooked Pocatello ex-cop and Mike left Pocatello with him before joining the Navy.

Archer catches planes from Pocatello to Salt Lake City to Los Angeles, goes to his apartment at 3:00 Thursday morning for a gun, and finds Stella there, let in by his manager. She says Tom called and asked her to meet him at the Santa Monica bus station with some money. She missed him last night and will try again tonight. Archer takes Stella to stay with Susanna Drew, who says she once knew Sipe.

Archer drives to the Barcelona, where he finds Sipe in a cluttered room dead drunk and with Tom's sweater nearby. Archer goes to Daly's gas station, phones Daly, and asks him to watch the hotel for Sipe while he looks for Tom. He learns that Tom boarded a Santa Monica bus. Archer and Daly search for Sipe but find him in the rear yard digging a grave. Mike lies on the ground, stabbed with a knife caught in his ribs. Daly guards Sipe with Archer's gun while Archer searches Mike's pockets. Sipe gashes Daly's head with his shovel. Daly shoots him dead. Daly summons the authorities. Bastian speeds the release of both Daly and Archer.

Archer returns for Stella, who says she eavesdropped unseen as Hillman visited Susanna, talked intimately with her, and left with her for breakfast. Archer drives with Stella to LPS and learns from a student there that Tom said he thought he had been adopted. Archer takes Stella to her parents and counters their criticism of her by saying they should trust and help her for a change.

Archer goes to the Hillman home, sees Leandro in the driveway, and learns from him that Elaine is alone. When Archer mentions the name Susanna Drew, Elaine reveals this: Hillman led aerial engagements at Midway (1942), regarded lost pilots as his lost sons; in January or February 1945 his ship was kamikazed and returned to San Diego; Hillman, on leave then, and Susanna spent intimate nights at the Barcelona; Sipe sold Elaine an incriminating snapshot; Hillman scared Sipe off later; Elaine forgave Hillman, who used her family money to start his business; Hillman, sterile, and Elaine adopted Tom, through Dr. Elijah Weintraub, a naval surgeon formerly serving under Hillman and now practicing in Los Angeles; on "that Sunday" (just before Tom was committed to LPS) Hillman argued violently with Tom; Hillman spends much time with Leandro, whose photograph Archer takes along.

Bastian tells Archer this: Carol and Mike could have been killed by the same knife; Daly knew Sipe through car sales; Carol's father is at City Hotel in Los Angeles. Archer tries to see Daly, but he won't look at Leandro's photograph. Visiting Weintraub, Archer learns that the Hillmans adopted Tom, born December 12, 1945. Weintraub won't name Tom's parents.

Archer drives to Susanna's apartment. She returns from work about 5:00 P.M. and invites him in. When he tells her he knows about her love affair with Hillman, she reveals this: Susanna met Hillman at a navy-movie preview in March 1945; they slept together at the Barcelona that night (she says, "First time drunk, first time bedded"); she fell in love, saw him for "a few weeks"; on April 14, 1945, Harold Harley took the photo Sipe used for extortion; Elaine learned of the affair, confronted Susanna in Carol's presence, and Carol, whom Susanna housed at Hillman's request, calmed both women down; Carol, when pregnant, was treated by Weintraub, who arranged the adoption; Hillman phoned Susanna Tuesday to get their stories straight; she saw him this morning, for the first time since 1945; he proposed marriage. When Susanna adds that this afternoon a lad came to her asking for Weintraub's address, Archer shows her Tom's photograph, which she says is that of her visitor. Paged, Weintraub phones that Tom burst in on him; he told Tom that Mike and Carol were his parents; Tom slugged him and stormed out. Archer tells Weintraub to inform the police.

On his way to Santa Monica to seek Tom, Archer stops at the Barcelona and encounters Harold on the beach. He admits he photographed couples in compromising positions for Sipe but did not snap any of Hillman with Susanna. Archer takes Harold to see Daly, at his gas station. The two reminisce. Archer produces Leandro's photograph, and Daly identifies him as a man who drove a late-model blue Chevrolet to the Barcelona with a companion last night. At the Santa Monica bus station Archer finds Stella awaiting Tom, who shows up promptly at 9:00 P.M. Archer persuades them to return home. On their drive back, Tom says this: Carol called and told him the truth a few weeks ago; they met near Dack's; he liked her and Mike, his father, whom he met on the Saturday he borrowed the Carlsons' car; Carol half-suspected Mike, who could be nice when he was not abusive, of the kidnap plot; Carol told Tom about his Pocatello grandfather; Tom despises Hillman and his money. Tom still won't discuss the car accident.

Archer takes Stella home and to her father's embrace. On the way to the Hillmans, Tom won't say what happened "that Sunday." The Hillmans welcome Tom. Tom goes upstairs to bathe. Elaine criticizes Hillman's domineering manner, which, admittedly, is toned down. Archer clears Tom of wrongdoing and suggests prep school and college for him. Hillman wonders where Leandro is. Bastian, having phoned, arrives with the weapon used on Mike and perhaps Carol, and despite Hillman's lies identifies it as a knife Hillman bought in town from Botkin. Hillman won't let Bastian talk with Tom tonight. Archer asks Bastian to check on Leandro's Chevy. When Hillman suggests bribing Archer and also Botkin, Archer counters with a demand for the truth. It emerges: Tom on "that Sunday" threatened Elaine with a gun and was committed to the reform school; Tom probably left the knife in his room; Tom is Hillman's natural son by Carol, who slept with him once, gloriously (Hillman gloats), at the Barcelona; Susanna was a later, poor replacement (this enrages Archer); Carol said Mike was an impotent pervert; Hillman got Weintraub to tell Elaine that Hillman was sterile. By phone, Bastian reports that Leandro borrowed a girlfriend's blue Chevy to drive to the Barcelona.

Elaine looks up from her needlework to upbraid Hillman. Tom, in the kitchen eating, tells Archer he left the Barcelona at about 8:00 P.M. Mike was there; Sipe was drunk; Tom didn't see Leandro. When Leandro, summoned by Hillman, arrives, the two talk with Archer. Leandro reports this: Elaine said the kidnapper wanted more money; Leandro drove her to the Barcelona; she visited it alone; Leandro heard an owl-like scream. Elaine reappears, having heard everything, and vilifies Hillman for bringing his bastard into their home. She offers to bribe Archer. When he fakes an interest to gain information, she confesses using the knife on Carol, whom Mike had beaten unconscious, and killing Mike because he suspected her of killing Carol. Tom staggers upstairs, and Hillman follows. Leandro saunters off for a drink. Elaine renews the bribe offer, but Archer declines. When he will not let her go get a handful of sleeping pills or a gun, she abruptly hammers her steel knitting needles into her breast and dies on Friday.

The Far Side of the Dollar was condensed as "The Far Side" in *Cosmopolitan* (September 1964). The British edition appeared in 1965 (London, Collins). A year later Bantam paid $7,500 and began a popular paperback run. The meaning of the title is made clear when Macdonald says Archer is unsuccessful when he asks Strip "flesh peddlers" to identify Carol from her disfigured death photograph because they "hated to be reminded of what was waiting on the far side of the last dollar." Abandoned titles were "The Black Hole of Calcutta," "The Black Yarn," "The Brass Bed," "The Deep Dark Night," "The Serpent's Tooth," "A Taste of Fire," "The Time Binders," "You'll Find Out on Judgment Day," "The Sea and the Highway," "The Underside of the Weave." Although most reviewers were enthusiastic, some noted the presence of too many coincidences. Macdonald's continuing popularity abroad was signaled to him by a report from his friend R.A.D. Ford* in 1978 that the popular USSR magazine *Ogonek* printed a pirated version of *The Far Side of the Dollar* with the title, as translated, *Path Leads to El Rancho*.

Bibliography: Bruccoli; Nolan; Schopen.

FARGEON, DON. In *The Drowning Pool*, he is a man mysteriously mentioned in Mildred Fleming's letter to Maude Slocum.

FARGO, MRS. SIMMY. In *The Chill*, she is the Surf Club photographer's wife. She helps him with his work.

FARGO, SIMMY. In *The Chill*, he is the Surf Club photographer. He identifies the gray-bearded man who talked with Dolly Kincaid.

FARNSWORTH, JERRY. In *The Galton Case*, he is the desk clerk at the Sussex Arms, a small San Francisco hotel. Farnsworth helps Archer find Roy Lemberg but betrays Archer by giving him a false lead to Reno. This results in Otto Schwartz's capturing Archer and having him beaten up. Archer returns to Farnsworth, warns him, and gets more information from him.

FARONESE. In "Guilt-Edged Blonde," he is a gangster not involved in Nick Nemo's murder.

FARRAND, DR. In *The Chill*, he taught at Pacific Point College. His coronary resulted in Helen Haggerty's replacing him.

FARRINGTON. In *The Drowning Pool*, he and his family live in the fashionable Staffordshire Estates.

FAUSTINO, MIKE. In *Find a Victim*, he is from Albuquerque, double-crosses Bozey after the hijacking, and is shot to death by Archer from ambush. Of Faustino's two cronies, Bozey names only Clincher.

FAWN, MOLLY. In *Meet Me at the Morgue*, she is the beautiful, vulgar blonde, twenty-one, who persuaded Bourke to hire Art Lemp. Howard Cross discovers her connection with Kerry Snow. This leads to her being detained by Sam Dressen, with Bourke, for their impossible attempt to rob Helen Johnson.

"THE FEAR OF DEATH." *See The Galton Case.*

"THE FEARFUL DETOUR." *See The Galton Case.*

FEATHERS, ALBERT. In *Trouble Follows Me*, he is a black sailor aboard Lieutenant Eric Swann's ship in San Diego harbor. Chester Gordon interviews him about Hector Land.

FELIX. In *The Moving Target*, he is the Filipino servant working for Ralph and Elaine Sampson. He resents being suspected when Ralph disappears. He cooperates with Archer, who treats him courteously.

FELLOWS, COLONEL HENRY. In *The Way Some People Die. See* Speed, Herman.

FELLOWS, MRS. HENRY. In *The Way Some People Die. See* Barron, Marjorie.

FENTON. In *The Dark Tunnel*, he is the FBI agent who assists Chester Gordon in Detroit. He meets Robert Branch and participates with Gordon in interviewing Rudolf Fisher.

FENTON. In *The Way Some People Die*, he is Danny Dowser's British servant. Dowser likes to hear Fenton pronounce big words.

FERGUSON. In *The Ferguson Affair*, he was a Scottish sheep rancher, migrated to Alberta, Canada, homesteaded at Wild Goose Lake, married, and had a son (*see* Ferguson, Colonel Ian). Ferguson joined the Scots Grenadiers and was killed at Vimy Ridge, France, in World War I.

FERGUSON, COLONEL IAN ("FERGIE"). In *The Ferguson Affair*, he was the son of a Scotsman in Alberta, Canada. After his father's death, he joined the Canadian army (1918). Oil was discovered on their Edmonton property. Ian's mother sent him to Harvard Business School, where he got Katie Mulloy (*see* Dotery, Kate) pregnant and abandoned her. Their daughter was Hilda Dotery. Ferguson pursued June Dotery, the movie actress, initially because she resembled Katie. The two married. Hilda impersonates June to fake her kidnapping for money. Ferguson, fifty-six, retains William Gunnarson to discover the truth. When June is identified (mistakenly) as Ian's own daughter, he vomits and says "Augh!" Ferguson sadly says money is "a root of evil in my life."

Bibliography: Speir.

FERGUSON, JUNE. In *The Ferguson Affair*, she is the daughter of James and Kate Dotery. Known as Holly May, June quit a movie career to marry Colonel Ian Ferguson, six months earlier. June, twenty-five, is taken by Hilda Dotery, her half-sister, and Hilda's lover, Larry Gaines, to a house near Mountain Grove, whereupon Hilda assumes her identity in a kidnap plot to gain money from Ferguson. William Gunnarson rescues June from the house when Hilda sets it on fire.

FERGUSON, MRS. In *The Ferguson Affair*, she was Colonel Ian Ferguson's mother. When widowed and rich, she sent him to Harvard Business School. Ferguson blames "blasted doctors" for her death.

THE FERGUSON AFFAIR (1960). Novel. (Characters: Abernathy, Asa Barker, Ella Barker, Judge Bennett, Arthur Bidwell, Hector Broadman, Chris, Mrs. Clement, Cline, Mrs. Cline, Velma Copley, Mrs. Denton, Augustine Donato, Manuel Donato, Secundina Donato, Frank Dotery, Hilda Dotery, Jack Dotery, James Dotery, June Dotery, Kate Dotery, Renee Dotery, Dorothy Drennan, Ferguson, Colonel Ian Ferguson, June Ferguson, Mrs. Ferguson, Frankie, Larry Gaines, Ed Gellhorn, Sergeant Pike Granada, Gunnarson, Sally Gunnarson, William Gunnarson, Adelaide Haines, Patrick Hampshire, Harry, Jack, Mahan, Mesa McNab, Barney Millrace, Mrs. Padilla, Tony Padilla, Perry, Joe Reach, Stephen Roche, Dr. Root, Salaman, Dr. Simeon, Mrs. Simmons, Whitey Slater, Smith, Michael Speare, Jimmie Spence, Ronald Spice, Ralph Spindle, Al Stabile, Mrs. Al Stabile, Keith Sterling, Torres, Arcadia Torres, Frank Treco, Jack Treloar, Dr. Trench, Walter Van Horn, Belle Weinstein, Detective-Lieutenant Harvey Wills, Jerry Winkler, Marguerite Wood, Sheila Wood, Claire Zanella.)

Ella Barker, a nurse, is in the county jail in Buenavista. She sold a diamond ring to Hector Broadman, a pawnbroker. It was identified as stolen, perhaps by a burglary ring. A stolen watch was found in Ella's apartment. William Gunnarson, attorney and narrator, is assigned to defend her. Ella tells him that, while she was on vacation in San Francisco, a man gave her an engagement ring, which she sold. When Broadman is slugged, Gunnarson accompanies Detective-Lieutenant Harvey Wills to the pawnshop. Manuel Donato, the tamale-shop owner next door, says he rushed to help Broadman, who, hysterical, is put in an ambulance by driver Whitey Slater, with Sergeant Pike Granada along, but dies before they reach the hospital.

Granada, who knows Manuel, his brother Augustine ("Gus") Donato, and Gus's wife, Secundina Donato, searches the shop with Wills. Wills tells Gunnarson that Broadman was probably a fence, and that Ella took care of Broadman in the hospital some months earlier. Jerry Winkler, a neighbor, beckons Gunnarson, accepts a bribe, and says he saw Gus, an ex-convict, take a tire iron into Broadman's shop, emerge, and load his truck with stuff.

Ella tells Gunnarson that Broadman proposed to her but drank too much, and that he introduced her to Larry Gaines, a poorly paid Foothill Club lifeguard. She and Gaines became lovers. Gaines gave her the ring and the watch, said he had some get-rich-quick schemes, and pestered her to tell him the name of her rich patients. She read about the burglary gang, suspected Gaines, caught him embracing another woman, and dumped him. Gaines threatened to have her killed by "a friend." She kept the watch but sold the ring to Broadman, to show up Gaines. Ella and Gunnarson suspect Gaines of engineering Broadman's death. Ella tells Wills that Gaines's new girlfriend may be the ex-actress Holly May.

Manuel tells Gunnarson he dislikes his evil brother Gus. Secundina, Gus's wife, defends Gus. Manuel says Secundina knows Tony Padilla, a bartender at the Club. Gunnarson drives there, is approached by a breezy guy from Miami named Salaman, who says he was Holly's lover until she married the aging Colonel Ian Ferguson and then picked up with some lifeguard. The police question Arthur Bidwell, the club manager. When they leave, Bidwell takes Gunnarson to his office and confesses to two awful mistakes: admitting Ferguson and his wife as club members, and hiring lover-boy Gaines as lifeguard. Ferguson, wildly drunk, bursts in, blames Bidwell for his wife Holly's disappearance with Gaines, threatens him, and starts to pull a gun. Gunnarson knocks him out. Padilla appears and offers to put Ferguson to bed.

Padilla gets Ferguson's car and, with Gunnarson along, drives him home. Padilla says Ferguson and Holly were happy, but she left, overly bejeweled, with Gaines last night. They pour coffee into Ferguson. He does not remember being decked by Gunnarson, who introduces himself. A kidnapper phones, demanding $200,000 for Holly's return. Ferguson says he will pay and wants no interference by authorities.

Gunnarson asks Padilla to drive him to Manuel's home. They learn he is in police custody, proceed to headquarters, and are told that Granada has shot and killed Manuel's brother, Gus. It seems that Granada got a tip, found Gus with loot from Broadman's shop, and shot him in self-defense. Both Padilla and Gunnarson taunt Granada. Secundina enters, screams at Granada, bites him, and curses him in colorful Spanish, which Padilla translates for Gunnarson. Home at midnight, Gunnarson munches a cold dinner. Sally, his pregnant wife, wakes up and complains that he is married to his job. The phone rings, and a blurry voice warns Gunnarson to drop the Ferguson case or Sally may be hurt. After fibbing to her about the call, he tosses uneasily in bed until dawn.

In the morning, while breakfasting at a café, Gunnarson reads in the newspaper about Gus's death and Granada's courage. Gunnarson alerts Wills to a possible Broadman-Ferguson connection. While in his office, he gets a call from Padilla: Ferguson needs help. Gunnarson drives over, warns him that Holly may be dead, but cannot persuade him to alert the authorities. Padilla reveals this: Broadman got scared; Gaines became leader of the burglary gang of which Granada was a member; Granada long sought Secundina's affections and may have killed Broadman after Gus merely clubbed him. Holly calls Ferguson with directions for a money drop.

Failing to find Secundina at home, Gunnarson tries unsuccessfully first to have Ella's bail reduced and second to learn more about Gaines. Reinterviewing Ella, he learns of a clipping in Gaines's wallet, left in her apartment. He goes there, talks with her landlady, Mrs. Cline, obtains the wallet, and reads in the clipping about a 1952 play featuring ten named people, including Hilda Dotery and Harry Haines. Could Harry Haines be Larry Gaines? At the morgue, Gunnarson asks the coroner Dr. Simeon whether Broadman might have been strangled in the ambulance. Simeon gives Secundina a prescription for sleeping pills. Outside, she tells Gunnarson that Granada probably told the burglars which mansions were not patrolled by fellow cops and that Gus called Larry Gaines "Harry."

Padilla drives up, says Ferguson dropped the money, and takes Secundina home. While Gunnarson is asking Whitey if Granada could have choked Broadman, a dispatch alerts Whitey to an accident involving Ferguson. Gunnarson drives to the scene. Ferguson confesses he was speeding, takes responsibility, is released by the police, and leaves with Gunnarson. Ferguson says he dropped the money by a pier, walked away, and saw Gaines grab it and drive off with Holly. Hiring Gunnarson for a $500 retainer, Ferguson reminisces: Ferguson fell in love with Holly's movie image, pursued her at a Vancouver film festival, married her; she seemed a perfect replacement for his one lost love; she never revealed her past. He names Michael Speare as her agent and Dr. Trench as her physician. Gunnarson says Trench is Sally's obstetrician.

Gunnarson briefly leaves Ferguson, who broke his nose in the accident, with Trench's partner, "bone man" Dr. Root. Gunnarson proceeds to his office, phones Speare, gets an appointment, and asks his secretary, Belle Weinstein, to find the California town where the ten persons in the clipping lived. Driven home by Gunnarson, Ferguson says Trench said Holly is two months' pregnant by Gaines.

On to Beverly Hills. Speare drinks in his office with Gunnarson, who says he is representing Ferguson. Both before and after Gunnarson says that, if divorced, Holly could return to acting, Speare reveals all this: Speare brought Holly along for three years; her real name is Dotty Dotery; she seemed ashamed of her family; she went to Las Vegas with pretty-boy Gaines; Ferguson wrecked Speare's plan for Holly by marrying her.

Going home for dinner, Gunnarson finds Sally knitting and worrying. She got an obscene phone call. He feels uneasy, but she says she can protect herself, especially if she gets out his service revolver. Returning to the morgue, Gunnarson learns from Dr. Simeon that Broadman was asphyxiated and also that Granada brought in Secundina earlier, dead allegedly from a sleeping-pill overdose. Padilla rushes in and tells Gunnarson this: Padilla loved Secundina, would have married her once Gus was gone; feels Granada killed Broadman, Gus, and Secundina. When Padilla and Gunnarson visit Arcadia Torres, Secundina's sister, they learn this: Holly, Gaines, and Gus two nights ago had a mountainside marijuana party; Holly stripped to show her figure; Gus was attracted; when

Secundina objected, Holly threatened her. Padilla will stay the night with Arcadia.

Gunnarson returns to his office. Belle, his secretary, has traced an Adelaide Haines to Mountain Grove, sixty miles away. Belle will stay overnight with Sally, since Gunnarson is summoned to Ferguson's mansion. Salaman is back, says Holly owes $65,000 for gambling and drug debts, and gives Ferguson one day to pay up. Although Gunnarson gets Ferguson to admit that Holly may be conning him, he says he will welcome her back on any terms. He will wait until Gunnarson checks his lead in Mountain Grove.

Gunnarson drives there, finds Adelaide Haines at home, and gleans the following from this demented ex-teacher of voice and piano: Henry Haines is her son; Hilda Dotery seduced him; he was falsely accused of breaking into houses, confessed in juvenile court to avoid the penitentiary, was discouraged by Speare from an acting career. Leaving Adelaide petting her cat and calling it Harry, her son, Gunnarson gets some food at a restaurant, finds James Dotery's name in a directory there, and drives to Dotery's home, which is over his variety store. His wife Kate Dotery, stupid but attractive, weaves a tawdry story: Of their five children, one son, Frank, is dead, the other, Jack, is in reform school; two daughters, June and Renee, have left home; Hilda, the oldest child, was corrupted at fifteen or sixteen by Henry Haines; Hilda soon left home, returned last month boasting of her oilman husband and glitteringly bejewelled. Kate hints James was not Hilda's father. Drunken James enters, slaps Kate for talking too much, apologizes, and orders her to bed. When Gunnarson gets in his car, Gaines is there with a gun, and forces him to drive to the old Haines mansion in the hills, where Holly, strung out, appears. Gaines wants to dress Gunnarson in his clothes and destroy him in a house fire. He boasts that others did the killings for him, and he and Holly will fly to South America. Holly gets suspicious when he cannot produce the airline tickets. Gunnarson suggests Holly return to Ferguson since Gaines may plan to flee with his mother. A fight ensues. Gaines slugs Holly; Gunnarson knocks him down; Holly shoots twice, hits Gunnarson, who passes out.

When Gunnarson comes to, the place is ablaze. He drags Holly to safety, and welcomes Whitey and Ronny, speeding in. They strap him down; Ronny prepares to asphyxiate him; Granada, following by police car, intervenes; Gunnarson kicks Ronny viciously; Granada has a shootout with Whitey and kills him. Awakening in the Buenavista hospital with a shoulder wound, Gunnarson learns this from Wills: Sally has given birth to a daughter; Ronny confessed he and Whitey were involved in "kidnapping" Mrs. Ferguson until Gaines double-crossed them; Granada, innocent, deserves Gunnarson's apology; Mrs. Cline bailed Ella out. Gunnarson does not tell Wills about Holly's probable complicity but says Gaines may be planning an escape to South America with his mother.

Ella thanks Gunnarson, who sees happy Sally. Trench says Holly lied to him when asked about being kidnapped and drugged. Gunnarson tells Trench that Holly may get arrested. Gunnarson tells Ferguson this: Salaman wants his money; Holly was drugged, is safe, must not have been in the car with Gaines, looks like Katie Mulloy, a girl he got pregnant in Boston twenty-five years ago and abandoned. When Gunnarson says that daughter may be Holly, Ferguson vomits and begs him not to tell Holly.

Gunnarson gets to Ferguson's house and finds Salaman there with a gun. Salaman is suddenly astonished when he checks Holly's face. She is not the actress he knew in Miami; so he leaves. Holly says she is June Dotery, Hilda's half-sister, and Hilda's father was an unknown guy in Boston. Arriving, Wills says a horribly charred body was found at the fire scene.

In two days the FBI cannot find Hilda or Gaines. Ferguson pays Gunnarson $2,000. The next evening, Gunnarson gets Speare to his office, pressures him into revealing this: Speare knew Gaines well, knew Hilda ran up gambling bills and was with Gaines; she had dental and plastic surgery in San Antonio to resemble photographs of June; Speare sought to have Hilda and Gaines wreck Ferguson's marriage so June would return to acting; Gaines is missing, but Hilda is at a certain beach shack near Malibu. While Speare goes out for a drink, Gunnarson calls Ferguson, who drives him to the shack. En route, Ferguson says this: He and June visited her forgiving mother yesterday, learned that Hilda always hated June, who at sixteen left home with a man named Sperovich (i.e., Speare); Hilda probably does not know Ferguson sired her. Speare suddenly speeds ahead of them, is shot at by Hilda, and drives into and kills her.

Highway patrolmen find Hilda's gun. A San Antonio dentist identifies the charred jawbone as Gaines's. Hilda shot and incinerated him. Adelaide Haines gets her son's body and inters it expensively. She sought to bribe Wills with thousands, the rest of which was found in her piano, along with an airline ticket to Rio de Janeiro for Cary Caine (Larry Gaines). When disrobed in the psychiatric ward, Adelaide shows off a diamond under her mourning dress.

Macdonald originally thought of titling *The Ferguson Affair* "Death Mask" and "The Silver Dollar Tree." His publisher, Alfred A. Knopf,* urged him not to follow *The Galton Case* with another Lew Archer mystery. Hence along came William Gunnarson, who behaves like Archer anyway and for whom Macdonald planned another novel that never materialized. *The Ferguson Affair* was immensely popular, was reprinted in hardcover three times in 1950, was sold to the movies for $16,500 but never translated to the screen, was sold to Collins of London for publication in "The Crime Club" series (with a £1,000 advance), and enjoyed paperback reprints (from 1963, with Collins/Fontana and Bantam). Macdonald's daughter, "Linda Jane" (*see* Millar, Linda), drove her car as dangerously as Colonel Ferguson does. In addition, Linda Jane Millar was in other ways almost as careless as Kate Dotery's daughters, Hilda (cf. Linda) and June (cf. Jane). Finally, was Macdonald deliberately echoing the letter "l" from Linda Millar's names in Belle, Bidwell, Ella, Padilla, and Sally?

Bibliography: Bruccoli; Nolan; Wolfe.

FERN, SERGEANT. In *The Way Some People Die*, he is a police officer whom Lieutenant Gary orders to deliver Archer. Sergeant Tolliver is with Fern on this peaceful assignment.

FIDELIS, JACK. In "The Suicide," he is a Las Vegas criminal whose search for Owen Dewar's money leads him to Clare Larrabee, whom he threatens. Archer intervenes and kills him.

FILLMORE. In *The Wycherly Woman*, he is the prissy, divorced manager of the Champion Hotel. He provides Archer with information.

FINCH, MARCELLA ("MARCIE"). In *The Moving Target*, she is a strident woman associated with Puddler. Archer follows her to a house where Dwight Troy is torturing Betty Fraley.

FIND A VICTIM **(1954).** Novel. (Characters: Tony Aquista, Lew Archer, Mrs. Archer, Bozey, Sal Braga, Chas, Hilda Church, Sheriff Brand Church, Clincher, Judge Craig, Danelaw, Devore, Ralph Devore, Sally Devore, Mike Faustino, Floraine, Allister Gunnison, Jr., Jerry Mae, Don Kerrigan, Kate Kerrigan, MacGowan, Meyer, Anne Meyer, Mrs. Meyer, Talley Raymond, Sammy, Jo Summer, Hairless Tarko, Dr. Treloar, Trotter, Marion Westmore, Sam Westmore.)

Thursday evening, October 15, 1953. Lew Archer, while driving to Sacramento to present evidence in a drug case, sees a man with a gunshot wound in the ditch. He takes him to a motel run by Don and Kate Kerrigan. Don Kerrigan recognizes the dying victim as Tony Aquista, a truck driver for Meyer. Kate calls an ambulance, which Archer follows to the Las Cruces hospital. Sheriff Brand Church arrives and recognizes Aquista. Church and Archer return by two cars to where Aquista was found. Sal Braga, Church's deputy and Aquista's cousin, has arrived. Church and Archer visit Kerrigan, for whom Church's wife Hilda Church's sister Anne Meyer works. Kerrigan rebukes Kate and needles Church about Anne's disappearance last Friday. Church bridles, apologizes, and leaves. Learning that Archer is a detective, Kate asks him about checking into her husband, who had "a thing . . . last year" with Anne. Kerrigan enters, slaps Kate, challenges Archer, and is flattened.

Wanting to help Kate and irritate Kerrigan, Archer follows Kerrigan when he drives to a restaurant. A gorgeous girl enters and starts dining with Kerrigan. Archer hears Kerrigan say Kate is suspicious but they cannot flee yet. She wants some "reefers" from Bozey, who owes Don money. Suddenly Kerrigan disappears. Archer follows the girl to her apartment, asks some neighbors where Meyer's company is, and goes there.

Archer chats up the watchman, who says this: Aquista liked Anne, who preferred others; Church caught Aquista stalking her, warned him; Aquista then liked a singer at the Golden Slipper Supper Club; Church got uppity after college, married Meyer's daughter Hilda, incurred Meyer's displeasure; a truck containing valuable whisky was hijacked.

Archer proceeds to Meyer's home. Hilda, dropped there by Church, admits him and calls her father. Meyer, a widowered, crusty truck owner, reveals much. He gave his wild daughter Anne a .38 for protection against Aquista. He dislikes Kerrigan, whose fine wife, Kate, is a judge's daughter. Kerrigan ordered the whisky shipment, but since Meyer did not deliver it, he stands to lose $7,000 (an uninsured tenth). He hires Archer to investigate and is surprised to learn that Anne, his other daughter, is missing.

Church does not return for Hilda. Archer drives her to her home. Hilda defends Anne, seems jealous of Anne's beauty, says she hates Las Cruces men, gives Archer permission to search Anne's apartment at Bougainvillea Court nearby, and hints that their father mistreated Anne. When she expresses a fear of the dark and of death, Archer kisses her good-night and proceeds to Anne's place. It has been broken into and rifled. He finds a year-old love letter from Tony Aquista. Church enters, gun in hand. Archer tells him that he is working for Meyer to find the truck and Anne, and that Hilda gave him permission to enter Anne's place. Church knocks him down with his gun. Threatening retaliation, Archer leaves.

Archer visits the Slipper. The owner says he bought the place this morning from Kerrigan. Archer bribes a bar-girl, who confides this: Aquista was demented; Jo Summer is an uppity singer; Jo has a grandpa in the mountains. The bar-girl gives him Jo's photo. Archer recognizes her as Kerrigan's companion at the restaurant. Archer proceeds to Jo's Cortes apartment, pretends Bozey sent him with reefers, and says Kerrigan will double-cross her. She escapes from Archer by pretending to shower before he is to drive her somewhere. When he follows her onto the street, Bozey knocks him unconscious with brass knuckles.

When Archer awakens, he is in his car, with his gun still in the glove compartment. He finds his way to the fine Kerrigan home, where, eavesdropping, he hears Kerrigan and Kate arguing about her house, their loveless marriage, his girlfriends, and his financial losses. When Kerrigan leaves, Archer drives after him, and sees Bozey give him a package, probably containing money. Archer follows Bozey to a deserted airport, where Bozey, in Meyer's missing truck, drives toward Archer and spins him into a ravine. Recovering, Archer follows Bozey along a mountain road, loses him, and is roadblocked by Church. Archer reports this to Church: Kerrigan, with Jo's help, set up Aquista, got money from Bozey for the whisky, sold the Slipper, and skipped town with Jo. Church warns Archer off the case.

Undeterred, Archer stops at Kerrigan's motel and finds him shot to death, his safe open and no money in it. Jo steals a sports car, tries unsuccessfully to run Archer down, and escapes. Braga, answering a call about a shot, tackles Archer but gets decked for his trouble. Archer drives to Kate's home, tells her how Kerrigan, dead, was involved. Kate has a mountain cabin, says Anne was there last Monday, gives Archer permission to search it, but asks him not to tell Church.

Friday. After little sleep, Archer drives to the messy cabin, finds one bed used, and drives back for gas. Sally Devore, the station owner, tells him this: Kate is a good woman; Kerrigan brought girlfriends, including Anne and Jo, to the cabin; last Saturday Aquista asked Mrs. Devore to use her phone, but she had none; Jo's grandfather, MacGowan, is caretaker at a nearby inn. She admits that when on the previous Monday she last saw Anne, driven by Kerrigan, Anne sat so inertly she might be dead. Archer visits MacGowan, who says he never liked Kerrigan, saw him drive by with a girl on Monday; they went up a hill and were digging a hole when he scared them away. Archer keeps a woman's heel found nearby. MacGowan says Jo, his granddaughter, was here last month with ugly Bozey, who said he was in the liquor business. He had lots of money and a gun; so MacGowan ordered them away. Archer tells him Bozey is a murderous hijacker, and Jo may be involved. On his way down, Archer sees Kate's car, stops, and learns this from her: Kerrigan dropped Anne as a lover but continued to employ her; Anne's father raped her when she was fifteen; last Monday Kate was with her close friend, Marion Westmore, the wife of Sam Westmore, Las Cruces's D.A., whom she recommends to Archer. They kiss briefly.

Archer reports to Meyer, who says Hilda has left Church. They take the shoe heel to Hilda, now at Meyer's house. She identifies it as Anne's. When Archer reports that Anne was with Aquista last Saturday at the cabin, Meyer is so critical of Anne that Hilda defends her and gets slapped. Archer accuses Meyer of raping Anne and quits working for him. Hilda leaves. When Archer catches up, she says Church threatened her. He drives up, warns Archer, and the two fight. Hilda prevents Church from shooting Archer. They turn friendlier; still, Archer accuses Church of not stopping Bozey after he drove the hijacked truck past his roadblock. Hilda goes home with Church.

Archer goes to Sam Westmore. He tells Archer that Bozey robbed an Oregon bank, passed some traceable money, probably paid Don with more, and skipped town with Jo and the looted whisky. Archer tells Westmore about Anne and Aquista at the cabin. When Westmore says Bozey used the same .38 to kill both Aquista and Don, Archer wonders whether the .38 Anne received from Meyer was the weapon. Westmore says the IRS is about to fine Kerrigan's wife Kate for unpaid taxes.

Kate is outside. MacGowan called to say he wanted to see Archer, who drives Kate home. She feels lost and guilty. Arriving, MacGowan says Jo visited him and he gave her a map to Traverse, Nevada, a deserted mining town where Bozey was to meet some cronies. Darkness falls. Archer drives MacGowan toward Traverse, but a sand slide into the road stops them. Jo suddenly drives down toward them but crashes into the slide. Kerrigan's money is in the car. She reveals this: Aquista peered through a window at a man with Anne at the cabin; Kerrigan left her corpse in her car in the desert; Bozey followed and drove Kerrigan back; she flagged down Aquista to stop his truck on the road; she stole Kerrigan's money only after finding him dead; three Albuquerque cronies of Bozey's just raped her, pommeled Bozey, and drove to Traverse.

Archer drives around the slide with MacGowan and Jo, proceeds to Traverse, and spots three men loading whisky cases into a van. Sneaking up, he shoots one to death and wounds another, who jumps into the moving van, which speeds off. Archer gets answers from groggy Bozey, left behind. He didn't kill Anne or Kerrigan, knows where Anne's body is, is in cahoots with a high-up official, and offers Archer a deal. They hear the van crash in the distance and explode.

Saturday dawns. Bozey directs Archer to Anne, dead of a .38 gunshot wound. At Las Cruces's morgue, Church views Anne's body and sobs. Archer goes to Westmore, chides him for believing Bozey did the killings, and challenges him to question Church. Westmore leaves. Archer gets Bozey to admit he was to steal the whisky truck Aquista was driving, but when it stopped Anne—was it?—drove Aquista away; Bozey then drove the truck past Church's roadblock, with Church's acquiescence. Church's identification officer reappears, says he checked Meyer's targets in his basement, found bullets matching those that killed Anne and Kerrigan, and has arrested Meyer.

Archer rushes to Hilda's house to see Church, who is away. Archer forces Hilda to let him in, and gets the deranged woman to confess that she shot Anne, Aquista, and Kerrigan. Why? Aquista told Hilda that her husband and Anne made love in the cabin. Hilda got Aquista to stop his whisky truck and get into her car. She killed him after he saw her .38. Since Kerrigan disposed of Anne's body and car and told Church, Hilda had to shoot Kerrigan. Church drives up, enters, surrenders the missing .38 to Archer, and explains. He married Hilda, who became mentally unbalanced; he fell for Anne; he let Bozey through the roadblock. He must now care for Hilda, who has gone outside, is tearing up flowers, and calls Church her father.

Alfred A. Knopf* criticized the first manuscript for *Find a Victim* for too much talk and too little drama, but did say Bantam editors liked it as it was. Macdonald admitted that he had toned down the direct violence out of disgust with the gory works of Mickey Spillane and made the later draft more graphic.

When a review of *Find a Victim* in *Time* (July 26, 1954) heralded Macdonald as "the successor to [Dashiell] Hammett and [Raymond] Chandler," his rise to respectability seemed assured. The novel was condensed for *Manhunt* (July 1954), was issued in London (Cassell, 1955) and was the first paperback Macdonald novel reprinted by Bantam Books (1955). Its title was inspired by a poem by Stephen Crane, asking whether it would be wiser to fear finding an assassin or a victim.

Bibliography: Bruccoli; Speir.

"FIND THE WOMAN" (1946, 1955). Short story. (Characters: Lew Archer, Mrs. Millicent Dreen, Ed, Lieutenant Harris, Gray Karp, Hilda Karp, Terry Neville, Ronald, Ensign Jack Rossiter, Una Sand.) Mrs. Millicent Dreen hires Archer to find her missing daughter (stage name: Una Sand). It develops that Una was frightened to death and drowned when Ensign Jack Rossiter, her husband, a navy pilot, flew low over the raft on which she and her lover, Terry Neville, were making love. Millicent sabotaged Jack's coming-home cable to Una because Una turned Jack away from her. Macdonald wrote "Find the Woman" in two nights while in the Navy at sea, and it won a $400 prize when published in *Ellery Queen's Mystery Magazine* (June 1946), with Rogers named as the detective. Macdonald revised it, with Archer as the detective, for a later collection of stories. In 1959 Macdonald sold "Find the Woman" for $750 for a CBS television show called "Pursuit," with the detective to be called Rogers, not Archer. The story is a kind of overture for future Archers, beginning with the missing-child theme, and with times and dates, sunsets and alcohol, drowning victim and coroner, cars and gas station, "sharp breast," eye imagery amid other similes, sarcastic tone, and distrust of cops.

FINNEY. In *The Barbarous Coast*, Mrs. Sarah Lamb names him as her adviser at the Spiritualist Church in Malibu.

FISHER, RUDOLF. In *The Dark Tunnel*, he is Peter Schneider's homosexual friend when Peter works at the Detroit bomber plant. When Peter abruptly leaves him, Rudolf is just dreadfully irate and sings to FBI agents Chester Gordon and Fenton.

FITZROY, PERCIVAL. In *The Galton Case. See* Brown, John (Jr.).

FLAHERTY, BOB. In *Sleeping Beauty*, he was Gloria Flaherty's first husband. He ran up debts, absconded with money, and left Gloria to pay.

FLAHERTY, GLORIA. In *Sleeping Beauty*, age twenty-seven, she is Martha Mungan's daughter, Martha's sister Alison Russo's niece, and Alison's son Tom Russo's cousin. Gloria tells Archer she is studying to be a dietitian and has a boyfriend named Harry. She and Harold Sherry, the latter wounded, check into a motel as Mr. and Mrs. Frank Sebastian.

FLAKE. In *The Barbarous Coast*, he is one of Leroy Frost's goons. Flake is so engrossed in a Western on television that Archer is able to knock him out with a lamp.

FLAVIN, MISS LETTY. In *The Zebra-Striped Hearse*, she is the maid of Colonel Mark Blackwell and Isobel Blackwell. With them only two months, Letty can provide little information to Archer, who does, however, get to observe "her excited little breasts bobbing under her uniform."

FLEISCHER, JACK. In *The Instant Enemy*, he is an ex-deputy in the Santa Teresa sheriff's office. He was sexually involved with Laurel Blevins (*see* Smith, Mrs. Laurel) and helped her cover up the murder of the man called Jasper Blevins, her husband. In reality, the murder victim is Stephen Hackett, Jasper's half-brother. Fifteen years later David Spanner seeks out his father (in reality, Jasper); so Fleischer resumes an investigation in hopes of money, bugs Laurel's apartment, records her conversation with Jasper, and tries to blackmail her. Archer investigates Fleischer, who winds up shot to death by Jasper, not David.

FLEISCHER, MRS. JACK. In *The Instant Enemy*, she is the betrayed, long-suffering wife of a crooked policeman. Between drinks, she tells Archer about Jack's girlfriend, Laurel Blevins (*see* Smith, Mrs. Laurel), fifteen years her junior. After Jack's murder, Mrs. Fleischer takes possession of tape recordings he made of Laurel, sells them to Keith Sebastian, and leaves the region.

FLEMING, MILDRED ("MILLIE"). In *The Drowning Pool*, she is a Hollywood movie-company executive. She has been Maude Slocum's close friend, ever since their Berkeley school days. Archer learns about Maude's relationship with Chief Ralph Knudson through Mildred, who tells Archer she has been unhappily married four times, her name now being Mrs. Mildred Fleming Kraus Peterson Daniels Woodbury.

FLETCHER, JACK. In *The Far Side of the Dollar*, he is a cocky Texan who plays poker in Reno. He won more than $20,000 of Mike Harley's ransom take from Ralph Hillman. Fletcher gave Mike $500 for his car, which when spotted led Archer to Reno. Fletcher tells Archer that Mike left for his home in Idaho.

FLORAINE. In *Find a Victim*, her name is on some graffiti near Jo Summer's apartment.

FLORENCE. In *The Moving Target*, she is a faded actress mentioned by Fay Estabrook.

FLORRIE. In *The Dark Tunnel*, she is the Tube's daughter and is a floozie at the brothel outside Arbana. She accommodates any male, even one whose nose has been destroyed by syphilis.

FOLEY, JUDSON ("JUD"). In *The Chill*, he is Sally Burke's sponging brother, an out-of-shape former football player and current ne'er-do-well. Archer spots him driving from Helen Haggerty's murder scene. Foley's background yields information for Archer. Foley tries to fight Archer, who, fifteen years his senior, easily handles him.

FORD, R.A.D. (1915–). Canadian diplomat, poet, and editor. Robert Arthur Douglas Ford was born in Ottawa, attended the University of Western Ontario (B.A., 1937) and Cornell University (M.A., 1939), where he taught history (1938–1940). He married Maria Thereza Gomes, of Rio de Janeiro (1946). Ford joined Canada's Department of External Affairs (1940) and began a distinguished diplomatic career, which took him to Colombia, Yugoslavia, Egypt, Sudan, Mongolia, and the Soviet Union, where he was Canada's ambassador (1964–1980). He was an adviser on East-West relations, disarmament, and security issues. Ford retired in Randan, France. Notable are Ford's *Our Man in Moscow: A Diplomat's Reflections on the Soviet Union* (1989) and *A Moscow Literary Memoir: Among the Great Artists of Russia from 1946 to 1980* (1995). A phenomenal linguist, Ford translated works from French, German, Portuguese, Russian, Serbo-Croatian, and Spanish. The best of his poetry and translations are in *Coming from Afar: Selected Poems, 1940–1989* (1990). They often depict bleak northern landscapes and emphasize pessimism and worldwide miseries.

Macdonald met Ford at the University of Western Ontario in 1934. They became friends. When Macdonald's daughter, Linda Millar,* was born (1939), Ford was her godfather. From Moscow in the mid-1940s, he wrote Macdonald fascinating letters about men of culture he met there. Macdonald dedicated *Blue City* (1947) to Ford. In 1955 the two met in

Ottawa after a seventeen-year hiatus. When Ford was assigned to Colombia (1957), Macdonald, Margaret Millar,* and their daughter planned to move to Bogotá, where Linda would attend a university. The plan came to naught. In 1971 Macdonald and Ford resumed a brief correspondence after being out of touch for seven years. Throughout their friendship, each admired the other's mind and writings.

Bibliography: Ralph Gustafson, "The World of R.A.D. Ford," in Robert A.D. Ford, *The Needle in the Eye* (Oakville, Ont.: Mosaic, 1983), pp. 11–15; Nolan.

FOREST. In *Meet Me at the Morgue*, he is an FBI agent brought into the case when authorities learn of Jamie Johnson's kidnapping. Forest works capably with Howard Cross.

FRALEY, BETTY. In *The Moving Target*, she is a recording pianist and an entertainer at the Wild Piano. She and Alan Taggert are lovers. Between twenty-five and thirty, Betty, a cocaine addict, and her brother, Eddie Lassiter, have criminal records. Archer gains information from her. His suspicions are soon aroused. During Ralph Sampson's kidnapping, Betty grabs the money and kills Eddie. Archer seizes her, but on the way to the authorities she steals his car, wrecks it, and dies.

FRAN. In *The Three Roads*, she is one of Larry Miles's abusively treated girlfriends.

FRANCE, FELICIA. In *The Drowning Pool*, a fat guest at Maude Slocum's cocktail party names Felicia as her daughter. The mother says Leonard Lyons (the famous *New York Post* columnist) has mentioned Felicia, a professional dancer, in several of his columns. Macdonald satirizes the conversation swirling through the alcoholic and musical haze at the party to reveal the intellectual vacuity of the pseudo-intellectuals inhabiting his southern California scene.

Bibliography: Schopen.

FRANKIE. In *The Ferguson Affair*, he is Tony Padilla's assistant at the Foothill Club bar.

FRANKS, DETECTIVE-SERGEANT SIMEON J. In *The Drowning Pool*, he works under Chief Ralph Knudson, brings Archer forcibly from a Quinto bar to Knudson, receives Archer's report about Pat Reavis, and illegally relays that information to Walter J. Kilbourne through Oscar Ferdinand Schmidt.

FRANZ. In *The Dark Tunnel*, he was a brave anti-Nazi Austrian in Munich. Robert Branch and Ruth Esch associate with him. Ruth writes Branch that Franz gave the Nazis no information when they fatally tortured him.

FREDERICK. In "The Sky Hook," he is the half-paralyzed man who, dying, dreams of a sky hook lifting him past his gold-rush comrades toward paradise.

FREDERICKS, MRS. NELSON. In *The Galton Case. See* Brown, Theodora.

FREDERICKS, NELSON. In *The Galton Case. See* Nelson, Fred.

FREDERICKS, THEODORE ("THEO"). In *The Galton Case. See* Brown, John (Jr.)

FRESNO GAMECOCK, THE. In *The Barbarous Coast. See* Torres, Tony.

FREY, DR. In *The Barbarous Coast*, he is psychiatrist who runs his own private Santa Monica sanitarium. One of his patients is Isobel Graff, nursed there by Rina Campbell. Archer gains information about Isobel from Rina and Frey.

FRIEDA. In "The Suicide," she is Edward Illman's nymphomaniacal companion.

FROST, LEROY. In *The Barbarous Coast*, he heads Simon Graff's Hollywood studio police force and is in league with Carl Stern. He and his goons torture Archer. Frost helped cremate Hester Wall's murdered body. Frost swaggers until Archer apprehends him in Las Vegas; then he grovels and pleads ill health.

FUNK, ANGEL. In "Gone Girl," he is a Palm Springs crime boss to whom Archer lies. When Funk sends Gino after Archer, Gino kills Donny, and Archer kills Gino.

G

GABLE, JESSIE. In *The Blue Hammer*, she was Jacob Whitmore's born-loser girlfriend. After his murder, she sells Archer some of his paintings, for money to buy Jacob a coffin, and provides Archer with some information.

GAHAGAN, JUDGE. In *The Chill*, he found Thomas McGee guilty of murdering his wife, Constance McGee. Archer's proves McGee's innocence.

GAINES, LARRY. In *The Ferguson Affair*, Larry was born Henry Haines, the son of Adelaide Haines of Mountain Grove. While a teenager, he seduced Hilda Dotery. They became fellow criminals. He joined a burglary gang in Buenavista and became a lifeguard at the Foothill Club. Larry, twenty-five or -six, and Hilda kidnap Colonel Ian Ferguson's wife, June Ferguson, who is Hilda's half-sister. They are helped by Whitey Slater and Ronald Spice, ambulance drivers they double-cross. Larry planned to double-cross Hilda and fly alone, as the Reverend Cary Caine, to Rio de Janeiro. When Hilda suspects him, she shoots and incinerates him.

GALLORINI, NICK. In *The Wycherly Woman*, he is the cabbie who drove Catherine Wycherly and Phoebe Wycherly to the *President Jackson* and back to San Francisco's St. Francis Hotel. He takes Archer to the Conquistador, near San Mateo, where he says he drove the rain-soaked Phoebe, helped her to her room, and undressed her for bed. Gallorini (rightly?) resents Archer's mild aspersions. Nick so volubly admires the Italian hero that his nickname has become "Garibaldi."

GALLOWAY, DR. In *The Dark Tunnel*, he is Midwestern University's smooth president. He was formerly a psychology professor. He doubts the evidence Robert Branch presents concerning Dr. Alec Judd's murder.

GALLOWAY, MRS. LEIGH. In *The Drowning Pool*, she plays the tough wife in Francis Marvell's play, *The Ironist*.

GALTON, ANTHONY ("TONY"). In *The Galton Case*, he is Maria Galton's long-missing son. He was twenty-two in 1936, studied mechanical engineering at Stanford, withdrew before graduation, named himself John Brown, wanted to become a populist writer, and married Theodora Gavin (*see* Brown, Theodora) (September 1936). Anthony last saw his mother that October. He and Theodora had a son, John Brown (Jr.) (December 1936). Fred Nelson, Theodora's former lover, beheaded Anthony and fled with Theodora and her baby to Canada. Maria hires Archer to find both Anthony and his son. Dr. August Howell, Maria's physician, tells Archer that Anthony was mainly "good at . . . boozing and fornicating."

GALTON, HENRY. In *The Galton Case*, he was Maria Galton's husband, wealthy through railroad- and oil-company holdings. He married in his late forties, cast his son Anthony Galton off, and died soon after Anthony disappeared.

GALTON, MARIA. In *The Galton Case*, she was rich Henry Galton's wife, has been widowed nearly twenty years, is seventy-three, and lives in an Arroyo Park mansion. Years after her only child, Anthony Galton, disappeared, she gets Gordon Sable, her attorney, to hire Archer to find Anthony and his son. Maria is demanding and querulous. When John Brown (Jr.) turns up professing to be her grandson, Maria lavishes attention, money, and plans on him. John Brown *is* her grandson.

***THE GALTON CASE* (1959).** Novel. (Characters: Angelo, Lew Archer, Barney, Chad Bolling, John Brown, Jr., Theodora Brown, R.C., Coney, Conger, Peter Culligan, Generous Joe Culotti, Lefty Dearborn, Dr. George T. Dineen, Mrs. Dineen, Fingers Donague, Jerry Farnsworth, Mrs. Fredericks, Anthony Galton, Henry Galton, Maria Galton, Mrs. Gorgello, Mrs. Haines, Mrs. Haskell, Cassie Hildreth, Dr. August Howell, Sheila Howell, Fran Lemberg, Roy Lemberg, Tommy Lemberg, Lempi, Gabriel R. Lindsay, James Matheson, Marian Matheson, Ronald S. Matheson, Merriweather, Dr. Meyers, Deputy Mungan, Fred Nelson, Ada Reichler, Ben Reichler, Mrs. Reichler, Rossi, Alice Sable, Gordon Sable, Otto Schwartz, Steele, Sheriff Trask, Dr. Trenchard, Turnell, Wellesley.)
Gordon Sable, a Santa Teresa estate attorney, wants his friend Archer to humor Maria Galton, a rich widow, seventy-three, by trying to find her

son, Anthony Galton, missing for about twenty years. Reporting to Sable's Arroyo Park home, Archer is delayed by the "houseman," Peter Culligan, and by Sable's wife, Alice, whom he married two years ago in his late forties. She is neurotic, alcoholic, and about half his age. Sable and Archer drive in two cars to the nearby Galton place. Present are Maria's physician, Dr. August Howell, his daughter Sheila Howell, eighteen and sexy, and Cassie Hildreth, Maria's relative and paid companion. Archer learns this: Tony, twenty-two in 1936, left Stanford shortly before graduation, got a girl named Teddy pregnant, married her, wanted to be a proletarian writer, and disappeared into the San Francisco slums. Tony stole jewels and money from Maria before he left; she treated him harshly but now wishes to forgive and be forgiven before she dies.

Alice calls Sable and asks him to come home. After taking lunch to Maria in her room, Cassie tells Archer this: Maria sent Cassie to an Eastern school; Cassie loved Tony (five years her senior); she remained with Maria after his disappearance; he wrote a poem titled "Luna, by John Brown" and published it in the San Francisco *Chisel*, edited by Chad Bolling. John sent Cassie a copy. She lends him the little magazine and photographs of handsome Tony. Archer chats with Sheila, who is critical of Maria. Archer calls Sable about being paid but is told that Culligan has just been stabbed to death.

Archer drives partway there but is stopped by a thug getting out of his wrecked, burning Jaguar. At gunpoint, he takes Archer's car. Authorities converge and take Archer to Sable's house, where he confers with Sheriff Trask. Sable tells Archer he recently hired Culligan off the wharf to protect Alice. Noting a gang-symbol tattoo on Culligan's body, Archer searches his room and learns this: Culligan had a 1941 San Francisco cooks' union card, had .38-caliber ammo but no gun, and kept a letter from his ex-wife Marian, now Mrs. Ronald S. Matheson of San Mateo, telling him to get lost. The letter mentions "L. Bay." While Alice moans in her room, Archer accepts $300 from Sable and prepares to fly to San Francisco to ascertain Culligan's background, since the Galton case seems to be going nowhere.

While aloft, Archer connects the "Luna" poem, "L. Bay," and Luna Bay, thirty miles from San Francisco. He finds Ronald S. Matheson's number, phones Marian, and persuades her to meet him at the airport. She reveals this: As a nurse's aide, she tended battered Culligan in a San Francisco hospital, married him, dumped him fifteen years ago, last saw him ten years ago, got a recent letter from him from Reno saying he had struck it rich; she won't discuss Luna Bay; knew no Anthony Galton or John Brown. Archer phones Bolling's home, learns that he is giving a poetry reading at the Listening Ear this evening, rents a car and gets a hotel room, dines well, and takes a cab to the Ear. After Bolling's affected rendition of idiotic poems, Archer has some drinks with him. Bolling recalls

John Brown of the 1930s, and says he visited Brown, his wife, and their baby, John, Jr., at Luna Bay.

Next morning Archer drives Bolling there and they find a shopping center under construction where the Browns lived. Archer locates Dr. George Dineen, the only physician who practiced there in the 1930s. Archer tells Dineen he hopes to help John Brown, Jr., long missing, gain an inheritance. Dineen reveals this: Brown's wife, nineteen or twenty, had scars from early abuse, flashed nice jewelry; Dineen delivered the baby; Mrs. Culligan, a nurse, helped afterwards; the three Browns suddenly left after Christmas 1936; five months ago the decapitated skeleton of a man in his twenties was found at the shopping center construction site; Dineen has seen John, Jr., within the last month. Dineen gives Archer a note to Deputy Mungan and the address of the gas station where John works.

With Bolling along, Archer learns this from John: His mother left him in an Ohio orphanage at age four; he escaped at sixteen, attended the University of Michigan, came to California, is twenty-two, would like to pursue an acting career, was recently shown bones by Mungan, but cannot believe they are his father's. Bolling says the lad's face and voice resemble those of the poet John Brown.

On to Mungan, tough and cooperative. Mungan reveals this: Luna Bay was full of criminals, including a gang led by Lempi, in the 1930s; the bones include a broken right arm. Archer phones Sable, who gets hold of Howell, who says Tony broke his right arm in prep school; Sable will drive up and confer with John. Archer phones Trask, and learns that his car has been found, and that the wrecked Jaguar, never reported stolen, was registered to Roy Lemberg, a car salesman living at San Francisco's Sussex Hotel.

Dropping Bolling off, Archer proceeds to the Sussex. The clerk, Jerry Farnsworth, leads him to Roy's wife, Fran Lemberg. Archer gains information from the sleazy blonde by pretending to want to buy the Jaguar. When Roy comes in, Archer scares him by saying his "stolen" Jaguar was involved in Culligan's murder. Archer tricks Roy into naming his boss— Otto Schwartz. Roy also admits his ex-convict brother Tommy Lemberg borrowed the car and promises to try to locate Tommy. Archer knows Roy is lying; so he pays Farnsworth to spy on Roy for him.

Just after 5:00 P.M., Archer proceeds to Redwood City, where Culligan's ex-wife, Marian Matheson, lives. She sends her husband Ronald and their son James, eleven, out to buy a cake and confesses this at Archer's insistence: Marian told Culligan about Brown's money and jewelry; Brown's criminal associate, called Shoulders, robbed and perhaps murdered Brown; Marian and Culligan moved to San Francisco, where five years later she divorced him, later marrying Ronald. Ronald returns, sees Marian weeping, and comforts her admirably.

On to Luna Bay. Archer grabs some food, reports to Mungan, and learns that Shoulders Nelson was a tough mobster with Culligan, did time in state prison, and says Shoulders may have killed John Brown. Archer bothers Mungan by asking him to get additional information on Shoulders from Sacramento. Mungan cooperates but only after Sable arrives, proves Tony's arm fracture matches Brown's, and names Anthony Galton in front of Mungan. Sable tells Archer he has put Alice in a nursing home, and accompanies Archer to Dineen's, where John is waiting.

Dineen vouches for John's birth, resents Sable's queries, brings in John, introduces him, and retires. Sable, Archer, and John proceed to John's rented room, where he proudly answers their questions. His mother, whom he remembers, told him his father's name, said he was born in California, left him at the Ohio orphanage; escaping, he hitchhiked to Michigan, was given room and board by Gabriel R. Lindsay, a widowered high school teacher now deceased, wrote Sacramento for his birth certificate based on his birthday (December 2, 1936) provided by the orphanage, read the place of birth, and recently came here. Sable seems satisfied, gets John to pack fast, and drives with him to Santa Teresa.

In the morning, Archer gets a note from Mungan about Nelson's criminal record. By phone Farnsworth tells him Roy phoned a Reno car dealer called Generous Joe. Archer flies to Reno, asks Joe Culotti about Roy, but is knocked unconscious from behind and comes to that evening in the presence of Roy's brother Tommy and Schwartz, their boss. When sassy Archer mentions Culligan's murder, Schwartz warns him, has him beaten badly, and jokes that he is to forget everything.

Archer awakens in the Reno hospital, with a broken jaw, a broken front tooth, and a damaged nose. Four days pass. The papers report Anthony's son John's happy reunion with Maria Galton, his wealthy grandmother. Archer, though ailing, sneaks a phone call to Sable, who comes, says John seems legitimate, the police have no leads on Anthony's long-ago murder and Culligan's recent one, and Maria will foot Archer's hospital bill. Archer insists he will prove John a phony.

A few days later Archer flies to San Francisco and terrifies Farnsworth, the Sussex clerk, into admitting that Roy ordered him to mislead Archer, and that Roy and Fran are at the Triton motel in Los Angeles. On to the Triton. Archer finds only Fran. Though reluctant and still loving Roy, she admits that Roy's brother Tommy killed Culligan and that Tommy and Roy are headed for some Ontario town north of Detroit.

Next morning Archer visits his dentist, and receives a check for $1,000 from Sable and a suspiciously sugary letter from John. He returns a phone call from Howell, is invited to lunch at his Santa Teresa club, hears an eavesdropper's click, and flies to the San Francisco airport, where Howell's daughter Sheila meets him. She admits to listening in and says she and John, whom his grandmother adores, have fallen in love. When Archer wonders whether she thinks John could be a phony, she cries, turns glum, drives him to the club, and goes for a swim. Archer and Howell agree John could be faking it. Howell says this: Maria may bequeath John a substantial fortune; Howell learned from a Cleveland associate that John's Ohio orphanage burned down, all records were destroyed, and the superintendent had a fatal heart attack; John pronounces "about" like a Canadian; Sheila likes John. Howell gives Archer a $500 advance to investigate John. When John courteously approaches Sheila at the pool, Howell bellows at him.

Archer visits Sheriff Trask, who says this: The police are holding Archer's recovered car; Trask lacks evidence to pursue Schwartz, whose minions have disappeared; Howell is "bankrolling" Archer; Trask also suspects John; Culligan was arrested in Detroit, January 7, five and a half years ago. Archer says this: John surfaced at Ann Arbor soon thereafter; Archer suspects the Syndicate could be behind a long-time plan against the Galton fortune and agrees Maria should be assigned police protection. Sable's secretary tells Archer her boss is with his wife, Alice, at Dr. Trenchard's institution. Archer takes a cab to the depressing "home," calls Sable aside, and learns this: Sable is no longer Maria's attorney; Howell and Sheila stand to gain if Maria's will remains unchanged; Sable also suspects John. Archer taxis to Maria's mansion, is greeted by Cassie, who praises John glowingly, and is ushered into Maria's presence. She thanks Archer for finding her grandson and says she does not want John to pursue a romantic relationship with Sheila but instead to study the theater in Europe for a while. John bursts in, drunk, swings at but misses Archer, and calls him Howell's spy. Hearing this, Maria denounces Howell and his daughter, says they won't get any of her money, and is touchingly comforted by John. Archer leaves for the airport.

At Ann Arbor, Archer learns that two days after Culligan's arrest in Detroit, John found protection in Lindsay, who died in February last year. John graduated in June from the University of Michigan, with honors as a speech major. His prissy landlady, Mrs. Haskell, liked him, attended plays in which he acted nicely, and says that a producer talked to him, and that Ada Reichler, his older, rich girlfriend, was angry when he disappeared in June. Archer feels the "producer" was an affiliate of the criminal Syndicate with a plan. Through the gardener of Ada's father, an automobile-parts dealer, Archer learns that Ada is vacationing in nearby Kingsville, Ontario. He goes there and talks with the frank, attractive young woman. Revealing his purpose and questioning her, he learns this: Ada loved and proposed to John; he rejected her, said his name was Theodore Fredericks, and led her to a slum sixty miles away at Pitt, where he pointed out his slatternly mother. Ada later returned and talked to the woman, who said her son, when sixteen, left her five years ago, permanently. When Ada weeps, Archer comforts her intimately. (The month, July, is mentioned.)

Archer drives to Pitt, locates the crummy rooming house run by drunk old Fredericks and his domineering wife (really Fred Nelson and Theodora Gavin Brown). He tells Archer he is glad his rubbishy son Theo is gone. Showing Theo's school picture (that of John Brown, Jr.), she tells Archer this: Theo stabbed her husband severely; she told the daydreaming lad his father was an English lord; Culligan boarded with her "years ago," told Theo his grandmother was wealthy in California and took him there. When Archer says Tommy Lemberg knifed Culligan, she says Tommy and Roy have been hiding here with her for two weeks. Archer awaits their return, decks Tommy, and makes both talk: Culligan shacked up in Reno with Alice, who owed money to Schwartz, who told Tommy to go scare Alice in Santa Teresa; Culligan drew a gun and a knife on Tommy, who conked him on the head, did not stab him, left the knife.

Tommy and Roy return with Archer to Santa Teresa and give their statements to Trask, who tells Archer that Sheila and John have just driven off. Howell and Archer learn that Sable has taken Alice home, where the surprising truth slowly emerges: Culligan, John, and Sable planned John's impersonation of Anthony Galton's son; Sable was the "producer" praising John's Ann Arbor acting and coached him to say he attended an orphanage Sable knew had been destroyed; Culligan was Alice's lover; Alice owed Schwartz $50,000 in Reno; Culligan learned about Anthony Galton's bones at Luna Bay; Cullen and John wanted to ease Sable out; Alice, long delusional, told Howell she had stabbed Culligan; Sable let her think so but killed Culligan himself; Maria, employing a different lawyer, may have named John as her heir. Howell phones the cops.

When Sable says he gave Sheila and John money last night and told them about Marian Matheson, Archer rushes to her and learns this: Sheila and John asked about Anthony; Marian accepted John as Anthony's son; the two are heading toward Ontario. Archer follows by air and car, learns from the Frederickses that the young couple are at a hotel in town and gets to them. They share and receive this information: Fred Nelson became John's mother's lover, was jailed, escaped, beheaded John's father; John thought Fredericks was his father, who abused him, but then Sable told him to impersonate Maria Galton's son's son; Lindsay and Dineen saw fineness in John; Culligan fed John many of these details. When John adds that his mother last night lied that Fredericks was his father, Archer tries with John and Sheila to find him. But first John's mother tells them this: Fredericks (really Nelson) has just hanged himself, thereby enabling her to break her vow of silence; Nelson axed Anthony, threatened her and baby John; she stood between the killer and her son until her son, when sixteen, left them. Sheila offers a welcome to John's mother, whom John forgives and embraces. She tells the youths to leave and love. A bird sings.

Before Macdonald fastened on *The Galton Case* for his title, he rejected the following: "The Castle and the Poorhouse," "The Decapitated Man," "The Enormous Detour," "The Fear of Death," "The Fearful Detour," "The Grand Detour," "The Imposter," "Luna Bay," "A Matter of Identity," "The Pelican Detour," and "The Skull Beneath the Skin." There are autobiographical elements in the novel. Note these similarities: John Brown, Jr. (born December 2, 1936, near San Francisco), dumped (age four) in an orphanage, moving to Canada; Macdonald (born December 13, 1936, near San Francisco), nearly left (age six) in a Canadian orphanage. It has been suggested that Macdonald used the name Galton because of the English scientist Sir Francis Galton's nature-versus-nurture theories. "Luna" was actually a poem Macdonald penned when sixteen. Regarding *The Galton Case* as his best work to its date—and always his favorite— he was disappointed when some reviewers regarded it as merely another Archer mystery-and-crime yarn, not a standalone novel. Sales of 4,000 called for only two printings in 1959 by Alfred A. Knopf,* followed by a Bantam reissue in paperback (from 1960). Macdonald has said that in *The Galton Case*, admittedly in part autobiographical, he is redacting the old legend of "Oedipus angry vs. parents for sending him away into a foreign country." The evidence is there, if but slight. In the thirty-two-chapter novel, the Oedipus parallel is first mentioned by Ada Reichler (Ch. 24), indirectly touched on by "Mrs. Fredericks" (Ch. 25), and repeated by young John (Ch. 32). Archer remains wrongheaded during three-fourths of his adventures, and pays for it with a beating reminiscent of the violence Macdonald found repellent in Mickey Spillane's fiction.

Bibliography: Bruccoli; Ross Macdonald, "A Preface to *The Galton Case*," in Thomas McCormack, ed., *Novelists on Their Novels* (New York: Harper & Row, 1968), pp. 146–159; Nolan; Eudora Welty, "Finding the Connections," in *IJ*, pp. 154–158; "WG."

GARBOLD. In *The Ivory Grin. See* Garibaldi, William.

GARIBALDI, WILLIAM. In *The Ivory Grin*, he runs the Ypsilanti numbers racket for the demented Leo Durano.

GARLAND, F. In *Blue City*, he is a homosexual, is a deadly shot, works for Roger Kerch, and is Joseph Sault's friend. John Weather calls him Gloria, antagonizes him, and at Wildwood is guarded by him. John breaks Garland's wrists. Freeman Allison kills Garland, identified as Jerry D. Weather's murderer.

GARLICK, DETECTIVE SERGEANT SAM. In *The Zebra-Striped Hearse*, he is a Los Angeles Police Department identification expert.

GARTH, BURTON. In *The Three Roads*, he is an ex-crook, in his mid-forties. Garth used Michigan black-market profits to buy the Cockalorum cocktail lounge in Glendale. Garth took Lorraine Taylor to her home but was beaten up by a man already there. Bret Taylor forces Garth to finger Larry Miles.

GARVIN. In *The Dark Tunnel*, he is the county prosecutor and decides not to press charges against Robert Branch.

GARY, LIEUTENANT. In *The Way Some People Die*, he is a Los Angeles Homicide Division officer. Once Peter Colton has vouched for him, Archer is allowed to work with Gary.

GAULT, WILLIAM CAMPBELL (1910–1995). Fiction writer. Gault was born in Milwaukee, attended the University of Wisconsin (1929), married Virginia Kaprelian (1942), had two children with her, was in the U.S. Army (1943–1945), and became a freelance writer of many short stories, mystery novels, and sports novels for juvenile readers. His twenty-nine mysteries, widely translated, appeared from 1952 through 1995. Their settings were almost without exception southern California, specifically Los Angeles. His series detectives are Brock Callahan and Joe Puma. Gault once explained that his fictional private eyes are simple dirty men doing seedy work in a wretched world. His first novel, *Don't Cry for Me*, won the 1952 Edgar Allan Poe Award.

Macdonald and Gault met at a party in San Diego in 1951 given by E.T. Guymon Jr., an avid collector of detective books. Gault moved from Pacific Palisades to Santa Barbara in 1958 and joined with Macdonald and others at regularly scheduled writers' lunches. In 1976 Macdonald asked Gault to suggest changes in *The Blue Hammer* at proof stage. Gault hesitantly did so and was pleased to note that passages he thought should be deleted were gone. Grateful, Macdonald dedicated the novel to Gault. Four years later, Gault was saddened, as many other friends were, to note Macdonald's tragic loss of memory.

Bibliography: Charles Cooper, "Brock the Rock Callahan: A Short Tribute to William Campbell Gault's Appealing Southern California Private Eye," *Armchair Detective* 25 (Spring 1992): 226–229.

GAYLEY, JACK. In *The Wycherly Woman*, he is a Medicine Stone garage owner. He and his son, Sam, help try to raise Phoebe Wycherly's Volkswagen from the Bay.

GAYLEY, MRS. In *The Wycherly Woman*, she is Jack Gayley's wife, Sam Gayley's mother, and a Medicine Stone café cook.

GAYLEY, SAM. In *The Wycherly Woman*, he is the son, eighteen, of Jack Gayley and his wife. He saw Robert Doncaster driving Phoebe Wycherly's Volkswagen toward the cliff. In diving gear, Sam retrieves a corpse, thought to be Phoebe's, from the submerged car.

GEISMAN, DR. In *The Chill*, he is the head of the department of modern languages at Pacific Point College and thus Helen Haggerty's administrative superior.

GELLHORN, ED. In *The Ferguson Affair*, he is a court reporter who takes down Ella Barker's statement professing her innocence.

GENSLER. In *The Instant Enemy*, he is Heidi Gensler's father, about forty. When Archer tries to talk to Heidi a second time, Gensler says he has sent her away to relatives.

GENSLER, HEIDI. In *The Instant Enemy*, she is Alexandria Sebastian's best friend. They are in high school together. Heidi tells Archer enough to lead to his conclusion that Alexandria's talk of suicide resulted from actions concerning sex and drugs.

GEORGE. In *The Chill*. *See* Bradshaw, Dean Roy.

GEORGE. In *The Way Some People Die*, he is a waiter at the waterfront café where Archer and Mario Tarantine eat and drink.

GEORGE. In *The Way Some People Die*, his is the café near the morgue. Mario Tarantine finds Galley Lawrence there, and they leave for Oasis.

GERHARDI. In *The Chill*, he is or was Madge Gerhardi's husband. She tells Archer he treated her nicely and she was foolish to leave him.

GERHARDI, MADGE. In *The Chill*, she is Thomas McGee's companion after his release from prison. She tells Archer that McGee wants to see him and that he can find McGee on Gil Stevens's yacht.

GERT. In *Blue City*, she is evidently a prostitute, buys marijuana from Joseph Sault, and is mercilessly teased by him.

GINO. In *The Way Some People Die*, he is the pigeon-chested, Mediterranean-type wrestler at the Arena.

GIRSTON, ALEC ("ALEX"). In *The Wycherly Woman*, he is the whining manager of the Conquistador. For $20, he tells Archer about the room Carl Trevor and Catherine Wycherly used up until early November.

GIRSTON, MRS. In *The Wycherly Woman*, she is the sick landlady of the Conquistador, where Carl Trevor and Catherine Wycherly had their bugged love nest.

GLEY. In *The Doomsters*, he is or was Mildred Hallman's father. He abandoned his wife and Mildred, then seven, went to Las Vegas, and never returned.

GLEY, MRS. In *The Doomsters*, she is Mildred Hallman's mother. In her late forties, she retains remnants of beauty and poise, but is alcoholic, whining, and possessive. When her husband disappeared, she ran a boardinghouse for ten years. It has been suggested that her name derives from Robert Burns's famous line: "The best-laid schemes o' mice and men gang aft a'gley."

Bibliography: Nolan.

GLOVER, MRS. In *The Goodbye Look*, this housekeeper works for John Truttwell and Betty Truttwell.

GODWIN, DR. JAMES. In *The Chill*, he is a big, forceful Pacific Point psychiatrist. He treated Dolly McGee (*see* Kincaid, Dolly), her mother, Constance McGee, and Dean Roy Bradshaw. When Dolly is threatened with arrest for Helen Haggerty's murder, Godwin shelters her. His treating her with sodium pentothal helps Archer rule out some puzzling evidence. It has been suggested that Macdonald chose the name Godwin because of William Godwin, the psychologist-novelist whose *The Adventures of Caleb Williams* (1794) was a precursor of crime fiction.

Bibliography: Nolan.

GODWIN, MRS. JAMES. In *The Chill*, she is the physician's "handsome," neglected wife. She tells Archer her husband burdens himself with patients' problems.

GOLDFARB. In *The Drowning Pool*, Mildred Fleming's humorous anecdote concerns Mr. Organic, who had to change his name to Goldfarb to do well in Hollywood.

GOMEZ, MISS. In *The Zebra-Striped Hearse*, she is the Mexicana Airlines stewardess who provides Archer with information about Harriet Blackwell and Bruce Campion, posing as Q.R. Simpson (*see* Simpson, Quincy Ralph).

"GONE GIRL" (1953, 1955, 1964). Short story. (Characters: Alfie, Lew Archer, Bartolemeo, Donny, Angel Funk, Gino Gretchen, Lorraine, Salanda, Ella Salanda, Mabel Salanda.) At Salanda's Emerald Bay motel, Archer happens upon the gangster Bartolemeo's murder. Clues lead to Palm Springs, where Angel Funk, a drug dealer, and his thugs batter Archer for information. He resists, lies, and is let go, to be followed. Archer discovers that Donny, Salanda's daughter Ella's weak-minded boyfriend, killed Bart to protect Ella. Gino, one of Funk's henchmen enters, shoots Donny dead, and is killed by Archer. The original title of "Gone Girl" was "The Imaginary Blonde." The 1964 reprint was titled "The Singing Pigeon."

THE GOODBYE LOOK **(1969).** Novel. (Characters: Lew Archer, Barnard, Chalmers, Estelle Chalmers, Irene Chalmers, Judge Harold Chalmers, Lawrence Chalmers, Nicholas Chalmers, Conchita, Miss Cowan, Mrs. Delong, Duke the Dude, Emilio, Mrs. Glover, Sidney Harrow, Helen, Joe Hespeler, Captain Oliver Lackland, Fast Phil Larrabee, Maclennan, Marco, Handy Andy Oliphant, Mrs. Samuel Rawlinson, Samuel Rawlinson, Mrs. Shepherd, Randolph Shepherd, Dr. Ralph Smitheram, Moira Smitheram, Roy Snyder, Eddie Sutherland, Eldon Swain, Louise Swain, George Trask, Jean Trask, Betty Truttwell, John Truttwell, Mrs. John Truttwell, Williams, Mrs. Florence Williams, Commander Wilson.)

On Tuesday, January (14 or 21) 1969, John Truttwell, a widowed lawyer in Pacific Point, hires Archer to investigate the theft of a Renaissance Florentine gold box, taken from the home of his across-the-street neighbors, Lawrence and Irene Chalmers, while the two were weekending in Palm Springs. Their son, Nicholas ("Nick") Chalmers, twenty-three, is engaged to Truttwell's daughter, Betty Truttwell, twenty-five. Archer interviews Irene. She reveals this: Lawrence's deceased mother (Estelle Chalmers) received the box from an admirer; it contained Lawrence's letters to his mother during World War II; Lawrence suspects Nick, who rebelled against his parents, disappeared last year, was found by detectives and returned to the university, but is missing again. Irene gives Archer Nick's campus address. Lawrence suddenly returns. Archer is distressed when Irene lies that Archer is an insurance man asking about the theft. Lawrence brusquely dismisses Archer.

Going to Nick's apartment, Archer finds Betty. She says this: Nick suddenly "quit caring," is involved with an older woman, Mrs. Jean Trask, and a bill collector from San Diego named Sidney Harrow. Last Friday, when the Chalmerses were away, Betty was checking Harrow's car near Nick's parents' home when Harrow emerged and slapped her; Nick appeared and decked Harrow. Both men pulled guns briefly. When the phone rings, Betty pretends she is Nick's answering service. On the phone, Mrs. Trask tells Nick to avoid the Montevista Inn, because her husband is watching. Betty tells Archer her mother was killed by a hit-and-run driver in 1945 (July 3), when Betty was a baby. She lives with her father.

Archer finds Jean Trask's cottage on the Montevista Inn grounds and overhears her telling her overly ardent husband, George Trask, that she is determined to find her father this time. George counters: Her father was a womanizing criminal, who abandoned his family. Archer flashes a useless badge and orders George out. While Jean, moderately attractive at about forty, mixes drinks, Archer spies the gold box in her bedroom. Loose-tongued, Jean solicits his help in her "nasty situation." She hired Harrow, who proved to be a "repo" man not a detective, and even pulled a gun on her young boyfriend; Harrow, useless now, is drinking on the beach at Sunset Motor Motel and won't return "the picture and stuff."

At the Sunset, Archer learns that Harrow has skipped town. In his room, Archer finds Nick's recent photo, which he keeps. He finds Harrow's car, described by the clerk. Inside is Harrow, shot dead. Archer phones the police, who take him to headquarters for questioning. Captain Oliver Lackland shows him an old snapshot. Archer silently guesses it is of Jean's missing father and demands to see his lawyer, Truttwell. Archer tells Truttwell that Nick probably stole the gold box, gave it to Jean Trask, who hired Harrow, who has been murdered. Truttwell drives Archer to see Betty. On the way he says his wife tried to scare off would-be burglars of the nearby Chalmers home and was run down and killed by a driver who was never caught. The car, stolen, was found in San Diego. Betty tells Archer that Nick phoned and plans to kill himself. Guessing he called from the Tennis Club, Betty takes Archer there. The bartender says Nick drank there for a while with a woman Archer figures was Jean. Betty and Archer drive to the Montevista and find Jean packing to leave. She too says Nick talked about suicide but then promised to go home, instead, and sleep off too many drinks. Betty and Archer go to Nick's apartment. He greets them at the door with a gun. Archer takes it and knocks Nick down. The revolver was fired once. Archer records its number. Deranged, Nick babbles about how "we" went to a hobo jungle, a man wanted him "to do a bad thing," and Nick shot him. Archer calls Nick's mother to say that he will bring the lad home. She agrees to call Dr. Ralph Smitheram, his psychiatrist.

Archer, with Betty's help, gets Nick home. Nick turns passively apologetic. Archer explains matters to Lawrence Chalmers, Nick's irresolute father, and tells him to summon Truttwell. He arrives, talks briefly with Lawrence, and walks over to his house. Archer follows, has him lock the revolver away, and learns that Nick has had psychotic "episodes," starting when he was assaulted at age eight by a "sexual psychopath." A Sacramento police friend, whom Archer asked to check the gun registration, reports that it was bought in 1941 by Samuel Rawlinson, a retired Pasadena bank president. Smitheram arrives and wants to hospitalize Nick, but Truttwell angrily insists that Nick must stay home for now.

After driving through evening traffic to Pasadena, Archer talks with Rawlinson, an eccentric octagenarian, and his housekeeper, Mrs. Shepherd. Archer proceeds to the nearby home of Rawlinson's daughter, Louise Swain, who is being visited briefly by Jean. A conversation with Rawlinson, Louise, and Jean gains Archer the following information: Louise married Eldon Swain; Jean, now thirty-nine, is their daughter; Swain, presently sixty-three, worked at Rawlinson's bank, embezzled $500,000 (July 1, 1945), ruining Rawlinson; Rawlinson gave Louise, alone with Jean, his revolver for protection; Swain disappeared into Mexico with Rita Shepherd, daughter of Mrs. Shepherd, divorced from Randolph ("Randy") Shepherd of San Diego; Swain returned in 1954, confronted Louise, seized her revolver; Nick, when a child, saw Swain at the Pacific Point railroad yard; Louise is unable to persuade Jean to return to George; Jean calls the gold box an heirloom belonging to her Rawlinson grandmother; Jean intends to locate her loving father, Swain. Louise, supporting herself for over twenty years as a sewing-machine demonstrator, remembers her mother's missing gold box, hopes Archer can recover what is left of Swain's loot, and gives Archer a photograph of Swain. After eating in Pasadena, Archer goes to his West Los Angeles apartment, writes up the facts of the case, and relays them by phone to Truttwell, who reports that he released the revolver to Lackland.

Wednesday at 7:00 A.M., Lackland phones Archer to come to his office. Lackland says the revolver killed Harrow, and he suspects that Nick had it. Archer clams up. Lackland produces a photograph. Archer names Eldon Swain as the subject. Lackland shows another photo, of a man in Mexican clothes, killed in the hobo jungle in 1954 and with his fingerprints scorched off. Lackland was a sergeant on the case then. He got the first photo from Harrow's pocket. Archer says the revolver went from Rawlinson to Louise to Swain, who was in Mexico. Lackland says Randy Shepherd was a suspect, soon released for lack of evidence.

Archer seeks Truttwell and finds him at the Chalmerses' home. Nick disappeared a few minutes earlier, with multiple sleeping pills. Archer offends the Chalmerses by saying the revolver that killed Harrow also killed a hobo in 1954. Truttwell can barely persuade the Chalmerses not to fire Archer. Truttwell tells Archer that Nick was distressed by a sexual experience Archer should ask Smitheram about. Archer goes to the Smitheram Clinic, established in Montevista (1967), and meets Smitheram's sympathetic, attractive wife, Moira Smitheram. Smitheram says Nick rambled about Jean and Randy. Archer phones George Trask's San Diego home and gets Jean. When she says she doesn't know Randy, Archer warns her: Nick may arrive there with sleeping pills. From Moira, Archer gets Randy's address in the Tijuana River Valley.

Archer drives to San Diego, arriving about noon. He locates the Trask house. The registration of a car parked in front names the owner as Randolph Shepherd, living at Conchita Cabins, Imperial Beach. That bearded fellow emerges from the house. Archer trips him up into revealing that Swain snatched Nick years ago. Releasing Randy, Archer enters the house and finds Jean stabbed to death and Nick unconscious from sleeping pills. Archer gets him to the hospital for stomach pumping, phones Irene to bring Smitheram down, anonymously phones the local police about Jean, and has breakfast. Archer talks to the physician who is handling Nick and who gives him a suicide note found in Nick's pocket.

Archer proceeds to the Conchita, gives $50 to Mrs. Florence Williams, the owner, and learns this: Randy often babbled about buried treasure, just sold his car, and is walking toward Mexico, where he has friends. Archer drives after him, grabs him short of the border, and assures him that he merely wants information. Randy states this: Randy's wife divorced him when he was in jail; he gardened for Swain in San Marino; Swain, possibly a child molester, must have snatched eight-year-old Nick; Swain's bank loot may be buried somewhere nearby on the U.S. side; Rita went to Mexico with Swain but never returned, though Swain did; Randy drove Swain to Pacific Point, doesn't know who killed him; Randy introduced Jean to Harrow. Archer gives Randy $50, and away he goes. For another $50, Mrs. Williams tells Archer this: Swain, while planning the bank heist, shacked up with pretty Rita at the Conchita during the war; Randy followed them here; the loot may be buried nearby; Harrow, here a week ago, may have received Nick's picture from Randy.

Archer finds Moira Smitheram at the San Diego hospital. Smitheram is consulting a brain surgeon, because Nick has a concussion—from a fall or a blow. Archer and Moira drive to La Jolla for a lush dinner. She shares a confidence: While Smitheram was a flight surgeon at sea out of San Diego in the 1940s, she had an affair (1943–1945) with "Sonny," one of Smitheram's La Jolla patients. Archer phones Trask, and Archer and Moira drive to see him. Trask says Randy killed Jean, Trask's wife, and should be executed. Archer privately asks Louise Swain, Jean's mother, also there, if her husband, Eldon, could still be alive. Maybe. Louise adds that Samuel Rawlinson, her father, had a "liaison" with Estelle Chalmers, Lawrence's mother, and gave Estelle the gold box. Louise wonders if Truttwell would buy it and also some possibly useful old pictures, now in Trask's home. Moira tells Archer that Trask described someone Jean was involved with; Moira figures it was Nick.

Archer and Moira return to the hospital. Archer finds Lawrence asleep but Irene alert. Irene says Nick is recovering and Truttwell said he was too busy to accompany them. Archer asks Irene to buy Jean's mother's pictures. No. Archer tells Irene he found Nick unconscious near Jean's corpse but has not informed the authorities. He shows her Nick's suicide note. Irene says he mustn't confer with Smitheram about Nick. Archer counters: Irene and Lawrence overprotect Nick, who is perhaps guilty, informs her he knows about the railroad-yard killing, and briefs her about Randy. She admits that Nick, when eight, told her and her husband he shot a man and left the gun at the railroad yard. Archer engages a guard, named Maclennan, for Nick. Archer phones Mrs. Williams, who says the cops are swarming, Randy has not reappeared, and she is selling the Conchita. Moira says her husband, a veritable "Trappist," is sleeping at the hospital and asks Archer to drive her home to Montevista. When Maclennan arrives, Archer orders him to guard Nick and not let him escape. Smitheram refuses to let Archer talk with Nick and even calls Archer a junior G-man. Archer drives Moira to her opulent, lonely house, and is allowed in. He will not use her to gain knowledge about Nick. Instead, the two make gentle love.

Thursday, 8:00 A.M. Archer visits Lackland, tells him Randy's motive for possibly killing Swain, and is told that Randy has been sighted heading north in a stolen car. Archer suggests Pasadena as his target, where both Randy and Swain have come from. When Lackland says Rawlinson's girl-friend was Estelle Chalmers, Archer departs, pondering Nick's attitude toward that. After breakfast and a shave, Archer goes to the Truttwell home. Betty says that the Chalmerses have dismissed Truttwell and that Truttwell ordered Betty to choose between her father and Nick. Truttwell enters, criticizes Betty, promises to pay Archer, says he is going to Louise Swain to buy some family movies, and asks Archer to follow. First, Archer talks with Betty, who explains that Nick removed his father's letters from the gold box, hid them in his school apartment, and Betty has them, with Nick's permission. Nick's father enjoyed reading from them to the boy when he was eight. Archer peruses three (one in 1943, two in 1945); they present Lawrence, as a naval pilot, lieutenant junior grade, evolving from idealistic to mature to fatigued. In the 1943 one, Lawrence mentions Rawlinson amiably. Betty releases the letters to Archer out of fear of her father. Archer challenges Betty to grow up but senses she feels irrationally guilty, somehow, of the deaths of her mother, Jean, and Harrow.

Lawrence drives home. To him Archer suggests a connection between his mother's death, that of Truttwell's wife, and Nick's taking of the gold box with its letters, and hints that Rawlinson might have looted his own bank and blamed Swain. Lawrence assumes that Archer is hinting at a financial relationship between his mother and Rawlinson, whom he calls "that whoremaster."

Archer gets to Pasadena and Truttwell, who is reviewing papers concerning "the Smitheram Foundation." Archer reveals Lawrence's letters. While they wait for Louise to arrive from San Diego, their talk reveals this: Randy may be gunning for Louise; Rawlinson's bank was robbed on July 1, 1945; Truttwell's wife was killed two days later; Lawrence's mother died of grief two weeks later; authorities opened her safe and found several hundred thousand dollars. Archer theorizes that perhaps Swain stole some bank money but Rawlinson took much more and stashed it with Lawrence's mother. Louise drives home, meets Truttwell, and says the authorities delayed her by grilling her about Randy Shepherd. Suddenly up drives Randy in his stolen black convertible, with his hair dyed red and his beard gone, but recognizable, and with the police on his tail.

Archer drives after both cars but soon loses them, winds up in front of Rawlinson's house, and spots the convertible nearby. He enters the house, finds Mrs. Shepherd, and acquaints her with enough facts to cause her to admit that Randy is hiding in the attic. Archer hustles old Rawlinson out, hints he may have stolen bank money to use with Estelle, and shows him the picture of Nick that Archer thinks Mrs. Shepherd treasured but Randy stole last week. Randy strolls out, disguised in Rawlinson's hat and coat. The police approach, Randy runs, and the police shoot him dead and hit Archer's left shoulder in the process.

Archer is treated in the Pasadena hospital. The police park his car nearby. After being questioned by the police, Mrs. Shepherd visits Archer and says her now-dead husband sold their daughter Rita to Swain and she died in Mexico. She doesn't think Rawlinson stole the bank funds. Archer shows her Nick's picture, which Randy took from her and gave Harrow. While Archer rests, Mrs. Shepherd gently filches the picture and leaves. Archer dreams she is Nick's grandmother.

Friday morning. Archer has some hospital breakfast, sneaks out, drives to his office, and returns two phone calls his answering service reported: Truttwell will see him at 4:30 P.M.; Betty, who will pick him up, says Nick is at Smitheram's clinic. Archer cooks himself a steak and waits for Betty. While she drives him to the clinic, Archer rummages through Chalmers's letters and finds one from overseas dated nine months before Nick was born on December 14, 1945. So Nick is not Lawrence's son. Moira is at the clinic, looks sad, fears she cannot help Nick, and says "Sonny" has reappeared—and is involved. Betty gets Archer to Truttwell's office building. Outside is the Chalmerses' car, from which Archer takes some vomit he dispatches Betty to have analyzed. Inside, Truttwell boasts that he gave Mrs. Shepherd the gold box in return for the family movies. Archer startles Truttwell by guessing Rita is Irene Chalmers. In the law-firm library, Archer encounters Irene, who says Lawrence is sick at home. Archer tells her he has the letters. She reveals this: She and Lawrence happily financed Smitheram's clinic, in gratitude for his helping Nick; Truttwell, back from San Diego, bought some dirt on the Chalmerses. When Archer presses her to admit it concerns Nick's being conceived while her husband was overseas, she rebukes him—but with "erotic underplay." Truttwell cockily says the movie was taken in San Marino, summer 1943, and runs it—to Irene's consternation: Jean, Irene (that is, Rita), a timid eighteen-year-old lad at a private pool; nearby, Louise Swain, also Rawlinson seated beside a beautiful woman (undoubtedly Estelle); Randy, working at a hedge; Swain cavorting with Jean and Rita.

In conversation that follows, Archer, who tells Irene the police just killed her father, is told this: Chalmers was the timid lad in the movie; Irene first met him that day; Randy destroyed Swain's fingerprints; Irene sent her mother Nick's photograph; Randy stole it, gave it to Jean, and asked her to get Harrow to look for Swain. Truttwell drives Archer and Irene to the clinic to interview Nick. Betty is there, and Truttwell behaves better toward her. In ensuing conversations, the following facts emerge: Nick, eight, was picked up by a man calling himself Nick's father and asking about the Chalmerses; when fondled at the railroad yard, Nick seized the stranger's belted gun, shot him, left the gun; Smitheram has protected Nick for years; Jean and Harrow told Nick that Chalmers was a criminal; Nick read enough letters from Chalmers to know he was not Chalmers's son; Nick said he killed Harrow, but didn't; Nick learned Swain was his father, and Jean's too. Smitheram whispers something to Moira. Nick says he swallowed sleeping pills, dropped from the window, and was hurt. Smitheram checks the letters; notes phrasing in them identical to what he wrote Moira from overseas; says Chalmers washed out of the Navy within months and got a job in the post office; concludes Chalmers sent partially copied letters to his mother about his battle exploits. How? Moira says she lived with Chalmers, her La Jolla "Sonny," until early 1945. Irene says she married Chalmers in July 1945. Moira loaned Chalmers the letters; Ralph knew about her adultery and let Chalmers finance his clinic for revenge. Moira tells Archer this confidentially: Smitheram has kept Chalmers balanced by heavy drugs; Chalmers could have been a threat to Nick; she is leaving Smitheram and will do social work. Betty says the drug tested was chloral hydrate, which unless vomited could have killed Nick. Irene admits Swain was "[p]robaby" Nick's father. Archer upbraids Irene for misleading Nick for fifteen years and making him feel guilty. Archer accuses Irene and Chalmers of filching from Swain, at Imperial Beach, the money he stole from the bank; of driving a stolen car to Pacific Point; of loading the loot in the family safe and running over Mrs. Truttwell when she rushed to investigate. Archer suggests this: Chalmers knew Nick was not his son; retrieved Swain's gun and burned his fingers; witnessed Nick, after he had written his suicide note and drugged himself, drop out the window; slugged him and drove him to San Diego to set him up as Jean's killer.

The party reaches the Chalmerses' house. Chalmers, dressed in his Navy uniform, has cut his throat and is dead. Irene says she and Chalmers were approached by Jean and Harrow and went to Palm Springs that weekend to escape them. When Irene callously asks Truttwell to continue as her lawyer and says she is sorry she and her Larry ran over his wife, he slaps her. Continuing, Irene laments the time she spent listening to her mother-in-law calling for her "Sonny," who must have finally silenced the blind old thing by confidentially telling her the truth. Truttwell summons the police.

Other titles for *The Goodbye Look* Macdonald considered were "The Stolen War" and "The Suicide Room." A passage in the novel explains that a "goodbye look" is the stare two soldiers, on opposite sides, give each other when they both want to kill and be killed. Published May 28, 1969, *The Goodbye Look* was what Macdonald called a unique, mainstream novel. The *New York Times Book Review* (June 1, 1969) featured not only a rave review of *The Goodbye Look* by William Goldman, author of the screenplay of *Harper* (based on *The Moving Target*), but also a profile-essay of Macdonald by the critic-journalist John Leonard. One week later the science-fiction writer Ray Bradbury wildly recommended *The Goodbye Look* and Macdonald's earlier books in a *Los Angeles Times* review. Bantam books paid $12,500 for reprint rights to *The Goodbye Look*. The novel was on bestseller lists into November, with more than 45,000 hardcover copies in print then. Macdonald's friend R.A.D. Ford* sent him word in 1972 that a Russian edition of *The Goodbye Look*, 100,000-copies strong, was being released. The plot of *The Goodbye Look* is Macdonald's most complex. Family relations are tangled, some hidden. Names are changed. Few characters are what they profess to be. Juxtapositionings, including reversed initials (S.R. and R.S.), heighten suspense without providing quick enlightenment. To summarize what followed when that gold box, twice compared to Pandora's box, was opened: Randolph Shepherd and Mrs. Shepherd (later housekeeper of Samuel Rawlinson, fond of Estelle Chalmers), produced Rita Shepherd (a.k.a. Irene Chalmers, wife of Lawrence "Sonny" Chalmers, Estelle's son, whom Moira Smitheram loved); Rita and Eldon Swain (Rawlinson's employee) produced Nick Chalmers (Moira's husband Dr. Ralph Smitherman's patient and later fiancé of Betty Truttwell, whose mother Irene and Lawrence killed); Swain and Louise Swain (Rawlinson's daughter), produced Jean Trask (George Trask's wife). Death ends the troubles of Eldon, Jean, Randolph, and Lawrence. Can Nick and Betty ever enjoy true love?

Bibliography: William Goldman, "The Macdonald Conspiracy," in *IJ*, pp. 143–147; Nolan; Speir; Wolfe.

GORDON, CHESTER ("CHET"). In *The Dark Tunnel*, he was Dr. Galloway's student and is a Detroit FBI agent. Robert Branch helps Gordon find Rudolf Fisher. Gordon helps Branch clear Ruth Esch and apprehend

Peter Schneider, Herman Schneider's son. In *Trouble Follows Me*, Gordon boards the Los Angeles-bound train to eye Sam Drake, who labels Gordon "a brunette Uriah Heep." They interview Laura Eaton in Santa Barbara. Gordon is of no help to Drake in Tijuana. Gordon says that their case is trickier than the one involving Herman Schneider.

GORGELLO, MRS. In *The Galton Case*, she is the Luna Bay landlady of the house in which John Brown (Jr.) lives.

GRAFF, ISOBEL ("BELLE"). In *The Barbarous Coast*, she is movie-mogel Peter Heliopoulos's daughter. Former actress and still attractive, she was Clarence Bassett's would-be lover, Simon Graff's psychotic wife, and Dr. Frey's patient. She spied on Graff in bed with Gabrielle Torres and shot her in the thigh. Bassett killed her and let Isobel think she had. Isobel hates Carl Stern, Graff's crooked partner. When Graff set up Hester Wall in a mansion, Isobel goes there to kill her but finds her murdered. Isobel witnesses Bassett's death.

GRAFF, SIMON ("SIME"). In *The Barbarous Coast*, evidently born in Greece, he partnered with movie-magnate Peter Heliopoulos and married Peter's daughter Isobel (*see* Graff, Isobel). Graff throws splashy parties. Sammy Swift writes tawdry movie scripts for Graff. Graff is in cahoots with Carl Stern to build a Las Vegas hotel-casino. Isobel used Graff's special .22 to shoot Gabrielle Torres. Clarence Bassett took Graff's .22 for blackmailing purposes. Hester Wall stole it. Stern got it. Bassett takes it. Graff buys it and tries but fails to bribe Archer into silence. It has been suggested that Macdonald based Graff in part on film-mogul Darryl Zanuck, one of whose lavish Palm Springs parties Macdonald and Margaret Millar* attended (February 1950).

Bibliography: Nolan.

GRAHAM, AUDREY. In *The Way Some Some People Die*, she is the gossipy nurse in the Pacific Point hospital where her ex-roommate, Galley Lawrence, nursed Herman Speed. Audrey disliked Galley's aggressive sexiness.

GRANADA, SERGEANT PIKE. In *The Ferguson Affair*, he is a Buenavista police officer. William Gunnarson suspects him of killing Hector Broadman, then Augustine Donato, and then Augustine's wife, Secundina, whom Granada loves. Granada saves Gunnarson when threatened by Whitey Slater and Ronald Spice, and donates a pint of blood to Gunnarson.

"THE GRAND DETOUR." *See The Galton Case*.

GRANTHAM. In *Black Money*, he was Mrs. Grantham's late husband and compared her memory to an elephant's.

GRANTHAM. In *Black Money*, she was Mrs. Grantham's daughter and knew Virginia Fablon in high school.

GRANTHAM, MRS. In *Black Money*, she was the Montevista landlady of Francis Martel, then known as Feliz Cervantes. She gives Lew Archer some helpful information.

GRANTLAND, DR. J. CHARLES ("CHARLIE"). In *The Doomsters*, he is a physician in Purissima, once hard-working and kind. Three years ago he met Zinnie Hallman, who played him for a sucker. Grantland performed Mildred Hallman's abortion; was partly responsible for the death of Alicia Hallman; gave Thomas Rica drugs; and hoped Zinnie would divorce her husband so he could marry into the Hallman wealth. After Grantland tries to kill Archer, Duane Ostervelt shoots Grantland dead.

GRAVES, ALBERT ("BERT"). In *The Moving Target*, he is an Ohio farmer's son, a self-made man, a University of Michigan law-school graduate, and a former Santa Teresa D.A. Graves, forty and single, has gone into private practice for big money. One rich client is Ralph Sampson, whose daughter, Miranda, Graves wants to marry. When Sampson is missing, Graves cooperates with his old friend Archer. After Alan Taggert is killed, Graves marries Miranda. When Archer finally locates Sampson, Graves slugs Archer and kills Sampson. Conscience-stricken, Graves turns himself in.

Bibliography: Schopen.

GREEN. In "Midnight Blue," he is a restaurant owner whose wife left him "years ago." When his daughter, Virginia Green, is murdered, he impulsively kills an innocent suspect.

GREEN, MISS. In *Trouble Follows Me*, she is Anderson's cheaply bejeweled companion on the train from Chicago. When she turns up in San Diego, Sam Drake follows her by taxi to Tijuana, where, as Señora Toulouse, she owns a brothel. After her spy ring is exposed, Miss Green, an ether addict, is imprisoned.

GREEN, MRS. In *The Wycherly Woman*, she is Sammy Green's wife, "a handsome young Negro woman."

GREEN, SAMMY. In *The Wycherly Woman*, he is the black steward of the *President Jackson*. He served Homer Wycherly during his two-month cruise. Green tells Archer that Wycherly could not have left the ship, gone to Atherton, and returned the evening of November 2.

GREEN, VIRGINIA ("GINNIE"). In "Midnight Blue," she is the oversexed high school blonde, seventeen, garrotted near the beach by Anita Brocco.

GREGORY. In *The Barbarous Coast*, he evidently represents the real-estate agency Teeny Campbell hired to sell her house.

GRETCHEN. In "Gone Girl," at her Palms Springs lingerie shop Archer gains information about Ella Salanda.

GRIMES, JUANITA ("NITA"). In *The Blue Hammer*, she is Paul Grimes's ex-wife and Paola Grimes's mother. Juanita, called a "half-breed," has a supply shop in Copper City, cooperates with Archer after Paul is murdered, and gives him money for Paola.

GRIMES, PAOLA. In *The Blue Hammer*, she is Paul Grimes's daughter, living in poverty and, after his murder, in fear as well. Her mother, Juanita Grimes, sends her money by Archer.

GRIMES, PAUL. In *The Blue Hammer*, he taught painting to Richard Chantry and William Mead in Copper City. After drug and prison troubles, Grimes became a Santa Teresa art dealer. Grimes, sixty and goateed, is murdered on the street. This prompts Archer to seek a connection to murders in 1943 and 1950.

GRINKER, MRS. DENISE. In *The Ivory Grin*, she is a Arroyo Beach hat maker. Una Durano bought a turban from her for Elizabeth Benning. Lucy Champion wore it when she went to visit Mrs. Charles A. Singleton, but panicked and dropped it. Sylvia Treen gives it to Archer for his use. Denise tells him Una has rented the Peppermill estate.

GRUNDLE, DR. In *The Wycherly Woman*, he cares for Carl Trevor in the Terranova hospital, after his coronary at Medicine Stone.

GRUPP, DR. HERMAN. In *The Wycherly Woman*, he is a martini-loaded chiropractor attending a St. Francis Hotel convention. Archer encounters him while looking for Phoebe Wycherly.

"GUILT-EDGED BLONDE" (1954). Short story. (Characters: Lew Archer, Arturo Castola, Faronese, Fats Jordan, Larue, Jeannine Larue, Harry Nemo, Mrs. Harry Nemo, Nick Nemo.) Nick Nemo hires Archer to be his bodyguard. Before Archer can start, Nick is killed by his sister-in-law, Mrs. Harry Nemo, who also kills Harry for selling to Nick her daughter by an earlier marriage.

"GUILTY KNOWLEDGE." *See The Blue Hammer*.

"THE GUILTY ONES." *See* "The Sinister Habit" and *Meet Me at the Morgue*.

GUNNARSON. In *The Ferguson Affair*, William Gunnarson mentions him as his father, a deceased Pennsylvania lawyer.

GUNNARSON, SALLY. In *The Ferguson Affair*, she is William Gunnarson's pregnant, neglected wife. While Gunnarson is in Mountain Grove following leads in the Ferguson case, she has a baby daughter in the Buenavista hospital.

GUNNARSON, WILLIAM ("BILL"). In *The Ferguson Affair*, he is a Buenavista attorney. He was a sergeant during the Korean War. Assigned to defend Ella Barker, Gunnarson is hired by Colonel Ian Ferguson to find June, his missing wife. Gunnarson's efforts lead him to policemen, physicians, and various suspects, including Hilda Dotery, June's look-alike half-sister. After Hilda shoots him, Gunnarson rescues June, who he thinks is Hilda. He uses Ferguson's $2,000 payment to start buying a house for his growing family. When Sally tells Gunnarson he is "nothing but a profession that walks like a man," Archer may be echoing Sue Archer's unrecorded complaint before she left him.

Bibliography: Speir.

GUNNISON, ALLISTER, JR. In *Find a Victim*, he is a guest at Don Kerrigan's motel. After hearing the shot that killed Kerrigan, he phoned the police. The high-strung, prissy Gunnison wears red pajamas. Jo Summer steals his red sports car.

GUTIERREZ, FLORIDA ("FLORIE"). In *The Ivory Grin*, she is Dr. Samuel Benning's receptionist. After Elizabeth fires her, Florie, plumply pretty but stupid, provides Maxfield Heiss and Archer with valuable information.

GWEN. In *The Doomsters*, she is the pretty Red Barn car hop. She mistakenly thought she spotted Carl Hallman foraging for food.

H

HACKETT, GERDA. In *The Instant Enemy*, she is the wife, in her early thirties, of Stephen Hackett (really Jasper Blevins). She is from Munich, Germany. Meeting abroad, the two married ten years ago. Her mother-in-law, Ruth Marburg, so dominates Stephen that Gerda has become passive and unhappy. She makes a pass, complete with fervid kiss, at Archer.

HACKETT, JASPER. In *The Instant Enemy. See* Blevins, Jasper.

HACKETT, MARK. In *The Instant Enemy*, he was the oil-rich husband of Henrietta R. Krug (*see* Marburg, Ruth). Their son was Stephen Hackett. Mark moved his Corpus Christi oil company to Long Beach and established a Malibu residence. Aware of his wife's infidelity, Mark rewrote his will to favor Stephen. Mark was murdered (May 24, 1952). His wife, remarried, is now Ruth Marburg. Archer's connecting Mark's murder with an unidentified man found beheaded and mangled four days later proves that Jasper Blevins, Ruth's son by Albert D. Blevins, killed Mark and Stephen and assumed Stephen's identity.

HACKETT, STEPHEN. In *The Instant Enemy*, he was the son of Mark Hackett and his wife, Ruth (*see* Marburg, Ruth). In Texas, Stephen had an affair with Laurel Dudney (*see* Smith, Mrs. Laurel) resulting in the birth of David (*see* Spanner, David). Having moved his family to Malibu, Mark learned of Ruth's infidelity and rewrote his will favoring Stephen. Ruth and Jasper Blevins, her son by Albert D. Blevins, Laurel's father-in-law, conspired to have Jasper murder Stephen at a ranch once owned by Ruth's parents. Jasper mangled Stephen's body and assumed his identity for the next fifteen years. Jasper and Lupe Rivera rape Alexandria Sebastian.

HAGEDORN, MAMIE. In *The Instant Enemy*, she is an ex-brothel madame in Rodeo City. Archer learns this from Mamie: Joseph L. Krug was nice; his wife, Alma R. Krug, is "a Bible-thumping sobersides"; Jack Fleischer kept Laurel Blevins (*see* Smith, Mrs. Laurel) as his girlfriend.

HAGGERTY, BERT. In *The Chill*, he is Helen Haggerty's ex-husband, in his forties. He met Helen in school in Bridgeton, Illinois. After an army hitch, he married Helen and they honeymooned on the G.I. Bill in Europe. He teaches journalism and English at Maple Park College and lives in Bridgeton with or near Helen's father, Earl Hoffman, who calls him a "pussy willow." Bert provides Archer with information.

HAGGERTY, DETECTIVE-SERGEANT. In *The Dark Tunnel*, he is an Arbana policeman. He disbelieves Robert Branch after Dr. Alec Judd's murder. Also doubting Branch's story, Helen Madden leads Haggerty to Branch outside Arbana. After Branch is cleared of suspicion, Haggerty drives Branch back to town.

HAGGERTY, HELEN. In *The Chill*, she had a crush on Luke Deloney in Bridgeton, Illinois, their hometown. She blamed her father, Earl Hoffman, when Luke died. She met Bert Haggerty in Bridgeton, when she was nineteen, and married him four or five years later. They honeymooned in Europe. Bert says she became promiscuous. Helen, in her forties, teaches French and German at Pacific Point College and evidently tried to blackmail Dean Roy Bradshaw there. While seeking Dolly Kincaid, Archer meets and is attracted to Helen. Solving her murder becomes part of his mission.

HAINES. In *The Doomsters*, Mildred Hallman names him as her boss in Purissima.

HAINES, ADELAIDE. In *The Ferguson Affair*, she is the articulate, demented mother of Henry Haines (*see* Gaines, Larry). Her second husband fell out a window; her third deserted her and their son. A former piano and voice teacher in Oakland and Sacramento, she lives in Mountain Grove. When William Gunnarson visits her, he senses "a darkness in her." She labels Hilda Dotery her Henry's "succubus." Adelaide has a cat she had "fixed" when he proved troublesome but now pets. After Henry's death, the police find his airline ticket to Rio de Janeiro in his mother's piano. She winds up in a mental asylum.

HAINES, HENRY ("HARRY"). In *The Ferguson Affair*. *See* Gaines, Larry.

HAINES, MRS. In *The Galton Case*, she is Gordon Sable's secretary. Her "feline" talk makes Archer think she "was looking for a successor" to a lost husband.

HALEY. In *The Zebra-Striped Hearse*, he works at the motel near Luna Bay with Vicky Simpson. Haley advised her to inform the police that her husband was missing.

HALFORD, GENE. In *Trouble Follows Me*, he is an opinionated war correspondent, forty and balding. Mary Thompson associates with him in Honolulu. Sam Drake takes an instinctive dislike to Halford, encounters him at the Burbank airport, and is wrongly suspicious of him.

HALLMAN, ALICIA. In *The Doomsters*, she was Senator Jeremiah Hallman's wife and the mother of Jerry Hallman and Carl Hallman. Alicia brought old Spanish land-grant money to her marriage. When she became depressed, Jeremiah dismissively said she was pampering herself. She took Mildred, Carl's wife, to Dr. J. Charles Grantland for an abortion. Mildred slugged Alicia; Grantland, with Thomas Rica's assistance, drowned Alicia and reported her death as suicide. To justify the abortion (and to give meaning to the title of this novel), Alicia quotes from "To an Unborn Pauper Child" by Thomas Hardy.

HALLMAN, CAPTAIN. In *The Ivory Grin*, he is a highway patrolman at the site of a burned Buick containing a body thought to be that of Charles A. Singleton, Jr., but really Maxfield Heiss's.

HALLMAN, CARL. In *The Doomsters*, he is a mental case. He married Mildred Gley (*see* Hallman, Mildred) in Berkeley, failed as a student, developed naive idealism, argued with his father, Senator Jeremiah Hallman, and mistakenly thought he caused the old man's death, as well as that of his mother, Alicia Hallman, earlier. At twenty-four, Carl escapes with Thomas Rica from the hospital, asks Archer to clear his name, hides in Mildred's home, emerges, is shot by Dr. J. Charles Grantland, but will recover.

HALLMAN, JERRY. (Real name: Jeremiah.) In *The Doomsters*, he is the son of Jeremiah and Alicia Hallman (both deceased), Zinnie Hallman's husband, and Martha Hallman's father. A failed attorney, thirty-four, and eager to control the Hallman estate, he commits his younger brother, Carl Hallman, to a mental institution. Jerry is outraged by Dr. J. Charles Grantland's attentions to Zinnie. Jerry is shot to death by Mildred, Carl's wife.

HALLMAN, MARTHA. In *The Doomsters*, she is the lovely daughter, three, of Jerry and Zinnie Hallman. Her nanny is Mrs. Hutchinson. Martha prefers Mildred Hallman, Jerry's sister-in-law.

HALLMAN, MILDRED ("MILLIE"). In *The Doomsters*, she is Mrs. Gley's daughter. Her father abandoned both when Mildred was seven. Mildred had Carl Hallman's baby aborted in Dr. J. Charles Grantland's office; slugged Carl's mother, Alicia, for insisting on the procedure; and married Carl and lived unhappily with him at the Hallman family ranch for two years. She drowned her father-in-law, Senator Jeremiah Hallman, in his bathtub. When Carl escapes from a mental institution, Mildred hides him in the home she shares with her mother. Mildred shoots Jerry and stabs Zinnie, tries twice to kill herself, and winds up making Archer, who is attracted to her, feel partly culpable.

Bibliography: Schopen.

HALLMAN, SENATOR JEREMIAH. In *The Doomsters*, he was a Pennsylvania German with "a lean rapacious face." He moved West, married wealthy Alicia, fathered Jerry Hallman and Carl Hallman, and became a state senator representing Purissima, where he had a ranch with extensive orange groves. Carl argued with him for grabbing land from Japanese-Americans interned during World War II and for abusing migrant Mexican workers. When Mildred Hallman, Carl's wife, killed the senator, Carl hallucinated that he had killed him.

HALLMAN, ZINNIE. In *The Doomsters*, Jerry Hallman met her, a divorcée, in a Los Angeles nightclub. They married. Two years later she gave birth to Martha, now three. Zinnie prefers Dr. J. Charles Grantland, plots to seize the Hallman wealth, is unaffected by Jerry's murder, and tries to seduce Archer to stop his investigation. She is stabbed to death at Grantland's place by Mildred, Jerry's brother Carl Hallman's wife.

HALLORAN. In *Trouble Follows Me*, he is a taxi driver who takes Sam Drake from San Diego to Tijuana. Drake gives him a note to deliver to Mary Thompson, which almost proves to be Drake's undoing.

HAMBERG, REX. In *The Galton Case. See* Lemberg, Roy.

HAMBLIN, MISS. In *The Barbarous Coast*, she is Clarence Bassett's secretary.

HAMMOND, JANE STARR. In *The Way Some People Die*, she edits radio scripts in a Hollywood office. Trim and attractive, she was in love with

Keith Dalling, who preferred Galley Lawrence. Archer seeks information from her.

HAMPSHIRE, JOYCE. In *Sleeping Beauty*, Tom Russo tells Archer she was his wife Laurel Russo's friend at a private school in Orange. Archer interviews her.

HAMPSHIRE, PATRICK. In *The Ferguson Affair*, his house was burglarized.

HANNA, JIM. In *The Zebra-Striped Hearse*, he works with Arnie Walters and helps him investigate activities at Colonel Mark Blackwell's Tahoe lodge.

HANSON, INSPECTOR RALPH. In *Blue City*, he is a city police officer on the take, who investigated Jerry D. Weather's murder inconclusively. Weather's son, John, helps him become honorable. Hanson rescues John from Dave Moffatt, another policeman. Weather goes with Hanson to Roger Kerch's office, where they find Kerch murdered.

HANSON, MRS. RALPH. In *Blue City*, she is the police inspector's whining wife.

HAPGOOD, CONNIE. In *Sleeping Beauty*, she is William Lennox's considerate live-in companion. She intended to marry him.

HARLAN. In "The Sinister Habit," he operated the Harlan School in Chicago. His children are J. Reginald Harlan and Maude Lister.

HARLAN, J. REGINALD ("REGGIE"). In "The Sinister Habit," he is Maude Lister's older brother, manages the Harlan School in Chicago, cannot get Maude away from her husband, Leonard Lister, and winds up shot dead.

HARLAN, MRS. In "The Sinister Habit," she is the mother of J. Reginald Harlan and Maude Lister. She divorced their father and married a drunk who died. She tells Archer she studies "spiritual auras."

HARLEY. In *The Far Side of the Dollar*, he is the irrationally religious father of Harold Harley and Mike Harley. He mistreated both. Old Harley, who has been in mental institutions in Pocatello, and his wife Martha live on their farm outside town. When Archer seeks information, he threatens Archer with a pitchfork.

HARLEY, CAROL. In *The Far Side of the Dollar*, she is the beautiful daughter, born about 1930, of Robert Brown and his wife. She was corrupted by and married Mike Harley, pursued an acting career in Hollywood in the early 1940s, and was forced to sleep with Ralph Hillman because he extricated Mike from deep trouble. She gave birth to Hillman's son, whom Hillman "adopted" and called Thomas Hillman. Carol resumed contact with Thomas, who lived briefly with her and with Mike. When Mike seeks to extort money from Hillman's wife, Elaine, she kills Carol and Mike. Carol's film name was Carol Cooper. Mike registers himself and Carol as "Mr. and Mrs. Rob[er]t Brown" at Dack's Auto Court.

HARLEY, HAROLD ("HAL"). In *The Far Side of the Dollar*, he is the son of old Harley and Martha Harley and is Mike Harley's younger brother. Harold was the Barcelona Hotel photographer and took a compromising picture of Ralph Hillman and Susanna Drew, which Otto Sipe used to blackmail Ralph's wife, Elaine. When Harold suggested by letter that Ralph could help Mike, the result was Mike's planning to kidnap Ralph's son, Thomas Hillman. Archer finds Harold and gains information from him enabling him to find Mike.

HARLEY, LILA. In *The Far Side of the Dollar*, she is Harold Harley's wife. When Archer finds Harold, Lila is away visiting her mother in Oxnard. She returns the next morning and, when Archer happens to look for Harold, is there and tells Archer that Mike is in Reno.

HARLEY, MARTHA. In *The Far Side of the Dollar*, she is the long-suffering wife, about seventy, of a demented Pocatello farmer. They have long since lost the love of their sons, Harold Harley and Mike Harley.

HARLEY, MIKE. In *The Far Side of the Dollar*, he is the sadistic son of old Harley and Martha Harley. Mike is Harold Harley's older brother and the sterile husband of the former Carol Brown (*see* Harley, Carol). Mike knew Ralph Hillman in the Navy. Mike's plan to cooperate with Otto Sipe, a Pocatello crony, and hold Thomas Hillman, the son of Ralph by Carol, results in Mike's extorting money from Ralph but gambling it away in Las Vegas. Elaine, who has already killed Carol, kills Mike. Mike registers himself and Carol as "Mr. and Mrs. Rob[er]t Brown" at Dack's Auto Court.

HARLOCK, DR. RICHARD. In *The Instant Enemy*, he signed the birth certificate of Henrietta R. Krug (*see* Marburg, Ruth) in Rodeo City.

HAROLD. In *The Underground Man*, he is a Sausalito detective working with Willie Mackey. He helps Mackey and Archer investigate Ellen Kilpatrick in Sausalito. Harold played for the Forty-Niners, the San Francisco football team.

HARRIS, LIEUTENANT. In "Find the Woman," he is Ensign Jack Rossiter's associate.

HARRIS, MRS. In "The Bearded Lady," she is Admiral Johnston Turner's housekeeper.

HARROW, SIDNEY. In *The Goodbye Look*, he is a San Diego bill collector. Randolph Shepherd gets him to work with Jean Trask to find her father. Harrow's efforts to do so get him murdered.

HARRY. In *The Ferguson Affair*, he is Adelaide Haines's cat. Although she pets and talks baby talk to him, she had him "fixed" because he was naughty.

HARRY. In *Sleeping Beauty*, Gloria Flaherty tells Lew Archer that Harry is her boyfriend, in the food business.

HARRY. In *The Wycherly Woman*, he is the Peninsula gas-station attendant who gives Archer information about the woman who phoned Robert Dorcaster and also about the man who followed her to the Siesta motel. The two are Phoebe Wycherly and Dr. Sherrill.

HARVEY, RHEA. In "Wild Goose Chase," she is Rod Harvey's distressed wife. When Rhea discovers his affair with Ruth Cave, she kills Ruth.

HARVEY, ROD. In "Wild Goose Chase," he is the defense attorney in Glenway Cave's trial on the charge of murdering Ruth Cave, his wife. Rhea Harvey, Rod's wife, discovered his affair with Ruth and killed her.

HASKELL, MRS. In *The Galton Case*, she was John Brown's Ann Arbor landlady. She gossips to Archer about Ada Reichler, Brown's girlfriend briefly.

HATCHEN, DR. KEITH. In *The Zebra-Striped Hearse*, he is a retired dentist. He met Pauline Blackwell (*see* Hatchen, Pauline) in Reno when both were getting divorces. They got married and moved to Ajijic, Mexico.

HATCHEN, PAULINE. In *The Zebra-Striped Hearse*, she is Colonel Mark Blackwell's ex-wife, Harriet Blackwell's mother, and Dr. Keith Hatchen's wife. She deserted Mark and Harriet, when the girl was eleven or twelve, because Mark fawned over Harriet and turned her against Pauline. When

Archer interviews Pauline, he finds her affected and imperious. Harriet appeals to Pauline for a show of affection; all she can offer is money, which she provides.

HATCHER, PRIVATE RODNEY. In *Trouble Follows Me*, he is a soldier returning from combat in Europe to go to the Pacific theater. When he boards the Los Angeles–bound train in Kansas City, he and Sam Drake talk and drink. Hatcher tells Drake that in 1937 he was in Nanking, where he saw Anderson, who is also on the train. Hatcher writes a letter to Laura Eaton. Anderson and Miss Green poison Hatcher's drink.

HAWKINS, MRS. In *The Instant Enemy*, she is employed in a Santa Teresa nursery school where Henry Langston, Jr., is placed.

HECKENDORF, COMMANDER JULIUS. In *Meet Me at the Morgue*, he was a naval officer serving on the *Eureka Bay*. Heckendorf praised Fred Miner.

HEFLER. In *Trouble Follows Me*, he is a Detroit FBI agent. He and Sam Drake share information about Hector Land and his wife, Bessie Land, who lives in Detroit. Hefler and Chester Gordon, another agent, also cooperate.

HEIDI. In *The Chill*, she is a Pacific Point College student Archer hears trying to explain something about Zeno's "infinite divisibility of space" to a perplexed male athlete and a fellow student.

HEISS, MAXFIELD ("MAX"). In *The Ivory Grin*, he was a Los Angeles private detective, forty to forty-five, lost his license, and still hustles. Calling himself Julian Desmond, he seeks reward money for finding Charles A. Singleton, Jr., who is missing. Archer knows and will not work with Max. Max gains information from Lucy Champion and Florida Gutierrez, but is murdered by Dr. Samuel Benning, dressed as Charles, and burned in Charles's Buick.

HELEN. In *The Drowning Pool*, she is a Quinto bar owner. She points out Gretchen Keck to Archer. Helen has "a rubber-lipped public smile."

HELEN. In *The Goodbye Look*, she works for Archer's answering service.

HELIOPOULOS, PETER ("HELIO"). In *The Barbarous Coast*, he was Isobel Graff's Greek-born father. After running a restaurant in Newark, New Jersey, he went to Hollywood. According to Dr. Frey, Heliopoulos, when widowed, "pushed her [Isobel] towards maturity, at the same time deprived her of true human contact." He refused to let her marry Clarence Bassett, who introduced her to Simon Graff, whom she married. Heliopoulos and Graff developed Helio-Graff, a moviemaking company. It has been suggested that Graff is based in part on movie-mogul Darryl Zanuck. If so, Heliopoulos may owe something to Spyros Panagiotes Skouras, the Greek-born Fox Film Corporation executive and producer often associated with Zanuck.

Bibliography: Nolan.

HENDRICKS, HARRY. In *Black Money*, Hendricks, thirty-eight, is hired by Kayo Ketchel and Kitty Ketchel to find Francis Martel. When Hendricks tries to photograph Martel, he is beaten up. Hendricks offers to split any fees with Archer, who pities but avoids him.

HENDRICKS, KITTY. In *Black Money*, she is Harry Hendricks's wife. Under thirty and gorgeous, she ignores her mother, Maria Sekjar, who lives nearby. Kitty consorts with Kayo Ketchel for the purpose of locating Francis Martel. Lew Archer finds her attractive but gets nothing but information from her.

HENDRYX, WALTER. In "The Bearded Lady," he is a dishonest millionaire who buys the stolen painting from Hilary Todd. Archer persuades Hendryx to return it for the purchase price.

HENRY. In *Blue City*, he is a fat bartender in a saloon where John Weather, by breaking up a fight, saves McGinis from Swainie and another thug.

HENRY. In *The Drowning Pool*, he and his wife own the Motel del Mar in Quinto. Archer gets a room there. Henry wants to sell the place; his domineering wife does not.

HERMAN, SHERIFF. In *The Wycherly Woman*, he is an official whose face resembles "carved redwood burl." Herman notifies Carl Trevor that Phoebe Wycherly's Volkswagen has been found under water. When Trevor identifies the corpse found inside and collapses, Herman takes Trevor to the hospital.

HESPELER, JOE. In *The Goodbye Look*, he writes his name on a wall in the Pacific Point police building to indicate he was there.

HILDRETH, CASSIE. In *The Galton Case*, she is Maria Galton's distant cousin. Now about thirty-seven, Cassie was sent to an Eastern school by Maria, was in love with Maria's son, Anthony Galton, and began to be

Maria's paid companion after Anthony disappeared twenty years ago. Cassie encourages Archer to find Anthony or at least his son. When John Brown (Jr.) appears and is reputedly that son, Cassie becomes enamored of him.

HILLMAN. In *The Far Side of the Dollar*, he was Ralph Hillman's father, an unsuccessful South Boston store owner.

HILLMAN, ELAINE ("ELLIE"). In *The Far Side of the Dollar*, she is the daughter of a Victorian-style, moneyed Boston family. A Radcliffe graduate, Elaine, thin, attractive, in her forties, is Ralph Hillman's undersexed wife. He used her money to establish a successful Pacific Point business. The two adopt Carol Harley's son (by Ralph), call him Thomas Hillman, and rear him as their own. Elaine kills Carol and her husband, Mike Harley, and—when the truth comes out—commits suicide with steel knitting needles.

HILLMAN, RALPH. In *The Far Side of the Dollar*, he is an M.I.T. graduate in engineering and Elaine Hillman's husband. During World War II, Hillman was a Navy combat pilot in the Pacific Theater of Operations. His jeep carrier was kamikazed and taken to Boston for repairs (early 1945). His terminal rank was captain. Hillman used his wife's money to establish Technological Enterprises, a successful firm. He was a philanderer with Carol Harley and Susanna Drew. He adopted his son by Carol and called him Thomas Hillman. The two argued, which generated the fake kidnapping of Thomas. This leads to Archer's being hired.

HILLMAN, THOMAS ("TOM," "TOMMY"). In *The Far Side of the Dollar*, he is the natural son of Ralph Hillman and Carol Harley, born December 12, 1945. Hillman adopted Tom and with his wife, Elaine, raises the boy as his own. The Hillmans dislike Tom's ambition to be a jazz pianist. When Carol gets in touch with Tom, seventeen, he makes trouble and Hillman commits him to the Laguna Perdida School. Tom escapes, finds Carol, and gets involved with her and her husband, Mike Harley. Mike extorts money from Hillman. Tom runs away and meets up with his girlfriend, Stella Carlson. Archer, hired by Hillman to locate Tom, finds both young people and persuades them to let him return them to their families. When Tom visits Susanna Drew, he calls himself Jackman. Sam Jackman is Tom's musician friend.

HIRSCHMAN. In *Blue City*, he heard news over the radio of Floraine Weather's murder.

HOFFMAN, EARL. In *The Chill*, he has been a married detective, for thirty-four years, in Bridgeton, Illinois. As a naval warrant officer, he served in San Diego and lived there with his wife and their daughter, Helen (*see* Haggerty, Helen). Helen blamed him for covering up Luke Deloney's 1940 murder. Hoffman's conscience has forced him into alcoholism. Archer's interviewing him so stirs his memories that he goes to the sight of Luke's murder, tries to arrest innocent people there, and is taken into custody.

HOFFMAN, MRS. EARL. In *The Chill*, she is the policeman's wife and Helen Haggerty's mother. When Helen is murdered, Mrs. Hoffman flies to Pacific Point to make the necessary arrangements. Archer meets her at the Los Angeles airport and gains information from her. When Mrs. Luke Deloney puts her up at the Surf House, Archer sees both women again.

HOLLY. In *The Ivory Grin*, she is a relative of Aunty Jones and cooks for her.

HOLLY MAY. In *The Ferguson Affair*. *See* Ferguson, June.

HOLMAN. In *The Blue Hammer*, she is Mrs. Holman's daughter, who cries when Archer questions her mother.

HOLMAN, MRS. In *The Blue Hammer*, she is a black nurse in La Paloma, a Santa Teresa convalescent home. Archer questions her about Betty Jo Siddon. Mrs. Holman tells him Mildred Mead and Sarah Johnson are related.

HOOPER, ALLAN. In "Sleeping Dog," he is Fay Hooper's wealthy husband, in his sixties. In 1945 he learned of her intimacy with George Rambeau and would have killed him, but Carlson (*see* Carlson, Sheriff) shot him first. When Otto, Fay's dog, is shot twenty years later, Allan buries him.

HOOPER, FAY. In "Sleeping Dog," she is Allan Hooper's wife, in her late thirties. In 1945 she fell in love with George Rambeau during a Canadian hunting trip. Twenty years later, Rambeau's brother, Fernando Rambeau, shoots Otto, Fay's dog. Fay says that for twenty years she has intended to divorce Allan.

HOOPER, SHERIFF. In *The Wycherly Woman*, he is an official who, according to Homer Wycherly, recommended Archer to him.

HOPE, DONNIE. In *Trouble Follows Me*, he and Alvin S. detained Private Rodney Hatcher in a Kansas City bar, as mentioned in the letter Hatcher wrote Laura Eaton.

HOPPE, WILLIE (1887–1959). William Frederick Hoppe was an American champion billiard player. In *Blue City*, Jerry D. Weather once played Hoppe in the old Weather House.

HOWELL, DR. AUGUST. In *The Galton Case*, he is Maria Galton's physician, in his fifties. His daughter is Sheila Howell. He and Maria's attorney, Gordon Sable, do not see eye to eye.

HOWELL, SHEILA. In *The Galton Case*, she is Dr. August Howell's sexy daughter, eighteen. Sheila doesn't like Maria Galton but hopes Archer can find her son, Anthony Galton. When Anthony's son, John Brown (Jr.) appears, Sheila falls in love with him, accompanies him to Canada, meets his mother, offers her genuine affection, and will undoubtedly marry John. Sheila resembles Linda Millar,* Macdonald's daughter.

Bibliography: Schopen.

HUMPHREYS. In *The Moving Target*, he is Santa Teresa's reliable D.A. He was a prosecutor when Albert Graves was the D.A. Humphreys enters the case of the missing Ralph Sampson when the kidnap note is received.

HUNT, RUSSELL. In *The Moving Target*, Hunt, formerly a Chicago reporter, is a movie writer. His agent is Timothy. When Archer follows Fay Estabrook to Swift's bar, he encounters his friend Hunt. This enables him to meet Fay.

HUNTER ("HUNT"). In *The Dark Tunnel*, he is a faculty member of Midwestern University's War Board. He speaks fifteen languages and hates Nazis. When Hunter questions the evidence Robert Branch offers concerning Dr. Alec Judd's murder, Branch tells him to go to hell.

HUTCHINSON. In *The Doomsters*, his wife or ex-wife, Mrs. Hutchinson, says he "wouldn't wait" while she wanted to train to become a nurse.

HUTCHINSON, MRS. In *The Doomsters*, she is employed by Jerry and Zinnie Hallman to care for their daughter, Martha. Mrs. Hutchinson, married about forty years, treats the lovely child coldly, calls her a "minx," but perceptively has the Hallman family in mind when she recites this from the Bible: "The fathers have eaten sour grapes, and the children's teeth are set on edge."

Bibliography: Schopen.

I

ILLMAN, EDWARD ("TEDDY"). In "The Suicide," he is Ethel Larrabee's rich ex-husband. Illman's companion is Frieda.

"THE IMAGINARY BLONDE." *See* "Gone Girl."

"THE IMPOSTER." *See The Galton Case.*

INDIAN SONEY. In "The Sky Hook," he was Frederick's trapper during his gold-rush days.

INNES, DR. IAN. In *The Blue Hammer*, he is a guest at Francine Chantry's cocktail party. He chomps on a cigar and checks out Archer with "surgical eyes" for symptoms.

INNES, MRS. IAN. In *The Blue Hammer*, she is a pale, tense, fluttering guest at Francine Chantry's party.

***THE INSTANT ENEMY* (1968).** Novel. (Characters: Lew Archer, Aubrey, Captain Robert Aubrey, Jacob Belsize, Arnold Bendix, Albert D. Blevins, Jasper Blevins, Dr. Converse, Fred Cram, Ralph Cuddy, Elaine, Jack Fleischer, Mrs. Jack Fleischer, Gensler, Heidi Gensler, Gerda Hackett, Mark Hackett, Stephen Hackett, Mamie Hagedorn, Dr. Richard Harlock, Mrs. Hawkins, Detective-Sergeant Janowski, Dr. Jeffrey, Alma R. Krug, Joseph L. Krug, Henry Langston, Henry Langston, Jr., Kate Langston, Bob Levine, Lippert, Mrs. Lippert, Willie Mackey, Ruth Marburg, Sidney Marburg, Paterson, Deputy Rory Pennell, Detective-Sergeant Prince, Lupe Rivera, Alex Santee, Alexandria Sebastian, Bernice Sebastian, Keith Sebas-

tian, Mrs. Sherrill, Al Simmons, Mrs. Laurel Smith, David Spanner, Edward
Spanner, Martha Spanner, Dr. Sunderland, Thorndike, Tom.)

One Thursday morning in early December 1957, Archer drives to the
Woodland Hills home of Keith Sebastian and Bernice Sebastian. They hire
him to find their missing daughter, Alexandria ("Sandy") Sebastian, seventeen. Sebastian, who works in a Los Angeles savings and loan office,
hopes his boss, Stephen Hackett, with whom Sandy went hunting earlier,
won't hear about this. Two nights ago Keith found Sandy with her boyfriend, David Spanner, nineteen, at a West Hollywood joint, threatened
to shoot him, and dragged Sandy home. Taking her father's shotgun and
shells the next morning, Sandy left in her green Dart but not for high
school. Archer accepts a $250 retainer from Bernice, who says she read
Sandy's diary and destroyed it, and lets him check Sandy's room. He finds
a threatening poem—by David?—and gets a description of Davy from
Sebastian, who rushes off to work. Archer speaks to Sandy's best friend,
Heidi Gensler, a neighbor. Heidi tells him Sandy was suicidal last summer
but is happy now. Heidi provides Davy's address.

Archer drives to the Laurel Apartments, where Mrs. Laurel Smith, the
owner, has given Davy an apartment and a pool-maintenance job. She
takes him to Davy. Sandy, frightened, is there too. When Archer alerts
Davy to his problem, Davy slugs him. Recovering in his car, Archer sees
a man across the street with a disk of recording tape. Sandy drives Davy
away; Archer follows toward Malibu, loses them, and returns to Laurel.
While praising Davy, she lets Archer search his place, where he finds self-
help books, a map of a place probably being cased, and pieces left when
a shotgun was sawed off.

Laurel says Jacob Belsize is Davy's probation officer. Archer knows him.
Over lunch, Belsize tells Archer this: Davy, an orphan, was adopted by
Edward Spanner and his wife, of Los Angeles; Davy stole cars, for "grief
riding," as he puts it; during six months in jail Davy got his high school
degree and read extensively; still a hothead, he wants to find his natural
parents; at about the time Davy was freed, a mean-spirited Santa Teresa
policeman named Jack Fleischer questioned Belsize about Laurel but
learned nothing.

Archer goes to Sebastian's office and finds him obsequious before Stephen Hackett. Once Hackett leaves, Sebastian tells Archer that Hackett
inherited oil money, which he has multiplied. Archer provides details
about Sandy and Davy, and shows Sebastian the map, which Sebastian
identifies as Hackett's art-filled Malibu estate. Because it may be the target
for a crime, Sebastian dispatches Archer to warn Hackett. Archer drives
to the place, is let in by a guard named Lupe Rivera, and meets Hackett's
wife, Gerda Hackett, a nervous, oppressed German. He is talking frankly
with her when Hackett drives up with his domineering, remarried
mother, Ruth Marburg. Archer warns the edgy threesome but peeves

them by neither accepting money nor overly praising the boastful Hackett's art collection.

On his way to the city, Archer stops to see Laurel but finds her beaten and unconscious. He phones for the police and an ambulance, looks through Laurel's belongings, and finds the names of Jacob Belsize and Mr. and Mrs. Edward Spanner and a Social Security card in the name of Laurel Blevins. When the authorities arrive, Archer goes to the house where he saw the man with the tape. A neighbor tells him the fellow rented the place from an agent named Alex Santee, remained two weeks with electronic equipment, and decamped an hour ago. Archer looks up Santee, from whom he learns that Fleischer rented the house on November 15. Archer calls Spanner to say that he is coming over and at sunset meets him and his wife, Martha. While they gently argue with each another—he is critical of Davy; she, forgiving—Archer learns this: The Spanners informally adopted Davy, six, from a Santa Teresa orphanage; chronically troubled, Davy was expelled from high school for slugging Henry Langston, his counselor; the Spanners then moved to Los Angeles; Edward, an ex-lay preacher, is a barber; an hour ago Davy and Sandy drove by, announcing plans to marry and joking about visiting "Daddy Warbucks" tonight, since Lupe will let Sandy in. Archer phones the Hacketts to warn them. Too late. Ruth Marburg answers and orders Archer to come immediately.

Archer arrives and is greeted by Sidney Marburg, Ruth's husband, a painter younger than Hackett. Sidney tells Archer "a chick and a boy with a shotgun" drove in, the chick cracked Lupe's skull with a tire iron, and the two marched in and kidnapped Hackett. Ruth says Gerda has "gone to pieces" upstairs and offers Archer $100,000 to find her son. Archer says he is working only for Sebastian but provides Ruth pertinent details and agrees to cooperate. Ruth wants no police interference. She phones Sebastian, pooh-poohs Archer when he says Davy's past may explain his behavior, and when Sebastian arrives tells him his "precious daughter has stolen" her son.

Sebastian confides in Archer: Sandy phoned from Santa Teresa's Power Plus gas station asking to be rescued, but the line suddenly went dead. While Sebastian drives Archer's car, Archer naps. The station attendant says Sandy stopped for gas, started to use his phone, but was hauled back to her Dart by a "big fellow." Sounds came from its trunk. Sebastian and Archer take motel rooms. Sebastian reassures his wife by phone. Archer phones Langston's house. The babysitter says he and his wife are out until midnight. Archer finds Fleischer's house. His drunk wife lets him in, offers him gin, tells him this: Fleischer lives half the time in Los Angeles; for years he has been chasing Laurel Smith; he recently took $1,000 from their savings for a get-rich-quick scheme; he is at Palo Alto's

Sandman Motel. While Mrs. Fleischer angrily breaks some dishes in the kitchen, Archer quietly departs.

Archer drives to Langston's home. His wife, worried and pregnant, has him wait until Langston returns after dropping off their babysitter. When Langston arrives, he says he investigated and learned that Davy's father was beheaded in a train accident near Rodeo City; Davy, three, sat beside him, traumatized, until Fleischer came to investigate. When Langston told Davy this in high school, Davy hit him and was expelled. Davy and Sandy came to Langston at 8:00 this evening and asked the Langstons to care for Sandy because Davy "had a job to do." Langston refused. Archer gets Langston to show him where the railroad accident occurred, near Rodeo City, outside Santa Teresa. Archer and Langston drive fifty miles north. On the way, they suddenly spot Sandy, dazed and sullen, in the road. She says Davy laid Hackett across some tracks, she escaped, and Davy took Hackett away and must have gone to a mountain house he mentioned. Finding nothing along the tracks, Archer drives Sandy and Langston back to Sebastian, at his motel. Archer calls a San Francisco detective named Willie Mackey and asks him to tail Fleischer in and out of Palo Alto's Sandman; drives Sebastian, Sandy, and Langston to Langston's home; drops Langston off; takes Sebastian and Sandy to Sebastian's car, at Malibu; and tells Sebastian to get Sandy a criminal lawyer. Past 4:00 A.M., Archer finds the nearest motel.

Friday. After breakfast, Archer drives to the Hackett mansion. Dr. Converse, summoned to tend to Lupe, who won't talk, tells Archer this: Ruth's first husband, Mark Hackett, was shot to death on the Malibu beach; Converse treated Sandy last summer but won't say for what. After Archer reports events to Ruth, she disagrees with his theory that Mark's murder and Hackett's being kidnapped are connected, permits him to cooperate with the police, and pays him a $1,000 retainer. Sidney, Ruth's husband, nonchalantly continues painting. Policemen arrive. Archer confides much in Captain Robert Aubrey but says nothing about Fleischer. Aubrey says Laurel has died.

At his office, Archer hears from Mackey that Fleischer visited a man named Albert D. Blevins in a seedy San Francisco hotel. Archer connects the name Blevins with Laurel's Social Security card. He flies to San Francisco, meets Mackey at 1:00 P.M., and learns that Mackey's associate tailed Fleischer to a photocopy shop. Archer finds out there that Fleisher copied an old newspaper clipping and the birth certificate of someone named Jasper. Archer goes to Blevins's hotel and learns this from the old fellow, now on welfare: Blevins, when twenty, married Henrietta R. Krug, seventeen, the daughter of Joseph L. Krug, an oil-company watchman, and Alma R. Krug, in San Francisco, March 3, 1927; later that year, Blevins delivered their baby, Jasper Blevins; Henrietta was injured during his birth; Henrietta and Blevins argued; their ranch house in Santa Teresa

County, given to them by the Krugs, partly burned; Henrietta deserted her husband and son; Blevins repaired the house minimally, tried to tame wild little Jasper, let Joseph and Alma Krug raise him; Jasper married Laurel Dudney, May 1948; their son, David Blevins, was born in Santa Monica, December 12, 1948, according to a letter Alma wrote to Blevins, dated December 14; Fleischer bought not only a clipping about Jasper's wedding, which Alma sent Albert, but also Jasper's birth certificate. Archer gives Albert $60 for his marriage certificate and Alma's letter.

Mackey tells Archer that Fleischer checked out and headed south. In Fleischer's motel room is a newspaper discussing the wealthy Hackett's disappearance. Archer flies back to Los Angeles, drives to the Sebastians, and helps them prevent Sandy's being jailed for assaulting Lupe. Archer asks Sandy's physician, Dr. Jeffrey, who is there, to check with Converse about Sandy. Sandy's mother rubs against Archer provocatively, will not say what she read in Sandy's diary, but lets him talk to Sandy. She says Davy wanted to find a partly burned mountain house where Laurel Smith, who told Davy she was his mother, left him and his father.

Archer tries to phone Blevins, but he is unavailable. Archer goes to the Krugs' old Santa Monica apartment address, locates Ralph Cuddy, the manager, who directs him to Mrs. Krug, in a nearby convalescent home. He finds the alert woman in a wheelchair and tells her he saw Blevins today and has met Davy, now nineteen. Mrs. Krug reveals that a wealthy Texan sent Laurel to California, then gives Archer directions to the "Krug ranch," near Rodeo City. As he is leaving, Archer sees Fleischer enter. Refused permission to see Mrs. Krug and rebuked by Archer, Fleischer pulls a gun. Archer disarms him. They talk outside. Archer reluctantly agrees to share information with him. They drive toward Rodeo City in Fleischer's car. Suddenly Fleischer slugs Archer, takes his revolver, leaves him on the road, and heads for the ranch. A trucker takes Archer to his car. He calls Langston and asks him to bring his car, a flashlight, and a gun.

They drive in rain past Rodeo City to Centerville and get information from a lunch-counter owner named Al Simmons. He says Fleischer kept a girlfriend at Mamie Hagedorn's local brothel and warns them that a flooded river may block their approach to the ranch. Wading across, Archer finds Hackett sprawled on the far shore. Hackett says Davy killed Fleischer with a shotgun, beat up Hackett, and drove away. Archer finds Fleischer's corpse, takes his car keys and the photocopies he made in San Francisco, and drives Hackett to Langston's car. They return to Centerville and wake up Simmons. Archer phones Deputy Rory Pennell in Rodeo City about Fleischer and gets an ambulance to take Hackett to his mother, whom Archer also phones. Simmons volunteers the gossip that fifteen years ago Fleischer and Laurel Blevins were lovers, often meeting while her husband, Jasper, was off hunting and painting. Riding in the ambulance, Archer learns this from Hackett: Sandy conked Lupe on the head; Davy put Hackett on some railroad tracks momentarily; Sandy escaped; Davy took Hackett to the ranch, smoked marijuana, called Hackett "Dad"; when Fleischer entered, Davy killed him and battered Hackett.

Saturday, shortly after 6:00 A.M., Ruth greets Hackett while Gerda hangs back. Ruth gives Archer a postdated check for $100,000. He feels unelated. Thorndike, an FBI agent on the scene, superciliously debriefs him and confers with Aubrey and Converse. Alone in Hackett's study, Archer checks the photocopies. Henrietta was born in Rodeo City, October 17, 1910. Mark Hackett was shot May 24, 1952; the unidentified railroad-track victim died May 28, 1952. Archer queries Aubrey, who says he investigated Mark's death. The murder weapon was found to be from his oil company's Long Beach office, reported missing earlier. When Archer says a man died on the railroad tracks four days after Mark's murder, Aubrey calls it a coincidence and isn't bothered when Archer names the second dead man as Jasper Blevins, Davy Spanner's father. Archer chats with Gerda. She suddenly kisses him passionately, laments that Ruth successfully competes for Hackett's love, and says she tutored Sandy in German. Gerda lets Archer search Lupe's living quarters over the garage, where he finds LSD cubes, samples of which he takes. Sidney appears and while driving Archer to Woodland Hills to his car offers this information: Sidney, a geological draftsman, worked for Mark at his Corpus Christi Oil Company; Ruth planned to divorce Mark and marry Sidney; Mark altered his will to favor Stephen; Ruth and Sidney had solid alibis when Mark was shot, at which time Stephen was studying economics in London; Ruth financed Sidney's study of painting in Mexico; he became adept; Ruth and Lupe may be lovers.

After breakfast, Archer drives to Heidi Gensler's house, is rebuffed by her father, and proceeds to the Sebastian home. Jeffrey is there. Sandy slashed her wrists, and he is sending her to a psychiatric hospital despite her father's cost-conscious objections. When Archer tells Jeffrey he found Lupe's LSD cubes, Jeffrey gets Sandy to reveal that Lupe "blew my mind" with LSD last August and that Gerda took her to Converse.

On to Long Beach and Hackett's oil-company building, where Archer is surprised to encounter Cuddy, the manager of Mrs. Krug's former apartment. Cuddy has been a security officer for Hackett for sixteen years. He tells Archer he knew and almost married Laurel Dudney before Jasper got her pregnant and married her. When Archer tries to question Cuddy about Sidney and the missing company revolver used to murder Mark, Cuddy pulls his gun and forces Archer to leave. Back at his office, Archer naps until the cops Prince and Janowski, irate at lack of cooperation, arrive. Archer pleases them by agreeing to go interview Fleischer's widow, who has clammed up.

In Santa Teresa Archer finds Mrs. Fleischer drunk and rambling thus:

Davy's parents were Jasper and Laurel; Fleischer killed Jasper; Laurel said the body was not Jasper's; Fleisher and Laurel dumped Davy in an orphanage to continue their love affair unabated; Pennell phoned Mrs. Fleischer that a fifty-man posse is hunting Davy in the north county and will shoot to kill; Mrs. Fleischer will sell her husband's taped recordings of Laurel but wants more than Archer's offered $1,000. Urging her to wait a bit, Archer phones Langston's wife, who says Langston has joined the posse. Archer drives to Rodeo City and visits Pennell, who doubts Archer's suspicion that Fleischer killed Jasper and forces Archer out with a gun. Archer locates Mamie Hagedorn and tells the old biddy that Simmons mentioned her. Only after Mamie phones the L.A.P.D. to confirm Laurel's death—she knows Fleischer is dead—does she reveal the following, which Laurel told her: Krug worked in Los Angeles for a rich man who married Krug's daughter, Henrietta; their son was Jasper; Laurel got pregnant by a rich Texan who gave her money to get to California; Laurel bribed Jasper to marry her and pretend he was her son Davy's father; Laurel killed Jasper with ax blows to the head; Jasper was unspeakably perverted; Fleischer, Laurel's "normal meat-and-potatoes" lover, put Jasper's unidentified body on the railroad tracks to cover up the crime; Laurel abandoned Davy, who would have been "evidence against her."

Archer drives to the Krug ranch, sees Langston there waving his pistol and Davy's shotgun, which he found in the receding river. They return in two cars to Centerville. Langston tries to phone home but gets no answer. When Simmons says the radio reported that Davy hitched a ride with a trucker to Santa Teresa, Langston speeds off. Archer follows, gets to the Langston home, and sees Mrs. Langston rush out bleeding. When Davy follows, Langston shoots and kills him. The cops come and congratulate Langston, who goes into shock.

On his way to Los Angeles, Archer stops to see Mrs. Fleischer. When he offers her $2,000 for the tapes, she boasts that she is selling them for $10,000—to a handsome man Archer figures is Sebastian—and is leaving town. Archer proceeds to Bernice Sebastian, who reports this: Sebastian plans to embezzle big money, is removing Sandy from psychiatric treatment; they will head for South America to avoid extradition; Sandy's diary revealed that last August she got bad LSD from Lupe, which made her sick, and that Lupe and another man abused her sexually.

Back in his office Archer gets a phone message from Cuddy, who says Mrs. Krug wants to see Archer again. She reveals the following: Stephen is Davy's father; Mark dispatched Stephen to Europe and bought Jasper's silence with $5,000; Jasper married Laurel, soon wanted more money; Jasper might have stolen the gun, which was under Krug's care in the oil-company office; Mark's murder troubled Krug's conscience and shortened his life; Mrs. Krug's daughter, Henrietta Ruth Krug, nicknamed "Etta," first married Albert Blevins, then Lupe Rivera (whom she divorced when he was jailed for smuggling), next Mark, and finally Sidney Marburg.

Driving toward Malibu, Archer spots Sebastian and follows his car to a beach house, where he boasts that he has money enough for himself and Sandy to live abroad. Sandy bolts into the ocean, trying to drown herself. Archer, with another man's help, rescues her and gets Sebastian to call Aubrey. Sebastian says he bought the tapes as part of a secret deal. When Sandy hears this, she blurts the following: Hackett is no doubt the mystery buyer; Lupe and Hackett raped her in this very beach house; she wrote about it in her diary, knowing her mother would read it and hoping her parents would comfort her; they did nothing; Davy, his motives confused, conceived of the kidnap idea; Laurel told Davy about his father. Sebastian says this: He doesn't want the $100,000 check Hackett gave him; he left Fleischer's recorder and tapes with Ruth Marburg; he will return Sandy to the psychiatrists.

Archer gets Aubrey to wait outside while he quizzes Ruth and her son, Stephen. Archer finds the pair in the mansion library playing the tapes. When Archer calls Ruth "Etta," she fumbles for a revolver, which Archer seizes. On the tapes, Laurel's voice tells Davy to call her "Mother," and Davy's voice wonders who killed his father. Against his mother's wishes, Stephen tells Archer this: Jasper, Stephen's half-brother, killed Mark over money; Stephen flew home from London to track the killer; he found Jasper and Laurel at the ranch; Jasper approached Stephen with an axe; Stephen seized and brained him with it; Davy, three, saw everything and was traumatized; Laurel planned the railroad-accident cover-up; last night, at the Krug ranch, Davy tortured Stephen, who admitted he was Davy's natural father; Davy released him. At this point, Ruth offers a million-dollar bribe to silence Archer. Instead, Archer plays more of the tape: Laurel's voice tells Davy the train ran over Stephen, his father; Davy leaves; entering, Stephen's voice says Fleischer just phoned; the voice asks who Davy is; when Laurel answers, "Don't you remember, Jasper?" blows follow and Laurel is silenced, forever.

So—for fifteen years Jasper pretended he was Stephen, to inherit from Mark and share with Ruth, whose affair with Sidney was known to Mark. Having presented that scenario, Archer adds that Jasper, as Stephen, went to Europe for a safe, bigamous marriage, and bribed Laurel; she got lonely and sought her son, which alerted Fleischer, who bugged Laurel's place. Jasper confesses that yesterday at the ranch he grabbed for Davy's gun, Davy got away, and Jasper shot Fleischer. Jasper suddenly trots toward Archer, and Archer shoots him in the leg. Alerted by the sound, Aubrey rushes in and arrests Jasper and his mother. Back at the office window, Archer makes confetti of his $100,000 check and lets it fall on sinners and "foolish virgins" alike.

The title *The Instant Enemy* is clarified when Davy Spanner proclaims himself such a person against his wrongdoers. Moreover, Archer is immediately inimical to those who through greed corrupt whole families. The novel was issued in England (London: Collins, 1969) and became a popular paperback (Bantam, from 1969; Fontana/Collins, from 1970). It was reviewed favorably and sold 10,000 copies fast. In 1976 Macdonald drafted a screenplay based on *The Instant Enemy* for a minor producer and in 1978 reworked it—to no avail. When Gerda shows Archer a Paul Klee maze painting, he muses that "[t]he man was in the maze; the maze was in the man." It has been suggested that mysteries are in the mind of Archer, whose outer world and Macdonald's amaze.

Bibliography: Nolan; Speir.

IRENE. In *The Way Some People Die*, she is Danny Dowser's albino-like girlfriend. He mistreats her, not least when she catches him cheating at canasta. Dowser calls her 'Rene.

Bibliography: Speir.

THE IVORY GRIN **(1952).** Novel. (Characters: Lew Archer, Dr. Samuel Benning, Mrs. Samuel Benning, Lieutenant Brake, Camberwell, Colonel Isaac Carlyle, Maria Valdes Carlyle, Carson, Lucy Champion, Cooley, Dewey, Donald, Leo Durano, Una Durano, Ethel, Garbold, Mrs. Denise Grinker, Florida Gutierrez, Captain Hallman, Maxfield Heiss, Holly, Aunty Jones, Captain Kennedy, Martinez, Elias McBratney, Norris, Alex Norris, Annie Norris, Pearce, Peppermill, Saddler, Santana, Schwartz, Mrs. Simpson, Charles A. Singleton, Jr., Major Charles A. Singleton, Mrs. Charles A. Singleton, Jame Spinoza, Jr., Paul Theuriet, Toby, Tom, Sylvia Treen, Sergeant Trencher, Van, Horace Wilding.)

Saturday morning. Una Durano (calling herself Una Larkin), in a leopard-skin coat, hires Archer to find a black woman named Lucy Champion in Bella City, east of Los Angeles. She says Lucy worked for her until she disappeared on September lst two weeks ago, describes her, and says she will be near Tom's store. Archer is to call about Lucy's actions and whereabouts but is not to confront her. Una will be in the Bella City's Mission Hotel. Archer drives there, spots Lucy, and follows her to a black section of town. He sees Lucy flirting with Alex Norris, a young black washing his car. While interviewing her next-door neighbor on a false pretext, Archer eavesdrops on an argument: Alex's mother evicted Lucy for entertaining a man in her room. Lucy taxis to the Mountainview Motel for a room. Archer gets an adjoining room and telephones Una, who soon arrives. Una cannot persuade Lucy to tell where a certain woman is, even though Una slaps her; it seems Una's brother needs to know. When Lucy goes to Dr. Samuel Benning's office, Archer follows, sees Benning's beautiful, black-haired wife (Elizabeth), and overhears him tell his receptionist

(Florida Gutierrrez) he cannot reason with Lucy. Archer follows Florie to the railroad station but is interrupted when Maxfield ("Max") Heiss, an alcoholic private detective he knows, approaches, says he too was hired but then fired by Una, and offers to share $5,000 for information. Alex drives by and picks up Lucy.

Archer grabs a bite, returns to the motel at 5:00 P.M., sees Lucy's key in her room door, enters, and finds her throat-slashed corpse and her face made up in white powder. He goes through her baggage and finds a letter from her mother urging her to return to Detroit, and also a newspaper clipping about a $5,000 reward offered by rich Mrs. Charles A. Singleton of Arroyo Beach for information about her son, Charles A. Singleton, Jr., missing for a week. Archer sees Alex, tells him about Lucy, phones the police, gets Alex to admit Lucy was trying to "pass" for white, and tells about Una Larkin to Lieutenant Brake when he arrives. Alex, though guarded by Sergeant Trencher, runs to his car and escapes.

At her Bella City hotel, Archer confronts Una, tells her he heard her argue with Lucy, says Lucy is dead, and returns Una's $100 retainer. Una's alibi is that she was phoning long distance at 5:00 P.M. While Archer is downstairs checking phone records—the call, just after 5:00, was to Garbold (William Garibaldi) in Ypsilanti—Una drives off.

When Archer goes outside, he happens to see Benning's receptionist, follows her to Tom's Café, and sees Max enter. Archer eavesdrops while Max sweet-talks the woman he calls Florie. Benning's wife enters and drags Florie out. Archer gets nowhere when he asks Max about Singleton, the man from Arroyo Beach; he does, however, shock Max with news of Lucy's death. Archer breaks into Benning's office, notes that Lucy Champion is not recorded as a patient, and sees in a closet a hanging, wired, tagged anatomical skeleton. Suddenly Mrs. Benning confronts him with a gun. When she almost faints at news of Lucy, Archer leaves.

Archer drives thirty miles west to coastal Arroyo Beach, finds the Singleton address in the telephone book, and goes there. A young lady, Sylvia Treen, admits him. He asks imperious old Mrs. Charles A. Singleton, missing Charles's mother, about a possible connection between Charles and Lucy, recently arrived and now murdered. She fancies Archer is like Max, who, she says, wanted her posted reward to find Charles. Sylvia sits with Archer in his car and confides in him. Her father and Charles's knew each other at Harvard. She fell in love with Charles, an Air Force pilot, after the war. She hired on as his mother's companion simply to be nearby. But Charles, who wants to escape his mother and her money and also to become a poet, has a tall, blonde girlfriend who has been with him in his mountain cabin on the Sky Route. Sylvia lends him a photograph of Charles and gives him a turban Lucy dropped when she approached the Singleton home but panicked and ran off.

At the Arroyo Beach bar, Archer asks the bartender and then a parking lot attendant named Dewey about Charles and the blonde. Dewey indicates that some time ago a dark-skinned woman drove away with a blonde, and a woman with a leopard-skin coat (i.e., Una) questioned him angrily about the pair. Archer finds the address of Denise Grinker, queries the beer-drinking hat maker, and learns that Una Durano in March bought the turban Lucy dropped and that Una has rented the Peppermill estate. Archer drives there, past midnight, peaks in a window, and sees Una and a white-coated orderly interrupt a card game to let a raving man they call Durano pretend to shoot them and then return to a barred upstairs room.

Sunday morning. Archer drives to the Sky Route, finds Horace Wilding, Charles's artist friend, and accompanies him to Charles's log cabin, now sealed by the police. Wilding tells Archer that Charles would never marry Sylvia Treen since for seven or eight years now Bess, the mysterious blonde, has been Charles's lover.

Archer drives to Benning's office and takes him to Brake's police station. The upshot of Archer's talks with the smiling Benning in his office, Alex's aggrieved mother, Mrs. Norris, and Brake at the station: Benning's wife is named Bess; Lucy, a nurse, arrived two weeks ago, rented Mrs. Norris's spare room, consulted Benning for "colonic spasm" aggravated by worry, entertained a man (i.e., Max), was evicted, left a thermometer stuck at 107°. Mrs. Norris laments her harshness toward Lucy, says Benning divorced Elizabeth, "a blonde Jezebel"; Archer tells Brake his client is Sylvia Treen but says nothing about Bess; Brake believes Alex, caught and jailed, killed Lucy, the weapon being a knife Alex's father, a Navy man now dead, sent him from the Philippines. Brake lets Archer interview Alex, who reveals that Lucy saw someone shoot Charles Singleton, was urged by a strange man (Max) to be a witness and share the reward, went toward the Singleton house, lost her nerve, got scared, borrowed Alex's knife, and was killed by it.

Brake, called to an accident in the mountains, lets Archer ride along. On the way, he tells Brake what Lucy witnessed. When they arrive, they discover an old Buick torched and Charles inside—identified by his initialed belt buckle. At noon Archer visits Bess Benning, who admits she knew Charles, summarizes her difficult childhood in Gary and Chicago, and her 1943 marriage to Benning, then in the Navy. She tries to seduce Archer until he says the body in the car is not Charles's. Benning returns, begins to bluster in front of Archer, but is intimidated by Bess. He swears she was home last night and gives Archer Florida ("Florie") Gutierrez's address. Going to Florie's landlord, Archer learns she owed rent, suddenly paid, and left with Max. Archer finds Florie in a sleazy hotel, hung over and deserted. She says Max, who drove an old Buick, bribed her into gossiping about Benning's blonde-turned-brunette wife. Archer pockets an unopened telegram sent to Max. Archer forces Florie to identify Charles's body in the morgue. It is Max's, recognizable by his teeth. Archer shows Brake the telegram. It concerns Leo Durano's Michigan-based criminal record and names William Garibaldi, Leo Durano, Una Durano, and Bess Wionowski. Archer theorizes that Una wanted to silence Lucy because Lucy saw Leo kill Charles. Archer escorts Brake to Benning, who says Bess left earlier for San Francisco and, when quizzed, shows a marriage certificate proving that he and Bess Wionowski married (Indiana, May 14, 1943). Archer theorizes that two weeks ago Benning treated mortally wounded Charles, whose blood Florie cleared away. When Brake expresses fear of any premature arrest of Bess, Archer leaves and drives to Una's house. Letting him see her brother, Leo, she reveals this: Leo became deranged in Detroit, remains nominally a lucrative numbers-racket boss; she brought him, with Lucy as nurse, to Bella City and the Bennings; Leo loved Bess, gut-shot Charles Singleton on learning she periodically visited Charles's cabin; will not say where Charles's body is.

On to the Singleton estate. Sylvia says Bess phoned from Los Angeles demanding $5,000 for information on Charles. The money is easily assembled. Bess phones again. Archer instructs Sylvia to tell Bess to drive by 10:00 P.M. to a West Hollywood address, which is in front of Archer's office. He and Sylvia rush there. Bess arrives. Gun in hand, Archer gets her into his office, with Sylvia secretly listening. Shown the money, Bess reveals this: Leo molested her; she married Benning but fell for Charles, who snubbed her in Boston; Leo bribed her out of a Detroit jail sentence, moved with Una to Arroyo; Bess resumed her liaison with winsome Charles; Lucy, Leo's nurse, witnessed his shooting Charles, who was taken to Benning; when he could not save Charles, Benning turned the body into nothing but a skeleton, which remains, hanging, to keep Bess in line. Sylvia cries out and faints. Una, who followed Bess, enters with a gun, kills Bess, and is killed by Archer. Archer proceeds to Benning and tells him Bess and Una are dead. Archer says he is aware that after Charles bled to death, Benning hid his clothes and car, processed his bones, killed Lucy, killed Max, dressed him as Charles, and torched both car and body. Archer denies Benning access to poison and collars him.

Charles's skull, hanging with his other bones in Samuel Benning's office, has what Archer labels "the ivory grin of death." Macdonald, whose working title for *The Ivory Grin* was "The Split Woman," regarded it as his best-plotted novel to date, with narration balanced by drama and with subtle psychosocial implications. It was well reviewed, did not sell satisfactorily, and was reprinted as *Marked for Murder* in its paperback edition (Pocket Books, 1953). In 1969 Macdonald was heartened by a Czech publisher's request for permission to issue an 80,000-copy edition of *The Ivory Grin*. Notable is Macdonald's sympathetic treatment of the behavior and fears of blacks and Chicanos.

Bibliography: Bruccoli; Nolan; Schopen; Speir.

J

JACK. In *The Ferguson Affair*, he owns a drive-in near Malibu. Hilda Dotery is holed up in a beach shack nearby.

JACK. In *The Three Roads*, in a personals column Theodora Swanscutt read, he and Sim are appealed to by Charlie to realize the deal is still on.

JACKMAN. In *The Far Side of the Dollar*. *See* Hillman, Thomas.

JACKMAN, MRS. SAM. In *The Far Side of the Dollar*, she is the wife of Sam Jackman, a trombonist at The Barroom Floor. Sam apologizes to Archer because the Jackmans' apartment is a mess since his wife must work.

JACKMAN, SAM. In *The Far Side of the Dollar*, he is a trombonist. Formerly a drug addict, Jackman encouraged Thomas Hillman to be a jazz pianist. Ralph Hillman, Thomas's father, got Jackman fired from a beach club and also criticized The Barroom Floor, where Jackman works. Archer describes Jackman as a light-skinned, "middle-aged Negro."

JACKSON, BEATRICE M. In *The Barbarous Coast*, she is Archer's cleaning lady. She leaves him a note alerting him to "mouse dirt in the cooler."

JACKSON, DR. In *The Dark Tunnel*, he is the Economics Department head at Midwestern University and the assistant of Dr. Galloway, the university president.

JAHNKE, RUSTY. In *Blue City*, he is a big, strong, stupid, loyal thug, from Pittsburgh, working for Roger Kerch. John Weather outboxes him to show Kerch his own usefulness. While Rusty is digging a grave at Wildwood for Joseph Sault and John, the latter slugs him and temporarily escapes. Rusty assists in the torture of Floraine Weather, is arrested, and gives faulty evidence concerning the murder of John's father, Jerry D. Weather.

JAIMET, ISOBEL. In *The Zebra-Striped Hearse, See* Blackwell, Isobel.

JAIMET, RONALD. In *The Zebra-Striped Hearse*, he was the first husband of Isobel Blackwell, whose second husband is Colonel Mark Blackwell, Jaimet's cousin. Jaimet was a Citrus Junction high school principal. A diabetic, he could not have children. While Jaimet and Blackwell were hiking, Jaimet broke his leg and died. Blackwell may have shoved Jaimet, indirectly causing his death.

JAKE. In *Trouble Follows Me*, he is the burly doorman at Miss Green's Tijuana brothel. Jake knocks Sam Drake out with a blackjack, at Miss Green's bidding.

JAKE, UNCLE. In *The Drowning Pool*, Archer fondly remembers this man, a boxer who fought Gunboat Smith fifteen rounds without a decision.

JAMES. In "The Sky Hook," he is the boy scared at the bus stop by Frederick's lurching gait and halting speech.

JAMIESON, MRS. PETER. In *Black Money*, she was old Peter Jamieson's wife and young Peter Jamieson's mother. She died twenty-four years earlier.

JAMIESON, PETER. In *Black Money*, he is young Peter Jamieson's father. They have long been neighbors of Roy Fablon, old Jamieson's roommate at Princeton University, and of Roy's wife (and widow) Marietta Fablon. Through his having been a member of the board of directors at the Montevista bank, Jamieson knows something about Francis Martel's finances. Jamieson, a genial alcoholic, perhaps finds pleasure with Vera, his housekeeper.

JAMIESON, PETER. In *Black Money*, he is the son of old Peter Jamieson, who disparages him. Young Peter, twenty-four, loves Virginia Fablon, who broke her engagement with him and disappeared with Francis Martel. Peter hires Archer to find Virginia. Peter's incurable gluttony amazes Archer.

JANE. In *The Drowning Pool*, she is Gretchen Keck's trailer bunkmate. Jane works at an all-night Quinto hamburger joint.

JANOWSKI, DETECTIVE-SERGEANT. In *The Instant Enemy*, he and Detective-Sergeant Prince answer Archer's summons after he finds Mrs. Laurel Smith beaten in her apartment. Archer notes that Janowski is of Baltic extraction.

JEFFREY, DR. In *The Instant Enemy*, he is the young, hurried physician Keith Sebastian calls in an effort to keep Alexandria, his daughter, out of jail. Jeffrey is reluctant to discuss her case with Archer.

JENKS. In *The Chill*, he was the upright father of Alice Jenks and Constance McGee in Indian Springs. He hated Constance's husband, Thomas McGee.

JENKS, MISS ALICE. In *The Chill*, she is Constance McGee's sister, fourteen or fifteen years older. She is Constance's daughter Dolly McGee's officious aunt. She talked the child into testifying that her father, Thomas McGee, shot Constance dead. Alice dislikes Gil Stevens, McGee's lawyer, and Dr. James Godwin, Dolly's psychiatrist. Alice pays more attention to her duties as a county welfare official than to her troubled niece. Archer despises her.

JENSEN, LORENZ. In *Trouble Follows Me*, this is the man who calls himself Anderson, the oil man. He was jailed in Joliet (1934); he and Mary Thompson were criminals in China (later 1930s); they are involved in passing information on U.S. naval ship movements out of Honolulu (1945). They hope to infiltrate the Manhattan Project. *See also* Anderson.

JEROME, DR. In *The Underground Man*, he is a Santa Teresa physician whose patients include Elizabeth Broadhurst, Stanley Broadhurst, and Frederick Snow.

JERRY MAE. In *Find a Victim*, she is a bar-girl at the Golden Slipper Supper Club. Archer gets information from her about Tony Aquista, Jo Summer, and Don Kerrigan.

JINX. In *The Moving Target*, this is a horse the waitress at The Corner hopes that Archer, who says he is a Las Vegas bookie, can offer her a tip on. When he cannot dissuade her from betting, he gives her $2 to bet on Jinx to show.

JOE. In *The Blue Hammer*, Archer and Captain Mackenridge have breakfast at Joe's place.

JOE. In *The Dark Tunnel*, he is Detective-Sergeant Haggerty's driver on the trip from the brothel back to town.

JOE. In *Trouble Follows Me*, Teddy Trask says Joe was his partner in their mind-reading act.

JOHANNES, MRS. In *Meet Me at the Morgue*, she is the police matron Molly Fawn evades.

JOHNNIE. In *The Dark Tunnel*, he is the drunk at the brothel outside Arbana. Peter Schneider, posing as Ruth Esch, stole Johnnie's car and clothes. Johnnie has an unnamed nude male companion.

JOHNSON. In *The Zebra-Striped Hearse*, in this woman's nearby car Dolly Campion's baby, Jack Campion, was placed after Dolly was murdered.

JOHNSON, ABEL. In *Meet Me at the Morgue*, he is a middle-aged man, wealthy from real-estate investments, living outside Pacific Point with his wife Helen and their son, Jamie. When Johnson learns that Jamie has been kidnapped, he leaves $50,000 as directed at the railroad station, and awaits results. He suspects his wife of infidelity, hires Art Lemp to shadow her, learns she is innocent, and confesses what he has done. She is outraged, and he storms to his room in chagrin and dies.

JOHNSON, FRED. In *The Blue Hammer*, he is the son, born in 1943 and now thirty-two, of Gerard Johnson and Sarah Johnson. Fred is an art student at the university in Santa Teresa and works at the local art museum. His girlfriend is Doris Biemeyer. Fred takes the Chantry painting to authenticate it. He goes to Copper City to try to find Mildred Mead. Archer returns Fred and Doris to town.

JOHNSON, GERARD ("JERRY"). In *The Blue Hammer*, he was a wounded army veteran. When released from a veterans' hospital in the Valley, he, his wife, Sarah, and their son, Fred, came to Francine Chantry's home (1950). William Mead, posing as Richard Chantry, Francine's husband, killed Gerard, buried him in their greenhouse soil, and posed as Gerard, Sarah's husband and Fred's father.

JOHNSON, HELEN. In *Meet Me at the Morgue*, she is Abel Johnson's young, beautiful wife. A lieutenant in the Navy nurses' corps, in 1945 she knew Fred Miner and other sailors. Helen married Abel for his money but is faithful. Their son, Jamie, is four. Howard Cross, Miner's probation officer, suspects her when Jamie is kidnapped. Helen is hoodwinked by Amy Miner. Cross intervenes, extricates Helen, and will marry her.

JOHNSON, JAMIE. In *Meet Me at the Morgue*, he is the son, four, of Abel and Helen Johnson. When Fred Miner, their driver, takes Jamie to their desert cabin, the kidnap plot engineered by Amy Miner and Art Lemp begins. Howard Cross, the county probation officer, saves Jamie.

JOHNSON, SARAH. In *The Blue Hammer*, she is Fred Johnson's mother and after her husband Gerard Johnson's murder pretends to be the wife of William Mead, who has assumed Richard Chantry's identity. Sarah is a nurse in the Santa Teresa hospital and then at La Paloma, a nursing home nearby. She brazenly rationalizes her every act when Archer corners her.

JOHNSTONE, AMOS. In *The Underground Man*, he is a ghetto wino paid to watch Frederick Snow's car for a friend. Johnstone tells Archer the whereabouts of Jerry Kilpatrick and Susan Crandall.

JONES, AUNTY. In *The Ivory Grin*, she is a gentle, family-oriented black Bella City widow. Archer courteously seeks information from her about her ghetto neighbors.

JORDAN, FATS. In "Guilt-Edged Blonde," he is a gangster not involved in Nick Nemo's murder.

JUAN. In *The Doomsters*, he is a Filipino servant for Jerry and Zinnie Hallman. Juan knows and likes Sam Yogan, another Hallman employee. Dr. J. Charles Grantland lures Juan into driving Yogan to Mildred Hallman's house, beside which Jerry's station wagon is parked, with Zinnie's corpse inside.

JUDAS. In *The Way Some People Die*, this is the nickname Archer gives one of Danny Dowser's goons.

JUDD, DR. ALEC. (Full name: Alexander Judd.) In *The Dark Tunnel*, he is an English Department professor, thirty-nine, at Midwestern University. He co-edits a Middle English dictionary there. He is engaged to Helen Madden, his secretary. He is Robert Branch's closest friend. Before leaving to join the U.S. Navy, Judd telephones Branch to say that he has some evidence against Dr. Herman Schneider, of the German Department. Branch goes to meet Judd, only to see him plunge from his office window to his death.

JURGENSEN, EVELYN. In *The Zebra-Striped Hearse*, she is Bruce Campion's sister and lives with her husband, Thor Jurgensen, in Menlo Park. Evelyn and Thor visit Bruce in the hospital, but the surly fellow orders them out, saying they neglected him earlier when he needed help.

JURGENSEN, THOR. In *The Zebra-Striped Hearse*, he is Evelyn Jurgensen's husband, Thor Jurgensen, Jr.'s father, and Bruce Campion's brother-in-law. Jurgensen is afraid that acknowledging Bruce will hurt him in his business and will damage his son's reputation.

JURGENSEN, THOR, JR. In *The Zebra-Striped Hearse*, he is Thor Jurgensen's son. Thor fears acknowledging Bruce Campion will damage young Thor's "fraternity connection."

K

KARP, GRAY. In "Find the Woman," he is a Hollywood agent.

KARP, HILDA. In "Find the Woman," she is Una Sand's best woman friend.

KARP, NELSON. In *The Zebra-Striped Hearse*, he is the night clerk at the Travelers, in Saline City. Archer gets him to remember whether he saw Bruce Campion and his wife on May 5th, the night Dolly Campion, Bruce's wife, was murdered.

KAUFMAN. In *Blue City*, he is a harmless anarchist, seventy-five. Kaufman runs a secondhand shop, from which the weapon used to kill Jerry D. Weather was stolen. Kaufman tells John Weather about his granddaughter, Carla Kaufman, and her ex-lover, Joseph Sault.

KAUFMAN, CARLA. In *Blue City*, she is Kaufman's granddaughter. Kaufman reared her, from age eleven, after Carla's abandoned mother died. He threw her out when she started flirting. She became Joseph Sault's girlfriend, but he now pimps for her. Carla is a Cathay Club girl and lives near Francesca Sontag, Sault's sister. John Weather meets her, sleeps briefly with her, and gains information and help. Carla is shot in the shoulder by Freeman Allison during his dispute with Roger Kerch. John plans to marry Carla.

KECK, GRETCHEN. In *The Drowning Pool*, she is Pat Reavis's girlfriend, seventeen, and evidently two months pregnant. Gretchen is a dancer at Helen's bar. To assuage his conscience after indirectly causing Reavis's death, Archer gives Gretchen the $10,000 taken from him. Archer feels she may blow it fast.

KELSEY, JOE. In *The Underground Man*, he is a Forest Service officer. Archer meets him beside Stanley Broadhurst's open grave and near where the forest fire started. Kelsey cooperates with Archer somewhat.

KELVIE, CAPTAIN. In *The Three Roads*, he is in charge of the San Diego naval hospital where Bret Taylor is a patient.

KENNEDY, CAPTAIN. In *The Ivory Grin*, he is mentioned in the clipping about Charles A. Singleton, Jr., as an Arroyo Beach police officer to whom people are invited to give information.

KENNER, HUGH (1923–). Educator and literary critic. William Hugh Kenner was born in Peterborough, Ontario, and was educated at the University of Toronto (B.A., 1945; M.A., 1946), and at Yale University (Ph.D., 1950). He taught at Assumption College, Windsor, Ontario (1946–1950); at the University of California at Santa Barbara (1950–1973); and at Johns Hopkins University (1973–). He was a visiting professor at the University of Michigan (summer 1956) and at the University of Chicago (summer 1962). Kenner published books on the most challenging modern writers, including Samuel Beckett, T.S. Eliot, James Joyce, Wyndham Lewis, and Ezra Pound; his less specialized books deal with major Irish and major American writers. Kenner aims to elucidate literary art and improve readers' taste, using wit and irony, and pertinent trivia. Kenner married Mary Josephine Waite (1947); they had five children. A year after Mary Kenner died in 1964, he married Mary Anne Bittner; they had two children.

Macdonald met Kenner at Santa Barbara in 1950, rejoiced in his Canadian origin, and was impressed by his learning. Despite the fact that Macdonald helped Kenner shape some of his early academic writing, especially his book on Lewis, Kenner regarded Macdonald as a complicated person he never knew well. The liberal novelist and the conservative critic avoided arguing about politics. Margaret Millar* disliked academics in general and Kenner in particular. She once wrote Macdonald that Kenner was self-centered and had a lot of crust (July 15, 1951). Kenner felt Margaret's lack of balance had been passed on to her daughter, Linda Millar.* Macdonald reviewed Kenner's *Gnomon: Essays on Contemporary Literature* (1958) and his *The Invisible Poet: T.S. Eliot* (1959) (*San Francisco Chronicle—This World*, March 30, 1958; October 4, 1959). In 1962, to no avail, Kenner recommended for publication Macdonald's dissertation on Samuel Taylor Coleridge, which he had read and admired.

Bibliography: Hugh Kenner, "Learning," in *IJ*, pp. 55–58; Nolan.

KENNY. In *The Drowning Pool*, he is Detective-Sergeant Simeon J. Franks's driver.

KERCH, MRS. SELBY. In *Blue City*, she is Roger Kerch's mother, of Trenton, New Jersey.

KERCH, ROGER. In *Blue City*, he is a villainous, frog-faced businessman. He came to the city two years earlier, whereupon he blackmailed Floraine Weather, his wife but also Jerry D. Weather's bigamist "wife," into having him manage her Cathay Club, which she inherited from Jerry, who was murdered on Kerch's orders. He has victimized Carla Kaufman, who helps Weather's son, John, seek revenge. When Kerch discovers Floraine is Joseph Sault's lover and is conspiring to kill him, he kills Sault and Floraine at Wildwood. John forces Kerch to release material he used to blackmail Floraine and Freeman Allison, who kills him.

KERCH, SELBY. In *Blue City*, he is Roger Kerch's father, of Trenton, New Jersey.

KERRIGAN, DON ("DONNY") (full name: Donald Kerrigan). In *Find a Victim*, he has been Kate Kerrigan's husband for seven years, has slept with Anne Meyer and Jo Summer, and runs a motel near Las Cruces. Kerrigan, an ex-Marine and an alcoholic, conspired to hijack Meyer's truckload of whisky. Kerrigan tangles with Archer and gets decked. He is shot dead by Meyer's older daughter, Hilda Church.

KERRIGAN, KATE ("KATIE"). In *Find a Victim*, she is Judge Craig's daughter and has been married to Don Kerrigan for seven unhappy years. She asks Archer to help her but then defends Don. No sooner does Don leave with Jo Summer than he is murdered and the IRS threatens to seize Kate's property. Archer tells Kate to regard herself as young, beautiful, and intelligent, and to be happy that Don is dead.

KETCHEL, KAYO. In *Black Money*, he was a professional boxer and the criminal partner of Davis, the owner of the Scorpion Club in Las Vegas. He is living with Kitty, Harry Hendricks's presumed wife. Ketchel hires Harry to find Francis Martel, who has stolen money Davis and Ketchel have skimmed. Ketchel is now a paralyzed invalid in Santa Teresa and is tended by sarcastic Kitty, who remains only in the hope of retrieving the missing money. Ketchel's real name is Leo Spillman.

KETCHEL, KITTY. In *Black Money. See* Hendricks, Kitty.

KILBOURNE, MAVIS. In *The Drowning Pool*, she is Walter J. Kilbourne's beautiful wife. Kilbourne is blackmailing her into remaining with him. Archer tries to extricate her. She shoots Kilbourne, gets his crooked money, and asks Archer to share it—and her—in Mexico. Instead, Archer leaves her to tell the police she shot Kilbourne "in self-defense."

KILBOURNE, WALTER J. In *The Drowning Pool*, he is a pink-haired multimillionaire, who made money selling cars in the black market during World War II in Ypsilanti. Residing in the Staffordshire Estates outside Los Angeles, Kilbourne controls the Pacific Refining Company, owns a taxi fleet, and lusts for Olivia Slocum's oil-rich land. He is married to Mavis Slocum, whom he blackmails to stay married to him. Kilbourne paid Pat Reavis to kill Olivia, thought Reavis did so, gives him $10,000 in hush money, and has Reavis killed. Archer outwits him and rescues Mavis, who shoots him "in self-defense."

KILLORAN, CAPTAIN. In *The Dark Tunnel*, he is a uniformed guard at the bomber plant outside Detroit. He helps FBI agent Gordon Chester.

KILPATRICK, BRIAN. In *The Underground Man*, he is Ellen Kilpatrick's ex-husband. Their son is Jerry Kilpatrick, who blamed his father when his mother ran off with Captain Leo Broadhurst (1955). Husky and about forty-five, Brian is a successful but irresponsible real-estate developer. He systematically extorts money from Elizabeth Broadhurst. Brian, an alcoholic, is engaged to an alcoholic beauty. When Archer exposes him, Brian shoots himself to death.

KILPATRICK, ELLEN. In *The Underground Man*, she is Jerry Kilpatrick's mother and Brian Kilpatrick's ex-wife. She taught art in high school in Santa Teresa, and knew Stanley Broadhurst, Al Sweetner, and Frederick Snow there. In 1955 Ellen ran away with Captain Leo Broadhurst, got a divorce in Reno, but was deserted. About forty, she is a painter in Sausalito of dark, depressing works. She helped Al locate Stanley when Stanley was looking for his father. She gives Archer information and offers to sleep with him. Her maiden name was Ellen Strome; her professional name, Ellen Storm.

KILPATRICK, FRANK. In "Wild Goose Chase," he is Janet Kilpatrick's ex-husband and the father of their child, Janie Kilpatrick. When Janet is murdered, Frank gains custody of Janie.

KILPATRICK, JANET. In "Wild Goose Chase," she was with Glenway Cave the night his wife, Ruth, was murdered. Janet is reluctant to testify for fear of losing custody of her daughter, Janie Kilpatrick. Janet loses out anyway, because Rhea Harvey kills her.

KILPATRICK, JANIE. In "Wild Goose Chase," she is the daughter, three, of Janet Kilpatrick and her ex-husband, Frank Kilpatrick, who ultimately gains custody of the sweet little girl.

KILPATRICK, JERRY. In *The Underground Man*, he is Brian and Ellen Kilpatrick's angry son. When Ellen ran off with Captain Leo Broadhurst (1955), Jerry blamed his father. Jerry, now nineteen, crews for Roger Armistead, on his *Ariadne*. When Jerry meets Susan Crandall, the two do drugs and decide to rescue little Ronald Broadhurst. They wreck the *Ariadne*, take Ronald to Jerry's mother, a Sausalito painter, but are caught by Archer and two associates. By talking sense to Jerry, Archer helps him become reconciled with his mother.

KINCAID, ALEX. In *The Chill*, he is Frederick Kincaid's domineered son and Dolly's brand-new husband. He hires Archer to find her when she disappears. Despite his father's objections, Alex sticks by Dolly when she is suspected of killing Helen Haggerty.

KINCAID, DOLLY (full name: Dorothy McGee Kincaid). In *The Chill*, she is the daughter of Thomas and Constance McGee. When Dolly was twelve, her mother was murdered, and her mother's sister, Miss Alice Jenks, persuaded her to believe Thomas was the killer and to testify in court. Dolly attended college for two years, and registered as Dorothy Smith at Pacific Point College, mainly to check into her father's case, married Alex Kincaid, but vanished after talking with McGee. Dolly is suspected of killing Helen Haggerty but is cleared by her psychiatrist, Dr. James Godwin. While calling himself Chuck Begley, McGee says his daughter is Mary Begley.

Bibliography: Nolan.

KINCAID, FREDERICK. In *The Chill*, he is in charge of the Channel Oil Corporation's Long Beach office. He disapproved of his son Alex's marriage to Dolly McGee (*see* Kincaid, Dolly). Archer calls Frederick "a bloodless bastard" to his sputtering face.

KINCAID, MRS. FREDERICK. In *The Chill*, she is Alex Kincaid's mother. Her husband Frederick beseeches Alex to return home to his sick mother.

KING. In *The Zebra-Striped Hearse*, Fawn King says her "ex was just a bookie."

KING, FAWN. In *The Zebra-Striped Hearse*, she is a call girl at the Solitaire, in State Line. She tells Archer, who observes she is "full and tender under her sweater," that she knew Quincy Ralph Simpson in South San Francisco, was his girlfriend in the Tahoe region, and knew he had an innocent crush on Dolly Campion. Fawn directs Archer to Dr. Edmund Burke Damis's cabin. Fawn tells Archer she dislikes her real name, Mabel.

KITO. In *The Zebra-Striped Hearse*, he is a houseboy working in the Tahoe region. Gossipers say he said Quincy Ralph Simpson stole something while there.

KLIFTER, DR. THEODORE. In *The Three Roads*, he is a Holocaust survivor and now a psychoanalyst practicing in Los Angeles. Paula West retained him as a technical adviser when she was rewriting a movie script. At her request, he examines Bret Taylor at the San Diego hospital. When Paula talks with Klifter at his Los Angeles apartment, he says Taylor should be told the truth. Klifter appears to be anti-Freud and anti-Jung, and regards Americans as materialistic optimists.

KNAPP, DELBERT. In *The Blue Hammer*, he manages the Southwestern Savings branch bank in Copper City. Jack Biemeyer tells Archer he knows Knapp.

KNOPF, ALFRED A. (1892–1984). (Full name: Alfred Abraham Knopf). Publisher. Born in New York City, Knopf graduated from Columbia University (1912), gained experience by working for two publishers, then founded his own firm (1915), financially backed by Blanche Wolf. The two married (1916) and had one son, Alfred ("Pat") Knopf, Jr., who became an independent publisher. The Knopfs succeeded because of Alfred's judgment and energy and Blanche's charm and critical acumen. Knopf published European writers first but soon counted the following among his American authors: James Baldwin, Willa Cather, Dashiell Hammett, Langston Hughes, H.L. Mencken, Samuel Eliot Morison, Wallace Stevens, and John Updike. Knopf merged with Random House (1960). Blanche Knopf died in 1966. The following year, Knopf married Helen Norcross Hedrick.

In 1947 Macdonald submitted *The Three Roads* to the Knopfs; they liked it but urged big cuts. Macdonald agreed, and Knopf secured him with a $500 advance. The two men corresponded regularly about stylistic problems, finances, reprint and movie rights, and much else. They first met in person in 1948, when Knopf, on tour to check on authors, bookstores, and librarians, stopped in Ann Arbor. Blanche Knopf persuaded Macdonald to pose for a publicity photograph—full-length silhouette, in trench coat, with fedora and cigarette lifted to mouth. Knopf used the result in ads for the next ten years. Knopf felt that *The Moving Target* was a weak novel, never liked the ending, and published it reluctantly. In 1950 Knopf advanced Macdonald $1,000 for *The Drowning Pool* and took options on his next two novels. When a Pocket Books editor criticized *Meet Me at the Morgue*, Knopf sent the report to Macdonald, who in an exceptionally long letter to Knopf (August 28, 1952) defended his artistry and blasted its defamer. Knopf provided needed advances when Macdonald's daughter, Linda Millar,* was involved in a hit-and-run vehicular homicide (1956). Macdonald and Knopf strengthened their friendship over the next decades, largely by mail. Margaret Millar* once remarked that Knopf was a troubled, troubling man. In 1976, Knopf and Helen Knopf, his second wife, gave a cocktail party for Macdonald at New York's St. Regis Hotel. The considerable Macdonald-Knopf correspondence is on deposit at the Harry Ransom Humanities Research Center, University of Texas, Austin.

Bibliography: Afred A. Knopf, *Portrait of a Publisher 1915–1965* (2 vols., New York: Typophiles, 1965); Nolan.

KNUDSON, CHIEF RALPH. In *The Drowning Pool*, he was a sergeant with the police force in Oakland, California. Though married to Eleanor Knudson, he was in love with a Berkeley student named Maude (later Maude Slocum) and got her pregnant. Unable to obtain a divorce, Knudson moved to Chicago, became a distinguished police lieutenant, but resumed his relationship with Maude in Quinto, by becoming Quinto's police chief. Knudson investigates Olivia Slocum's death, with and without Archer's cooperation. Knudson takes Cathy Slocum, Maude's and his daughter, away for treatment.

KNUDSON, ELEANOR. In *The Drowning Pool*, she was married to Chief Ralph Knudson when he was a sergeant on the Oakland, California, police force. She rented rooms to Maude Slocum and Mildred Fleming when they were sophomores at Berkeley. Mrs. Knudson discovered her husband's love affair with Maude but would not give him a divorce. Mildred describes Eleanor as "a frigid bitch" and "one of these hard righteous women."

KRAMM, HILDA. In *The Dark Tunnel*, she is the Midwestern University telephone switchboard operator. Robert Branch phones her for information about Dr. Alec Judd's last phone conversation.

KROMBERG, MRS. In *The Moving Target*, she is Ralph and Elaine Simpson's reliable housekeeper. Archer's courteous treatment of Mrs. Kronberg pays off.

KRUG, ALMA R. In *The Instant Enemy*, she was Joseph L. Krug's wife in Santa Monica and then Long Beach, and is the mother of Henrietta R. Krug (*see* Marburg, Ruth), Jasper Blevins's grandmother, and David Spanner's great-grandmother. Alma taught school at Centerville. She and Joseph owned a place, now dilapidated, still known as the Krug ranch. It is the scene of Stephen Hackett's murder in 1952 and Jack Fleischer's in 1967. Archer gains family data from the rigidly righteous Alma, probably well over seventy-five and in a pleasant Santa Monica convalescent home. Alma has been financed by hush money from Ruth and from Jasper Blevins, posing as Stephen Hackett. The initial "R." in her name stands for Ruth.

KRUG, JOSEPH L. ("JOE"). In *The Instant Enemy*, he was Alma R. Krug's husband. Formerly a rancher, Krug was head of security for Mark Hackett's Corpus Christi Oil Company building in Long Beach. When a revolver was stolen from his office and was used to kill Mark, Joseph felt the event so deeply that he soon died.

KUNTZ, SIMEON ("SIM"). In *The Moving Target*, he is Fay Estabrook's director at a University City studio visited by Archer. A Central European, Kuntz is patient with Fay, a has-been.

L

LACKLAND, CAPTAIN OLIVER. In *The Goodbye Look*, he is the Pacific Point captain of detectives. He and Archer cooperate only later in identifying Eldon Swain and understanding how he was killed.

LACKNER, ROY. In *The Blue Hammer*, he is the long-haired lawyer, thirty-one, whom Ruth Biemeyer consults tentatively for a divorce. Lackner becomes Fred Johnson's helpful lawyer. Lackner and Archer discuss alcoholism and dysfunctional families.

LAMB, MRS. SARAH. In *The Barbarous Coast*, she ran the snack bar for Clarence Bassett in the Channel Club. When her "legs give out," she rented Malibu cottages. One tenant was Hester Campbell (*see* Wall, Hester). Archer gains information concerning Hester from Mrs. Lamb.

LAMPSON. In *Sleeping Beauty*, he was Dr. Lampson's father, killed at Guadalcanal.

LAMPSON, DR. In *Sleeping Beauty*, he is a veterans' hospital physician. He treated Nelson Bagley and is informative when Lew Archer questions him.

LAND, BESSIE. In *Trouble Follows Me*, she is Hector Land's wife-turned-hooker, in Detroit. When Sam Drake questions her in a bar, she mentions Black Israel, a militant black organization. This results in her having her throat fatally cut. The police wrongly call her death suicide.

LAND, HECTOR. In *Trouble Follows Me*, he is a wardroom steward on Lieutenant Eric Swann's ship in Honolulu. He is unjustly suspected of raping and killing Sue Sholto. Land is involved in Black Israel, the anti-moderate black movement, and helps Anderson gain information on movements of American naval vessels. Land disappears. Sam Drake locates him in Tijuana, where Drake falsely tells him that Anderson killed Bessie Land, Hector's wife. Hector kills Anderson and then himself.

LANG, DOROTHEA S. ("DOLLY"). In *The Wycherly Woman*, she is Phoebe Wycherly's babbling sophomore roommate at Boulder Beach College. They shared a room in Mrs. Doncaster's house. With a "ghastly smile" and "rabbit-shaped," Dolly irritates Archer by saying "my quote unquote mind," but reveals much about Phoebe and Robert Doncaster. The typewriter on which she types her jargon-filled paper concerning juvenile delinquency provides a significant clue.

LANGDALE, DR. In *Sleeping Beauty*, he is a physician for William Lennox and Harold Sherry. He treats Harold's wound and mentions William's fatal heart attack.

LANGDALE, MRS. In *Sleeping Beauty*, she is Dr. Langdale's wife. When Archer telephones his office, she says her husband is out treating William Lennox.

LANGSTON, HENRY ("HANK"). In *The Instant Enemy*, he is a Santa Teresa high school counselor. When he tried to advise David Spanner, David slugged him and was expelled. Langston tells Archer about David and accompanies Archer toward the Krug ranch. Archer and Langston return Stephen Hackett to safety. David eludes a posse, makes his way to Langston, and terrifies his pregnant wife, Kate. Langston rushes up and fatally shoots David.

LANGSTON, HENRY, JR. In *The Instant Enemy*, he is Henry and Kate Langston's son. He is at his nursery school when his father kills David Spanner.

LANGSTON, KATE. In *The Instant Enemy*, she is Henry Langston's wife. Six months pregnant, she disapproves of his efforts to counsel David Spanner.

LANSING, DISTRICT ATTORNEY. In *The Blue Hammer*, he is the opinionated Santa Teresa D.A. Archer calmly lets Lansing grab what glory he can.

LARKIN, HORACE. In *The Ivory Grin*. *See* Archer, Lew.

LARKIN, UNA. In *The Ivory Grin. See* Durano, Una.

LARRABEE. In "The Suicide," he was the father of Clare and Ethel Larrabee. When his wife left him, Larrabee brooded, drank, and finally shot himself to death.

LARRABEE, CLARE. In "The Suicide," she is Ethel Larrabee's younger sister. She engages Archer to find Ethel. He wrongly suspects Clare, who is sweet and spunky.

LARRABEE, ETHEL. In "The Suicide," she is Clare Larrabee's generous but criminal older sister. She married Edward Illman, divorced him, married Owen Dewar, robbed and shot him, and finally killed herself with the gun her father used to commit suicide.

LARRABEE, FAST PHIL. In *The Goodbye Look*, he writes his name on a wall in the Pacific Point police building to prove he was there.

LARRABEE, MRS. In "The Suicide," she is or was the mother of Clare and Ethel Larrabee. When Mrs. Larrabee left her husband, he committed suicide.

LARUE. In "Guilt-Edged Blonde," he is or was Mrs. Harry Nemo's "rummy" first husband and Jeannine Larue's father.

LARUE, JEANNINE. In "Guilt-Edged Blonde," she is Mrs. Harry Nemo's blond daughter, guilty of nothing but bad luck.

LASHMAN ("LASH"). In *The Barbarous Coast*, he is one of Leroy Frost's guards at Simon Graff's movie company. He holds George Wall while Marfeld pistol-whips him. While Graff watches, Lashman knocks Archer unconscious. At the Dewdrop Inn in Las Vegas, Archer gun-butts Lashman's skull.

LASHMAN, SIMON. In *The Blue Hammer*, he is a Tucson artist, seventy-five, white-haired, and preoccupied with death. His paintings resemble Richard Chantry's. He was one of Mildred Mead's former lovers. He provides Archer with information.

LASHMAN, TONY. In *Sleeping Beauty*, he is Sylvia Lennox's simpering servant. When he tries to blackmail Marian Lennox, he gets murdered.

LASSITER, EDDIE. In *The Moving Target*, he is a crook, about thirty-five, from New York and more recently Las Vegas. Lassiter helps kidnap Ralph

Sampson by driving him from the Burbank airport. After he grabs the ransom money and splits, his sister, Betty Fraley, angry that he testified against her in a drug bust, shoots him and takes the money.

LATINO, JOHN "RAGS." In *The Moving Target*, Archer sees this name in the men's lavatory at The Corner. Latino calls himself a high school hurdler from Dearborn, Michigan.

LAWRENCE, DR. SAMUEL. In *The Way Some People Die*, he was Galley Lawrence's father and died when she was eight. His widow remembers him devotedly.

LAWRENCE, GALLEY. In *The Way Some People Die*, she was a Pacific Point nurse when Herman Speed, a drug pusher, was hospitalized wounded. Galley (real name: Galatea) met Speed's crooked associate, Joseph Tarantine, whom she married and whose betrayal of his cohorts inspired her murderous criminal career, spelling doom for Joseph, Keith Dalling, whom she led on, and Joseph's brother, Mario Tarantine. She circumvents the suspicions of Danny Dowser, Speed's boss, but Archer collars her for the authorities. Archer defines Galley thus: "Only the female sex was human in her eyes, and she was its only important member." Galley is the most depraved of Macdonald's several murderesses. Critics commenting on *The Way Some People Die* make too much of Galatea-Pygmalion overtones.

Bibliography: Nolan; Speir.

LAWRENCE, MRS. SAMUEL. In *The Way Some People Die*, she is Galley Lawrence's prim mother. Widowed for sixteen years and now in her fifties, she rents rooms in her Santa Monica home to tourists. Galley had Keith Dalling pose as an undercover policeman and scare her into hiring Archer to find Galley. Although Galley is responsible for several men's deaths, her mother regards her as innocent and plans to use the $30,000, which Galley gave her to hide, for her defense.

LAWSON. In *The Doomsters*, he is a deputy coroner under Duane Ostervelt. When Jerry Hallman is shot, Lawson examines the body and warns Archer about Ostervelt.

LEAH. In *Meet Me at the Morgue*, she is J. Thomas and Mabel Richard's black servant.

LEANDRO, DICK. In *The Far Side of the Dollar*, he is a protégé of Ralph Hillman, who sponsored him when his parents split up. Hillman sent him to college and got him a brokerage job. In his early twenties, Leandro is attentive to Hillman's wife, Elaine. Archer notes his Ivy League suit, his slight stammer, and "[h] handsome, healthy face." Leandro borrows a car from his girlfriend, Katie Ogilvie, and drives Elaine to the Barcelona Hotel, unaware of her murderous intent.

LEMBERG, FRAN. In *The Galton Case*, she is Roy Lemberg's sensual, alcoholic wife. Archer worms information out of her at San Francisco's Sussex Arms and Triton Motor Court.

LEMBERG, ROY. In *The Galton Case*, he is Tommy Lemberg's alcoholic brother and Fran Lemberg's husband. They are criminal associates of Otto Schwartz. The Lembergs hide in Pitt, Ontario. Archer encourages Roy to return to Santa Teresa, clear up matters with the law, and reunite with Fran. Roy registered at the Triton Motor Court as Rex Hamburg.

LEMBERG, TOMMY. In *The Galton Case*, he is Roy Lemberg's criminal brother, paroled to Roy's care. Otto Schwartz, their boss, wanted Tommy to scare Alice Sable into repaying a gambling debt. Peter Culligan answered her door and shot Tommy in the arm. Tommy knocked him out and fled. Aware that the police think Tommy killed Culligan, Tommy and Roy flee to Pitt, Ontario. Archer finds them there, sucker-punches Tommy, but persuades him to return and clear his record.

LEMP, ART ("ARTIE"). (Original name: Arthur George Lempke.) In *Meet Me at the Morgue*, he was born June 14, 1892, in Pittsburgh, was a college scholarship student, worked his way through law school, and was a lieutenant in World War I. He married Florabelle (*see* Seifel, Florabelle) in Chicago, practiced there, corrupted a witness, and served time in Joliet. He briefly kidnapped his and Florabelle's son (*see* Seifel, Lawrence), when the boy was three. Lemp was committed to a mental hospital. In 1922 he was in San Francisco, where he became a corrupt police officer. In 1951, his friend Molly Fawn persuaded Bourke, a Los Angeles detective, to hire Lemp. Lemp was involved with Molly, Fred Miner, and Kerry Snow. Lemp and Molly concocted the kidnapping of Jamie Johnson. Amy Miner spoils their plot by killing Lemp and taking the ransom money. When Howard Cross finds Lemp's corpse, he notices "A.G.L." on his comb case. Lawrence sees his father after three decades only when he is dead.

LEMPI. In *The Galton Case*, Deputy Mungan says Lempi led a Luna Bay gang in the 1920s. They ran rum-running and gambling operations in the Red Horse Inn, their brothel. Theodora Gavin (*see* Brown, Theodora) associated with the Red Horse group. Lempi, jailed on Alcatraz (1932), died there.

LEMPKE, ARTHUR. In *Meet Me at the Morgue*, he was Art Lemp's father, a Pittsburgh ironworker.

LEMPKE, TRINITY. In *Meet Me at the Morgue*, she was Art Lemp's mother, a Pittsburgh housewife.

LENNOX, JACK. In *Sleeping Beauty*, he is William Lennox's son, about fifty; Marian Lennox's husband; and Laurel Russo's father. He married Marian (1944 or 1945), consorted before and after that with Alison Russo, served in the Navy with Captain Benjamin Somerville (May 1945) aboard the *Canaan Sound* to Okinawa. An explosion aboard ended their naval careers. Jack worked for his father in the oil business. When Laurel is missing, Jack looks for her.

LENNOX, MARIAN. In *Sleeping Beauty*, she is Jack Lennox's unhappy wife. Her knowledge of Jack's 1945 affair with Alison Russo sparks much action.

LENNOX, SYLVIA. In *Sleeping Beauty*, she is the estranged old wife of William Lennox, the oil-company owner, and is the mother of Jack Lennox and Elizabeth Somerville. Sylvia puts up most of the ransom when Laurel Russo, her granddaughter, is allegedly kidnapped.

LENNOX, WILLIAM. In *Sleeping Beauty*, he is Sylvia Lennox's estranged husband, in his seventies, the father of Jack Lennox and Elizabeth Somerville, and Jack's daughter Laurel Russo's grandfather. William owns the Lennox Oil Company. An oil spill threatens his concerns. His live-in companion is Connie Hapgood. While driving a tractor to clear the beach of oil, he suffers a fatal heart attack.

LEONARD, LANCE ("MANNY"). (Baptismal name: Manuel Purificación Torres.) In *The Barbarous Coast*, he is Tony Torres's tough nephew, called Lance, in his early twenties, and lovely Gabrielle Torres's cousin. He was a Channel Club lifeguard, boxed, was jailed for throwing fights, and associated with Leroy Frost, a criminal. Lance changed his name to Lance Leonard, and became a handsome movie actor. He associates with Simon Graff, a dishonest movie producer, and his criminal cronies, including Carl Stern. When Archer tries to interview Hester Wall, Lance's girlfriend, Lance sucker-punches him. When Hester is murdered, Lance tells how to dispose of her body. Lance's last act is to collect Stern at the airport.

LEONARD, MRS. WESLEY. In *The Zebra-Striped Hearse*, she is Sergeant Wesley Leonard's wife, helps care for Vicky Simpson, and prepares sandwiches for Archer. She deplores her husband's attentiveness to Vicky.

LEONARD, SERGEANT WESLEY. In *The Zebra-Striped Hearse*, he is a Citrus County police officer, who alerts Archer to the discovery of Quincy Ralph Simpson's corpse. He helps Simpson's widow, Vicky, enough to peeve his wife. Leonard helps Archer crack the case by lending him the icepick used to murder Simpson.

LESTINA, MRS. In "The Suicide," she operates the Mission Rest Home in San Diego where Ethel Larrabee, suffering from a beating, commits suicide.

LEVERETT, COLONEL. In *The Dark Tunnel*, he is a faculty member of the Midwestern University War Board. A former West Point teacher, he commands troops on Midwestern's campus.

LEVERETT, SERGEANT. In *The Blue Hammer*, he checks on Paul Grimes, who has been fatally battered.

LEVIN, DR. In *The Doomsters*, he examined Carl Hallman in Berkeley when the fellow lost interest in sex and turned gloomy. Although Dr. Levin said Carl should be institutionalized, Carl's father, Senator Jeremiah Hallman, pooh-poohed the idea.

LEVINE, BOB. In *The Instant Enemy*, he is an associate of Willie Mackey, a San Francisco detective friend of Archer's. Levine tails Jack Fleischer and provides information about him.

LEVINSON, DR. In *Meet Me at the Morgue*, he was the physician who diagnosed Fred Miner, in the Navy, as a potential alcoholic around 1943.

LEVY, BELLA. In *The Three Roads*, she and her husband, Bill Levy, live in La Jolla and are very much in love. At a cocktail and dance party at their home, Paula West meets Bret Taylor.

LEVY, BILL. In *The Three Roads*, he and his wife, Bella Levy, are too much in love, Paula West thinks, to give a really good party at their La Jolla home. Paula meets Bret Taylor at one such gathering.

***LEW ARCHER, PRIVATE INVESTIGATOR* (1977).** Collection of nine reprinted short stories. The contents are "Find the Woman" (1946, 1955), "Gone Girl" (1953, 1955), "The Bearded Lady" (1948, 1955), "The Suicide" (1953, 1955), "Guilt-Edged Blonde" (1954, 1955), "The Sinister Habit" (1953, 1955), "Wild Goose Chase" (1954, 1955), "Midnight Blue" (1960), and "Sleeping Dog" (1965).

Bibliography: Otto Penzler, "On Publishing Ross Macdonald," in *IJ*, pp. 83–88.

LEWISOHN. In *The Drowning Pool*, he and his family live in the fashionable Staffordshire Estates.

LINDA. In *Meet Me at the Morgue*, she is Lawrence Seifel's "feline" secretary, with "wine-dark eyes and chartreuse hair."

LINDSAY, GABRIEL R. ("GABE"). In *The Galton Case*, he was an Ann Arbor high school teacher and counselor. He befriended John Brown (Jr.), who, known as Theodore Fredericks, took the name John Lindsay. When Gabriel died two winters before, he willed John $2,000.

LINDSAY, JOHN. In *The Galton Case. See* Brown, John (Jr.).

LINEBARGE, ALEX S. In *Meet Me at the Morgue*, he is the deputy probation officer under Howard Cross. Once a police officer, Alex is competent, as is proved by his thorough report concerning Fred Miner.

LION. In *The Far Side of the Dollar*, he is the black German shepherd belonging to Ringo. Lion grins at Archer "with his fangs."

LIPPERT. In *The Instant Enemy*, he has "a nose like a beagle," according to his wife, who for that reason won't drink with Mrs. Laurel Smith.

LIPPERT, MRS. In *The Instant Enemy*, Mrs. Laurel Smith rents her an apartment, according to their conversation recorded by Jack Fleischer. She declines to have a drink with the alcoholic Laurel.

LISTER, LEONARD. In "The Sinister Habit," he is a mercenary would-be filmmaker, in his late forties. He abandons Stella Dolphine, his landlord Jack Dolphine's wife, marries Maude Harlan (*see* Lister, Maude), and is to be arrested for trying to bury Stella's body.

LISTER, MAUDE. In "The Sinister Habit," she is J. Reginald Harlan's younger sister, in her thirties. She quits teaching, marries Leonard Lister, and is enmeshed in murderous intrigue.

LITTLE, EMERSON. In *Sleeping Beauty*, he is, according to Captain Benjamin Somerville, Sylvia Lennox's attorney. When Jack asks Archer for a person to recommend him and Archer mentions John Truttwell, Jack says he knows Little, Truttwell's former associate. Little vouches for Archer when Jack telephones him.

"THE LIVING EYE." *See The Zebra-Striped Hearse.*

LOFTIN, MRS. In *Black Money*, she is Dr. George Sylvester's square-faced, intimidating secretary.

LORRAINE. In "Gone Girl," she works in Salanda's motel.

LUGER, SAMMY. In *The Three Roads*, he was, according to Mrs. Joe Berker, her daughter Lorraine Taylor's friend from Michigan. He is now a sergeant stationed in Berlin.

LUIS. In *The Moving Target*, he is Dwight Troy's contact in Mexico to provide illegal immigrants. When Luis is driving Troy's car, Archer saves Betty Fraley by stopping Luis and knocking him unconscious.

"LUNA BAY." *See The Galton Case.*

M

MABEL. In *Blue City*, she is a Cathay Club prostitute, as is Carla Kaufman.

MAC. In *The Three Roads*, he is the Los Angeles tailor who mends Bret Taylor's ripped navy jacket.

MacGOWAN. In *Find a Victim*, he is Jo Summer's grandfather. He is a watchman at the Inn near Lake Perdida, gives Archer information about Jo, and tells him where the hijackers of Meyer's truck are hiding.

MacGOWAN, JOSEPHINE. In *Find a Victim. See* Summer, Jo.

MACKENDRICK, CAPTAIN. In *The Blue Hammer*, he is a Santa Teresa police officer. When he got out of the Army (1945), he became a patrolman and knew Richard Chantry. Mackendrick investigates Paul Grimes's murder. He clashes with Archer, who is put off by the man's "crumpled face"; but the two finally cooperate.

MACKENDRICK, MRS. In *The Blue Hammer*, she is evidently Captain Mackendrick's wife. She answers Archer's phone call with impatient resignation.

MACKEY, MRS. WILLIAM. In *The Underground Man*, she is the brand-new wife of Archer's San Francisco detective friend. From her eager arms Archer summons him.

MACKEY, WILLIAM ("WILLIE"). In *The Wycherly Woman*, he is a San Francisco detective, in his late forties, whom Archer knows professionally. Homer Wycherly hired Mackey to seek the source of poison-pen letters he received, then abruptly discharged him. Mackey gives Archer copies of the letters. In *The Instant Enemy*, Mackey and his assistant, Bob Levine, provide Archer information about Jack Fleischer. Archer mentions that for twenty years he has known Mackey, who spends "his money on women and clothes." In *The Underground Man*, Archer enlists Mackey to help him locate Ellen Kilpatrick in Sausalito. Mackey is diverted from his new bride to do so and, employing an assistant named Harold, succeeds.

MACLENNAN. In *The Goodbye Look*, Archer employs him to guard Nicholas Chalmers in the San Diego hospital.

MACON, MISS. In *The Drowning Pool*, she is the tiny, monkey-like nurse who sadistically aids Dr. Melliotes. Archer disarms her and warns her to get lost.

MACREADY, LETITIA O. In *The Chill. See* Bradshaw, Mrs. It has been suggested that Macdonald chose the name Macready to suggest that its bearer is greedy.

Bibliography: Speir.

MACREADY, VAL. In *The Chill*, he was Letitia O. Macready's divorced husband. Mrs. Hoffman says Macready "had meat-packing money on his mother's side" in Bridgeton, Illinois.

MADDEN, HELEN. In *The Dark Tunnel*, she is Dr. Alec Judd's secretary and fiancée. When Judd is killed and Robert Branch asks her to help him escape Arbana police officers, she brings Detective-Sergeant Haggerty to the rendezvous point instead, apologizes later to Branch, and announces that she has joined the Red Cross.

MAE. In *The Moving Target*, she is a former actress, mentioned by Fay Estabrook as forgotten.

MAHAN. In *The Ferguson Affair*, he is a policeman to whom Whitey Slater speaks briefly.

MALDON, JOHN. In *The Dark Tunnel*, he is a deaf-mute out hunting for rabbits, with a friend, when Robert Branch encounters him. Branch buys his shotgun and shells but fails to use the weapon effectively while pursuing Peter Schneider.

MALKOVSKY, ERIC. In *Black Money*, he is the Montevista Tennis Club photographer. He gets Archer a photograph of Kayo Ketchel, Kitty Ketchel, and Francis Martel. Archer pays him decently.

MALLOW, MRS. In *The Far Side of the Dollar*, she is the alcoholic house mother of Laguna Perdida School's East Hall. A broken-down social psychologist, she is friendly to students and gossips to Archer about the school administration.

MALTEONI. In *Blue City*, he owns an establishment from which Joseph Sault reports to Roger Kerch that Floraine Weather telephoned Sault. This is a lie, which Kerch does not believe.

MANDEVILLE, CAPTAIN THEODORE. In *The Wycherly Woman*, he owned the house in Atherton that Ben Merriman sold to Catherine Wycherly. Merriman would not share the excessive profit with Mandeville. Mandeville tells Archer that Catherine moved to Sacramento's Champion Hotel.

MANDEVILLE, LIEUTENANT. In *The Wycherly Woman*, he was Captain Theodore Mandeville's son. When Mandeville tells Archer his son was shot down at Okinawa, Archer replies that he, too, was at Okinawa.

MANDEVILLE, MRS. In *The Wycherly Woman*, she was Captain Theodore Mandeville's wife. Mandeville tells Archer that when she died he decided to sell their Atherton house.

MARBURG, RUTH ("ETTA"). In *The Instant Enemy*, she was born Henrietta R. Krug, October 17, 1910, the daughter of Joseph L. and Alma R. Krug, in Santa Teresa County. (The "R." in each woman's name stands for Ruth.) Ruth married Albert D. Blevins in San Francisco (March 3, 1927). Their son is Jasper Blevins. In the early 1940s she married Lupe Rivera, who was then a young criminal in San Diego. He was arrested for smuggling; so she divorced him. When her father got a job with Mark Hackett in the Los Angeles area, she married Mark. They had a son named Stephen Hackett, who murdered Mark (May 24, 1952) and was murdered by Jasper (May 28, 1952). Jasper assumed Stephen's identity for fifteen years. Ruth married Sidney Marburg, a painter younger than Stephen, thus becoming Ruth Marburg. When Archer connects Mark's and Stephen's murders, and that of Mrs. Laurel Smith, Albert Blevins's daughter-in-law, Mrs. Marburg offers him a million-dollar bribe. He refuses and turns her and Jasper over to the police.

MARBURG, SIDNEY. In *The Instant Enemy*, he is Ruth Marburg's young painter husband. While still married to Mark Hackett, she was having an affair with Marburg, then a geological draftsman in Mark's company. When Mark wised up, she had him murdered. She sent Marburg to Mexico for a year to study art when she thought he might have become suspicious. To continue his own life of ease, Marburg hangs on.

MARCO. In *Black Money*, he is the Montevista Tennis Club's quick-eyed bartender. He gives Archer useful information. In *The Goodbye Look*, Marco tells Archer about the movements of Nicholas Chalmers and Jean Trask.

MARFELD, THEODORE. In *The Barbarous Coast*, he was a county policeman for fifteen years before becoming a thug employed by Leroy Frost, one of Simon Graff's goons. Marfeld pistol-whips George Wall when that foolish man threatens Graff. Marfeld participates in concealing Hester Wall's murder. When Marfeld and others find Rina Campbell at the Dewdrop Inn in Las Vegas, Archer gun-butts him between the eyes.

MARIA. In *The Chill*, she is Mrs. Bradshaw's Spanish maid.

MARIANO, CHARLES ("CAPPIE"). In *The Drowning Pool*, he was a criminal whose capture by Ralph Knudson, then a lieutenant in the Chicago police force, was so widely reported that Maude Slocum, Ralph's lover, read about it, located him, and renewed her relationship with him.

MARIE. In *The Doomsters*, she was scared when a bum, incorrectly identified as Carl Hallman, approached her on the beach near Purissima.

MARIE. In *The Zebra-Striped Hearse*, she runs Marie's Salon de Paris beauty parlor at State Line, happily criticizes Fawn King to Archer, and tells him where Fawn lives.

MARIO. In *The Chill*, he is an auto mechanic who worked on Mrs. Bradshaw's Rolls and gives Archer her address.

MARKS, JERRY. In *The Chill*, he was Bridget Perrine's defense counsel in the Pacific Point court. He has a "homely Middle-European face" improved by "intelligent brown eyes." Archer gets Marks to represent Dolly Kincaid. He reads the transcript of the trial of Thomas McGee, Dolly's father, and says he was framed. Marks witnesses Dr. James Godwin's questioning of Dolly under the influence of sodium pentothal.

MARSLAND, STAN. In *Meet Me at the Morgue*, he is a police officer at the county jail where Amy Miner is held.

MARTEL. In *Black Money*, he was Francis Martel's grandfather, a French engineer educated in Paris. He went to Panama, lost his money investing in French efforts to build the Panama Canal, and married a Panamanian.

MARTEL, FRANCIS. In *Black Money*, as Pedro Domingo, he grew up in the Panama City slums with his mother (*see* Rosales, Secundina), fantasized his descent from Sir Francis Drake and French aristocracy, and jumped ship off California. As Feliz Cervantes, he studied under Allan Bosch at Los Angeles State College, met Taps Tappinger, who teaches at Montevista College, and through him met Virginia ("Ginny") Fablon. He and Ginny fell in love. He became a Montevista Tennis Club bar-boy and associated with Leo Spillman (*see* Ketchel, Kayo), a Las Vegas criminal who financed his schooling in Paris. As a Panamanian diplomat, he stashed away skimmed money for Ketchel, stole from Ketchel, and returned to Montevista, calling himself Francis Martel, a little over thirty and suave. He persuades Ginny to marry him, but their escape to France is thwarted when he is murdered.

MARTHA. In "The Sky Hook," she is Frederick's loving, considerate old wife.

MARTIN. In *Black Money*, he is the Los Angeles State College placement officer. He provides Lew Archer with information concerning Feliz Cervantes (*see* Martel, Francis).

MARTINEZ. In *The Ivory Grin*, he is a resident, sixty-three, in Bella City's Chicano ghetto. He tells Archer that Florida Gutierrez left the neighborhood with Maxfield Heiss.

MARVELL, FRANCIS. In *The Drowning Pool*, he is an affected Britisher, supposedly a lord's nephew from Oxford. He lives in Quinto, has written a play titled *The Ironist*, and casts James Slocum among other locals in it. His friendship with Slocum is too close for the comfort of those nearby. Slocum thinks his wife, Maude Slocum, has killed Olivia, his mother. After Archer disputes this theory with Slocum, he and Marvell calmly renew their chess game.

MATHESON, JAMES ("JIMMY"). In *The Galton Case*, he is the delightful son, eleven, of Marian and Ronald S. Matheson. Archer talks with him before his mother arrives.

MATHESON, MARIAN. In *The Galton Case*, she is Ronald S. Matheson's wife and James Matheson's mother. Twenty-one in 1936, Marian was a nurse's aide in San Francisco, cared for Peter Culligan, who was hospitalized after a dock brawl, and married him. After John Brown (Jr.), Theodora Brown's son, was born (December 1936), Marian helped Theodora briefly. Fifteen wretched years later, Marian divorced Culligan and told Archer in Luna Bay that she had not seen Culligan for ten years. Happily married in Redwood City, she reluctantly answers Archer's questions about Culligan. Brown and his girlfriend, Sheila Howell, visit Marian, gain information about Culligan and Fred Nelson, and tell her they are going to Canada after Nelson. Telling Archer this enables him to find Brown.

MATHESON, RONALD S. ("RON"). In *The Galton Case*, he is Marian Matheson's husband and James Matheson's father. The three live comfortably in Redwood City, where Ronald is a business executive. When Matheson learns about his wife's dreadful past, she fears his anger; however, he offers genuine comfort.

"A MATTER OF IDENTITY." *See The Galton Case*.

MATTHEWS, MARTHA. In *The Barbarous Coast*, she is a pretty guest at Simon Graff's Channel Club party. For a stunt, Graff orders her to pull off her dress, jump into the pool, and let him rescue her.

MAUDE ("MAUDIE"). In *The Doomsters*, she runs the Buenavista Inn, a brothel near Purissima. She welcomes and tries to hide Thomas Rica. When Maude asks her bouncer, Dutch, to eject Archer, who is seeking Rica, Archer knocks him out—twice. She comes at Archer with a gun, but he disarms her. Rica tells Archer that Maude tried to help him over his heroin addition.

McBRATNEY, ELIAS. In *The Ivory Grin*, according to Archer's answering service, McBratney called twice and will call again.

McCUTCHEON, DR. In *The Way Some People Die*, he performs Joseph Tarantine's autopsy and agrees with Archer that death could have come from drowning, smothering, or freezing.

McEACHERN. In *The Wycherly Woman*, he is the *President Jackson* master-at-arms. While seeing off her ex-husband, Homer Wycherly, for his cruise, Catherine Wycherly became obstreperous and McEachern was summoned to take her ashore. He tells Archer that Catherine was "looped" and vulgar, and left with Phoebe Wycherly by taxi, probably for the St. Francis Hotel. He describes the taxi driver accurately.

McGEE, CONSTANCE ("CONNIE"). In *The Chill*, she was Thomas McGee's wife and the mother of Dolly McGee (*see* Kincaid, Dolly). She was murdered by Mrs. Bradshaw, jealous of Constance's affair with Roy Bradshaw. McGee was convicted of the crime.

McGEE, THOMAS ("TOM"). In *The Chill*, he is Dolly Kincaid's father. Although innocent, he was convicted of murdering his wife, Constance, in their Indian Springs home. His attorney, Gil Stevens, got the sentence reduced to ten years at San Quentin. Once released, he began to live with Madge Gerhardi. He found Dolly, worked (as Chuck Begley) at a liquor store, and hides when Dolly is suspected of murdering Helen Haggerty. Archer finds McGee on Stevens's yacht.

McGINIS. In *Blue City*, he is a feisty fellow at Henry's saloon. McGinis, sixty-five, tells John Weather that his father, Jerry D. Weather, was murdered. When McGinis is robbed by Swainie and another thug, John Weather steps in, knocks the thieves down, and helps McGinis on his lonely way.

McMINN. In *Black Money*, he is a Montevista bank manager who gives Archer information on Mrs. Bagshaw and old Peter Jamieson.

McNAB, MESA. In *The Ferguson Affair*, her name appears in the clipping in Larry Gaines's wallet.

MEAD. In *The Blue Hammer*, he was Mildred Mead's father. Simon Lashman tells Archer that Mead once did him "a serious disservice."

MEAD, MILDRED. In *The Blue Hammer*, she is over seventy and, sad at losing her astonishing beauty, tells Archer she is "the hag of the universe." Mildred when fourteen left her Denver family for Copper City, Arizona. She had many lovers, including Sheriff Brotherton, Simon Lashman, Jack Biemeyer, and finally Felix Chantry, whom she married. They had a son whom they named Richard. William Mead, who was her son by Jack, was supposedly Felix's. Jack bought the Chantry house near Copper City and gave it to Mildred. She modeled for various painters. When Richard was murdered (1943), Mildred, lying, said his mangled body was William's. She sold her house (July 1975) to religious zealots for a commune, moved to Santa Teresa, got money from Jack but demanded too much, and moved to La Paloma, a nursing home. When Mildred is exposed, Archer prevents her from committing suicide.

MEAD, WILLIAM ("WILL"). In *The Blue Hammer*, he was supposedly the son of Felix Chantry and his wife Mildred (*see* Mead, Mildred) in Copper

City. In reality, William was hers by Jack Biemeyer. William and his half-brother, Richard Chantry, were painters. When William was drafted into the Army (1942), Richard stole some of William's work. On leave back home (summer 1943), William killed Richard and buried him in William's uniform. William assumed Richard's identity, took over his wife, Francine, and moved with her to Santa Teresa. William, still professing to be Richard, disappeared (July 1950)—this after killing Gerard Johnson. William assumed Johnson's identity, pretended to be Johnson's wife Sarah Johnson's husband and her son Fred's father, and turned alcoholic and demented. William killed Jacob Whitmore (October 1975) and then kills Paul Grimes, to prevent either from blowing his cover. Archer exposes the truth.

MEET ME AT THE MORGUE (1953). Novel. (Characters: Bourke, Carol Bourke, Dr. Campbell, Lieutenant Cleat, Howard Cross, Ann Devon, Mrs. Sam Dressen, Sam Dressen, Captain Angus Drew, Eddie, Molly Fawn, Forest, Commander Julius Heckendorf, Mrs. Johannes, Abel Johnson, Helen Johnson, Jamie Johnson, Leah, Art Lemp, Arthur Lempke, Trinity Lempke, Dr. Levinson, Linda, Alex S. Linebarge, Stan Marsland, Amy Wolfe Miner, Ella Miner, Fred Miner, First Lieutenant Elmer Morton, Ray Pinker, Jason Thomas Richards, Mabel Richards, Sandy, Secundina, Florabelle Seifel, Lawrence Seifel, Kerry Snow, Sturtevant, Simmie Thatcher, Joe Trentino, Miss Hilda Trenton, Watkins, Daniel Wolfe.)

At Pacific Point, Fred Miner drove while drunk in February, killed an unidentified man, and the charge against him was pleaded down by attorney Lawrence Seifel to a fine and probation—this owing to Fred's good record, including wartime service. His probation officer is Howard Cross. Fred and his wife, Amy, work for Abel Johnson and his young redhaired wife, Helen, whom Cross admires. About 9:00 A.M., Saturday, May 10, 1952, Fred, after speaking furtively to Cross, takes Jamie, the Johnsons' son, four, for a drive in Abel's Jaguar. Both disappear. At 9:30, Abel gets a letter demanding $50,000 to be left behind the railroad station magazine rack at 10:58 A.M., three minutes before the train leaves for San Diego, which Abel is to board. Otherwise, Jamie will die. Abel follows orders. Cross, Ann Devon (his assistant), and Amy drive to the Johnsons' home. Helen says Seifel drove after the train to intercept it at Sapphire Beach, its next stop. Helen dined last night at Seifel's and his mother's home. Abel and Seifel return. Jamie remains missing. Abel forbids anyone to notify the authorities and reluctantly goes and lies down. When cocky Seifel banters at Ann, she says he broke their dinner date to dine with Helen.

Helen permits Cross to investigate. In town he learns from Joe Trentino, a blind newsstand owner, that a bellhop named Sandy, who works across the street at the Palace Inn, picked up the ransom suitcase. Cross pumps Sandy, brash until threatened, and learns he gave the suitcase to a middle-aged man whom he describes and who limped toward the harbor. Hoping to locate him, Cross crosses the tracks and finds a dead man in a car, an icepick in his neck. The only identification is a comb case initialed A.G.L.

Cross phones the police and Helen. Helen, Amy, Ann, and Cross meet at the morgue. None identifies the corpse. Lieutenant Cleat, a detective, questions Amy about Fred, her missing husband, and holds her. Forest, an FBI agent, enters, goes with Cross and Ann to Cross's office, and consults Fred's record. Ann confidentially tells Cross she saw the dead man earlier with Seifel during Fred's trial in February. Ann, who unrequitedly loves Seifel, drives Forest to the Johnsons, and Cross reviews Fred's file: Fred had an exemplary military career, was wounded aboard the carrier *Eureka Bay* (1945); he has received counseling for alcoholism; his unknown DUI victim had also been drinking. Seifel visits Cross. He admits he knew the dead man, a Los Angeles detective who told Helen he might be able to identify the man Fred ran over. Seifel reminisces crazily about his divorced parents in Chicago and about being briefly kidnapped, at age three, by his mentally ill father. Cross accompanies Seifel to his office to get the name of the detective's agency, the Acme. Seifel's mother enters and rebukes him.

Late afternoon. Cross learns from Sam Dressen, Cleat's identification man, that the man Fred killed was wearing a suit stolen from J. Thomas Richards. Cross alerts Dressen as to the Acme Investigative Agency. Cross phones the Richardses, but they are at their club. He phones the Acme, talks to Bourke, its owner, sees him, and describes the man killed with the icepick. Bourke identifies him as Art Lemp and reveals this: Molly Fawn, a would-be actress, persuaded Bourke to hire Lemp, an ex-cop (October); Abel Johnson suspected his wife Helen of cheating, asked Bourke to investigate (last fall); Bourke assigned Lemp, fired him (December) for trying with Molly and an unnamed photographer (i.e., Kerry Snow) to blackmail Abel; the photographer lives in Sunset Hotel. Cross suggests Bourke share the Johnson file with FBI agent Forest, who just phoned and is coming over. But the file is missing.

Cross gets Molly's apartment address, goes there, but finds only Molly's gossipy landlady, Miss Hilda Trenton. She says Molly entertained the man in the photographs of Fred's DUI victim (calling him Kerry), and gives Cross a *Eureka Bay* camera left in Molly's room. Cross finds the residence of Richards, whose suit was stolen. He is a retired movie director; Mabel, his wife, a former actress. It seems that the thief sweet-talked Mabel into letting him in to photograph their home. Along with the suit, he took a watch, which police found pawned by a Pacific Palisades photographer. Mabel visited his shop with her insurance agent. With the help of Cross's photographs and descriptions, she identifies the thief as Kerry, the man in the shop as Lemp, and his associate as Molly. Mabel tells Cross where Kerry's shop is.

Cross drives past Sunset Boulevard to the shop, finds Molly in, and shows her dead Kerry's photograph. She says she loved him but when he left with Lemp in February she replaced him with Lemp. When Lemp abused her, she dumped him. At the shop and while they are driving after 11:00 P.M. to Lemp's Long Beach hotel, Molly tells Cross this: Kerry, a naval photographer aboard the *Eureka Bay*, got involved with a red-head woman, went AWOL with official cameras, was fingered by the red-head, spent six years in prison, and vowed revenge; Lemp located the woman. They get the hotel clerk's permission to search Lemp's room. Among sleazy items is a note detailing kidnap plans: Mail kidnap instructions Friday evening; Miner to take boy to desert Saturday early; train leaves at 11:00 A.M.; "plane leaves Int. Airport 2:20 P.M." Cross also finds Kerry's wallet.

Cross drives Molly to Dressen, and Dressen and Forest query her. While having a bite to eat, Cross shows Amy the hit-and-run photos; she identifies Kerry as Fred's *Eureka Bay* shipmate. Dressen takes Molly home to his wife. After brainstorming with Cross, Forest recalls that in 1946 Seifel, a Navy courts-martial lawyer, fingered Kerry, who was then imprisoned. Forest says Abel just died and Seifel is at Helen's home comforting her. Cross drives out past the spot where Fred killed Kerry (with Lemp probably watching in the shadows), to Helen's house, where he finds Seifel drunk. Helen is voluble: Abel remorsefully confessed he hired Lemp to spy on her, raved until he died; Seifel proposed to her within hours thereafter; she admits she wed old Abel for his money but cared faithfully for him; she admires Cross. When he mentions the possibility that Fred took Jamie into the desert, she says she and Abel have a desert cabin two hours away. Cross finds Seifel sick, learns from him that Helen told him in 1946 where to find Kerry on the AWOL charge, and tells Seifel they are going for a drive.

Sunday, 3:00 A.M.: Cross drives the Johnsons' Lincoln into the desert. Dawn breaks. They find the cabin. Jamie is safe outside. When Fred emerges with a gun, he speaks to Helen. Seifel, who held her shotgun, shoots him in the arm. Fred drives the Jaguar away. Cross, alone, follows in the Lincoln. Fred crashes horribly, tells Cross that Helen ordered him to protect Jamie, and dies. Cross returns to the cabin with Fred's body. Forest, summoned by Seifel, senses that Cross loves Helen and theorizes that Fred, worried that Kerry was gunning for him after his jail sentence, killed Fred with Lemp's aid, and called it a hit-and-run.

Back at the Johnson residence, Cross sees Jamie playing in the pool and accepts sandwiches from Helen. When told that Fred said she ordered him to protect Jamie, Helen denies any part in the kidnapping and denies she was the redhead who betrayed Kerry. She admits that she gave Kerry's name to Seifel to give to the FBI at Fred's request.

Asleep in his apartment, Cross dreams that Lemp was carrying Larry Seifel as a boy in his arms. Forest's phone call awakens Cross. It seems that Lemp, as George Lempke, went to law school, was in the Army, practiced law in Chicago, was jailed for suborning perjury from a witness, was a mental patient, and resurfaced in San Francisco as Arthur Lemp (1922). Cross pays a visit to Larry Seifel's mother, Mrs. Seifel, calls her Mrs. Lempke, and hears her confirming explanation, ending that "George" found her here last November. She thinks her son doesn't know Lemp was his father. Cross rushes to the morgue, finds Seifel there with Ann, and senses that Seifel knows the truth.

The next morning, Cross testifies before a grand jury (without mentioning any redhead), learns that Molly has run off, and at a nearby restaurant sees Seifel and Ann. Seifel says he "had it out" with his mother, will marry Ann and move to Seattle with her, and is sorry he shot Fred. Sam phones Cross: Molly has been spotted hitchhiking north. They proceed to her photo shop. She is there with Bourke, discussing how to split the loot. Both are arrested. Phoning the Johnson home, Cross that learns Helen is driving Amy to Amy's family home near San Diego.

By police dispatch they learn that Amy's father, Daniel Wolfe, runs a La Jolla grocery store. They arrive, and Cross grills the upset, talkative man. Wolfe gives Cross a package Amy mailed to herself. It contains the ransom money. When Helen drives up, Amy rushes for the package. But the jig is up. Amy reveals this: She used to have dyed red hair, loved Kerry, married Fred; Lemp told Kerry where Amy was, Amy got Fred drunk, ran over Kerry; let Fred be blamed; Lemp forced her into the kidnap plot; Amy told Fred that Helen wanted him to drive Jamie to the cabin; Amy watched the money drop, icepicked Lemp after he took it to his car, mailed the loot to herself in care of her father; Amy is sad no one loves her and she cannot have a baby now. Cross and Helen somberly agree to get married soon.

Macdonald did research for Cross's character by visiting a receptive Santa Barbara probation office. Alfred A. Knopf* agreed to publish *Meet Me at the Morgue* only after persuading the Pocket Books editor to guarantee a paperback reprint. When the editor carped a bit at both the characters and the plot, Macdonald sent Knopf a five-page defense (August 28, 1952). Pocket Books also wanted the title to be "The Convenient Corpse." Macdonald offered "Message from Hell" and "The Guilty Ones" instead, but the title remained *Meet Me at the Morgue*—until *Cosmopolitan* paid $5,000 to condense the novel (March, 1953) as "Experience with Evil"; that title was used for the London book edition (Cassell, 1954). The novel was well enough reviewed but sold sluggishly.

Bibliography: Bruccoli; Nolan; Speir.

MEISINGER, DR. BILL. In *The Dark Tunnel*, he is an Arbana hospital surgeon, with a "long, intelligent Savonarola face." When Robert Branch chances to expose his arm, Meisinger recognizes that the hypodermic shot Peter Schneider gave Branch contained sodium pentothal.

MELLIOTES ("MELL"), DR. In *The Drowning Pool*, he is Walter J. Kilbourne's sadistic companion and fellow criminal. A hairy Mediterranean, Melliotes helps Enrico Murratti capture Archer, kills Oscar Ferdinand Schmidt, supervises Archer's recapture at the Quinto pier, and tortures him in his Angel of Mercy Nursing Home, in Venice, California, where he specializes in water treatments. Archer escapes, slugs Melliotes, and evidently lets the police take over from that point.

MERCERO. In *The Barbarous Coast*, he is a California Highway Patrol employee whom Archer knows. Archer asks Mercero to check on the ownership of the Jaguar that Lance Leonard drives. Mercero reports that Lance is the owner.

MERRIMAN, BEN. In *The Wycherly Woman*, he was the Camino Real real-estate agent involved in a scam to buy Captain Theodore Mandeville's house in Atherton and sell it to Catherine Wycherly. Five years earlier, Merriman married Stanley Quillan's sister (*see* Merriman, Sally). Ben's being interested in Jessie Drake, Stanley's girlfriend, infuriated Stanley. Ben and Stanley were involved in blackmailing Catherine. After Archer stumbles on Ben, a murder victim, he determines that Ben was asked to resign his naval commision (1945), was a gambler, and blackmailed Catherine with Stanley's connivance.

MERRIMAN, SALLY. In *The Wycherly Woman*, she was originally Sally Quillan, Stanley Quillan's sister, an actress, and the long-time friend of Jessie Drake, Stanley's girlfriend. Unhappily married to Ben Merriman for five years, Sally drinks too much. Before and after Ben's murder, she plays up to Archer, who is mildly responsive long enough to obtain a tape Stanley made and Ben hid in his office safe.

MERRITT, MR. In *The Zebra-Striped Hearse*, he was Archer's high school teacher. In a dream, a "snooty" girl in Merritt's class tells Archer he will fail; he replies not so, he is a detective.

MERRIWEATHER. In *The Galton Case*, he was superintendent of the Crystal Springs orphanage, near Cleveland. Gordon Sable and John Brown (Jr.) concoct the lie that Brown lived there from ages four to fourteen. In reality, a fire at the orphanage destroyed the records and caused Merriweather to suffer a fatal heart attack.

MERRIWELL, MRS. In *Trouble Follows Me*, she is a racist from South Carolina. A widow, she lives in Honolulu and has a secretarial position at Hickam Field. She falsely accuses Hector Land, a black, of raping and killing Sue Sholto.

"A MESS OF SHADOWS." *See The Chill*.

"MESSAGE FROM HELL." *See Meet Me at the Morgue*.

MEYER. In *Find a Victim*, he is a crotchety, widowered truck-line owner. He is the father of Hilda Church and Anne Meyer. He argued with his wife the day their second daughter was born female, since he wanted a son. His wife died that day. He committed incest with Anne when she was fifteen, rationalizing that he was lonely, and, anyway, she was occasionally nude around the house. Meyer hires Archer to find a truck of his, hijacked and loaded with whisky. When Archer learns about him, Archer tosses his retainer back at him, thus freeing himself to operate independently.

MEYER, ANNE ("ANNIE"). In *Find a Victim*, she was old Meyer's gamey daughter, twenty-five. Anne's older sister, Hilda Church, is jealous of Anne's beauty. At fifteen, Anne was given shelter by Hilda and her husband, Brandon Church. Anne worked for Don Kerrigan four or five years, slept with him, was pursued by but disliked Tony Aquista, and disappeared some days before her father's whisky-loaded truck was hijacked. Hilda discovered Anne was also sleeping with her husband. In a demented daze, Hilda killed Anne, and Don disposed of her body and car.

MEYER, CHARLES. In *The Barbarous Coast*, he is a Las Vegas taxi driver. He takes Archer to where he drove Rina Campbell the night before. Meyer complains that drink, women, and gambling have ruined him. Bribed, Meyer returns with Leroy Frost, Lashman, and Theodore Marfeld to put Archer in harm's way.

MEYER, MANNY. In *The Zebra-Striped Hearse*, he is a Los Angeles art critic appealed to by Archer. Meyer identifies paintings Archer shows him as by Bruce Campion, whose talent he praises. When Archer tells him Campion may have murdered his wife, Meyer hopes Campion eludes capture and goes on painting well. Archer is astonished that Meyer does not believe in evil, since his father was a Buchenwald victim.

MEYER, MRS. In *Find a Victim*, she is Meyer's deceased wife. The day she gave birth to their second daughter, Meyer griped that he wanted a son. She promptly died.

MEYER, STANLEY. In *The Blue Hammer*, he is a Santa Teresa hospital orderly. Jessie Gable tells Archer that Meyer, who paints and sells his works, told her Sarah Johnson sold Jacob Whitmore the missing Chantry painting.

MEYERS, DR. In *The Galton Case*, he is mentioned as a Luna Bay physician, between thirty and thirty-five, hence too young to have known Anthony Galton.

MICHELANGELO ("ANGELO"). In *The Zebra-Striped Hearse*, he is Dr. Edmund Burke Damis's hawk.

"MIDNIGHT BLUE" (1960, 1977). Short story. (Characters: Lew Archer, Al Brocco, Alice Brocco, Anita Brocco, Mrs. Al Brocco, Franklin Connor, Stella Connor, Green, Virginia Green, Sheriff Pearsall.) About to practice Sunday morning target shooting in a canyon near a town outside Los Angeles, Archer finds the garrotted body of Virginia Green. Her sweater is midnight blue. A religious derelict runs from an empty gatehouse nearby. After much confusion, during which the innocent fellow is shot dead by Virginia's hot-tempered father, Archer pins Virginia's murder on Anita Brocco, a police dispatcher, outraged when Virginia's high school counselor dumped Anita for a romantic rendezvous with Virginia, overseen by Anita.

MILES, LARRY. In *The Three Roads*, he was a tough, cocky boxer, called Adonis, in Syracuse. He was intimate with Lorraine Taylor, slugged Burton Garth, and is blackmailing Paula West because of her efforts to protect Bret Taylor. When Miles sees Taylor knocked out by Sollie, the Golden Sunset Café bartender, he takes him home, calls himself Harry Milne, and wants to continue shaking Paula down. Taylor learns through Garth that Miles was the last one to see Lorraine alive and pursues him to a motel. The two fight. When the police come and Miles resists, they kill him.

MILLAR, ANNA ("ANNIE") MOYER (c. 1875–1936). Macdonald's mother. Anna Moyer trained for nursing at Winnipeg General Hospital and worked in Alberta, Canada, until she contracted typhoid fever from a patient. She and John Macdonald Millar* married in Calgary, Alberta (September 1909). They lived in Alberta and British Columbia, moved to San Diego (1913), then Los Gatos, California, where Anna Millar, after three stillbirths, gave birth to Kenneth Millar (later writing as Ross Macdonald), December 13, 1915. Macdonald's father abandoned his wife and son in Vancouver (1919). The two moved to Kitchener, Ontario (1920), and lived with members of Anna's family, then in furnished rooms. Poverty forced Anna (1921) to consider putting her son into an orphanage but instead was allowed to send him to Rob Millar, a second cousin, and his wife, Elizabeth, who lived north of Kitchener in Wiarton, on Georgian Bay. Anna and her husband were briefly reconciled in Kitchener (1928). She helped get him admitted to a Toronto hospital (1932), where he died. Anna used money from his insurance policy amounting to $2,212 to finance Macdonald's education at the University of Western Ontario. He persuaded her to share his London, Ontario, apartment (1935). Anna developed a brain tumor and died (January 26, 1936). Money inherited from her sister Adeline's small estate and bequeathed to Macdonald financed his visit to Europe (1936–1937). Troubled mother-son relationships figure in much of Macdonald's fiction.

Bibliography: Nolan.

MILLAR, JOHN ("JACK") MACDONALD (1873–1932). Macdonald's father. He was born in southern Ontario, to which his father had migrated in 1856 from Galashiels, Scotland. John Millar was a silver miner in Colorado, lived with Indians near Great Slave Lake, and was a newspaperman in Greenwood, British Columbia, and Granum, Alberta. He aided Japanese fishermen during the 1907 anti-Japanese riots in Vancouver. He met Anna Moyer in Red Deer, Alberta (1908), delighted her by reciting his poems written in Scottish dialect, and married her in Calgary, Alberta (September 1909). For four years, John Millar ran three different newspapers in British Columbia and Alberta, then moved with his wife to California and back to Vancouver, with their son. John Millar suffered a mild stroke, obtained sea captain's papers, and during World War I was a harbor-boat pilot. He deserted his wife and their son (1919). He clerked for a Kitchener insurance company and tried unsuccessfully to reconcile with his family (1923). He became a common seaman for a while, returned ill to Kitchener (1928), saw his son again, was in a charity ward, was hospitalized (September 1932) for incurables in Toronto, and soon died. Macdonald visited his father in the Toronto hospital. Unable to speak, John scribbled lines of what his son recognized as rhyming couplets. Preserved in the library at the University of California, at Irvine, is a two-page letter (July 1, 1928) in which the father offers his son practical advice about hard work, study, and consideration for others. John Millar left an insurance policy for $2,212, which his widow used to finance their son's college education. In several works, Macdonald transmutes into fiction the agonies he suffered because of his father's misbehavior. The search for the lost father is a major motif.

Bibliography: Nolan; Schopen.

MILLAR, LINDA ("LIN") (1939–1970). (Full name: Linda Jane Millar Pagnusat.) Macdonald's daughter, born June 18, 1939, in Toronto. Macdonald was thrilled; but his wife, Margaret Millar,* felt trapped by motherhood, soon developed a heart condition, read mysteries, and began to write. Linda, bright but rebellious, had a troubled childhood, worsened by unsavory friends, underage drinking, and experiments with drugs. One evening in February 1956 she got into her car in Santa Barbara, drank too much wine, hit two boys and threw them seventy feet, killing one, grazed a third, sped off, crashed into another car minutes later, and rolled over. When she was detained, she lied to the authorities. Ray Pinker, a detective (who figures in *Meet Me at the Morgue*), investigated. After legal maneuvering and psychoanalysis, Linda wrote a confession, was pronounced guilty on two felony counts (June), and was imprisoned at Camarillo. Terms of her release (August) were generous: eight years' probation, no drinking, no driving, regular counseling. A $65,000 wrongful-death suit was dismissed with prejudice; Macdonald settled the injured boy's suit for $10,800 (plus court costs).

Linda enrolled in high school at Menlo Park (September 1956), graduated a year later, and enrolled at the University of California at Davis (September 1957). By January 1958 she was caught drunk twice but avoided probation-violation consequences. Despite having done well academically, Linda disappeared with two men (May 1959). A massive search followed, involving police, and radio, television, and newspaper appeals. Macdonald hired Armand and Thelma Girola, a husband-and-wife detective team in Reno, Nevada. They found Linda there. A friend drove Macdonald from Santa Barbara to Bishop, California, where Girola turned her over to him. She was hospitalized in Los Angeles, wrote a statement outlining her eccentric behavior, was given only a suspended sentence and probation extension, and began working in a Santa Monica hospital. Linda enrolled at UCLA, became a senior (September 1961), married a missile-guidance technician named Joseph Pagnusat, worked as a secretary with him for a computer company, and gave birth to their son, James Pagnusat* (1963–1989). Linda worked as a medical assistant, suffered a slight stroke (1968), and died of what Macdonald called "a cerebral incident" (November 5, 1970).

Details of Linda's life, many of which remain obscure, are adumbrated in Macdonald's fiction, after—and often, uncannily, before—they occurred. For two examples, *see* Cathy Slocum (*The Drowning Pool*) and Laurel Russo (*Sleeping Beauty*). The Girola pair figure as Arnie Walters and his wife Phyllis Walters in some of Macdonald's fiction.

Bibliography: Bruccoli; Nolan.

MILLAR, MARGARET (February 5, 1915–March 26, 1994). Novelist and Macdonald's wife. Margaret Ellis Sturm was born in Kitchener, Ontario;

attended the Kitchener-Waterloo Collegiate & Vocational School, where she met Macdonald; took classes at the University of Toronto (1933–1937); and married Macdonald (June 2, 1938), with whom she had one child, Linda Millar,* a year later. Margaret developed a heart problem, was confined indoors often, and began to read mystery novels, which led to her writing some herself. *The Invisible Worm* (1941) came first. Five more followed. While Macdonald was at sea with the U.S. Navy, Margaret, living with Linda at Santa Barbara, wrote for Warner Brothers (1945–1946).

Macdonald and Margaret had different natures. She was high-strung, did not like to entertain, traveled reluctantly, and was often surly. He was calm, hospitable, and peripatetic. The two cooperated professionally. He constantly praised her work. She was helpful, not least by typing many of his manuscripts. (He never learned to type.) She was successful as a writer before he was. Twenty-one of her twenty-five novels were mysteries. Three of them featured Paul Prye; two, Inspector Sands; and three, Tom Aragon. The others were not series, as Macdonald's eighteen Lew Archer ones were. This may have hurt Margaret's sales; however, her *Beast in View* (1956) and her *Banshee* (1983) won Edgar Allan Poe awards. By 1978 their incomes demonstrate Macdonald's greater popularity: his, $136,000; hers, $14,000. In the 1970s Margaret's health began to decline. She had operations for facial and lung cancers. She also developed symptoms of macular degeneration, which four operations failed to impede. Macdonald's memory loss, beginning as early as 1971, distressed Margaret. His onset of Alzheimer's disease (1980) was a horror for both, but her response was a harsh stoicism. She was declared legally blind (1982). In the year of her husband's death (1983), however, Margaret published another mystery novel; in 1985, her final one appeared. Her memoir is *The Birds and Beasts Were There* (1968). Margaret Millar died in Santa Barbara.

Bibliography: Hugh Kenner, "Learning," in *IJ*, pp. 55–58; Margaret Millar, "Highlights," in *IJ*, pp. 43–44; Nolan; Obituary, *New York Times*, March 29, 1994; Wolfe.

MILLRACE, BARNEY. In *The Ferguson Affair*, he shares a suite of law offices with William Gunnarson. According to Gunnarson, Millrace, a middle-aged tax and probate specialist, is an alcoholic "on his way down."

MILNE, HARRY. In *The Three Roads. See* Miles, Larry.

MINER, AMY. (Full name: Amy Wolfe Miner.) In *Meet Me at the Morgue*, she is the graying wife, formerly with dyed red hair, of Fred Miner, an ex-sailor employed, as Amy is, by Abel Johnson and Helen Johnson. Amy and Fred were married ten years earlier (in 1942), have no children, but seem happy. She and Art Lemp deliberately ran over Kerry Snow, their enemy, and staged the murder to look like a DUI homicide committed by Fred. Amy and Art plan the fake kidnap of the Johnsons' son, Jamie. Art grabs the $50,000 Abel leaves, but Amy murders Art. Howard Cross, Fred's probation officer, unravels the mystery, and Cross and Sam Dressen, a police officer, apprehend Amy, whose remorseless babblings are close to idiotic.

MINER, ELLA. In *Meet Me at the Morgue*, she is or was Fred Miner's older sister. After their mother died, Ella helped raise him.

MINER, FRED. (Full name: Frederick Andrew Miner.) In *Meet Me at the Morgue*, he was born in Ohio (1916), had an arduous childhood, enlisted in the U.S. Navy (1940), and married Amy Wolfe (*see* Miner, Amy) in San Diego (September 18, 1942). Fred joined the crew of a jeep carrier the *Eureka Bay* (1943), was demoted for alcoholism (later checked), served loyally, and was crippled during a Japanese kamikaze attack. After hospitalization in San Diego, he was mustered out on a partial disability pension (1946). Fred began chauffeuring for Abel Johnson and Helen Johnson. Amy got him drunk (February 1952) and made him think he had run over and killed Kerry Snow. Howard Cross, Fred's probation officer, got the charge reduced to probation. Amy told Fred (May 10) that Helen wanted him to take her son, Jamie, to the Johnsons' desert cabin. This "disappearance" sets in motion the fake kidnap plot, the result of which is that Lawrence Seifel shotguns Fred, and he drives away, crashes the car, and dies.

MOFFATT, DAVE. In *Blue City*, he is a crooked plainclothes policeman who, at Roger Kerch's bidding, takes John Weather out of town and slugs him. Moffatt arrests and beats Weather in police headquarters. After Inspector Ralph Hanson rescues him, Weather promises to get even with Moffatt eventually.

MONA. In *The Barbarous Coast*, she is Archer's casual friend. She passed out at a pre-Christmas party both attended. She sends him a Christmas card. He remembers that Mona's husband was killed in Korea and that her young son died in the hospital.

MORAN. In *The Dark Tunnel*, he is a police officer who investigates Dr. Herman Schneider's automobile accident.

MORENO, GILBERT. In *The Way Some People Die*. *See* Mosquito.

MORGAN, MRS. KATE. In *Trouble Follows Me*, she is Bessie Land's roommate in a rundown Detroit apartment.

MORTON, FIRST LIEUTENANT ELMER. In *Meet Me at the Morgue*, he was the damage-control officer on the *Eureka Bay* when Fred Miner was aboard. Morton praised Miner's diligence and devotion to duty.

MOSQUITO. In *The Way Some People Die*, he is a drug pusher. Archer strong-arms him, rescues Ruth from him, and forces him to take him to Herman Speed, his supplier. Mosquito is run over and killed, on orders from Danny Dowser, who calls him "Gilbert the Mosquito." His real name is Gilbert Moreno.

THE MOVING TARGET (1949). Novel. (Characters: Andrews, Lew Archer, Sue Archer, Helene Chadwick, Chasen, Chico, Claude, Peter Colton, Morris Cramm, Mrs. Morris Cramm, Mrs. Ruth Dickson, Clyde Drew, Millicent Drew, Fay Estabrook, Felix, Marcella Finch, Florence, Betty Fraley, Albert Graves, Humphreys, Russell Hunt, Jinx, Mrs. Kromberg, Simeon Kuntz, Eddie Lassiter, John "Rags" Latino, Luis, Mae, Ollie, Puddler, Bob Sampson, Elaine Sampson, Miranda Sampson, Ralph Sampson, Franklin P. Schneider, Joe Spanner, Swift, Alan Taggert, Timothy, Dwight Troy.)

On May 7, Archer takes a cab to the Santa Teresa seaside residential compound of crippled Elaine Sampson, who wants him to find her missing husband, Ralph Sampson, a rich oilman. Archer meets Elaine's stepdaughter, Miranda Sampson, and Alan Taggert, Ralph's pilot, who has a cottage on the grounds and whom Miranda, twenty, lusts for.

Felix, a Filipino servant, chauffeurs Archer, Miranda, and Taggert into town. Albert Graves, Archer's friend and Sampson's attorney, says that Elaine wants her husband's estate, not a divorce, and that Graves, forty and single, wants Miranda. Taggert flies Archer and Miranda to Burbank. Archer inquires about Sampson's going there in a limousine; taxis to the Valerio, a Los Angeles hotel complex where Sampson has a bungalow; and in its astrologically decorated red bedroom finds a photograph signed "Fay."

Archer learns from Morris Cramm, a journalist, that Fay Estabrook is a fading actress at a University City studio set. Archer follows her from there when she drives to her Pacific Palisades mansion, then into Swift's, a Hollywood and Vine establishment. He sees Russell Hunt, a movie writer. When Fay's silver-haired companion leaves, Hunt calls him Dwight Troy, her ex-husband, allegedly an importer. Hunt introduces Archer to Fay, whose acting he flatters and who drunkenly discusses astrology. Driving her car, he barhops with her to the Valerio cantina. She says her friend Sampson is in Nevada. Suddenly entering, Miranda and Taggert whisper that Sampson has written Elaine to get $100,000 ready. Archer suspects a kidnapping and tells the two to alert Graves, the Los Angeles police, and the FBI. Archer gets Fay home in her car. Once she is asleep, he cases the place and spots $8,000 to 10,000 in a bedroom drawer. The phone rings; he answers it, and, when asked, says yes he is Troy. Betty, the caller, says she is at the Piano and, when asked, adds that she doesn't know where Sampson is. Troy, enters, flourishes a gun, seems satisfied when Archer says he merely brought Fay home, goes into the bedroom to check on the money, and warns Archer about Fay's nasty friends. A cabby takes Archer to the Wild Piano in West Hollywood. He finds Betty Fraley, a cocaine-addicted recording pianist, and praises her music. Betrayed by his ignorance, he admits he is a private detective. When he scares her by asking about Sampson and she recognizes his voice from their phone talk, she calls Puddler, the bouncer, who pummels him outside. Puddler gets conked on the head by Taggert, who was at the Piano looking for Sampson. They taxi to Swift's for Archer's car and gun, break into Fay's home, find notes concerning cash receipts, and discover the cash gone. A blue truck approaches. Taggert, armed by Archer, foolishly fires at the truck, which speeds off. Archer declines to fly with Taggert to Santa Teresa, promises to drive there tomorrow, and goes home to bed.

Next morning. Archer discreetly mentions the possible kidnapping of Sampson to Peter Colton, a friend working in the office of the D.A., Humphreys, requests his cooperation, and learns that Troy and Fay are the Piano's crooked owners. Archer drives to Santa Teresa, sees Elaine, who shows him her husband's letter requesting $100,000 for a business deal, and warns her that Sampson may be kidnapped by shady associates. Archer witnesses Elaine and Miranda squabbling, and when Elaine leaves talks sensibly with Miranda, who loves Taggert but is loved by Graves. Graves brings the money. There is talk about workers striking on Sampson's ranch near Bakersfield, and about "The Temple in the Clouds," financed by Sampson and run by Claude, his astrologist friend. While Miranda freshens up, Graves says he is jealous of Taggert. Taggert pops in after a swim. Archer tells him to arm himself and guard the place. Archer gets Graves to arm himself as well and alert the police. The two discuss Sampson's possible financial involvement with Troy.

While Archer is driving Miranda through beautiful mountain country to "The Temple," they discuss how he quit being a cop when he realized that stopping evil was not easy. They meet the shabby, bearded sunworshipper Claude, whom Miranda ridicules. He lets them check around. Only an Indian girl is there, cooking. But Archer notes the track of the truck Taggert shot at. Returning after sunset, they see a retreating limousine and find a message left in Sampson's mailbox. It orders the money dropped at an intersection outside Santa Teresa at 9:00 P.M.—or else. The police, including a deputy sheriff, arrive; Archer officiously orders fingerprints taken from the note and the FBI alerted. He phones Colton, who reports on one suspicious limo, rented by a Lawrence Becker. Archer hears a second phone in the Sampson house click. At 9:00 Graves and Taggert drop the money, while Archer, lagging behind in his car in the fog, hears a car skid and then a shot, and sees a cream-colored convertible driven by a woman speed away. He locates the limo, ditched and its driver shot dead. In his pocket is a matchbook labeled "The Corner." It is a roadhouse near Buenavista.

After Graves and Taggert say the money was picked up, Archer tells them to alert the authorities and drives to Buenavista. He describes the dead man to a Corner waitress and learns that he is "Eddie" from Las Vegas. Enter the deputy sheriff, whom Archer briefs on events. Puddler drives up in the blue truck, sees the deputy's car, and speeds into the hills. Archer follows by car, eavesdrops, and overhears Puddler and a Marcie wonder where Eddie is. When Puddler drives away, Archer follows him to the Temple but is jumped by Mexicans emerging from the truck. In the morning, Troy appears, tells Claude to deliver the Mexicans and get lost, and offers the trussed-up Archer a third of the $2,100 ransom sum. Archer startles him by saying $100,000 was dropped, Eddie was shot, and a cream-colored convertible took off. Puddler reveals that Betty grabbed the drop in the convertible. Troy pretends all's well, orders Puddler to take Archer to a Rincon pier, and leaves. Puddler drives Archer in his car to a pier, drags him into a tool shed, and awaits instructions from Troy. Archer calls Puddler so many derogatory names that he unties him for a boxing match. Archer grabs a file and rakes it across Puddler's eyes. They struggle outside and into the water. Archer holds Puddler under water until he drowns.

Archer, hot-wiring his car (Puddler kept the ignition key), drives to Santa Teresa. Felix helps him clean up and eat. Archer phones Graves, who reports that Sampson is still unlocated, drives in, and tells Archer the FBI report says Eddie Lassiter's record includes a New York cocaine bust with his sister Betty. Hearing Betty Fraley named as probably that very Betty prompts Felix to say Taggert collects Fraley musical recordings. Graves, pleased that Taggert is suspected, will get the FBI after Betty. While Taggert has breakfast, Archer searches his cottage, remembers he saw Taggert discarding disks into the ocean, and dives for and retrieves one. Taggert watches. After they play the record and Archer fits Taggert into the kidnapping scheme, Taggert draws a gun. Graves enters and shoots Taggert dead. Archer goes to Miranda, says Sampson is probably still alive but Graves just shot Taggert, and is surprised when she reveals a schizoid personality first by asserting she merely used Taggert sexually and next by rushing to kiss Archer. When they visit Graves, the police are already there. She kisses Graves and says she will marry him. Taggert's body is photographed and removed. Archer mollifes Sheriff Spanner, who is angry, by explaining that illegal immigrants from Mexico are probably being trucked to Bakersfield.

Archer finds Marcie (real name: Marcella Finch) near The Corner. She accuses him of killing her Eddie. Archer says Betty Fraley probably did, leaves, and drives after Marcie and her car, until past Beverly Hills she gets into Troy's car, driven by a dark stranger. They go to a house past the Palisades. Archer sneaks close and, unable to intervene, hears Troy torture Betty into saying the $100,000 is in the Buenavista bus-station locker. She surrenders the key. Archer blocks Troy's car, orders the driver out and knocks him unconscious, gets Betty's locker key from Fay, makes her drive him back to the house, wounds Troy as he emerges, rescues Betty, drives with her to his car, keeps Troy's ignition key, and away they go. Betty asks Archer to split the $100,000 with her secret partner, will take Archer to Sampson, tied up at the deserted Sunland Beach Club, and admits she killed her abusive brother Eddie. When Archer says Taggert is dead, Betty in anguish says they were secret lovers and planned the kidnapping. Archer phones Graves about Sunland and Colton about the Mexican illegals, probably used as strikebreakers. Driving to Sunland, Archer removes his car key, approaches the place, is knocked unconscious, but comes to with Graves there. They find Sampson dead. Archer's car is gone. Betty used his hot-wires on it. Graves says he couldn't get hold of Spanner earlier and drops Archer at the bus station, where he finds the money. Returning, Graves reports Betty crashed Archer's beloved convertible and is dead. Spanner arrives. When he tells Archer he was on duty, Archer knows Graves lied and confronts him with the truth: Graves, having married Miranda that afternoon, killed Sampson for his estate. Graves slumps, drops Archer at the Sampson home, and drives away. Archer tells Elaine her husband is dead. Goody, she will control enormous wealth. Giving Miranda the $100,000, Archer shocks her with the truth. She goes with him to Humphreys. Graves, already there, has confessed. Archer could take advantage of vulnerable Miranda but instead drives her home.

Alfred A. Knopf* accepted *The Moving Target* reluctantly and only after Macdonald agreed to call it anything other than *The Snatch* and also to clarify Albert Graves's motivation. Knopf never liked the ending. The title of the novel is somewhat clarified when Miranda tells Archer that while driving fast, she likes to pretend she will meet "a moving target in the road." The novel was well reviewed and sold nicely. Knopf reissued it (1949); it appeared in paperback (Pocket Books, beginning 1950; then Bantam, 1970) and enjoyed a London edition (Cassell & Company, 1951). *The Moving Target* was the basis for the movie *Harper* (Warner Brothers, 1966), starring Paul Newman (playing Archer), Shelly Winters (Fay), Robert Wagner (Taggert), and Arthur Hill (Graves). Macdonald's pay for film rights was only $12,500. In England, the movie title reverted to that of the novel. *The Moving Target* is the first Lew Archer novel and Macdonald's first novel to dramatize the corrosive effects not only of money but also of war. He also has Archer comment on women at one point. While carrying Betty Fraley to safety, he generalizes thus: "It seemed to me then that evil was a female quality, a poison that women secreted and transmitted to men like a disease."

Bibliography: Nolan; Heta Pyrhönen, *Mayhem and Murder: Narrative and Moral Problems in the Detective Story* (Toronto: University of Toronto Press, 1999), pp. 178–187; Schopen; George Sims, "The Dark Backward," in *IJ*, pp. 127–136; Speir.

MULLOY, KATIE. In *The Ferguson Affair. See* Dotery, Kate.

MUNGAN, DEPUTY. In *The Galton Case*, he is the big, competent Luna Bay policeman. He tells Archer about the skeletal remains found in Luna Bay, and fills Archer in concerning Lefty Dearborn, Lempi, Fred Nelson, and Rossi. In *The Zebra-Striped Hearse*, Mungan, called Patrick and Pat, is Captain Royal's assistant. He helps Archer in connection with Dolly Campion's murder.

MUNGAN, ETHEL. In *Sleeping Beauty*, she is Ralph P. Mungan's other "wife," whom Ralph hopes to continue living with because she is well-to-do.

MUNGAN, MARTHA ("MARTIE"). In *Sleeping Beauty*, she is Alison Russo's sister, Tom Russo's aunt, and Gloria Flaherty's mother. Martha, an alcoholic, is still Ralph P. Mungan's wife, because their Mexican divorce is invalid.

MUNGAN, RALPH P. In *Sleeping Beauty*, he is Martha Mungan's legal husband because their Mexican divorce is invalid. He lives with Ethel Mungan and hopes Archer will discreetly handle information he provides.

MURAT, HENRY. In *The Drowning Pool. See* Murratti, Enrico.

"MURDER COUNTRY." *See The Zebra-Striped Hearse.*

"MURDER IS A PUBLIC MATTER." *See* "The Bearded Lady."

MURPHY, DR. In *The Far Side of the Dollar*, he is a El Rancho hospital physician. He treats Archer's head wound, the result of his fight with Mike Harley.

MURRATTI, ENRICO ("RICO"). In *The Drowning Pool*, he is a versatile criminal working for Walter J. Kilbourne, whose wife, Mavis, says Murratti may be from Chicago. Mavis flirts with him to enable Archer to get the home movie Kilbourne has used to blackmail her with.

MUSSELMAN, BUD. In *The Drowning Pool*, Archer meets him at a Las Vegas saloon and pays him to drive him to Quinto with Pat Reavis.

MUSSELMAN, MORRIS McNEIL (1899–1952). Writer. Born in Wichita, Kansas, Musselman cowrote film scripts for *Straight, Place and Show* (1938), *Kentucky Moonshine* (1938), *The Three Musketeers* (1939), *Rhythm of the Islands* (1943), *Shady Lady* (1945), and *Tangier* (1946). He also wrote *The Honeymoon Is Over: A Comedy in One Act* (1941) and the following books: *The Wheels in His Head: Father and His Inventions* (1945), *It Took Nine Tailors* (a biography of actor Adolphe Menjou, 1948), *I Married a Redhead* (1949), *Get a Horse! The Story of the Automobile in America* (1950), and *Second Honeymoon* (1952).

Soon after moving to Santa Barbara (1946), Macdonald and Margaret Millar* became friendly with Musselman, who was busy in Hollywood. Both visited Musselman in a Santa Monica hospital (1952), where he had fatal pancreatic cancer. Margaret told Tom Nolan, Macdonald's biographer, that "Mussey was my darling." Macdonald probably had Musselman in mind when he sketched the frustrated Hollywriter Sammy Swift in *The Barbarous Coast*.

Bibliography: Larry Langman, *A Guide to American Screenwriters: The Sound Era, 1929–1982, vol. I, Screenwriters* (New York & London: Garland Publishing, 1982); Nolan; Obituary, *New York Times* (April 24, 1952).

MUSSO. In *The Drowning Pool*, he owns a lunch place where Mildred Fleming suggests that she and Maude Slocum should meet. In *The Barbarous Coast*, Archer recalls that Leroy Frost, on an expense account, once bought Archer's lunch at Musso's and now feels superior.

MUSTIN. In *The Three Roads*, he is a naval chief petty officer. Mustin and Bret Taylor argued at the Golden Sunset Café about the adulterous Mustin's criticism of his adulterous wife. When Sollie the bartender knocks Taylor out to end their fistfight, Mustin helps Larry Miles take Taylor to Larry's car.

MYRIN. In *The Barbarous Coast*, a female diver at the Channel Club tells Archer that when she saw Hester Wall at Myrin's a week earlier, Hester snubbed her. "Hester" must have been Rina Campbell, her look-alike sister.

N

THE NAME IS ARCHER (1955). Collection of seven reprinted short stories. The contents are "Find the Woman" (1946, rewritten as a Lew Archer story), "Gone Girl" (1953), "The Bearded Lady" (1948, rewritten as a Lew Archer story), "The Suicide" (1953), "Guilt-Edged Blonde" (1954), "The Sinister Habit" (1953), and "Wild Goose Chase" (1954).

NELL. In *The Chill*, she is one of Dr. James Godwin's mentally infirm patients. She makes ceramic ashtrays and takes walks.

NELSON, FRED ("SHOULDERS"). In *The Galton Case*, he is a vicious criminal. Marian Matheson tells Archer a man named Shoulders escaped from San Quentin and murdered John Brown (Sr.). Deputy Mungan says Fred Nelson belonged to Lempi's Red Horse Inn gang, worked on the San Francisco docks (1920s), was a Lempi enforcer (beginning 1928), was suspected of murder (1930), served time in "Q" for grand theft (1932), and escaped (1936). Fred's girlfriend was Theodora Gavin (*see* Brown, Theodora). He killed her husband and told her to marry him or he would kill her son, John Brown (Jr.). The three escaped to Pitt, Ontario, where, calling himself Nelson Fredericks, he and his wife ran a boardinghouse. When Peter Culligan told Brown that Fredericks had murdered his father, Brown stabbed him and escaped to Michigan. When Archer exposes Nelson, he hangs himself.

NEMO, HARRY. In "Guilt-Edged Blonde," he is Jeannine Larue's stepfather, about forty. His wife kills him for selling Jeannine, her daughter, to his older brother, Nick Nemo.

NEMO, MRS. HARRY. In "Guilt-Edged Blonde," she is an ex-cop who tried to make Harry go straight. When Harry sells her daughter, Jeannine Larue, to his brother, Nick Nemo, Mrs. Nemo kills both men.

NEMO, NICK. In "Guilt-Edged Blonde," he is a gangster. When his younger brother, Harry Nemo, sells his stepdaughter, Jeannine Larue, to Nick, Jeannine's mother, Harry's wife, kills both men.

NESTERS, AL. In *The Underground Man*. *See* Sweetner, Al.

NEVILLE, TERRY. In "Find the Woman," he is a movie actor and Una Sand's lover on the raft.

NICKERSON. In *The Underground Man*, he is a part-time Santa Teresa construction worker and Martha Crandall's father.

NICKERSON, MARTY. In *The Underground Man*. *See* Crandall, Martha.

NOBLE, HARVEY. In *The Underground Man*, he is a San Francisco travel agency proprietor. At Stanley Broadhurst's request, he checked on Captain Leo Broadhurst's alleged voyage to Honolulu about July 6, 1955.

"THE NOON OF NIGHT." *See The Blue Hammer*.

NORRIS. In *The Ivory Grin*, he was Anna Norris's husband, Alex Norris's father, and a naval chief petty officer in the U.S. Navy, deceased during the war. He sent Alex a bolo knife from the Philippines. Alex gave it to Lucy Champion, whose throat was fatally cut with it.

NORRIS, ALEX. In *The Ivory Grin*, he is Anna Norris's son, nineteen, and Lucy Champion's loving boyfriend. He is detained after her murder. Archer proves his innocence.

NORRIS, ANNA ("ANNIE," "AUNTY"). In *The Ivory Grin*, she is Alex Norris's widowed mother. She rented a room to Lucy Champion. Anna referred Lucy to Dr. Samuel Benning when she was ill.

NORTON. In *The Zebra-Striped Hearse*, he is the owner of a Citrus Junction mortuary parlor where Quincy Ralph Simpson's body is placed.

O

OBER, HAROLD (1881–1959). Literary agent. Ober was born near Lake Winnepesaukee, New Hampshire, graduated from Harvard (1905), traveled in Europe, and worked for Paul R. Reynolds and Son (1907–1929), except for service during World War I in France with the American Red Cross (1917–1918). Establishing Harold Ober Associates in New York City (1929), Ober soon represented many fine authors, including Faith Baldwin, Pearl Buck, William Faulkner, F. Scott Fitzgerald, and J.D. Salinger.

Margaret Millar* asked Faith Baldwin in 1943 for advice with publishers. Baldwin suggested she get an agent and recommended Ober. Macdonald was soon working with two Ober associates, Ivan von Auw* and Dorothy Olding.* When Macdonald got tired of calling himself Kenneth Millar on his title pages (1948), he decided on "John Macdonald" for *The Moving Target*. This prompted John D. MacDonald, the successful writer of mystery and detective fiction, to protest by letter to Ober. Ober thought matters were smoothed over when Macdonald agreed to call himself John Ross Macdonald, which he did beginning with *The Drowning Pool* (1950) and continuing through *Find a Victim* (1954). But when John D. MacDonald saw the name John Ross Macdonald as the author of "Experience with Evil," the March 1953 *Cosmopolitan* condensed version of *Find a Victim*, J.D. MacDonald wired his agent, Max Wilkinson, to demand that Macdonald stop calling himself John Ross Macdonald. Ober's associate, von Auw, mediated; after a flurry of letters, both authors agreed neither could do much but continue to write well. By letter to von Auw (April 27, 1966), Macdonald terminated his agreement with Ober to share his movie and television income.

Bibliography: Nolan.

OGILVIE, KATIE. In *The Far Side of the Dollar*, she is Dick Leandro's girlfriend and lends him her blue Chevrolet, which he uses to drive Elaine Hillman to the Barcelona Hotel.

OGILVY. In *The Chill*, he is the attorney Gil Stevens's associate.

OLDING, DOROTHY (1910–1997). Literary agent. She was born in New York City, attended Columbia University (1927–1929) and became assistant fiction editor of *American Magazine* (1929–1938). She worked with Harold Ober,* head of Harold Ober Associates, Inc., a literary agency, rising from assistant (1938) to executive vice president (1949–1972) and president (1972–1990). She married Edward V. McKeown (1946). (He died in 1951.)

In 1943, Ober began representing Margaret Millar.* A year later Ivan von Auw,* one of Ober's associates, became Macdonald's agent when he placed *The Dark Tunnel* with the publishing firm of Dodd, Mead. Olding visited Macdonald at Santa Barbara (1956); thus began a solid, loving professional relationship. During a 1960 visit, she was sympathetic when he complained of alleged mistreatment, returned to New York, and saw to it that circumstances improved for him. A year later he dedicated *The Wycherly Woman* to her. Their correspondence was not one-sided; even as Olding was smoothing commercial matters for Macdonald, he was suggesting writers she might wish to handle, including Robert Easton,* whose 1972 *Black Tide* she placed. When Macdonald was honored by the Mystery Writers of America at a banquet in New York's Essex House, he happily sat with Olding (May 3, 1974). When his mind was obviously failing, Macdonald haltingly wrote Olding of her value to him and his devotion to her (August 5, 1980).

Bibliography: Nolan.

OLIPHANT, HANDY ANDY. In *The Goodbye Look*, his name is on a wall in the Pacific Point police building, simply to attest that he was there.

OLLIE. In *The Moving Target*, he is a rookie cop who chases Betty Fraley in Archer's car. She crashes and is killed. Ollie pulls her out, is devastated by the sight, and is comforted by an older policeman.

OLSEN, INSPECTOR HAROLD. In *Black Money*, he is a Montevista police officer who does not cooperate with Archer after Marietta Fablon's murder.

***ON CRIME WRITING* (1973).** Two essays. In "The Writer as Detective Hero," Macdonald says that detective heroes are based on their authors and reflect their values. After touching on the romantic, rebellious, idiosyncratic heroes of Edgar Allan Poe and Sir Arthur Conan Doyle, Macdonald turns to the disenchanted views of urban life shown by Charles Baudelaire, Dashiell Hammett, and Raymond Chandler. Macdonald accuses critics of Hammett and Chandler of moral bias. He says he followed Chandler from the time of *Blue City* (1947) until *The Doomsters* (1958), after which his plots stopped essentially creating scenes and became "a vehicle of meaning." His Archer acts, questions, and displays intelligent unselfishness. In "Writing the Galton Case," Macdonald begins with a discussion of James Pagnusat* (his grandson), summarizes his false starts in writing *The Galton Case*, and analyzes Oedipal and other autobiographical elements in that novel. Macdonald dedicated *On Crime Writing* to Donald Davie.*

O'NEILL. In *The Dark Tunnel*, he owns a barn near the brothel outside Arbana. He is holding a square dance there when Robert Branch enters seeking to purchase a gun. O'Neill, who once shot a toe off, won't oblige Branch but gives him some beer.

ORGANIC, MR. In *The Drowning Pool. See* Goldfarb.

OSBORNE, LETITIA ("TISH"). In *The Chill. See* Bradshaw, Mrs.

OSBORNE, SENATOR. In *The Chill*, he was a U.S. senator and the father of Mrs. Luke Deloney and Mrs. Bradshaw. Mrs. Deloney tells Archer her father died on December 14, 1936. Mrs. Bradshaw has a portrait of him that Archer sees. Archer's noting its resemblance to a picture of Osborne helps him unravel much evidence. When Mrs. Hoffman tells him the Osbornes rode to the hounds, Archer replies, "Good for them."

OSTERVELT, DUANE ("OSTIE"). In *The Doomsters*, he is Purissima's sheriff and coroner, in office over twenty-five years. A widower, he tries to seduce Mildred Hallman and investigates Jerry Hallman's murder and that of his wife Zinnie. He tangles with Archer, slugs him once, and warns him repeatedly. When he shoots Dr. J. Charles Grantland, he says, "I don't like to kill a man. It's too damn easy to wipe one out and too damn hard to grow one." Archer admires Ostervelt for saying this. It has been suggested that Macdonald often humanizes "evil" characters by such humanizing touches.

Bibliography: Schopen.

OTTO. In "Sleeping Dog," he is Fay Hooper's German shepherd, shot by Fernando Rambeau and buried by Allan Hooper, Fay's husband.

OWEN, DR. In "Shock Treatment," Evelyn names him as her physician, in the city far away.

OX-TAILBY, OSWALD. In "The South Sea Soup Co.," he is murdered by Peter P. Soup for saying Peter did not put veal in the chicken soup.

P

PADILLA, MRS. In *The Ferguson Affair*, she is Tony Padilla's superstitious mother. She believes in *susto* (i.e., a bad sickness coming from an evil spirit).

PADILLA, TONY. In *The Ferguson Affair*, he is the Football Club's main bartender. He once belonged to "the ice-plant gang," with Augustine Donato, Pike Granada (*see* Granada, Sergeant Pike), and Secundina (*see* Donato, Secundina). Tony loved Secundina. Punchy from boxing matches, he is loyal to Colonel Ian Ferguson and helps William Gunnarson in his work for Ferguson.

PAGNUSAT, JAMES ("JIMMIE") (1963–1989). Macdonald's grandson. His mother was Linda Jane Millar Pagnusat (*see* Millar, Linda); his father, Joseph Pagnusat, an engineer. When Jimmie was four, he wrapped himself in a towel, laughing happily but then also pretending he was a scary monster; Macdonald theorized that the child was somehow thus grappling with primordial fears. Macdonald delighted in his grandson, taught him to swim, and incorporated some characteristics of his personality in Ronald Broadhurst in *The Underground Man* (1971). James Pagnusat died of a drug overdose in Las Vegas.

Bibliography: Nolan; "WG."

PANGBORN, JACK. In *The Three Roads*, he was Paula West's alcoholic husband. Paula divorced him (1940).

PARISH, ROSE. In *The Doomsters*, she is an unmarried psychiatric social worker in the hospital where Carl Hallman and Thomas Rica are patients.

She advises Archer about Carl, whom she likes, and shows Archer Rica's record. Mildred Hallman, Carl's wife, "maul[s]" Rose conversationally. Rose treats Carl's niece, Martha Hallman, affectionately. Rose helps Archer come to terms with the disastrous consequences of his having neglected Rica earlier.

PARK, DR. CHARLES. In *Black Money*, he is a Santa Teresa physician who gives Dr. George Sylvester the address of Leo Spillman (*see* Ketchel, Kayo). Sylvester gives it to Archer.

PATCH, MR. In *The Far Side of the Dollar*, he is Laguna Perdida School's East Hall supervisor. At age forty-nine, he has twenty-five years of juvenile work under his belt. He knocked Thomas Hillman down, swaggers, and stops some boys from playing ping-pong by stepping on their ping-pong ball.

PATERSON. In *The Instant Enemy*, he is the head of the drafting department of the Hackett family's oil company in Long Beach. He tells Archer a great deal about Sidney Marburg.

PEACHES. In *Find a Victim. See* Church, Hilda.

PEARCE. In *The Ivory Grin*, he is a Bella City police department worker. Lieutenant Brake tells Pearce to take Alex Norris's statement.

PEARCE, DONALD R. (1917–2000). Writer and educator. His middle name, Ross, was in honor of his godfather, Ross Macdonald, Canadian House of Commons Speaker. Born in Brantford, Ontario, Pearce studied at the Western University of Ontario, London, Ontario (B.A., 1940), and at the University of Michigan (M.A., 1941; Ph.D., 1948). He detailed his military service in *Journal of a War: North-West Europe, 1944–1945* (1965). His teaching career proceeded from instructor to associate professor of English, University of Michigan (1948–1961), and professor of English, University of California, Santa Barbara (from 1962). Pearce published journal articles and published and edited books on William Blake, Samuel Taylor Coleridge, John Keats, John Milton, Ezra Pound, and William Butler Yeats; an overarching interest in these works is the interrelationship between history and art. Pearce met Macdonald at the Western University of Ontario and admired his tact, sincerity, humor, and intellect. Pearce had met Margaret Sturm (*see* Millar, Margaret) at Kitchener years before she married Macdonald (1938). Pearce regarded her as witty, charming, but sometimes neurotic. Pearce and Macdonald studied under W.H. Auden* at Michigan (1941). Macdonald dedicated *Trouble Follows Me* (1946) to Pearce. Macdonald preceded Pearce to Santa Barbara, California (1946). Macdonald flourished the bulky typescript of *The Ivory Grin* (1952) at Pearce, read aloud its last three sentences, and explicated them as meaning modern man is incomplete because modern woman is uncompleted. When Macdonald and his family moved briefly to Menlo Park, California, the Pearces bought their Santa Barbara house (1956). When Macdonald underwent psychotherapy and was often egocentric and abrasive (1956–1957), Pearce remained sympathetic, as he was with Macdonald's wayward daughter, Linda Millar.* Once Macdonald returned to Santa Barbara (1957), the two friends often sailed together. Macdonald failed in his bid to teach creative writing at Santa Barbara (1958), despite Pearce's backing. Pearce tried unsuccessfully (1961) to interest Indiana University Press editors in Macdonald's dissertation on Samuel Taylor Coleridge. Pearce despised *The Chill* (1964), because in it Dean Roy Bradshaw, an academic character, was partly modeled on Pearce and his marital problems. This caused a rupture in his friendship with Macdonald.

Bibliography: Nolan.

PEARSALL, SHERIFF. In "Midnight Blue," he is the local law official who investigates Virginia Green's murder.

PEDRO. In *The Underground Man*, he is Carlos's fisherman friend who works for Roger Armistead. Pedro saw Susan Crandall foolishly climb the mast of Armistead's sloop the *Ariadne* and dive into the ocean.

"THE PELICAN DETOUR." *See The Galton Case*.

PENNELL, DEPUTY RORY. In *The Instant Enemy*, he works in the Rodeo City sheriff's office. Archer tells him about Jack Fleischer's murder. Rory, who stammers, mans the radio when the posse seeking David Spanner sends messages to him.

"THE PEOPLE WATCHER." *See The Zebra-Striped Hearse*.

PEPPERMILL. In *The Ivory Grin*, this is the name of the family whose lavish estate, outside Arroyo Beach, Una Durano rents. In it, she cares for her demented brother, Leo Durano.

PEREZ. In *The Far Side of the Dollar*, he and his wife are Mexican servants working for Ralph Hillman and Elaine Hillman. He is currently vacationing in Mexico.

PEREZ, JOSÉ. In *The Zebra-Striped Hearse*, he is the bartender at the *Cantina* in Ajijic. He eavesdrops when Archer is talking with Claude Stacy, then tells Anne Castle that Archer is investigating Bruce Campion.

PEREZ, MRS. In *The Far Side of the Dollar*, she is the Spanish-speaking servant of Ralph and Elaine Hillman. She likes their son, Thomas Hillman, and tells him about her home in Sinaloa, "a land of many rivers."

PERLBERG, CAPTAIN. In *Black Money*, he is a Montevista police officer who investigates Francis Martel's murder and cooperates with Archer.

PERRINE, BRIDGET. In *The Chill*, she was tried for something in a Pacific Point court. Archer's testimony helped acquit her. Her defense counsel was Jerry Marks. Knowing about her guilty conduct in other activities, Archer resists her drunken advances. It has been suggested that Macdonald created her name out of those of Brigid O'Shaughnessy and Effie Perrine in *The Maltese Falcon* by Dashiell Hammett.

Bibliography: Nolan.

PERRY. In *The Ferguson Affair*, this is the name of neighbors whose loud radio bothers William and Sally Gunnarson.

PETE. In *Blue City*, he is a delivery boy on whose truck John Weather rides to avoid the police. Pete boasts about his amatory successes with Rose.

PINKER, RAY. Police officer. Pinker was a Los Angeles forensic chemist, the so-called "test-tube detective" made famous by appearing on the radio and the television crime show *Dragnet*. In *Meet Me at the Morgue*, Pinker, who lives in Westwood, is identified as Sam Dressen's friend. Macdonald consulted Pinker to validate details concerning Fred Miner's DUI homicide of Kerry Snow. Fiction became reality when in 1956 Macdonald's daughter Linda Millar* caused a DUI homicide and Pinker was called to Santa Barbara to examine her car for evidence.

Bibliography: Nolan.

PISCATOR, PETER. In *Blue City*, this is the imaginary man John Weather says he fishes with.

PLANTER, ARTHUR. In *The Blue Hammer*, he is a well-known art critic and a supercilious guest at Francine Chantry's cocktail party. He tells Archer a certain painting could be by Jacob Whitmore and mentions Whitmore's death by drowning.

PLIMSOLL, COLONEL. In *Black Money*, he was a friend, living in Washington, D.C., of Major General Hiram Bagshaw, whose widow suggests Plimsoll may help Archer identify Francis Martel. Archer follows this lead succesfully.

"PORTRAIT OF THE ARTIST." *See The Blue Hammer*.

"PORTRAIT OF THE ARTIST AS A DEAD MAN." *See The Blue Hammer*.

PRATT, JACKIE. In *The Blue Hammer*, he is a guest at Francine Chantry's cocktail party. Archer thinks Pratt resembles a Charles Dickens juvenile. On closer observation, Archer believes him to be fifty or more.

PRINCE, DETECTIVE-SERGEANT. In *The Instant Enemy*, he and Detective-Sergeant Janowski investigate the beating of Mrs. Laurel Smith at her Pacific Palisades apartment. When Archer proves uncooperative, Prince, an ex–Golden Gloves welterweight in his late thirties, seems tempted to punch him.

PROCTOR. In *Black Money*. *See* Fablon, Marietta.

PUDDLER. In *The Moving Target*, he is the ex-pugilist working for Betty Fraley and Dwight Troy at the Wild Piano and elsewhere. He punches Archer until Alan Taggert rescues him. Archer follows Puddler to Claude's temple, is captured by Troy's illegal immigrants, and is turned over to Puddler to take to a pier off Rincon. The two fight, and Archer drowns him. In *The Wycherly Woman*, Archer tells Catherine Wycherly that eleven or twelve years ago he killed a man named Puddler, who was trying to kill him. In *The Blue Hammer*, Archer recalls having killed Puddler and therefore subdues, instead of killing, the villainous Rico "as an equalizer" of that sin.

PURVIS, HENRY. In *The Blue Hammer*, he is the Santa Teresa deputy coroner. He tells Archer that Jacob Whitmore drowned in the ocean but later says he must have been murdered in fresh water. Purvis examines the bones of the murder victim who turns out to be Gerard Johnson and says they reveal shrapnel wounds.

PURVIS, VAUGHAN. In *The Underground Man*, he is the deputy coroner when Stanley Broadhurst's body is exhumed. Purvis knew Stanley in school and envied the Broadhurst family wealth.

Q

QUILLAN, STANLEY. In *The Wycherly Woman*, he is the boyfriend of Jessie Drake, who lives next door to the San Mateo apartment Catherine Wycherly rented from Girston. Stanley abuses Jessie and calls her his "pig." Stanley is Ben Merriman's wife Sally's brother. Stanley owns a record shop, is a sound expert, and bugs Catherine's room. He and Ben start a blackmailing scheme. When Ben is murdered, Archer warns Stanley, who, however, is also murdered.

R

RACHEL. In *The Far Side of the Dollar*, she is the babysitter hired by the wife of Tony, The Barroom Floor bartender.

RADER, JEREMY. In *The Blue Hammer*, he is a guest at Francine Chantry's cocktail party. He is hairy, jovial, and "in the last late flush of his youth."

RADER, MOLLY. In *The Blue Hammer*, she is a guest at Francine Chantry's cocktail party. She may be Jeremy Rader's wife. Archer regards Molly, thirty-nine or so, as "the most beautiful thing I'd seen in weeks."

RAINE, EVA. In *Trouble Follows Me*, she lives in Santa Barbara near Laura Eaton, who was visiting her when Anderson broke into her home looking, unsuccessfully, for Private Rodney Hatcher's letter to her.

RAISCH. In *The Way Some People Die*, he is the self-made landlord who rented Pacific Point apartments to Galley Lawrence and Audrey Graham. He tells Archer about Galley. Raisch, who has a bad heart, expects to die within two years.

RALPH. In *The Blue Hammer*, he is a Santa Teresa art-museum worker who matches the subject in the photo of the so-called Chantry painting to a portrait by Simon Lashman.

RALSTON, DR. HOMER L. In *The Three Roads*, he was the Los Angeles physician who stitched up Burton Garth's eyelid after Larry Miles slugged him.

RALSTON, GEORGE. In "Shock Treatment," he is one of Tom's business acquaintances. Evelyn, Tom's wife, reminds him that Ralston declined to lend him money for his business venture.

RAMBEAU, FERNANDO. In "Sleeping Dog," he is a veterinarian, married to Marie Rambeau. He shot Otto, Fay Hooper's German shepherd, because in 1945, when Fernando was seven, Allan Hooper, Fay's husband, shot the dog belonging to Fernando's brother George Rambeau.

RAMBEAU, GEORGE. In "Sleeping Dog," he was a Canadian hunter. He was the guide during the 1945 hunting trip of Allan Hooper, Fay Hooper, Carlson (*see* Carlson, Sheriff), and his wife. Rambeau got intimate with Fay and was pursued by Hooper and Carlson. Hooper shot George's dog. About to shoot Allan, George was shot by Carlson.

RAMBEAU, MARIE. In "Sleeping Dog," she is Fernando Rambeau's wife.

RAMONA. In *Sleeping Beauty*, Charlene tells Lew Archer that Ramona is or was Harold Sherry's girlfriend. Archer finds Ramona, twenty-nine, heavily beautiful, and learns from her that Harold has been looking for a car.

RANDALL, ISAAC. In *Trouble Follows Me*, he is a man answering Anderson's description and seen driving toward San Diego. This lead, pursued by the FBI, proves false.

RANDY. In *Trouble Follows Me*, he is a Detroit police fingerprint specialist who appears at Bessie Land's death scene.

RAOUL. In *Trouble Follows Me*, he is a Mexican pimp who directs Sam Drake to Miss Green's Tijuana brothel.

RASMUSSEN. In *Black Money*, he is Ward Rasmussen's father. They live together in a shabby Montevista house.

RASMUSSEN, DR. In *The Dark Tunnel*, he examines Dr. Alec Judd's body, after his fatal fall.

RASMUSSEN, WARD. In *Black Money*, he is an intelligent, ambitious Montevista policeman. He knew Virginia Fablon and Kitty Sekjar (*see* Ketchel, Kitty) in high school. Ward, in whom Archer sees his own youthful self, cooperates with Archer ably.

RASSI. In *The Way Some People Die*, he sold the *Aztec Queen* to Mario Tarantine.

"RATTLESNAKE." *See The Underground Man.*

RAWLINS. In *The Underground Man*, he is Mrs. Joy Rawlins's son. Joy must work to send the boy to school.

RAWLINS, MRS. JOY. In *The Underground Man*, she has worked at the Yucca Tree Inn for Lester Crandall, its owner, for fifteen years. When Joy is unable to hold his daughter, Susan Crandall, for him, Crandall fires her. She tells Archer, to whom she gives information, that her name should be "Sorrow." After Archer rebukes Crandall, he rehires Joy.

RAWLINSON, MRS. SAMUEL. In *The Goodbye Look*, she was the retired Pasadena banker's wife and Louise Swain's mother. Louise says her mother owned the gold box, which disappeared when she died.

RAWLINSON, SAMUEL. In *The Goodbye Look*, he is the Pasadena Occidental Bank's feisty, arthritic ex-president, eighty. His daughter, Louise, married Eldon Swain, a bank employee who stole money from it (July 1, 1945) and escaped toward or into Mexico. Rawlinson, who bought a revolver (September 1941), gave it to Louise for her protection (1945) but says it was stolen from her (1954). Archer wonders whether Rawlinson did the embezzling. Rawlinson liked Estelle Chalmers, Lawrence Chalmers's mother, and gave her his deceased wife's gold box. Lawrence calls Rawlinson "that whoremaster."

Bibliography: Wolfe.

RAYM. In *The Dark Tunnel*, he is Captain Killoran's assistant at the bomber plant. Raym produces the file on Ludwig Vlathek (really Peter Schneider).

RAYMOND, TALLEY. In *Find a Victim*, he was engaged to Kate Kerrigan but was killed during World War II. Her ruinous marriage to Don Kerrigan followed.

REACH, JOE. In *The Ferguson Affair*, he is "the D.A.'s wheelhorse." His twenty years of experience enable him to advise William Gunnarson.

REAVIS, PAT. In *The Drowning Pool*, he is a criminal with a U.S. Marine Corps dishonorable discharge (December 1942). Walter J. Kilbourne planted him as a chauffeur working for Olivia Slocum, to spy on her.

Reavis gets intimate with Olivia's granddaughter, Cathy Slocum. When Olivia drowned, Reavis said he killed her, demanded $10,000 from Kilbourne as hush money, and fled to Las Vegas, where his sister, Mrs. Elaine Schneider, hid him. Archer finds him and drives part-way back to Quinto with him. Kilbourne's men, led by Oscar Ferdinand Schmidt, block the road. Schmidt kills Reavis and burns his body. Archer, spared by Schmidt, retains the money, which he gives to Reavis's pregnant girlfriend, Gretchen Keck. Reavis's real name was Patrick Murphy Ryan.

REEVES, DR. ANTHONY, JR. In *The Barbarous Coast*, he treated George Wall at Las Vegas's Southern Nevada Hospital and leaves a message about George with Archer's answering service. Reeves tells Archer he mustn't talk with George, but Archer does so anyway.

REICHLER, ADA. In *The Galton Case*, she was briefly the girlfriend of John Brown (Jr.) in Ann Arbor. She is some years older than John and drove a Cadillac. When she proposed marriage, John declined, called her "a dollar slob," but self-demeaningly told her about his mother in Pitt, Ontario. Archer visits Ada in Kingsville, Ontario, and she gives him information enabling him to find John's mother. Archer admires Ada thoroughly.

REICHLER, BEN. In *The Galton Case*, he is Ada Reichler's father. He is a well-to-do Detroit auto-parts dealer with a family summer home in Kingsville, Ontario.

REICHLER, MRS. In *The Galton Case*, she is Ben Reichler's wife and Ada Reichler's mother. Archer goes to their summer home in Kingsville, does not meet Mrs. Reichler, but interviews Ada there.

REYNOLDS, CHAUNCEY. In *The Zebra-Striped Hearse*, he is an affected, alcoholic painter, from New York with a little independent income. He purchased the unprofitable *Cantina*, in Ajijic, Mexico. Reynolds tells Archer that he knows Burke Damis (*see* Campion, Bruce) and that Burke associated with Annie Castle. Reynolds also says he argued about art with Bill Wilkinson's wife Helen. These leads help Archer.

REYNOLDS, GLADYS. In *The Zebra-Striped Hearse*, Chauncey Reynolds says that she is his ex-wife, a big ex–burlesque queen from the Bowery. Reynolds initially thought Gladys, ignorant of his whereabouts, hired Archer to "ferret" him out.

RICA, THOMAS ("RICKEY," "TOM," "TOMMY"). In *The Doomsters*, he escapes with Carl Hallman from the hospital where Carl is a mental patient and Rica is being treated for heroin addiction. Three years earlier, Rica sought help from Archer, was aided, and needed advice. Rica had wanted to tell Archer he helped Dr. J. Charles Grantland dispose of Alicia Hallman, but Archer rebuffed him. As a result, misery follows, and Archer partly blames himself. Archer and Rica, twenty-eight or -nine, apologize to each other.

RICEYMAN, REVEREND LOWELL. In *The Underground Man*, he was a minister, deceased, who advised Stanley and Jean Broadhurst. Aware of Stanley's obsessive search for his father, Riceyman urges him to think of the present, not the past, which is of little use. It has been pointed out that this advice partly echoes the philosophy of Blaise Pascal.

Bibliography: Speir.

RICHARDS, JASON THOMAS. In *Meet Me at the Morgue*, he lives in Westwood with his wife, Mabel. He is a peppy ex–movie director. Kerry Snow's murdered corpse is dressed in Richards's stolen suit, which occasions Howard Cross's visit to Richards for information.

RICHARDS, MABEL. In *Meet Me at the Morgue*, she is Jason Thomas Richards's gently henpecking wife. Retired, she was a nice actress, whom Richards directed.

RICO. In *The Blue Hammer*, he is a worker, dumb but virile, for Francine Chantry and William Mead. In 1950 Rico buried the body of Gerard Johnson, murdered by William, who then disappears. Francine paid for Rico's subsequent silence with sex. On her orders, Rico digs up Gerard's bones. Archer catches Rico and delivers him to Captain Mackendrick.

RILEY, RARING. In "The South Sea Soup Co.," he informed Herlock Sholmes that Black Bleerstone was Josephine Bailey's lover.

RINGO. In *The Far Side of the Dollar*, he owns the auto yard where Rhea Carlson's wrecked car has been placed. Archer visits him and examines the car.

RISKO, COLONEL. In *The Barbarous Coast*, he is named in a silly television commercial Archer hears while being held at Carl Stern's hideout.

RIVERA, LUPE. In *The Instant Enemy*, this young Mexican was living in San Diego when he became Ruth Marburg's second husband. When he was arrested for smuggling, she divorced him. After her third husband, Mark Hackett, was murdered, and while she is Sidney Marburg's wife, she employs Lupe to guard her son Stephen Hackett's residence. Lupe got Alexandria Sebastian sick on bad LSD, whereupon he and Jasper Blevins raped her. Alexandria later hits Lupe with a tire iron.

ROBERTS, MRS. In *The Three Roads*, she is Paula West's officious servant. She objects when Paula doesn't partake of the roast she has prepared for her dinner.

ROBERTSON, COMMISSIONER. In *The Chill*, he was the commissioner of police in Bridgeton, Illinois. Mrs. Luke Deloney tells Archer that Robertson, deceased, ordered his subordinates to call Luke's murder an accidental suicide.

ROCHE, STEPHEN. In *The Ferguson Affair*, his name appears in the clipping in Larry Gaines's wallet.

ROD. In *The Three Roads*, he is a bartender at the Golden Sunset Café.

ROLLINS, JAMES ("JIMMIE"). In *The Three Roads*, he is a disreputable bartender at the Golden Sunset Café. Bret Taylor promises Rollins $100 for information about the last man who picked up his wife, Lorraine Taylor, before her murder. Rollins willingly fingers Burton Garth, because Garth promised him a job but gave it to Lefty Swift instead. Taylor gives Rollins only $40.

ROMANOVSKY. In *The Drowning Pool*, he and his family live in the fashionable Staffordshire Estates.

RON. In *Blue City*, he is one of Dave Moffatt's dishonest cops.

RONNIE. In *The Way Some People Die*, this drug pusher and motel clerk, nineteen or twenty, pimps for Ruth. Archer rescues Ruth and forces Ronnie to talk about Herman Speed, his drug source.

ROOT, DR. In *The Ferguson Affair*, he is a physician who treats Colonel Ian Ferguson's broken nose and William Gunnarson's gunshot wound.

ROSALES, RICARDO. In *Black Money*, he is the vice president of a Panama City bank. He married Francis Martel's mother, the former Secundina Domingo (*see* Rosales, Secundina). The two conspire to receive stolen money sent them by Martel.

ROSALES, SECUNDINA. In *Black Money*, she is the mother of Pedro Domingo (*see* Martel, Francis). They lived in Panama City, where she was a prostitute. She and her recently acquired husband, Ricardo Rosales, receive money from Martel that he stole from Leo Spillman (*see* Ketchel, Kayo). When Martel is murdered, Secundina flies to Los Angeles, gets to Montevista, and wants his body and—more to the point—his money.

ROSE. In *Blue City*, she is supposedly Pete's girlfriend. Pete boasts of his alleged success with her.

ROSIE. In *The Chill*, she and a male companion are sunbathing on the roof of Luke Deloney's apartment building when Earl Hoffman seeks idiotically to arrest them in connection with Deloney's murder. Archer prevents violence.

ROSSI. In *The Galton Case*, he was a member of Lempi's Red Horse Inn gang.

ROSSITER, ENSIGN JACK. In "Find the Woman," he was Una Sand's husband, buzzed her raft with his aircraft, and caused her to drown.

ROSSITER, MRS. JACK. In "Find the Woman." *See* Sand, Una.

ROURKE. In *Blue City*, he is one of Dave Moffatt's dishonest cops.

ROWLAND, JIM. In *The Zebra-Striped Hearse*, he is the owner of the land in Citrus Junction where Harriet Blackwell buried Quincy Ralph Simpson's corpse. After Isobel Jaimet sold her house there to Rowland, it was demolished for highway construction.

ROYAL, CAPTAIN LAMAR. In *The Wycherly Woman*, he is the San Mateo police officer quoted in the *Chronicle* to the effect that Ben Merriman's murder was the result of hoodlums. Not so. Carl Trevor knows Royal. In *The Zebra-Striped Hearse*, he is mentioned as off duty.

RUDY. In *The Barbarous Coast*, he is a Las Vegas taxi dispatcher through whom Archer gets with touch with Charles Meyer, who drove Rina Campbell to the region of seedy motels.

RUNCEYVALE. In *The Way Some People Die*, he is an Oasis area police officer, who with Archer inspects Mario Tarantine's murder scene.

RUNYMEDE, FLICKA. In *Blue City*, according to a hand-painted invitation, she is to offer a reading in the public library through which John Weather runs while escaping the police dragnet.

RUSSO. In *Sleeping Beauty*, he was unfaithful Alison Russo's husband until she was murdered. He is Tom Russo's father and Laurel Russo's father-in-law. He worked in the Bremerton shipyards during the war and knew Captain Benjamin Somerville and Jack Lennox.

RUSSO, ALISON ("ALLIE"). In *Sleeping Beauty*, she was Martha Mungan's sister, Russo's wife, and Tom Russo's mother. She was intimate with Captain Benjamin Somerville and Jack Lennox. Her murder is a central crime of the novel.

RUSSO, LAUREL. In *Sleeping Beauty*, she is the daughter, thirty, of Jack and Marian Lennox, William Lennox's granddaughter, and Tom Russo's unhappy wife. Archer finds her lamenting the death of a bird killed by the oil spill. She steals Archer's sleeping pills and disappears. Laurel is partly Macdonald's portrait of his daughter, Linda Millar.*

Bibliography: Nolan.

RUSSO, THOMAS ("TOM"). In *Sleeping Beauty*. He is the son, thirty-one, of Russo and Alison Russo, Martha Mungan's sister. Thomas, a pharmacist, is troubled by memories of his mother's murder (1945). He hires Lew Archer to find his wife, Laurel. When Harold Sherry is wounded, Thomas takes bandages to Gloria Flaherty, Harold's companion.

RUTH. In *The Way Some People Die*, she is a teenage drug addict, supplied by Ronnie. To Archer, who rescues her, she says she saw someone identified as Keith Dalling emerging from the ocean near where Mario Tarantine's *Aztec Queen* was wrecked. Archer takes her to Peter Colton, who begins Ruth's possible rehabiliation.

RYAN, PATRICK MURPHY. In *The Drowning Pool. See* Reavis, Pat.

S

S., ALVIN. In *Trouble Follows Me*, in his letter to Laura Eaton, Private Rodney Hatcher says that "Alvin S." drank with him in Kansas City before Hatcher boarded the train to Los Angeles.

SABLACAN. In *The Galton Case. See* Sable, Gordon.

SABLE, ALICE. In *The Galton Case*, she is Gordon Sable's unstable, alcoholic wife. She was a model in Chicago, endured a bad marriage, and lost a child. She incurred gambling debts owed to Otto Schwartz of Reno, where she was also Peter Culligan's lover. She is periodically in Dr. Trenchard's mental institution. When Culligan is killed, Sable lets her believe she did it. Dr. Trenchard and others jog Alice's memory and protect her from police inquiries.

SABLE, GORDON. In *The Galton Case*, he is a member of the Santa Teresa law firm Wellesley and Sable. He got married, when nearly fifty, to young Alice. They live in Arroyo Park. Sable is Maria Galton's estate-planning lawyer. He hires his friend Archer to find her son Anthony. Sable, Peter Culligan, and John Brown (Jr.) get Brown to represent himself to Maria as her son's son. He hires Culligan as his "houseman." Fearing Culligan and Brown want to cheat him, Sable kills Culligan and lets Alice, who is psychotic, imagine she did so. Archer forces Sable to confess. In two aborted starts of *The Galton Case*, Sable was named Dr. Dawson and Sablacan.

Bibliography: Bruccoli.

SADDLER. In *The Ivory Grin*, Maxfield Heiss reminds Archer about the Saddler case. Archer did investigative work for the prosecution, while Heiss "combed the jury panel for the defense."

SALAMAN. In *The Ferguson Affair*, he is a Miami gangster to whom Hilda Dotery, posing as Holly May (*see* Ferguson, June), owes $65,000. Salaman recognizes that June Ferguson, Colonel Ian Ferguson's wife, is not Hilda. Salaman is arrested in Los Angeles on a gun-possession charge.

SALAMANDER, PROFESSOR. In *Blue City*, he conducts a sleazy religion-and-medicine program over the radio. Roger Kerch gets Salamander, formerly a physician, to stitch Floraine Weather's mutilated face. Inspector Ralph Hanson brings Salamander in for questioning.

SALANDA. In "Gone Girl," he owns the Emerald Bay motel near where Bartolemeo is murdered. Salanda hires Archer to clear him.

SALANDA, ELLA. In "Gone Girl," she is Salanda's daughter, tried for a singing career as "Fern Dee," and got snared by criminals. Ella survived when Donny, her loyal friend, killed Gino, her pursuer.

SALANDA, MABEL. In "Gone Girl," she is Salanda's enormous second wife. Salanda says Mabel drove his daughter, Ella, away.

SALE, OFFICER. In *The Dark Tunnel*, he is a constable investigating Dr. Alec Judd's murder. About thirty, tall, with a broken nose, Sale pursues Robert Branch when he finds Dr. Herman Schneider murdered.

SAMMY. In *Find a Victim*, he is the owner of Sammy's Oriental Garden, a Las Cruces restaurant where Don Kerrigan rendezvouses with Jo Summer.

SAMPSON, BOB. In *The Moving Target*, he was Ralph Sampson's son, by his first marriage, and Miranda Sampson's brother. He was a Navy pilot killed flying over Sakashima in World War II. Ralph was permanently in despair over Bob's death.

SAMPSON, ELAINE. In *The Moving Target*, she was Ralph Sampson's mistress and now his second wife. Paralyzed in a horse-riding accident, Elaine uses a wheelchair. Younger than Ralph, she is greedy to grab his estate. She hires Archer to investigate Ralph's disappearance. Elaine verifies the ransom demands as written by Ralph.

SAMPSON, MIRANDA. In *The Moving Target*, she is Ralph Sampson's daughter, twenty, by his first marriage, and is Elaine Sampson's step-daughter. Miranda was expelled from Radcliffe for insubordination. She loves Alan Taggert, her father's pilot. Albert Graves, her father's attorney, loves her. Archer finds Miranda attractive, but her schizoid personality disquiets him. In *The Way Some People Die*, Archer is told by Joshua Severn, a friend of Miranda's with a Santa Teresa beach house, that she has moved to Hawaii.

SAMPSON, RALPH. In *The Moving Target*, he is a rich, eccentric, alcoholic oilman whose wealth comes from Oklahoma and Texas. Children by his first marriage are Bob and Miranda Sampson. He sleeps with Fay Estabrook, a fading actress. He is involved in smuggling illegal Mexicans to his farm. His second wife is crippled Elaine Sampson, who hires Archer to find Ralph when he disappears. Betty Fraley, who helped kidnap Sampson, once thought he had "faggot blood." Archer locates Sampson only after he has been murdered.

SAND, UNA. In "Find the Woman," she was Mrs. Millicent Dreen's daughter, Ensign Jack Rossiter's wife, and Terry Neville's lover. She was a retired actress, whose stage name was Una Sand. Jack, a pilot, buzzed the raft she and Terry were on and caused her to drown.

SANDERS. In "The Sinister Habit," he is a Los Angeles travel agent through whom J. Reginald Harlan buys tickets for a flight to Chicago.

SANDERS, DR. In *The Drowning Pool*, he prescribed strychnine sulphate for Olivia Slocum. Maude Slocum, her daughter-in-law, committed suicide by overdosing on it.

SANDERSON. In *Black Money*, he and his family were guests at the Montevista Tennis Club (September 1959).

SANDIMAN, DR. R.A. In *The Dark Tunnel*, he is a Canadian World War I veteran. Now a physician at the Kirkland Lake hospital where Ruth Esch is recovering, Sandiman helps Robert Branch.

SANDMAN, RALPH. In *The Blue Hammer*, he is a guest at Francine Chantry's cocktail party. Archer notes that Sandman and Larry Fallon "comprise a pair."

SANDRA. In *Trouble Follows Me*, she was Sam Drake's girlfriend in Detroit. When he returns home, he learns that she has married a Navy pilot and they are living in Pensacola.

SANDRA. In *The Way Some People Die*, she is Irene's Beach Club friend. Irene tells Danny Dowser that Sandra saw Galley Lawrence at Palm Springs.

SANDY. In *Meet Me at the Morgue*, he is the Pacific Inn bellhop who innocently gave Abel Johnson's suitcase of money to a man (Art Lemp) he describes to Howard Cross.

SANFORD, ALONZO P. In *Blue City*, he is a sanctimonious businessman. He was in cahoots with Jerry D. Weather, John's deceased father. Sanford hires strike-breakers to intimidate underpaid workers in his polluting rubber factory. He bought the Weather House from Floraine Weather and turned it into the Palace Hotel. He cooperates with dishonest Roger Kerch. John is treated coolly by Sanford but shames him into possibly reforming.

SANTANA. In *The Ivory Grin*, he is a lawyer whom Anna Norris says she has asked to defend her innocent son, Alex Norris.

SANTEE, ALEX. In *The Instant Enemy*, he is the Pacific Palisades real-estate agent who rented the house near Mrs. Laurel Smith to Jack Fleischer, who bugged Laurel's place. Santee tells Archer about Fleischer.

SAULT, JOSEPH ("JOE," "JOEY"). In *Blue City*, he is Francesca Sontage's slickly handsome brother, Carla Kaufman's boyfriend and then pimp, Floraine Weather's current lover, and the criminal associate of Roger Kerch, F. Garland, and others. Two years earlier, Sault stole the weapon used to shoot Jerry D. Weather but concealed details from Inspector Ralph Hanson. When Kerch discovers that Sault and Floraine are plotting to kill him, he kills them both.

SAVO, LIEUTENANT. In *Trouble Follows Me*, he is a naval physician in Honolulu. When Sue Sholto dies, he examines her body, and that of rape suspect Hector Land, and says no rape occurred.

"THE SCENE OF THE CRIME" (1984). Lecture. In 1954 at the University of Michigan, Macdonald gave this lecture, which was recorded, edited, and transcribed. In it Macdonald displays enormous knowledge of fiction, mostly American and British; deplores the false distinctions between serious and "popular" literature; suggests that many novels not called mysteries have heroes who are essentially detectives and murderers who must be seen as tragic; locates the source of crime writers' fascination with atrocities in society's "spiritual malaise"; and especially praises works by Fyodor Dostoevsky, Sir Arthur Conan Doyle, William Faulkner, Dashiell Hammett, Edgar Allan Poe, and Mark Twain.

Bibliography: *IJ*, pp. 11–34.

SCHILLING. In "The Sinister Habit," he is the head of the university Speech Department and gives Archer information about Leonard Lister.

SCHMIDT, OSCAR FERDINAND. In *The Drowning Pool*, he is a policeman under Chief Ralph Knudson in Quinto but on Walter J. Kilbourne's payroll. Schmidt learns Pat Reavis's whereabouts, kills him, and burns his body. Archer squeezes him for information. Dr. Melliotes, another Kilbourne thug, kills Schmidt.

SCHNEIDER, DR. HERMAN. In *The Dark Tunnel*, he is a Heidelberg Ph.D., was Ruth Esch's professor in Munich, and protested against the Nazis. Schneider, a widower, moved to Midwestern University (1935) and heads the German Department there. Dr. Alec Judd tells Robert Branch he suspects Schneider of espionage. When Judd is murdered, Branch suspects Schneider. Schneider provides housing for his son, Peter Schneider, and Peter's transvestite lover, Captain Carl von Esch. They kill Dr. Schneider and implicate Branch. In *Trouble Follows Me*, Chester Gordon says that the current espionage case is trickier than the one involving Schneider, brainy though he was.

SCHNEIDER, FRANKLIN P. In *The Moving Target*, Archer sees this name in The Corner men's room. Schneider defines himself as a deaf-mute from Osage County, Oklahoma.

SCHNEIDER, MRS. ELAINE. In *The Drowning Pool*, this woman, formerly Elaine Ryan Cassidy, is Pat Reavis's brother. When Pat is in trouble, Elaine hides him. Through his papers, Archer traces Elaine and finds Reavis. Elaine, a cheap dancer, has "enough paint to preserve a battleship" and a "chest . . . like a battleship's prow."

SCHNEIDER, PETER. In *The Dark Tunnel*, he is Dr. Herman Schneider's pro-Nazi, homosexual son, so pale he resembles an albino. Left behind, in Germany at age fifteen (1935), Peter became an engineer, migrated to America (1941), and worked in several factories, sometimes calling himself Ludwig Vlathek. While at the Detroit bomber plant, he gathered information for German agents and roomed with Rudolf Fisher, a homosexual. Peter and Captain Carl von Esch, pretending to be his sister, Ruth Esch, whom they threw down a mine shaft to die, pressured Dr. Schneider, at Midwestern University, into housing them. When he opposes their work, they kill him and blame Robert Branch. Branch traces him to Canada and causes his capture.

SCHREIBER, CHIEF. In *The Way Some People Die*, he is the Pacific Point harbormaster and helps locate Mario Tarantine's *Aztec Queen*.

SCHRENCK, DR. OTTO. In *The Chill*, Archer learns that he prescribed Helen Haggerty sleeping pills. Thompson, the pharmacist, or one of his associates, filled the prescription in Bridgeton, Illinois (June 17, 1962).

SCHULTZ, MRS. MARGUERITE. In *The Three Roads*, she was Lorraine Taylor's neighbor, heard a scream while Lorraine was being murdered, but thought it was a sound effect during a radio program.

SCHWARTZ. In *The Ivory Grin*, he is a police officer Lieutenant Brake orders to guard Alex Norris.

SCHWARTZ, OTTO. In *The Galton Case*, he is a Reno criminal, almost forty, with "green glacial eyes" and "a lean quick body." His thugs include Peter Culligan, Roy Lemberg, and Tommy Lemberg. While looking for Maria Galton's grandson, Archer questions Schwartz's thugs. Schwartz lures Archer to Reno and has him beaten up. Since Schwartz is not involved with the Galtons, he spares Archer's life.

SCOTT, BELLE. In *The Doomsters*, she is Glenn Scott's wife, away visiting their first grandchild.

SCOTT, GLENN. In *The Doomsters*, he is a retired Los Angeles detective, living with his wife Belle on their avocado ranch outside Purissima. Since he investigated Alicia Hallman's supposed suicide, Archer, who regards Scott as a "master," consults with him about the case.

SCOTT, JOE. In *Trouble Follows Me*, he sublets Sam Drake's Detroit bachelor apartment. When Drake returns, Scott, a reporter, provides information concerning Hector Land, whose brother's death in the 1943 race riots contributed to Hector's turning subversive.

SCOTT, LIEUTENANT CHET. In "Sleeping Dog," he works with Sheriff Carlson but must arrest him for murdering Allan Hooper.

SCOTT, UNCLE. In *The Chill*, Mrs. Luke Deloney tells Archer that Uncle Scott, deceased, was "the guardian of our trust," that is, hers and her sister Tish's. (For Tish, *see* Bradshaw, Mrs.) Scott was probably the murdered Luke Deloney's brother; if so, his name was Scott Deloney.

"THE SEA AND THE HIGHWAY." *See The Far Side of the Dollar*.

SEBASTIAN, ALEXANDRIA ("SANDY"). In *The Instant Enemy*, she is the daughter, seventeen, of Keith and Bernice Sebastian. Fed bad LSD by Lupe Rivera, Sandy was raped by Lupe and Stephen Hackett. Sandy described the event in her diary, knowing her mother would read it and hoping she would intervene. Bernice read it but did nothing. Her father found Sandy and David Spanner, her boyfriend, in a strip joint, threatened David, and took Sandy home. She slugs Lupe, and they kidnap Hackett. Archer locates her and gets her home again.

SEBASTIAN, BERNICE ("BERNIE"). In *The Instant Enemy*, a former model, she is Keith Sebastian's wife and Alexandria's mother. Bernice let Alexandria down by doing nothing after the girl was raped. Bernice rubs seductively against Archer, whom Keith hires to find Alexandria after she runs away.

SEBASTIAN, FRANK. In *Sleeping Beauty. See* Sherry, Harold.

SEBASTIAN, KEITH. In *The Instant Enemy*, he is Bernice Sebastian's husband, about forty, and Alexandria's father. His wife calls the handsome, simple fellow "a boy scout." They live in Woodland Hills. Keith works in Stephen Hackett's Los Angeles savings-and-loan company. When Alexandria disappears, he hires Archer to find her. When he does so, he talks Keith out of his idiotic scheme to shake down Hackett and go with Alexandria to South America.

SEBASTIAN, MRS. FRANK. In *Sleeping Beauty. See* Flaherty, Gloria.

SECUNDINA. In *Meet Me at the Morgue*, she works at a hotel called the Delmar. She tells her probation officer, Howard Cross, that a man resembling Art Lemp had a room there. Soon thereafter, Lemp is murdered.

SEELEY, MISS. In *The Barbarous Coast*, she is the dancing teacher Anton's assistant. Bony-figured and attracted to Archer, she gives him information about Lance Leonard.

SEIFEL, FLORABELLE. In *Meet Me at the Morgue*, she is Lawrence Seifel's conceited, domineering mother. She tells Howard Cross she married George Lempke (*see* Lemp, Art), had his son in Chicago, had his father institutionalized, and moved to Pacific Point.

SEIFEL, LAWRENCE ("LARRY"). In *Meet Me at the Morgue*, he is Florabelle Seifel's browbeaten, unbalanced son, briefly kidnapped at age three in Chicago by his deranged father (*see* Lemp, Art). Seifel went to law school, did court-martial work in the U.S. Navy, and, tipped off by Amy Miner in San Diego (1945), fingered deserter Kerry Snow. Seifel does estate work in Pacific Point, and yearns to marry Helen Johnson should her rich, ailing husband Abel die. Ann Devon loves Seifel. The next time

Seifel sees his father is at the morgue. Seifel helps Howard Cross but renders himself suspicious by shooting Fred Miner. Seifel and Ann will marry and move to Seattle.

SEKJAR. In *Black Money*, he was Kitty Ketchel's father and died in the County Hospital.

SEKJAR, MARIA. In *Black Money*, she is Kitty Ketchel's poor widowed, judgmental mother. Maria, about fifty, is a nurse's aid. From a photograph, Maria identifies Kayo Ketchel for Archer.

SELF-PORTRAIT: CEASELESSLY INTO THE PAST (1981). Essays. Of the twenty-one essays in this collection, eighteen were previously published. Ralph B. Sipper, a Bay Area bookseller and a devoted friend of Macdonald's, edited the book and provided an appreciative afterword. Eudora Welty furnished a laudatory introduction.

Three original essays are "In the First Person," an autobiographical sketch; "The Death of the Detective," based on remarks at a 1978 conference concerning the detective's personality; and "F. Scott Fitzgerald," defining Fitzgerald as an epoch-ending Romantic. Five subjective pieces concern detective and suspense fiction: "Homage to Dashiell Hammett" (1964); "The Writer as Detective Hero" (1965); symposium comments (in "The Writer's Sense of Place," *South Dakota Review* 13 [Autumn 1975]: 83–84); "Down These Streets a Mean Man Must Go" (1977); and an introduction to his edition of *Great Stories of Suspense*, 1974. One is a publication of Macdonald's adoring remarks on Welty that he presented at a 1977 Santa Barbara writers' conference. Six entries reprint Macdonald's introductions to collections of his novels (1967, 1970, 1979), short stories (1952, 1977), and reviews (1979); they shed light on his parents, childhood, favorite authors (including Samuel Taylor Coleridge, Edgar Allan Poe, Hammett, and Raymond Chandler), and professional problems and successes. One is a reprint of "Writing the Galton Case" (*see On Crime Writing*). Three essays deal with environmental concerns—the endangered condor ("A Death Road for the Condor," 1965) and oil spills ("Life with the Blob," 1969; and "Black Tide," 1972—*see* Easton, Robert). The most amusing piece is the introduction to "Kenneth Millar/Ross Macdonald—A Checklist" (1971), by Matthew J. Bruccoli,* in which Macdonald says the list resembles the "rap sheet . . . [of] a three-time loser." Finally, Sipper includes his interview of Macdonald.

"THE SERPENT'S TOOTH." *See The Far Side of the Dollar*.

SEVERN, JOSHUA. In *The Way Some People Die*, he is a radio-show executive. He released Keith Dalling for drunkenness. Jane Starr Hammond leads Archer to Severn. In *The Barbarous Coast*, Clarence Bassett tells Archer that Severn, a television producer, recommended Archer.

SHANLEY, DR. In *The Far Side of the Dollar*, he examined Thomas Hillman after he wrecked Rhea Carlson's car.

SHANTZ, MRS. In *The Dark Tunnel*, she is Dr. Herman Schneider's servant. He brought her from Germany, calls her "an ignorant peasant," but says she cooks well.

SHANTZ, SERGEANT ("SHANTZIE"). In *Sleeping Beauty*, he is a policeman who, with Captain Dolan, investigates the wounding of Jack Lennox.

SHAW. In "The Bearded Lady," he is Walter Hendryx's gate guard.

SHELL, MISS. In *Sleeping Beauty*, she is a veterans' hospital nurse who remembers Nelson Bagley.

SHEPHERD, MRS. In *The Goodbye Look*, she is Randolph Shepherd's wife, almost sixty, and the mother of Rita Shepherd (*see* Chalmers, Irene). She divorced her husband when he was imprisoned and is Samuel Rawlinson's housekeeper in Pasadena. She visits Archer in the San Diego hospital, where she was once a nurse's aide. He shows her a photograph of Nicholas Chalmers, her grandson, and lets her take it.

SHEPHERD, RANDOLPH ("RANDY"). In *The Goodbye Look*, he is Mrs. Shepherd's ex-husband. He fathered Rita Shepherd (*see* Chalmers, Irene), gardened for Eldon Swain in San Marino (summer 1943), gave Rita for sexual purposes to Swain (presumably into Mexico, 1945–1954), and became a criminal. Randy saw Swain killed in Pacific Point (1954). Randy persuades Sidney Harrow to go with Jean Trask, to find her father. Archer finds Randy in and near San Diego and grills him. The police shoot him dead in Pasadena. Mrs. Shepherd says, "He was a bad husband and a bad father, and he came to a bad end."

Bibliography: Wolfe.

SHEPHERD, RITA. In *The Goodbye Look*. *See* Chalmers, Irene.

SHERRILL, DR. In *The Wycherly Woman*, he is a Palo Alto psychiatrist, forty-five or fifty. He treats Phoebe Wycherly and helpfully, if unprofessionally, shares his diagnosis with Archer.

SHERRILL, MRS. In *The Instant Enemy*, she works in the office of Jacob Belsize, the probation officer. Her recommendation enables Alexandria Sebastian to remain out of jail.

SHERRY, HAROLD ("HARRY"). In *Sleeping Beauty*, he was a schoolmate of Laurel Lennox, who ran off with her to Las Vegas, was expelled, and grew vengeful. Now thirty-three, Harold pretends he has kidnapped Laurel (Mrs. Thomas Russo), and demands $100,000. He and her father, Jack Lennox, exchange shots; wounded, Harold goes with Gloria Flaherty to a motel, checking in as Mr. and Mrs. Frank Sebastian. Archer persuades Harold's mother to give him Harold's gun and money, and call the police.

SHERRY, MRS. In *Sleeping Beauty*, she is Harold Sherry's mother. Archer persuades her to turn the wild lad in.

SHERRY, ROGER. In *Sleeping Beauty*, he was Harold Sherry's vicious father, long gone.

SHINY. In *The Dark Tunnel*, he is an Arbana taxi driver. Robert Branch recognizes him outside town by his "central European nose" and dark eyes.

SHIPSTAD, CAPTAIN ARNIE. In *The Underground Man*, he is a captain of detectives in Los Angeles. Archer, who calls him "a fresh-faced Swede," has known Arnie from their Hollywood days. Arnie tells Archer about Al Sweetner's criminal record.

"SHOCK TREATMENT" (1953). Short story. (Characters: Evelyn, Dr. Owen, George Ralston, Tom.) Tom and Evelyn, married a week, are honeymooning at a remote lake cottage. Evelyn, a wealthy, diabetic airhead, adores her husband. Tom, a sarcastic brute, needs to inherit her money for a business venture. So he secretly breaks her bottle of insulin, lets her dose herself from a bottle he bought of a different strength, and talks demeaningly to her until she dies.

SHOLMES, HERLOCK. In "The South Sea Soup Co.," he is the detective, whose deductions do not rival those of Sherlock Holmes, whose name Macdonald was not the first spoofer to spoonerize. *The Adventures of Herlock Sholmes* reprints eighteen "Herlock Sholmes" stories by Charles Harold St. John Hamilton (1876–1961) from 1915 and 1916 issues of *The Greyfriars Herald*; its introduction mentions earlier parodies featuring Sherlaw Kombs (1892), Picklock Holes (1893), and finally Herlock Sholmes, in *Arsène Lupin contre Herlock Sholmes* (1908) by Maurice Leblanc (1861–1941).

Bibliography: Peter Todd [i.e., Hamilton], *The Adventures of Herlock Sholmes*, introduction by Philip José Farmer (New York: Mysterious Press, 1976).

SHOLTO, HENRY ("HANK"). In *The Zebra-Striped Hearse*, he is a Lake Tahoe handyman who tells Archer and Arnie Walters about Harriet Blackwell and Bruce Campion, Kito, Quincy Ralph Simpson, and Colonel Mark Blackwell. Macdonald gets in a gratuitous comment about California racism when he has Sholto add that "you can't always trust these Orientals," meaning Kito.

SHOLTO, MOLLY. In *The Zebra-Striped Hearse*, she is Henry Sholto's wife. She says Harriet Blackwell complained that Bruce Campion "was taking advantage of her love."

SHOLTO, SUE. In *Trouble Follows Me*, she is an attractive little Jewish girl. She and Mary Thompson are Honolulu radio disk jockeys. Sue has been Lieutenant Eric Swann's girlfriend about about a year. When Sue suspects Mary is transmitting naval secrets, Mary murders her.

SID. In *Blue City*, he owns a hamburger stand near where Dave Moffatt dumped John Weather.

SIDDON. In *The Blue Hammer*, he was Betty Joe Siddon's father. Siddon, a writer, took her to see Richard Chantry when she was four or five. She tells Archer she didn't like her family.

SIDDON, BETTY JO. In *The Blue Hammer*, she is a pro-feminist Santa Teresa newspaper reporter, just under thirty. Archer meets her at Francine Chantry's cocktail party. Archer finds Betty "well-shaped but rather awkward." They cooperate, competitively, to find Mildred Mead. She succeeds, but Gerard Johnson kidnaps her. Archer rescues her. The two sleep together in his motel room their second night and again, more calmly, the third. He cares for her and feels renewed by her love.

SILCOX, DR. W. In *The Underground Man*, he works in the Santa Teresa hospital, tells Archer that Captain Leo Broadhurst was shot with a .22 but killed by a butcher knife, and clams up when asked for more details.

"THE SILENT HAMMER." *See The Blue Hammer*.

SILLIMAN, DR. In "The Bearded Lady," he is the San Marcos art museum curator.

SILVADO, MRS. In *The Wycherly Woman*, she is the Champion Hotel clerk on duty when Archer, pretending to be Homer Wycherly, asks about his "wife."

"THE SILVER DOLLAR TREE." *See The Ferguson Affair.*

SIM. In *Blue City*, he is evidently a black servant working for Alonzo P. Sanford.

SIM. In *The Three Roads*, in a personals columns Theodora Swanscutt read, he and Jack were told by Charlie that their deal was still on.

SIMEON, DR. In *The Ferguson Affair*, he is the Buenavista hospital coroner who examines the bodies of Hector Broadman and Secundina Donato. William Gunnarson persuades him to reconsider his opinions. In the presence of corpses, Simeon speaks with improper levity.

SIMEON, JUDGE ERNEST. In *Blue City*, he is a city judge. Dave Moffatt displeases Simeon by presenting prisoners who have obviously been beaten. Roger Kerch evidently forced Freeman Allison to write Simeon a letter incriminating Allison.

SIMMIE. In *The Drowning Pool*, he is a bartender at Las Vegas's Green Dragon, which Mrs. Elaine Schneider frequents.

SIMMIE. In *The Way Some People Die*, he is a courteous black janitor, eighteen, at the Point Arena. He is ambitious to become a boxer. He talks to Archer more than his girlfriend Violet will. Mario Tarantine's chasing Simmie into the black neighborhood dramatizes racial tensions in Pacific Point.

SIMMONS, AL. In *The Instant Enemy*, he is a Centerville lunch-counter owner. He provides Archer and Henry Langston with information about past activities of Mamie Hagedorn, Mrs. Laurel Smith, and Jack Fleischer, and the recent movements of Fleischer and David Spanner.

SIMMONS, MRS. In *The Ferguson Affair*, she owned the diamond ring Larry Gaines stole and gave to Ella Barker.

SIMON, MAX. In *The Dark Tunnel*, he is the janitor at the apartment building where Robert Branch lives. When Branch is hospitalized, Simon brings him clean clothes.

SIMPSON, MRS. In *The Ivory Grin*, she is a police matron who guards Florida Gutierrez.

SIMPSON, QUINCY RALPH. In *The Zebra-Striped Hearse*, he is called Ralph. Simpson was in the army in Korea with Bruce Campion, married Vicky (*see* Simpson, Vicky), gambled and pretended he was a detective, worked for Colonel Mark Blackwell, and stayed with Fawn King. Dead two months, Ralph's body was found in July, near the former home of Isobel Jaimet (*see* Blackwell, Isobel). The truth comes out: Ralph planned to blackmail Blackwell; but Blackwell's daughter, Harriet Blackwell, killed and buried him. Simpson never appears in the novel.

SIMPSON, STANLEY. In "The Suicide," he is the La Jolla taxi driver who tells Archer he took Clare Larrabee to Gretchen Falk's home.

SIMPSON, VICKY. In *The Zebra-Striped Hearse*, she is Quincy Ralph Simpson's pretty wife. In late May, she reported he had been missing two months. Sergeant Wesley Leonard, a Citrus County policeman, identifies Ralph's body. Leonard's wife regards Vicky as a threat to her marriage. Vicky tardily tells Archer that she suspected Ralph killed Dolly Campion.

SIMS, DR. LAMBERT. In *The Three Roads*, he was the assistant medical examiner who checked Lorraine Taylor's corpse and said she was strangled.

"THE SINGING PIGEON." *See* "Gone Girl."

SINGLETON, CHARLES A., JR. ("CHARLIE"). In *The Ivory Grin*, he was the Singleton family scion, twenty-nine. His mother is Arroyo Beach's wealthy widow, Mrs. Charles A. Singleton of Arroyo Beach. Young Charles entered Harvard (1941), became a combat Air Force pilot, wanted to be a poet, loved and was loved by Elizabeth Benning, attended Harvard Law School, and tried to abandon opulence by doing farm work. Elizabeth's other lover, Leo Durano, fatally shot Charlie. Dr. Samuel Benning, Elizabeth's husband, converted his corpse into a grinning office skeleton. Maxfield Heiss is murdered, dressed in Charlie's clothes, and torched in Charlie's Buick. The $5,000 reward posted by his mother occasions much action. Sylvia Treen hopelessly loved Charlie. He never appears in the novel.

Bibliography: Speir.

SINGLETON, MAJOR CHARLES A. In *The Ivory Grin*, he was Charles A. Singleton, Jr.'s father.

SINGLETON, MRS. CHARLES A. In *The Ivory Grin*, she is the missing Charles A. Singleton, Jr.'s wealthy, reserved mother and has posted $5,000 for information about him. Archer interviews her and informally begins working for her. He gains information about Charles from Sylvia Treen, the old lady's companion, who hopelessly loved him.

"THE SINISTER HABIT" (1953, 1955). Short story. (Characters: Lew Archer, Jack Dolphine, Stella Dolphine, Harlan, J. Reginald Harlan, Mrs. Harlan, Leonard Lister, Maude Lister, Sanders, Schilling.) J. Reginald Harlan hires Archer to find his sister, Maude, who married Leonard Lister. To do so, Lister deserted his landlord's wife, Stella Dolphine, whose husband, Jack Dolphine, strangled Stella for still wanting Leonard. The result: Jack aims at the Listers but shoots Reginald dead, whereupon Archer kills Jack. The original title of "The Sinister Habit" (i.e., Archer's habit of asking tricky questions) was "The Guilty Ones." In 1952 Macdonald structured "The Guilty Ones" like a television drama, in a fruitless attempt to attract a TV contract for a thirteen-week Archer series.

Bibliography: Nolan.

SIPE, OTTO. In *The Far Side of the Dollar*, he is an ex-policeman from Pocatello. In the 1940s he and Mike Harley went to California together. Sipe got a job as the Barcelona Hotel detective. Harold Harley took a compromising photograph of Ralph Hillman and Susanna Drew, which Mike used to extort money from Elaine Hillman, Ralph's wife. Encountering Sipe when he is watchman at the bankrupt Barcelona, Archer describes his face as that "of a horribly ravaged baby who had never been weaned from the bottle." Sipe, hopelessly drunk, finds Mike stabbed to death, is about to bury him when Archer and Ben Daly interrupt him, and fights Daly, who shoots him dead.

"THE SKULL BENEATH THE SKIN." *See The Galton Case.*

"THE SKY HOOK" (1948). Short story. (Characters: Joe Brewer, Frederick, Indian Soney, James, Martha, Soapy Smith, Starr.) Martha, seventy, gently kisses Frederick, who has been her husband for fifty years, and watches the half-paralyzed fellow limp out for a short walk. Frederick remembers trips half a century ago to the Alaskan gold fields. His group once wished they had a sky hook to hoist them over a crevasse. Now he needs such a hook as he stumbles across a street. He looks at the distant mountains, falters, and as he falls, dying, feels that sky hook lifting him above "Martha safe in the garden," high over a line of tiny gold-seeking men "crossing . . . to the promised land."

SLATER, WHITEY. In *The Ferguson Affair*, he is an ambulance driver, works with Ronald Spice, and seems obsessed by death. He and Spice murder Hector Broadman and Secundina Donato and try to kill William Gunnarson.

SLEEPING BEAUTY (1973). Novel. (Characters: Mrs. Archer, Lew Archer, Nelson Bagley, Blanche, Dr. Lawrence Brokaw, Charlene, Wilbur Cox, Captain Dolan, Dr. Larry Drummond, Leroy Ellis, Mrs. Ellis, Bob Flaherty, Gloria Flaherty, Joyce Hampshire, Connie Hapgood, Harry, Lampson, Dr. Lampson, Dr. Langdale, Mrs. Langdale, Tony Lashman, Jack Lennox, Marian Lennox, Sylvia Lennox, William Lennox, Emerson Little, Ethel Mungan, Martha Mungan, Ralph P. Mungan, Ramona, Russo, Alison Russo, Laurel Russo, Thomas Russo, Sergeant Shantz, Miss Shell, Harold Sherry, Mrs. Sherry, Roger Sherry, Smith, Captain Benjamin Somerville, Elizabeth Somerville, Joseph Sperling, Deputy Stillson, John Truttwell, Sheriff Whittemore.)

Wednesday. Archer is flying back from a case in Mazatlán, Mexico, to Los Angeles, when he sees a bad oil spill near the coast, caused by the Lennox oil company. He gets his car and heads to Pacific Point, eats at Blanche's seafood place, and sees an old man and a young man. On the beach, Archer encounters a girl holding an oil-killed bird. She says she is Laurel Russo, seems lost, and lets him drive her to his place, where she will phone her husband Thomas Russo. She steals Archer's sleeping pills and skips.

Archer phones Laurel's husband, a Westwood pharmacist, goes to him, and learns this: Laurel is the granddaughter of William Lennox of El Rancho and Sylvia Lennox of Seahorse Lane, Pacific Point; the daughter of Jack Lennox, their son, and his wife Marian, of Cliffside, Pacific Point; the niece of Captain Benjamin ("Ben") Somerville and his wife Elizabeth ("Liz"), of Bel-Air; and the friend from school days of Joyce Hampshire, of Greenfield Manor. Tom hires Archer to find Laurel, who has left him before.

At Tom's house, Archer meets Jack and Marian, and Tom's cousin Gloria Flaherty. Tom is buying his father's house, where Alison Russo, Tom's mother and Gloria's aunt, died. Tom's father lives in Inglewood.

Archer learns this from Joyce at Greenfield Manor: Laurel, when fifteen, ran off with a senior named Harold Sherry; the two faked her being kidnapped and got $1,000 from her father; Sherry was prosecuted, but family money saved Laurel.

Archer visits Ben's home, meets Smith, his black servant, loyal from their Navy days together. While they talk in the pool house, Ben is inside on the phone and his wife, "Liz," is nearby. Archer enters, says Laurel is missing and Tom hired him, and learns that Jack just phoned: Laurel has been kidnapped. Only Sylvia Lennox can provide the $100,000 demanded.

Liz tells old Ben, sleepless because of working at the oil spill, to go to bed. Then, while driving with Archer to her brother Jack's, Liz tells him this: Ben commanded the *Canaan Sound* off Okinawa (May 1945), with Jack as a junior officer; the ship caught fire, wrecking Ben's career; William employed Ben in his oil company; William, estranged from Sylvia, has young Connie Hapgood as his live-in. When they arrive, Marian explains the ransom sum, which Sylvia will furnish by noon.

They visit old Sylvia, who requires Archer to accompany Jack to the drop-off. Archer and Liz search Laurel's room in Sylvia's guest house and find a love letter from Tom. Liz tells Archer that Ben had a mistress both before and after he married her (in 1944). Liz and Archer suddenly sleep together.

In the morning, they find a corpse, with burn scars and bruises, in the water nearby. The man's suit label says Joseph Sperling of Santa Monica tailored it in 1955 for Ralph P. Mungan. Sylvia and her servant, Tony Lashman, enter, and the police are summoned. Archer locates Mungan, who says he left the suit in his ex-wife Martha's apartment. On his way to Martha, Archer stops at Tom's and finds him raving that he killed his mother. Gloria, also there, says his mother (her aunt) was murdered more than twenty-five years ago, but refuses to provide details.

Archer finds Martha Mungan in an apartment she manages near the coastal highway. She is startled when he tells her Ralph's suit was on a drowned man. She says she gave the suit to a beggar some weeks ago.

Archer interviews Blanche, who says the two men she saw last night asked directions to Seahorse Lane. At the oily beach, Archer observes picketing environmentalists and evades a reporter's questions about the corpse. Ben arrives, and follows Archer to Sylvia's. Lashman feels left out, wants to hire Archer, but is refused. Jack and Archer drive with the money to a location only Jack knows about. They argue. Jack shows a gun, orders Archer out of the car, and drives to his hunting lodge. Following on foot, Archer sees Jack and the young man from Blanche's exchange shots. Jack suffers a head wound; the other man staggers off with the money and escapes in a green Falcon. Archer tells the police about the shooting, the wounded man, and the drowned man, but nothing about Laurel.

Archer drives Jack's car to William's estate, meets Connie, and they discuss Jack, who is hospitalized, and the possibility that Laurel and a friend have faked the kidnapping. Showing Archer a yearbook with pictures of Laurel and Harold Sherry, Connie says that Harold's expulsion caused his parents' breakup and that his mother lives in El Rancho. Harold may be the wounded man.

Archer visits Harold's widowed mother, obtains his photograph, and learns of his relationship with Laurel. When informed that he may be wounded, she tells Archer that Lawrence Brokaw is his doctor.

Returning to Sylvia, Archer tells her and Liz that Harold is probably the kidnapper. Lashman is missing. Liz irrationally feels responsible for the ruinous oil spill because she mistreated Ben. Going to the hospital, Archer informs Jack and Marian that Harold and Laurel may be colluding for the money. After briefing the police somewhat, Archer sees murdered Lashman's body and the beach victim's both in the morgue. The latter is identified by Leroy Ellis, Ben's associate, as Nelson Bagley, a seaman long missing off the *Canaan Sound*, on which Ellis also served with Ben.

At a cafeteria near Dr. Brokaw's Long Beach office, Archer learns from Harold's former girlfriend that his new girlfriend has a green car, has a protective mother, and spoke of moneymaking plans. Brokaw tells Archer this: Brokaw treated Harold, who was wounded, at a motel on Highway 101; someone answering Laurel's description was there, and he also treated Bagley, whom Harold had brought to him earlier. Archer asks Brokaw to investigate Bagley's medical history at the veterans' hospital. At the motel, Archer learns that Harold was there with a girl in a green car. At the hospital, Dr. Lampson informs Archer that Bagley suffered long-term memory loss, raved about killing Alison Russo, felt the *Canaan Sound* explosion was God's vengeance, and left Tuesday night with Harold and Gloria.

At Tom's house, Tom's father tells Archer that he worked at the Bremerton shipyards in the 1940s, Bagley slept with Alison Russo but killed her when she found another man, and Alison's sister Martha accused him of the murder. When Tom returns, Archer says Harold shot Jack and the police are looking for Harold. Tom says Laurel introduced him and Gloria to Harold but caused an argument leading to Laurel's moving out. Russo gets Tom to agree that Bagley killed Alison and to feel that his letting Harold into their home triggered Gloria's interest in revenge.

Archer returns to Martha, Gloria's mother, who confesses that when she gave the old suit to Bagley, Gloria and Harold were accompanying him. Harold had them watch as Ben was interviewed on television discussing the oil spill. She doesn't think Bagley killed Alison.

Archer goes to Liz's home. Liz says Marian shouldn't be alone; so Ben fetches her. Archer says Ben and Nelson were both involved with Alison, who was killed May 2, 1945. Liz reads from her diary to prove Ben was at home with her that night and shipped out to Okinawa May 3; it also asserts that Jack, who shipped out with Ben, and Marian and Laurel all shared the Bel-Air house. Liz says Alison blackmailed Ben, by bringing little Tom (earlier in 1945). Ben and Marian return. Archer links Alison's, Bagley's, and Lashman's murders. Ben suggests some sleep for Marian, worried about Laurel, who Archer says could be a fourth victim. Alone, Ben says he slept with but didn't kill Alison; received clippings of her murder while at sea off Okinawa; saw a would-be suicide gunshot by Bagley, who probably got clippings also, caused by its flash the ship explosion; Ben let Ellis pretend he ordered excessive tank pressure while loading aviation gasoline, which contributed to the fire and which Ben may have ordered; Ben rewarded him by permanent employment. Archer says Harold excited Bagley by showing him Ben on television.

Smith located in Somerville's garage the tube of pills Laurel stole. He gives Archer the empty container. Liz and Marian, entering, conclude that Laurel was there. Marian phones Tom to inquire about Laurel, and Smith drives her home.

Home again and asleep after thirty hectic hours, Archer is alerted by his answering service that Martha has news. Gloria is with her. She tells Archer that Tom preferred Laurel to her and that Harold has the $100,000 and was driven off by an older woman. Martha says that, though married, Alison fell for Ben in Bremerton and soon wanted a divorce. When Ben married Liz, Alison blackmailed her by showing her little Tom. Phoning Connie, Archer learns that William is missing. Archer drives to Mrs. Sherry's, sees blood in her car, and talks with Harold. His mother has the money, and he hasn't seen Laurel for a week. Harold says Bagley told him Jack shot at him aboard the ship off Okinawa and caused the explosion. When Gloria told Harold about the murder of Alison, he concluded that Jack caused that death too. Harold arranged for Bagley to see Jack and Ben on television. Jack must have pushed Bagley over the cliff, after which Harold blackmailed Jack. But then who killed Lashman? Martha says she called Dr. Langdale to come treat Harold's wounds but learned that the doctor was out of the office ministering to William, who had fallen off a tractor. Archer retrieves the money and Harold's gun from his mother, whom he persuades to notify the police. Dr. Langdale enters, with news of William's death by a heart attack. Archer goes to the hospital and tells Jack about Harold and about Lashman's death. Jack denies killing Alison and wounding Bagley. Archer suspects Jack killed Bagley at the cliff or is covering for someone who did. Marian phones the hospital to announce the death of William, Jack's father. Gloating about his sudden wealth now, Jack offers Archer $100,000 to protect Laurel, who is home again. Jack says that when someone sent clippings about Alison's death, he suspected Bagley; when they argued, Jack shot at him and started the fire. Did Tom, though little, send the clippings? Sylvia enters, expresses compassion for William, and wonders who killed Lashman. Archer goes to Jack's house. Marian says this: Marian has sedated Laurel, whom she saw kill Bagley; Laurel, who played with Tom in early childhood, may have seen Bagley kill Alison; Jack visited Alison his last night ashore; Marian herself sent the clippings. Suddenly Marian turns viciously critical of all men, admits killing Alison, and adds that Laurel saw her kill Bagley. She also killed Lashman for attempting a shakedown. While Archer is bending over beautiful, sleeping Laurel, Marian jumps out the window to her death on the rocks below.

Macdonald considered the following titles before choosing *Sleeping*

Beauty: "The Forever Room," "The Fugitive Daughter," "The Money Cart," "The Sleep Walkers," "Spill," "The Spill," "The Survivor," and "The Unknown." He wrote Ashbel Green, an Alfred A Knopf* editor (January 16, 1973), that *Sleeping Beauty* was "the book which is the most important to me." Despite lukewarm reviews, it was a moderate bestseller for six weeks. Macdonald and Margaret Millar* actively protested the oil spill off Santa Barbara (January 1969). At that time, he and Robert Easton* founded the Santa Barbara Citizens for Environmental Defense and also GOO (Get Oil Out), to aid opponents of the oil companies. The first simile in *Sleeping Beauty* is Macdonald's finest, and most frequently quoted. It compares the the oil platform offshore to "the metal end of a dagger that had stabbed the world and made it spill black blood." In *Self-Portrait: Ceaselessly into the Past*, Macdonald says this: "Over the years I developed my own system of imagery." Triggering trouble a quarter of a century before the oil spill was the fuel spill (and fire) aboard the *Canaan Sound*. Such spills are analogous to the polluting, corrupting money seeping down through decades of family members and igniting murders. It has been suggested that *Sleeping Beauty* is a fairy tale: Archer, as Prince Charming, seeks to find and awaken Laurel, the Sleeping Princess; his climactic action is to kiss her "warm forehead."

Bibliography: Bruccoli; Ross Macdonald, "Life with the [oil-spill] Blob," *Sports Illustrated* (April 21, 1969): 50–52, 57–60; Nolan; Schopen; Richard Snodgrass, "Down These Streets, I Mean, a Man Must Go," *South Dakota Review* 24 (Spring 1986): 7–27; Speir; Wolfe.

"SLEEPING DOG" (1965, 1977). Short story. (Characters: Lew Archer, Mrs. Carlson, Sheriff Carlson, Allan Hooper, Fay Hooper, Otto, Fernando Rambeau, George Rambeau, Marie Rambeau, Lieutenant Chet Scott.) Fay Hooper, the beautiful wife of rich old Allan Hooper, hires Archer to find Otto, her missing German shepherd. Archer's investigation exposes the shooting, and the killers, of a dog and a man in Canada in 1945, followed twenty years later by the shooting of Otto and Allan.

SLOCUM. In *The Drowning Pool*, he was Olivia Slocum's husband, dead and buried in the grounds of their ranch home outside Quinto, California.

SLOCUM, CATHY. In *The Drowning Pool*, she appears to be the daughter, fifteen, of James and Maude Slocum. Cathy flirts with Pat Reavis, pulls away, implicates him in the drowning death of her grandmother, Olivia Slocum, and confuses Archer during his investigation. Cathy sent Maude, whom she hates, the letter hinting at Maud's adulterous conduct, to split up her squabbling parents and let her be alone with James, whom she adores. Cathy, gently treated by Archer, is Maude's daughter by Chief Ralph Knudson; Cathy killed Olivia, in the hope that inheriting Olivia's wealth would cause her "parents" to argue.

SLOCUM, JAMES ("JIMMIE"). In *The Drowning Pool*, he is Olivia Slocum's spoiled, unemployed son and Maude Slocum's indifferent husband. His closest friendship, with a hinted-at homosexual basis, is with valueless playwright Francis Marvell. James's accusation that Maude killed Olivia drives Maude to suicide. Archer tells Marvell to get James some competent medical treatment.

SLOCUM, MAUDE (MAUDIE"). In *The Drowning Pool*, she has been married to James Slocum for sixteen years. With their daughter, Cathy Slocum, they live in a ranch home near Quinto owned by his domineering mother, Olivia Slocum. When Maude receives a letter hinting that she is an adulteress, she hires Archer to investigate. Maude's friend, Mildred Fleming, helps. When Olivia drowns, James accuses Maude of murder. Maude commits suicide, leaving a note to "Dear Heart"—Chief Ralph Knudson, her lover from her Berkeley student days (1932) and Cathy's father.

SLOCUM, OLIVIA. In *The Drowning Pool*, she is James Slocum's mother, Maude Slocum's mother-in-law, and Cathy Slocum's grandmother. Olivia and her husband bought a ranch and land at Nopal Valley thirty years earlier. He is buried there. Olivia, spry and vain of her fading beauty, controls the family wealth and the family. She resists the oilman Walter J. Kilbourne's efforts to drill a well into her beautiful property. Olivia Slocum drowns in the family pool.

SLOVEKIN, EUGENE ("GENE"). In *The Doomsters*, he is the Purissima *Record* police reporter. Archer meets him at Jerry Hallman's murder scene and sees him again at the Red Barn interviewing Gwen. Slovekin tells Archer that his father, an Austrian Jew, left Vienna "one jump ahead of the storm troopers."

SLOVELL, SAM. In *The Three Roads*, at the La Jolla party given by Bill and Bella Levy, this musician was drunk and therefore used the electric organ to play some boogie-woogie.

SMITH. In *The Ferguson Affair*, this is the detective whom Michael Speare tells William Gunnarson he hired to find Holly May (*see* Ferguson, June).

SMITH. In *Sleeping Beauty*, he is Captain Benjamin Somerville's black shipmate from *Canaan Sound* days off Okinawa. Smith, now Somerville's loyal servant, helps Archer.

SMITH, DOROTHY. In *The Chill. See* Kincaid, Dolly.

SMITH, KERRY. In *Meet Me at the Morgue. See* Snow, Kerry.

SMITH, MISS. In *The Wycherly Woman. See* Wycherly, Phoebe.

SMITH, MR. In *The Wycherly Woman. See* Doncaster, Robert.

SMITH, MRS. In *The Wycherly Woman. See* Wycherly, Catherine.

SMITH, MRS. In *The Wycherly Woman. See* Wycherly, Phoebe.

SMITH, MRS. LAUREL. In *The Instant Enemy*, she was born Laurel Dudney, evidently in Texas, married Jasper Blevins (May 1948), and bore their
son, David Blevins (December 12, 1948). They lived briefly in Santa Monica with Joseph L. Krug and Alma R. Krug, Jasper's grandparents. After
Jasper murdered Stephen Hackett and assumed his identity (1952), Laurel abandoned David. By the time David found his alcoholic mother
(1967), she had been bribed by Jasper and, as Mrs. Laurel Smith, owned
and was running a Pacific Palisades apartment building. Jack Fleischer, a
crooked ex-policeman, learns of David's activities and bugs her apartment. Archer interviews Laurel briefly. Jasper finds her apartment and
kills her. Fleischer's tape-recording of this action leads Archer to solve
Laurel's murder.

SMITH, RALPH. In *The Underground Man. See* Broadhurst, Captain Leo.

SMITH, SOAPY. In "The Sky Hook," he was a murderer during Frederick's gold-rush days.

SMITHERAM, DR. RALPH. In *The Goodbye Look*, he is a psychiatry specialist. When he was serving aboard the *Sorrel Bay*, a naval escort carrier
under Commander Wilson, as a flight surgeon out of San Diego (1943–
1945), his wife, Moira Smitheram, committed adultery with Lawrence
Chalmers in La Jolla. Knowing of Chalmers's discharge from the Navy for
mental instability, Ralph treated Chalmers for years and let him fund the
Smitheram Clinic in Montevista (1967). Smitheram treated Chalmers's
alleged son, Nicholas. When Smitheram learns that Chalmers copied letters Smitheram had written Moira from overseas (1943–1945), pretending
he was a brave Navy pilot, he decides to expose Chalmers.

SMITHERAM, MOIRA. In *The Goodbye Look*, she was born in Chicago
and trained at the University of Michigan in psychiatric social work. When
her husband, Dr. Ralph Smitheram, joined the Navy and went to sea out

of San Diego (1943–1945), she stayed in La Jolla and lived with Lawrence Chalmers. Moira, who is attractive but has become hopelessly sad, now works for her husband in his Montevista clinic. The Smitherams tend Nicholas Chalmers in San Diego; when her husband sleeps at the hospital there, Moira and Archer dine together, discuss her past, drive to her home, and sleep together one night. She tells Archer, "Disaster. I can feel it in my bones. I'm partly, Irish, you know." After Moira and Smitheram help expose Lawrence, she tells Archer she will leave her husband and return to social work.

SMYTHE. In *Black Money*, he is the manager of Montevista's Breakwater Hotel, where Harry Hendricks and Kitty Hendricks live. Archer finds Kitty there.

"THE SNATCH." *See The Moving Target.*

SNELL, DR. In *Trouble Follows Me*, he is named as a fictional dentist in patter Sam Drake uses to entertain Mary Thompson.

SNIDER, DEPUTY. In *The Wycherly Woman*, he is a police official quickly appearing at the scene after Stanley Quillan is killed.

SNOW. In *The Underground Man*, he was Mrs. Edna Snow's husband. She tells Archer she had to be strong, because her husband was "ailing," weak, irrational like their son, Frederick, and held jobs only occasionally.

SNOW, FREDERICK ("FRITZ"). In *The Underground Man*, he is Mrs. Edna Snow's mentally challenged, overprotected son, about thirty-five. Fritz, Al Sweetner, and Marty Nickerson (*see* Crandall, Martha) stole a car and were caught; Fritz, also wrongly blamed for Marty's pregnancy, served time in the Forestry Service. He buried Captain Leo Broadhurst and his car (1955). Fritz bought a disguise (August 1970) to hide his harelip and chase girls, unsuccessfully.

SNOW, KERRY. In *Meet Me at the Morgue*, he was a Navy photographer aboard the *Eureka Bay*, with Fred Miner. When Snow went AWOL, he was fingered by Fred's wife, Amy, court-martialed by Lawrence Seifel, and imprisoned. Released when about thirty, Snow associated with Molly Fawn, established a Pacific Point photography shop, and wanted revenge. Amy, with Art Lemp's help, staged Snow's murder in a way that implicated Fred. Lemp took Snow's car, registered to Kerry Smith.

SNOW, MRS. EDNA. In *The Underground Man*, she is the over-righteous, rationalizing, widowed mother of Frederick Snow, whom she smother-loves. She was Elizabeth Broadhurst's housekeeper and Al Sweetner's reluctant benefactor. To commit murder, she steals Frederick's disguise. Exposed by Archer, Mrs. Snow half-boasts of stabbing Captain Leo Broadhurst (that "fornicator"), axing Stanley Broadhurst, and stabbing Sweetner, Frederick's companion.

SNYDER, ROY. In *The Goodbye Look*, he is a Sacramento detective who traces, at Archer's request, the registration number of the revolver in Nicholas Chalmers's possession.

SOLLIE. In *The Three Roads*, he is a big Central European waiter-bartender at the Golden Sunset Café. When Bret Taylor and Mustin fight, Sollie decks Taylor with a bottle.

SOMERVILLE, CAPTAIN BENJAMIN ("BEN"). In *Sleeping Beauty*, he is Elizabeth Somerville's unfaithful husband, old enough to be her father. He consorted with Alison Russo (1945), commanded and shipped out aboard the *Canaan Sound*, with Jack Lennox, Nelson Bagley, and Leroy Ellis as crew members. Off Okinawa there was an explosion that ended Somerville's naval career. As a civilian, Somerville began to work for William Lennox, Elizabeth's father.

SOMERVILLE, ELIZABETH ("BETH," "LIZ"). In *Sleeping Beauty*, she is the daughter of William and Sylvia Lennox, and Jack Lennox's sister, Laurel Russo's aunt, and old Captain Benjamin Somerville's wife. In 1944, Elizabeth, twenty-one, graduated from Vassar College and married Somerville. Elizabeth helps Archer when he is hired by Thomas Russo to find his wife, Laurel. Aware of Ben's former infidelity and frustrated by his fatigue, she sleeps one night with Archer, memorably for him. Such affairs are rare with Archer, who next morning too coldly watches her pop out of bed, "her breasts swinging."
Bibliography: Nolan.

SONNY. In *The Goodbye Look. See* Chalmers, Lawrence.

SONTAG, FRANCESCA ("FRANCIE"). In *Blue City*, she is Joseph Sault's sister and Carla Kaufman's neighbor in the same apartment building. Francesca is the lover of Freeman Allison, who supports her. Allison's married status enables Roger Kerch to blackmail him. Disgusted at Allison's ultimate pusillanimity, she shoots him.

SOPER, MRS. KINGSLEY. In *The Way Some People Die*, she is a Casa Loma resident. Her neighbors include Galley Lawrence, Joseph Tarantine, and Keith Dalling.

SOTWUN. In "The South Sea Soup Co.," he is Herlock Sholmes's monkey-ugly assistant.

SOUP, PETER P. In "The South Sea Soup Co.," he killed Oswald Ox-Tailby.

"THE SOUTH SEA SOUP CO." (1931, 1982). Short story. (Characters: Josephine Bailey, Black Bleerstone, Oswald Ox-Tailby, Raring Riley, Herlock Sholmes, Sotwun, Peter P. Soup.) Herlock Sholmes, bright young detective, hopes the South Sea Soup Co. will hire him to find oysters in the oyster soup. No luck—until he is called by the company to solve the murder of Oswald Ox-Tailby. Sholmes and Sotwun, his ugly assistant, rush there. Sholmes names as the murderer Black Bleerstone, who is unattractive Josephine Bailey's lover; Bleerstone's calling her beautiful makes Sholmes think he is the killer. But Peter P. Soup confesses he killed Ox-Tailby when he accused Peter of not putting veal in the chicken soup. Peter knocks Sholmes through a window, swallows a slot-machine mint, and dies singing "Rock of Ages." Hired, Sholmes finds only oyster-shell buttons in the oyster soup. A so-so parody, published in the Kitchener-Waterloo Collegiate and Vocational School *Grumbler* with a Kenneth Miller [sic] byline. (He should have called himself Men Killer.)

Bibliography: Bruccoli; Ralph B. Sipper, ed., *Early Millar: The First Stories of Ross Macdonald & Margaret Millar* (Santa Barbara: Cordelia Editions, 1982).

SPANNER, DAVID ("DAVY"). In *The Instant Enemy*, he is the son of Jasper Blevins and Laurel Dudney (*see* Smith, Mrs. Laurel), born December 12, 1948. He remembers their living at a dilapidated place once owned by Joseph L. and Alma R. Krug, his mother's parents. Jasper murdered Stephen Hackett (1952), assumed his identity, and he and Laurel abandoned David. He went to a Santa Teresa orphanage and at age six was informally adopted by Edward Spanner and Martha Spanner. Thereafter called David Spanner, he slugged Henry Langston, his high school counselor, stole cars, and was jailed. At nineteen, he met Alexandria ("Sandy") Sebastian and found his mother, calling herself Mrs. Laurel Smith. Archer locates Laurel and sees David. David and Sandy kidnap rich Stephen Hackett (really Jasper). At the Krug ranch, David is about to kill Jasper, until he says he is David's father. When Jasper kills Fleischer, who has pursued him, David escapes, hitchhikes to the Langston home for help, but is shot to death by Henry Langston.

SPANNER, EDWARD. In *The Instant Enemy*, he and his wife, Martha Spanner, informally adopted David Blevins in Santa Teresa. They called him David Spanner. He was expelled from high school after he slugged

Henry Langston, his counselor. When David spent time in jail, the Spanners moved to West Los Angeles, where Archer interviews them about David.

SPANNER, MARTHA. In *The Instant Enemy*, she is Edward Spanner's wife. David Spanner, whom the two informally adopted, caused both of them grief. She is more forgiving than her husband.

SPANNER, SHERIFF JOE. In *The Moving Target*, as the Santa Teresa sheriff he begins investigating Ralph Sampson's disappearance after the kidnap note is received. He and Archer argue over the handling of evidence. An untruthful statement by Albert Graves regarding Spanner leads to Graves's undoing.

SPAULDING. In *The Doomsters*, he is the Purissima *Record* editor, hence Eugene Slovekin's supervisor.

SPEARE, MICHAEL ("MIKE"). In *The Ferguson Affair*, he is a Hollywood agent. As Sperovich, a salesman, he met Hilda Dotery, sixteen. As an agent, Speare handled Holly May (*see* Ferguson, June) and advised Larry Gaines not to pursue an acting career. Speare rehearsed and polished Holly for three years but lost her when she married Colonel Ian Ferguson. Speare leads William Gunnarson to Hilda Dotery, who impersonates Holly and whom Speare accidentally kills.

SPEED, HERMAN. In *The Way Some People Die*, he is a middle-level drug dealer, in his forties, under Danny Dowser and over Mosquito. Speed's partner, Joseph Tarantine, rips off Dowser and Speed. To recoup, Speed, as Colonel Henry Fellows, marries Marjorie Barron, and steals her money and car. Archer locates Speed, who surrenders a stash of Dowser's heroin and jumps off the Golden Gate Bridge.

SPENCE, JIMMIE. In *The Ferguson Affair*, his name is among others in the clipping in Larry Gaines's wallet.

SPERLING, JOSEPH ("JOE"). In *Sleeping Beauty*, he is a Santa Monica tailor, made Ralph P. Mungan a suit, and helps Archer locate Ralph.

SPEROVICH. In *The Ferguson Affair*. *See* Speare, Michael.

SPICE, RONALD ("RONNY"). In *The Ferguson Affair*, he is an ambulance driver with Whitey Slater. Together, they smother Hector Broadman and Secundina Donato, and try to kill William Gunnarson.

SPILLMAN, LEO. In *Black Money. See* Ketchel, Kayo.

SPINDLE, RALPH. In *The Ferguson Affair*, he drove the car that killed Frank Dotery, according to Kate Dotery, Frank's mother.

SPINOZA, JAMES, JR. In *The Ivory Grin*, according to Archer's answering service, this man, the proprietor of the of Spinoza Beach Garb, left him a message.

SPONTI, DR. In *The Far Side of the Dollar*, he is the Laguna Perdida School administrator. He hires Archer to find Thomas Hillman. Mrs. Mallow, a school employee, tells Archer that Sponti's degree is worthless because it is from a diploma mill and his dissertation was on boarding-school kitchen logistics.

SPURLING, MRS. In *The Wycherly Woman*, she is the manager of the Siesta Motel, where Robert Doncaster and Phoebe Wycherly stay briefly. Mrs. Spurling tells Archer her first husband was killed in the war.

SQUERRY. In *The Far Side of the Dollar*, he is the Laguna Perdida School comptroller. Dr. Sponti orders him to give Ralph Hillman a full refund when Thomas Hillman, Ralph's son, runs away.

STABILE, AL. In *The Ferguson Affair*, he is a carouser whose wife wants a divorce. William Gunnarson represents his wife. Al Stabile's name resembles that of Alvin Stump,* a Santa Barbara sports journalist Macdonald knew.

STABILE, MRS. AL. In *The Ferguson Affair*, she wants a divorce, and William Gunnarson represents her.

STACY, CLAUDE. In *The Zebra-Striped Hearse*, a middle-aged American, he is the Ajijic *posada* night clerk. He tells Archer about Pauline Hatchen and her second husband, Dr. Keith Hatchen. Pauline hints that Stacy is a homosexual. After Archer is finished there, Stacy generously drives Archer to the airport.

STAN. In *Blue City*, he is one of Dave Moffatt's crooked cops.

STANDISH, MRS. CAROLINE. In *The Way Some People Die*, she left messages Monday and Tuesday with Archer's answering service. He was too busy to get back to her.

STANISLAUS. In *The Far Side of the Dollar*, he owns Dack's Auto Court and tells Archer that Mike Harley and Carol Harley posed as Mr. and Mrs. Robert Brown. After Carol is murdered, the police are irate because Stanislaus recorded no patrons' car-license numbers.

STANLEY ("STAN"). In *Black Money*, he is the Montevista Tennis Club lifeguard. By pumping him, Archer learns that Francis Martel is moving out.

STARR. In "The Sky Hook," he was Frederick's partner during their gold-rush days. Frederick remembers Starr's being frozen to death near Skagway, fifty years ago.

STEELE. In *The Galton Case*, James Matheson tells Archer that "Mr. Steele" is his Little League coach.

STEFAN. In *The Barbarous Coast*, Clarence Bassett, while drunk, tells Archer that Simon Graff stole his girlfriend, Isobel Heliopoulos (*see* Graff, Isobel) and stole Stefan, his Channel Club "maître dee, too," the latter for Graff's Las Vegas hotel-casino.

STELLA. In *The Chill*, she is the efficient waitress at a restaurant in Pacific Point. Archer has breakfast there and likes her "flashing smile."

STERLING, KEITH. In *The Ferguson Affair*, he is the Buenavista D.A. William Gunnarson appeals to him, without success, to have Ella Barker's bail reduced.

STERN, CARL. In *The Barbarous Coast*, he is a Los Angeles drug dealer with connections in New York, New Jersey, Cleveland, and Detroit. He cannot get a license in Nevada; so Simon Graff fronts for him in their hotel-casino operation. Hester Wall introduced Rina Campbell, her sister, to Stern. Rina tells Archer that Stern is a pederast. Hester stole Graff's .22 and gave it to Stern for blackmailing purposes. Clarence Bassett traced it to Stern, killed him, and took the .22.

STEVENS, GIL. In *The Chill*, he is a clever lawyer who has practiced in Pacific Point for forty years. He defended Thomas McGee; when he was convicted of murdering his wife, Constance McGee, Stevens got him a lighter sentence. Archer finds McGee, released from prison, hiding on Stevens's yacht. Stevens is portrayed as compassionate through awareness of past missteps.

Bibliography: Wolfe.

STEVENSON, ROBERT LOUIS. In *The Dark Tunnel*, when Robert Branch asks the policeman guarding him in the Arbana hospital his name, the man unaccountably calls himself Robert Louis Stevenson.

STILLSON, DEPUTY. In *Sleeping Beauty*, Martha Mungan urges her daughter Gloria Flaherty, who is in danger, to talk to Deputy Stillson, who, Martha says, always liked her.

"THE STOLEN WAR." *See The Goodbye Look*.

STOLL, RETO. In *Black Money*, he is the Montevista Tennis Club manager. From him, Lew Archer learns that Francis Martel can be violent.

STONE, ELIZABETH ("LIZ"). In *The Zebra-Striped Hearse*, she and Jack Stone are Dolly Campion's parents and Jack Campion's grandparents. Long-time Citrus Junction residents, they were grateful when Isobel Jaimet (*see* Blackwell, Isobel), once their neighbor, befriended Dolly. After Dolly was murdered, they took care of Jack. Mrs. Stone tells Archer that when Isobel married Colonel Mark Blackwell, she and Jack sent her a silver icepick and corkscrew as a gift. She describes Bruce Campion, Dolly's husband, as a drinker and a liar.

STONE, JACK. In *The Zebra-Striped Hearse*, he is Elizabeth Stone's husband and Dolly Campion's father. He works in a laundry and is a good though uncultured man.

STORM, ELLEN. In *The Underground Man. See* Kilpatrick, Ellen.

STRANG, MRS. In *The Drowning Pool*, she is Olivia Slocum's servant and Olivia's granddaughter Cathy Slocum's devoted friend. She will accompany Chief Ralph Knudson when he takes Cathy to Chicago for treatment.

STROME. In *Black Money*, he is Ella Strome's second husband, a widowered lawyer. Describing him as older and "peculiar," Ella tells Archer the two split after six years.

STROME, ELLA. In *Black Money*, she is the Montevista Tennis Club secretary. She provides information about guests to Archer, who arouses her unrequited amatory interests.

STROME, ELLEN. In *The Underground Man. See* Kilpatrick, Ellen.

STROME, WILLIAM. In *The Underground Man*, he was probably Ellen Kilpatrick's father. He had a mill and lumber company.

STUMP, ALVIN ("AL") (1916–1995). Sports writer. Stubb was born in Colorado Springs, Colorado, attended the University of Wisconsin, and was a war correspondent during World War II. He became a prolific writer, best known for ghostwriting a dishonest, sanitized autobiography of Tyrus ("Ty") Cobb (1886–1961) titled *My Life in Baseball: The True Record* (1961), his sensational, syndicated 1961 exposé of Cobb in *True* magazine, and his admirable *Cobb: A Biography* (1994). The 1994 movie version of Cobb's life, based on Stump's *True* piece, starred Tommy Lee Jones as old Cobb and Robert Wuhl as Stump. Stump died in Newport Beach, California.

Soon after moving to Santa Barbara (1949), Macdonald met Stump, dropped into his office often, and swam, dined, drank, and walked with him. Stump got into trouble with Macdonald (1956) for telling him that Linda Millar,* Macdonald's daughter, was drinking and taking drugs. When Linda disappeared (1959), Stump helped Macdonald track her down. Macdonald gratefully dedicated *The Ferguson Affair* (1960) to Stump. Stump fondly remembered Macdonald for his observational powers, intelligence, and reserve. Macdonald copyedited the *True* piece, for which Stump earned $4,500.

Bibliography: Nolan.

STURTEVANT. In *Meet Me at the Morgue*, he is Lawrence Seifel's semi-retired law partner. Sturtevant was Pacific Point's leading estate lawyer.

"THE SUICIDE" (1953, 1955). Short story. (Characters: Lew Archer, Owen Dewar, Gretchen Falk, Jake Falk, Jack Fidelis, Frieda, Edward Illman, Larrabee, Clare Larrabee, Ethel Larrabee, Mrs. Larrabee, Mrs. Lestina, Stanley Simpson.) Meeting Clare Larrabee by chance on the train to Los Angeles, Archer agrees to search for her missing sister, Ethel Larrabee, who divorced Edward Illman, married Owen Dewar, stole from him, was beaten by him, and shot him. When found in San Diego and confronted with the truth by Archer and Clare, Ethel commits suicide. The original title of "The Suicide" was "The Beat-Up Sister."

"THE SUICIDE ROOM." *See The Goodbye Look*.

SULLIVAN. In *The Way Some People Die*, he is one of Danny Dowser's thugs. Dowser orders him to go to Ensenada to see Torres, in an effort to find Joseph Tarantine. Sullivan is among those arrested when Peter Colton raids Dowser's house.

SUMMER, JO. In *Find a Victim*, she is MacGowan's beautiful but wayward granddaughter, about twenty. She was an attractive but drug-addicted singer at Las Cruses's Golden Slipper Supper Club. She consorted with Don Kerrigan and Bozey. She goes with Bozey to Traverse, Nevada, where his three Albuquerque cronies betray him and rape her. When Jo escapes, Archer apprehends her. Archer's conscience bothers him after he gives her "reefers" in exchange for information.

SUNDERLAND, DR. In *The Instant Enemy*, he treated Lupe Rivera after Alexandria Sebastian injured his skull with a tire iron.

SUTHERLAND, EDDIE. In *The Goodbye Look*, he is a junior member of John Truttwell's law firm.

SUTHERLAND, LAURA. In *The Chill*, she is the Pacific Point College dean of women. She accompanies Dean Roy Bradshaw to Reno for a meeting at the University of Nevada. After he gets a divorce from Letitia O. Macready (*see* Bradshaw, Mrs.), he and Laura marry. To mislead Mrs. Bradshaw, Bradshaw suggests that he is in love with Helen Haggerty, whereupon Mrs. Bradshaw murders her.

SUTHERLAND, MONA. In *The Zebra-Striped Hearse*, she is the "busty" airhead girlfriend of Ray Buzzell. As such, she is one of the beach bums in and out of his zebra-striped hearse. When Archer matches a loose leather button with similar buttons on a coat Mona was wearing at Malibu, she readily gives him the coat. Mona and her friends say they found it washed ashore.

SWAIN, ELDON. In *The Goodbye Look*, this criminal, born in 1905, worked for the Pasadena bank president Samuel Rawlinson and married his daughter, Louise; fathered Jean Swain (*see* Trask, Jean) (1929); employed Randolph ("Randy") Shepherd as his gardener in San Marino, made home movies (summer 1943); stole $500,000 from Rawlinson's bank (July 1, 1945); deserted his wife and daughter; absconded with the stolen money to San Diego and perhaps Mexico with Randy's daughter, Rita Shepherd (1945–1954); and had a son, Nicholas Chalmers, by her (December 14, 1945). Rita (*see* Chalmers, Irene) and Lawrence Chalmers stole Swain's loot (July 1945). Swain confronted Louise and took her revolver (1954). In Mexican garb and accompanied by Randy, Swain went to Pacific Point to find his son, who, then age eight, resisted being fondled, seized Swain's gun, and killed him. Swain's fingerprints were burned off to make identification difficult.

Bibliography: Wolfe.

SWAIN, LOUISE. In *The Goodbye Look*, she is Samuel Rawlinson's daughter, Eldon Swain's wife, and the mother of their daughter, Jean (*see*

Trask, Jean). They lived well in San Marino. Swain disappeared with Rita Shepherd (*see* Chalmers, Irene). Rawlinson gave Louise a revolver to protect herself and Jean. Swain returned and took her revolver (1954). For more than twenty years she has supported herself demonstrating sewing machines. John Truttwell buys home movies from her that Swain took (summer 1943).

SWAINIE. In *Blue City*, he is a pug-ugly who with another thug tries to rob old McGinis in Henry's saloon. John Weather flattens both would-be thieves.

SWANN, HELEN. In *Trouble Follows Me*, she is Lieutenant Eric Swann's wife. Their home is in Detroit. When Swann is home on leave, the Swanns, Sam Drake, his Navy friend, and Drake's girlfriend Mary Thompson dine out together. Helen, who is childless, is both clinging and demanding.

SWANN, LIEUTENANT ERIC. In *Trouble Follows Me*, he is a naval officer, born in Toledo and now thirty. While stationed in Honolulu, Swann, though married to Helen Swann, has a girlfriend named Sue Sholto. When she is murdered, Swann and his friend, Sam Drake, interrogate Hector Land, whom they wrongly suspect. Swann goes to Detroit on leave. He and Drake, also in Detroit, talk with Hector's wife, Bessie Land, who is soon murdered. Swann, then stationed in San Diego, helps Drake and FBI agent Chester Gordon develop leads.

SWANSCUTT, FRANKLIN ("FRANK"). In *The Three Roads*, he was one of George Watt Taylor's graduate students. When Taylor discovered his wife sleeping with Swanscutt, Taylor beat him up. The guilty pair left for Cincinnati, where Swanscutt's family lived. The two married. Swanscutt lost a job and turned wimpish. The two moved to Los Angeles, where he is supported by his wife.

SWANSCUTT, THEODORA. In *The Three Roads*, she is Bret Taylor's mother. She was married to George Watt Taylor, Bret's juiceless philosopher-professor father, more than ten years her senior. She began to sleep in their house with Franklin Swanscutt, one of Taylor's graduate students. Bret, four, discovered the pair one night and attacked his mother with his fists. The guilty pair decamped for Cincinnati. Bret fantasized that he had killed his mother. Theodora married Swanscutt, moved to Los Angeles with him, and opened a lending library. Theodora happens to read Paula West's personals column asking Bret Taylor to call. She telephones Paula, goes to Paula's for tea, learns about her son, and tells Paula about her past. Taylor sees Theodora, trim and "nearly fifty," enter and leave Paula's house but never meets her.

SWEETNER, AL. In *The Underground Man*, he is a Santa Teresa resident. He, Frederick Snow, and Marty Nickerson (*see* Crandall, Martha) stole a car. Mrs. Edna Snow, Frederick's mother, housed Al to keep him from going to the reformatory. Al saw Frederick bury Captain Leo Broadhurst in his car (1955). Al learned that Leo's son, Stanley Broadhurst, was seeking his father, tries to shake him down, but is stabbed to death in Stanley's Northridge house. Elegant, a girlfriend Al victimized, tells Archer that Al called himself Al Nesters.

SWIFT. In *The Moving Target*, his is the fancy establishment near Hollywod and Vine where Archer meets Fay Estabrook.

SWIFT, LEFTY. In *The Three Roads*, he was hired by Burton Garth to work at his Cockalorum cocktail lounge in Glendale, even though Garth promised the job to James Rollins.

SWIFT, RONALD ("RONNIE"). In *Blue City*, he is a Cathay Club tenor. Although he introduces himself as "sensational," his singing is at best "limply endearing."

SWIFT, SAMMY. In *The Barbarous Coast*, he is an intelligent screenwriter from Galena, Illinois. For five years, he has worked for Simon Graff. Swift drowns his regrets at selling out to Hollywood in alcohol. He tells Archer that he and Graff plan to fly to Italy to film a movie based on *Salammbô* by Gustave Flaubert. Swift is to give the tragedy a happy-ending twist. It has been suggested that Swift is partly modeled on Hollywood writer Morris McNeil Musselman,* whom Macdonald and Margaret Millar* knew.

Bibliography: Nolan.

SYLVAN, DR. AMBROSE. In *The Wycherly Woman*, he is a chiropractor attending a convention in San Francisco. He elbows himself into the telephone booth Archer vacates after trying to call Willie Mackey.

SYLVESTER, AUDREY ("AUD"). In *Black Money*, she is Dr. George Sylvester's alcoholic wife. She bailed him out when he gambled ruinously but since then has become suspicious of his relationship with Virginia Fablon.

SYLVESTER, DR. GEORGE. In *Black Money*, he is a Montevista physician. He gambled with Kayo Ketchel, lost heavily, and worked off part of the debt by treating Ketchel professionally. George's wife, Audrey Sylvester, grew angry because of his debts and dislikes his friendship with Virginia Fablon, his receptionist for a while. Sylvester reluctantly helps Archer, best by getting Ketchel's address for him.

SYLVESTER, JOE ("JOEY"). In *The Far Side of the Dollar*, he is an alcoholic Hollywood agent, baby-faced, white-haired, and with "crafty eyes." When appealed to, Sylvester tells his old friend Archer about Carol Harley and Susanna Drew.

SYLVIE. In *The Dark Tunnel*, he is the police fingerprint expert in Arbana. He finds nothing of importance.

SYMONS, JULIAN (1912–1994). Man of letters, born in London. With no formal schooling after age fourteen, Symons became a self-educated, voracious reader, developed leftist tendencies, and founded and ran *Twentieth Century Verse* (1937–1939). He married Kathleen Clark (1941), had two children, served in the British army reluctantly (1942–1944), and with his wife's support became a freelance writer (1947). Symons's bibliography is incredible. Among much else, the following may be mentioned: seven critical biographies, including ones of Charles Dickens (1951), Thomas Carlyle (1952), Edgar Allan Poe (1978), Sir Arthur Conan Doyle (1979), and Dashiell Hammett (1985); twenty-eight crime novels (from 1945); six short-story collections (1961–1995), five books of verse, and radio and television plays. Symons's classic 1972 *Bloody Murder: From the Detective Story to the Crime Novel* (U.S. title: *Mortal Consequences: A History from the Detective Story to the Crime Novel*, 1972), was twice revised and updated (1974, 1985).

Macdonald's association with Symons began when Symons praised *The Ivory Grin* in two London *Times* pieces (November 20, 1953; December 7, 1958). The two met at a Mystery Writers of America annual dinner at the Hotel Astor, New York (1965). They corresponded diligently. When Macdonald and Margaret Millar* went to London (1969), his British publisher, Collins, gave a lunch in his honor and Symons attended (October 19); the next day, Symons interviewed Macdonald for a BBC radio broadcast. When Macdonald and Symons attended the Second International Convention of Crime Writers in New York (March 1978), Symons sadly noticed that his old friend's mental acuity was slipping. Three years later, Symons visited Macdonald in Santa Barbara but felt that Macdonald did not recognize him. In his *Bloody Murder*, Symons especially praises *Blue City, The Blue Hammer, The Far Side of the Dollar, The Galton Case,*

The Underground Man, and *The Zebra-Striped Hearse*; he calls "Macdonald's achievement . . . unique in the modern crime story."

Bibliography: Nolan; Julian Symons, "A Transatlantic Friendship," in *IJ*, pp. 59–66.

T

TAGGERT, ALAN. In *The Moving Target*, he is a former P-38 combat pilot and now the rich oilman Ralph Sampson's private pilot flying out of Santa Teresa, Burbank, and Los Angeles. Taggert is indifferent to death and unable to adjust to civilian life. Sampson's daughter, Miranda, likes Taggert, who, however, likes the cocaine-addicted Betty Fraley. Taggert and Betty kidnap Sampson, which causes their ruination. Taggert is a tragic figure.

Bibliography: Schopen.

"TAKE MY DAUGHTER HOME." *See The Wycherly Woman.*

TAPPINGER. In *Black Money*, he is the older son, about eleven, of Taps Tappinger and Bess Tappinger.

TAPPINGER. In *Black Money*, she is the daughter, six or seven, of Taps Tappinger and Bess Tappinger.

TAPPINGER, BESS. In *Black Money*, she is Taps Tappinger's wife, twenty-nine. The scandal of Taps's getting Bess pregnant while he taught and she was his student at the University of Illinois, though followed by marriage, drove him to the local college at Montevista. Bess despises Taps for his seven-year affair with Virginia Fablon. Bess comes on to Archer, who is initially responsive.

TAPPINGER, TAPS. In *Black Money*, an Army veteran, he is a so-so professor of French, forty-one. Twelve years earlier at the University of Illinois, he got Bess, his student, pregnant. Although they married, the scandal forced their departure. He teaches at the local state college at Montevista. They have three children. Seven years earlier, he started a love affair with another student, Virginia Fablon, of Montevista. He took her to a festival at Los Angeles State College, at the invitation of Allan Bosch, his former student then (and still) teaching there. Bosch's student, Pedro Domingo (*see* Martel, Francis), saw Virginia. Tappinger's seven-year affair with Virginia Fablon of Montevista leads to the murders of Virginia's parents, Roy and Marietta Fablon, and that of Francis Martel, also Virginia's lover.

TAPPINGER, TEDDY. In *Black Money*, this son, three, of Taps Tappinger and Bess Tappinger, was conceived when Bess unsuccessfully sought to reawaken his interest in her.

TAPPINGHAM. In *The Drowning Pool*, he and his family live in the fashionable Staffordshire Estates.

TARANTINE, JOSEPH ("JOE," "JOEY"). In *The Way Some People Die*, he was Sylvia Tarantine's younger son and Mario Tarantine's brother. Handsome Joe graduated from shoplifter to drug dealer, married Galley Lawrence, double-crossed drug dealers Danny Dowser and Herman Speed, stole Mario's boat, and was murdered by Galley and Keith Dalling. In the morgue, his mother calls Joey her Giuseppe.

TARANTINE, MARIO. In *The Way Some People Die*, he is Sylvia Tarantine's older son and Joseph Tarantine's brother. Mario owns a boat for commercial fishing until Joseph steals it. Mario is beaten up on orders of Danny Dowser, Joseph's suspicious drug supplier. When Mario forces Galley Lawrence, Joseph's wife, to look for missing drug money, she kills Mario.

TARANTINE, MRS. JOSEPH. In *The Way Some People Die. See* Lawrence, Galley.

TARANTINE, SYLVIA. In *The Way Some People Die*, she is the widowed, pious mother of Mario and Joseph Tarantine.

"THE TARANTULA HAWK." *See The Blue Hammer.*

TARKO, HAIRLESS. In *Find a Victim*, he is the watchman at Meyer's truck-line parking area. Archer gains information from Tarko, who got his nickname when a truck exploded and burned off his scalp.

"A TASTE OF FIRE." *See The Far Side of the Dollar.*

TAYLOR, BRET. In *The Three Roads*, this psychologially troubled man was the son of George Watt Taylor, a puritanical philosophy professor in Indiana. Bret, four, discovered his mother, Theodora Taylor (*see* Swanscutt, Theodora) in bed with Franklin Swanscutt. Having attacked her hysterically, Bret was persuaded by his father to believe he had killed her. Bret studied at the University of Chicago, entered the U.S. Navy, and rose to full lieutenant. He met and fell in love with Paula West on leave in La Jolla (winter 1943), argued with her (fall 1944), and while drunk married Lorraine Berker (*see* Taylor, Lorraine). In action off Iwo Jima (1945), his carrier was kamikazed and he was blown into the water. He returned to Los Angeles, went with Paula to Lorraine's home (May 23, 1945), and found her murdered. Now an amnesiac, about thirty, in a San Diego naval hospital, Bret gets out and searches frantically for his wife's killer despite Paula's desire for him to find love rather than justice. After confronting several suspects, Bret ultimately recalls the dark past, with himself as the killer.

TAYLOR, GEORGE WATT. In *The Three Roads*, he was Theodora Taylor's husband, more than ten years older than she; was Bret Taylor's father; and taught philosophy in Indiana. Bret, four, discovered his mother in bed in their home with Franklin Swanscutt, one of Taylor's students. Alerted when Bret attacked his mother, Taylor knocked Swanscutt down, ordered both lovers out, let Bret think he had killed his mother, and repeatedly told him all women are sinful. When Bret was twenty, Taylor died, at age sixty-five.

TAYLOR, LORRAINE. In *The Three Roads*, she was the daughter of Joe Berker, an alcoholic, and his dumpy wife, of Michigan. Lorraine was an attractive but sluttish drunk, nineteen or twenty. Bret Taylor picked her up in San Francisco, slept with her, and married her (1944). She was murdered (May 23, 1945), in a Los Angeles home he bought for her.

TEAGARDEN. In *Blue City*, he originally owned the gun that killed Jerry D. Weather, according to Inspector Ralph Hanson.

TERHUNE, TERRY. In *Blue City*, he is Floraine Weather's neighbor. When he sees John Weather running from her house, Terhune chases him, bravely but unsuccessfully.

TESSINGER, MRS. In *Trouble Follows Me*, she is a high-breasted passenger, in her fifties, with her daughter, Rita Tessinger, on the Chicago–Los Angeles train. Although Teddy Trask, another passenger, would prefer Rita, Mrs. Tessinger quickly gets him into her berth.

TESSINGER, RITA. In *Trouble Follows Me*, she is Mrs. Tessinger's pretty daughter, eighteen. They are passengers on the train to Los Angeles. Rita eyes Chester Gordon, but Teddy Trask eyes her. She gets neither man.

THATCHER, SIMMIE. In *Meet Me at the Morgue*, Bourke, who runs the Acme Investigative Agency, names Thatcher as an employee.

THEO. In *The Chill*, he and his girlfriend are sunbathing on the roof of Luke Deloney's building in Bridgeton, Illinois, when Earl Hoffman tries to arrest them in connection with Luke's death. Archer rescues the innocent pair.

THEURIET, PAUL. In *The Ivory Grin*, Elizabeth Benning tells Archer that Theuriet joined her in a dance act in Montreal and American cities ending with Detroit, where he abandoned her.

THOMAS. In *The Dark Tunnel*, he is a chimpanzee in the Zoological Gardens in Munich. Ruth Esch's telling Robert Branch she wants to go see Thomas makes Branch jealous—briefly.

THOMPSON. In *The Chill*, he or his drugstore in Bridgeton, Illinois, filled a prescription for sleeping pills (June 17, 1962) for Helen Haggerty.

THOMPSON, MARY. In *Trouble Follows Me*, she is a beautiful disk jockey, working with Sue Sholto at a Honolulu radio station. Sam Drake meets her and lures her away from Gene Halford, a war correspondent. After Sue is murdered, Mary and Drake meet in Detroit, take a Chicago–Los Angeles train, and sleep together overnight in her berth. In Tijuana, she tells him this: Mary, orphaned at nine, turned shoplifter, then prostitute; Lorenz Jensen (*see* Anderson) was her pimp. Later, back from the Far East with "Anderson," Mary helped him radio naval information in Honolulu. She killed Sue and stuck with Drake to frustrate his detective work. Hector Land kills Mary.

THORNDIKE. In *The Instant Enemy*, he is the FBI agent called in by Keith and Bernice Sebastian after their daughter, Alexandria, disappeared.

THORNE. In *The Wycherly Woman*, he is the policeman Captain Lamar Royal orders to jail Archer.

***THE THREE ROADS* (1948).** Novel. (Characters: Aunt Alice, Ellie Berker, Joe Berker, Mrs. Joe Berker, Charlie, Dr. Clark, Miss Davis, Edie, Fran, Burton Garth, Jack, Captain Kelvie, Dr. Theodore Klifter, Bella Levy, Bill

Levy, Sammy Luger, Mac, Larry Miles, Chief Petty Officer Mustin, Jack Pangborn, Dr. Homer L. Ralston, Mrs. Roberts, Rod, James Rollins, Mrs. Marguerite Schultz, Sim, Dr. Lambert Sims, Sam Slovell, Sollie, Franklin Swanscutt, Theodora Swanscutt, Lefty Swift, George Taylor, Lieutenant Bret Taylor, Lorraine Taylor, Lieutenant Samuel Warren, Lieutenant Weising, West, Paula West, Mrs. Wionowski, Commander Wright.) The novel is in four titled parts: "Saturday," "Sunday," "Monday," and "Doomsday."

Lieutenant Bret Taylor of the Navy met Paula West, a Hollywood writer, in La Jolla, California (winter 1943). They compared backgrounds, fell in love, and sadly argued (fall 1944). He got drunk in San Francisco, met Lorraine, and married her the next day. Paula visited Lorraine in Los Angeles in a home that Bret started to buy but never actually lived in. In combat on a carrier, he was kamikazed and burned (April 1945), returned home, found Lorraine murdered (May 23, 1945), and has been in a California hospital for nine months with partial amnesia. Paula is nearby.

"Saturday" (February 1946). Commander Wright, a naval doctor treating Bret, is attracted to Paula. Dr. Theodore Klifter, practicing in Los Angeles, is to psychoanalyze Bret. Paula tells Klifter about Bret, including this: Bret phoned Lorraine, who was out drinking, phoned Paula, drove toward Malibu with her, and returned with her to Lorraine's home—only to find her strangled. By a lover, still unidentified?

"Sunday." Bret lies musing in his hospital bed. His mother died when he was four. His puritanical father died, "unloved in his sleep," when Bret was twenty. Bret left Indiana for the University of Chicago, studied and boxed well, published a book on the Age of Reason, and was commissioned in the Navy. He swam with Paula in La Jolla, was intimate with her then felt revulsion, corresponded with her while at sea, staying on leave with her in a San Francisco hotel suite she rented. He criticized her high income and was told to leave. He knows it is February 24, 1946. The name Lorraine pops up. In a San Francisco bar he picked up the pliable Lorraine; they made love and got married. Carefully questioning Bret, Wright triggers more memories; says Lorraine is dead; says that Klifter, treating Bret, believes Bret conflates mother and wife. Klifter, who thinks Wright is stalling on Bret's cure because of his love of Paula, encourages Bret to talk about his childhood, his dead mother, and his father's coldness. When Bret wonders what happened to Lorraine, Klifter gives him newspaper clippings that Paula entrusted to him, reporting Lorraine's murder by someone unknown.

"Monday." Wright lets Paula drive Bret to Los Angeles, to consult Klifter further. Bret says he wants to interview the bartender, James Rollins, who worked at the Golden Sunset Café, was named in the newspapers accounts, and spoke with Lorraine just before her death. Bret and Paula argue, and he gets out of the car and walks away. Paula goes on home and phones Larry Miles, a flashy friend. She tells him to avoid both the

Golden Sunset and Bret. He agrees, if bribed with another $200. Instead, Larry tells his girlfriend, Fran, to get lost, and heads for the Golden Sunset. Meanwhile, Bret goes there too and starts drinking heavily. A chief petty officer introduces himself as Mustin and maunders to Bret that he got married in 1940, was faithless, but cannot forgive his wife when she confesses her own infidelity. When Bret tells him to go apologize to his wife, Mustin turns nasty. They fight. Bret knocks him out but is decked by the bartender. Larry, there and watching, gets the bartender to help him put his friend Bret into his car, drives to his apartment, and gets Bret inside. Larry tells Bret his name is Harry Milne. Bret sleeps there overnight.

"Doomsday." In the morning, Larry lends Bret some clothes and takes Bret's torn trousers to a tailor. Larry is in clover, with $200 from Paula and prospects for more. Bret leaves a thank-you note and proceeds to the Golden Sunset, where he treats his hangover with breakfast. Rollins is there, and Bret bribes him with $40 for information. Rollins saw a man with Lorraine (May 23). He is Burton Garth, an ex-crook who bought a Glendale cocktail lounge. Bret takes a taxi there, and makes the little fellow admit he drove Lorraine, who was drunk, to her home, tried to enter, but was slugged in the eye by a big, flashy, blond fellow. The taxi delivers Bret and Garth to the doctor who stitched Garth's cut eye and who confirms Garth's story. Bret finds the house where Lorraine lived and died. Living there are Lorraine's parents, Joe Berker, a drunk, and his slatternly wife. They tell Bret that Miss West brought them there from Michigan. They are unable to identify Lorraine's killer. Bret returns to Milne, finds Paula there, leaves with her, gets his uniform at the tailor's and leaves there the clothes borrowed from Milne. Bret suspects Milne of being Lorraine's murderer; argues with and leaves Paula; summons Garth, returns with him to Milne for his hat and tie, shows Milne to a hidden Garth, who identifies him as Lorraine's final male guest; buys a gun from Garth; breaks into the absent Milne's place; taxis to Paula's; and sees a strange woman park and approach her home.

Now turn to Mrs. Theodora Swanscutt. She is Franklin Swanscutt's wife and a lending-library owner-operator. Today she sees in a personals column a plea for "Bret Taylor" to phone "P.W." at a certain number. She dials, learns that "P.W." is Paula West, says she is Bret's mother, and accepts Paula's invitation to tea. Paula tells her Bret is a naval officer and a mental case. Theodora confirms what Paula thought she knew about Bret's mother's death by confessing this: Theodora married George Taylor, old and soon sexless; took his student Swanscutt for a lover right in the Taylor residence; was seen in bed with Swanscutt by four-year-old Bret, whose yells brought George, who evicted the lovers that night; was divorced, married Franklin in Cincinnati, and moved west. While Theodora is enjoying a sandwich, Paula gets a phone call from Larry, warning

her about Bret and ordering her to meet him at Hollywood's Mexicana
Motel. Taking an automatic, she leaves. Bret, in his taxi, sees the strange
woman leave but follows Paula to the motel and hears her argue with
and threaten a man. After she departs, Bret goes toward the man's room,
followed briefly by the motel owner. Paula proceeds to Klifter's apartment
and argues with him over Bret's treatment. Klifter wants to administer
cold truth to jar Bret's memory; Paula prefers to protect him, because
the truth would cause him to dump her. Bret raps at the motel room
door and is admitted by the man he calls Milne. Pulling his gun, Bret
forces Milne (i.e., Larry) to confess that he and Paula planned a blackmail
scheme. Larry charges Bret; they fight; Larry gets Bret's gun; the police,
alerted by the motel owner, order them to surrender; Larry fires, is killed.
Meanwhile, Paula waits and waits. The police deliver Bret to her. He
wonders why she paid this Milne fellow. The truth suddenly emerges.
Bret caught Lorraine, whose lover scampered away and whom Bret then
strangled. Bret turns indifferent to Paula until she says she was not with
Bret when he entered Lorraine's home but was blackmailed into silence
by Larry, who planned to blackmail Bret. The two survivors cannot tell
the authorities. Does Paula fear Bret now? No. Bret wanted justice, not
love, but must settle only for merciful love. Paula wanted love, not truth,
and gets both.

At the urging of Alfred A. Knopf,* Macdonald speeded up the pace of
The Three Roads by repacking the action into four days and cutting
10,000 words. Knopf also bridled at the scatalogical diction. So Macdonald sanitized his prose, leaving, however, the image Bret conjures up of
himself picking up the promiscuous Lorraine: "a second-class private in
the nocturnal army that had bivouacked on her young *mons*." Satisfied,
Knopf sent a welcome $1,000 advance. *The Three Roads* was issued by
Dell in paperback (1949), in London (Cassell & Company, 1950) and in
many Bantam paperback editions (from 1960). It is Macdonald's first
novel cast in California and his only one told from the third-person point
of view. Its epigraph—reading in part "O ye three roads . . . and narrow
outlet of three ways"—is from Sophocles's *Oedipus Tyrannus*, even
though Bret thinks he has killed his mother, not his father. The three
roads may refer to the intertwining of past, present, and future ("the
impossible future superimposed upon the ugly present in the presence
of the regretted past") or perhaps what may emerge from infinity ("grief,
or ecstasy, or death"). The controversial psychological contents of *The
Three Roads* triggered mixed reviews.

Bibliography: Bruccoli; Nolan; Schopen; Speir.

"THE TIME BINDERS." *See The Far Side of the Dollar.*

TIMOTHY. In *The Moving Target*, he is Hollywood writer Russell Hunt's agent. Timothy wants to leave Swift's for Chasen's, which has his required unique au gratin potatoes.

TOBIAS, JOSEPH ("JOE"). In *The Barbarous Coast*, he is an intelligent, observant black Channel Club lifeguard, twenty-five. A Korean conflict veteran, Tobias liked but was teased by Gabrielle Torres, attends junior-college classes, and is loyal to Clarence Bassett. Tobias tells Archer that when Lance Torres (*see* Leonard, Lance) corrupted his cousin, Gabrielle Torres, Tobias informed her father, Tony Torres.

TOBY. In *The Ivory Grin*, he is Aunty Jones's neighbor, who says he has a radio and a television.

TODD. In *The Zebra-Striped Hearse*, he is the security officer at the Solitaire, in State Line. He tells Archer that Marie, a beauty-parlor owner, may be able to tell him where Fawn King lives.

TODD, HILARY. In "The Bearded Lady," he is a San Marcos art dealer. His plan to steal a valuable painting by Hugh Western and sell it to Walter Hendryx goes awry, after which Todd helps Alice Turner dispose of the murdered Western's body. Alice then kills Todd.

TODD, SAM. In *The Wycherly Woman*, he is the Champion Hotel "day man." He delivered meals to Phoebe Wycherly, who was posing as her mother, Catherine Wycherly.

TOKO. In *The Barbarous Coast*, he is evidently a chauffeur employed by Simon Graff.

TOLLIVER, SERGEANT. In *The Way Some People Die*, he is a police officer that Lieutenant Gary sends, along with Sergeant Fern, to bring Archer to headquarters. Archer kids him by saying his name is undoubtedly pronounced Taliaferro.

TOM. In *The Galton Case. See* Brown, John (Jr.)

TOM. In *The Instant Enemy*, he is a Los Angeles County sheriff's deputy. He wants to arrest Alexandria Sebastian for hitting Lupe Rivera with a tire iron. Mrs. Sherrill, from the probation office, talks Tom out of arresting Alexandria for assault.

TOM. In *The Ivory Grin*, at his café and liquor store Archer encounters Lucy Champion and later Florida Gutierrez.

TOM. In "Shock Treatment," he kills Evelyn, his doting wife, by secretly substituting a wrong dosage of insulin and letting her take it.

TONIA. In *The Wycherly Woman*, she is a Champion Hotel cleaning lady. She tells Archer she believes in spirits. She theorizes that Phoebe Wycherly, when crying and overeating, was feeding the spirits of her dead and crying for them. Tonia's sister is Consuela, who was ill until a *curandero* lifted a spell cast on her.

TONY. In *The Far Side of the Dollar*, he is the bartender at The Barroom Floor. He gives Sam Jackman's address to Archer.

TORRES. In *The Ferguson Affair*, he is Arcadia Torres's husband, jailed for non-support.

TORRES. In *The Way Some People Die*, he is a Mexican contact in Ensenada in Danny Dowser's drug business.

TORRES, ARCADIA. In *The Ferguson Affair*, she is Secundina Donato's sister and an irresponsible man's wife. After Secundina is murdered, Arcadia will care for her children.

TORRES, GABRIELLE. In *The Barbarous Coast*, she was Tony Torres's beautiful niece, twenty-one when murdered (March 21st, almost two years earlier). Lance Torres (*see* Leonard, Lance), her cousin, taught her to drink and wanted to pimp for her in Los Angeles. In the Channel Club, Gabrielle worked for Mrs. Sarah Lamb's snack bar and was a lifeguard. When Isobel Graff caught her husband Simon Graff in bed with Gabrielle, she shot Gabrielle in the thigh, after which Clarence Bassett killed Gabrielle.

TORRES, TONY. In *The Barbarous Coast*, he is an ex-pugilist, formerly known as "The Fresno Gamecock." Tony is the father of Gabrielle Torres, whose murder he vows to avenge. Tony is now the Channel Club watchman. When Gabrielle is corrupted by Tony's nephew, Lance Torres (*see* Leonard, Lance), Tony ends their friendship. When he learns that Clarence Bassett, the club manager, killed Gabrielle, Tony shoots him dead. Archer arranges the killing to look like self-defense.

TOULOUSE, SEÑORA. In *Trouble Follows Me. See* Green, Miss.

TRASK, GEORGE. In *The Goodbye Look*, he is the long-suffering husband of Jean Trask, the daughter of Eldon Swain, whom she is obsessed with finding.

TRASK, JEAN. In *The Goodbye Look*, she is the daughter (born 1929), of Eldon and Louise Swain, who is Samuel Rawlinson's daughter. Married to George Trask for twenty years in San Diego, Jean obsessively seeks her missing father. Randolph Shepherd encourages her to hire Sidney Harrow of San Diego to help. In Pacific Point, Jean locates Nicholas Chalmers, her half-brother, and disturbs the nervous lad. Archer meets Jean, finds her marginally attractive but addicted to gin, and warns her that Nicholas may be dangerous. Archer soon finds Jean stabbed to death and Nicholas, unconscious, near her body.

TRASK, SHERIFF. In *The Galton Case*, he is a leading Santa Teresa police official. Trask gives Archer a lead concerning Roy Lemberg. Archer persuades both Roy and his brother, Tommy Lemberg, to return from Canada to Santa Teresa and provide information clearing them both.

TRASK, TEDDY. In *Trouble Follows Me*, Teddy, named after Theodore Roosevelt, is a magician and entertained troops in Europe. He is on the Chicago–Los Angeles train with Sam Drake, Mary Thompson, Anderson, Mrs. Tessinger, and her daughter, Rita Tessinger. Teddy helps Drake figure out how signals could be transmitted by a disk jockey in Honolulu to Japanese submarines. Teddy would like to sleep with Rita but settles for her mother instead.

TREADWITH, RITA. In *The Drowning Pool*, she is named as the costume maker for *The Ironist*, Francis Marvell's play.

TRECO, FRANK. In *The Ferguson Affair*, his name appears in the clipping found in Larry Gaines's wallet.

TREEN, SYLVIA. In *The Ivory Grin*, she is the naive girl, twenty-one, hopelessly in love with Charles A. Singleton, Jr. Their fathers attended Harvard together. Her father teaches philosophy at Brown. She faints when she hears details of Charles's death, then witnesses the killings of Elizabeth Benning and Una Durano.

TRELOAR, DR. In *Find a Victim*, he is the Las Cruses pathologist who examines Anne Meyer's body.

TRELOAR, JACK. In *The Ferguson Affair*, his name is among others in the clipping found in Larry Gaines's wallet.

TREMAINE, SHERIFF. In *The Underground Man*, he is the Santa Teresa sheriff who cannot talk much with Archer because he is directing men trying to extinguish a forest fire.

TRENCH, DR. In *The Ferguson Affair*, he is the Buenavista hospital obstetrician, short and forty. His treats June Ferguson and Sally Gunnarson. When Salaman threatens June and Colonel Ian Ferguson, Trench appears, levels a shotgun at him, calls himself a skeet shooter, and persuades Salaman to depart.

TRENCHARD, DR. In *The Galton Case*, he is the physician who runs the private mental institution where Gordon Sable places Alice, his unnecessarily conscience-stricken wife.

TRENCHER, SERGEANT. In *The Ivory Grin*, he is the Bella City police officer ordered by Lieutenant Brake to watch Alex Norris. When Alex escapes, Brake orders Trencher to chase him.

TRENTINO, JOE. In *Meet Me at the Morgue*, he is a blind newsstand owner, forty, at the Pacific Point railroad station. He provides Howard Cross details about the dropping and picking up of the ransom money after Jamie Johnson was allegedly kidnapped.

TRENTON, MISS HILDA. In *Meet Me at the Morgue*, she rented an apartment to Molly Fawn, disapproved of her gentlemen friends, and kept Molly's boyfriend Kerry Snow's camera when Molly departed without it. Miss Trenton gossips valuably to Howard Cross.

TREVOR, CARL ("CULLY"). In *The Wycherly Woman*, he is the husband, fifty-three or -four, of Helen Trevor, the sister of Homer Wycherly, whose oil-and-land corporation Trevor manages. Trevor and his wife have no children (and no sexual relations). He is devoted to Phoebe Wycherly, supposedly the daughter of Homer and his wife Catherine Wycherly but really his and Catherine's, born after he was married and Catherine was about to marry Homer. Trevor and Catherine resumed a love relationship that went sour, after which he kills her, kills Ben Merriman, her real-estate agent, and kills Stanley Quillan, who with Ben planned a blackmail scheme. When it is thought that Phoebe is in her submerged Volkswagen and a corpse is shown him for identification, Trevor says it is Phoebe's and faints after having a second coronary. Archer solves everything, confronts Trevor in the hospital, and forces him to sign a confession. Trevor asks Archer to hand him his supply of digitalis, so he can overdose and die.

TREVOR, HELEN. In *The Wycherly Woman*, she is Homer Wycherly's sister and Carl Trevor's fussy wife. Carl works for Homer. Helen lost a child and turned frigid. Now about fifty, with "a face like a silver hatchet," Helen discourages Archer from trying to find Phoebe Wycherly.

TRICK CURLEY. In *The Way Some People Die*, he is a lobsterman who saw Mario Tarantine's boat leave the pier. She soon ran aground.

TRIM. In *The Way Some People Die*, Violet warns Simmie to shut up, because Trim is home. Trim never appears.

TROTTER. In *Find a Victim*, he is one of a gang of peppy black lads near Jo Summer's apartment. He gives Archer directions to Meyer's truck-line lot.

TROUBLE FOLLOWS ME **(1946).** Novel. (Characters: Anderson, Baker, Baroness, Bob, Bob, Lieutenant Cassettari, Detective Cram, Dee, Joe Doss, Sam Drake, Laura Eaton, William Eaton, Edwards, Albert Feathers, Chester Gordon, Miss Green, Gene Halford, Halloran, Private Rodney Hatcher, Hefler, Donnie Hope, Jake, Joe, Bessie Land, Hector Land, Mrs. Merriwell, Mrs. Kate Morgan, Eva Raine, Isaac Randall, Randy, Raoul, Alvin S., Sandra, Lieutenant Savo, Joe Scott, Sue Sholto, Dr. Snell, Helen Swann, Lieutenant Eric Swann, Mrs. Tessinger, Rita Tessinger, Mary Thompson, Teddy Trask, Dr. Simeon Wanless, Lieutenant Will Wolson, Major Wright.) The novel is in four titled parts: "Oahu," "Detroit," "Transcontinental," and "The End of the Ride."

"Oahu" (February 1945). Sam Drake, the narrator, is a Navy ensign from Detroit, off combat duty, and awaiting mainland leave. He parties at the Honolulu House with his Detroit buddy, Lieutenant Eric Swann, Swann's attractive Jewish girlfriend, Sue Sholto, a correspondent named Gene Halford, Halford's friend from Cleveland, Mary Thompson, and others. Another drinker, Mrs. Merriwell, a South Carolinian widow, uses the "n" word about Hector Land, a black wardroom sailor (from Detroit) serving at a buffet. When Sue shouts she prefers "Negroes" to "unreconstructed Southern whites," the party dissolves. Sam, ogling Mary, accompanies her to the radio station where she and Sue are disk jockeys. They return to look for Sue, find Eric drunk, and Sue hanged by a drapery rope from the second-floor ladies' room window. Authorities arrive. Mrs. Merriwell says she saw Land upstairs and shouts rape and murder. After examining Sue's body and Land, Lieutenant Savo, a Navy doctor, denies the rape accusation. Halford, however, seconds the murder charge. Land admits being upstairs seeking women's leftover liquor bottles. Sam and Eric rest in Eric's cabin on board ship. At 5:00 A.M. they check Land's record, which includes recent transfers of money to his wife, Bessie. He explains that he won huge sums shooting dice. At the inquest, Sue is declared a suicide. Mary and Sam seek relief by a swim and dinner. Halford has been repeating rumors about enemy agents in Hawaii. Is Sue's death connected somehow? Antiaircraft practicing downshore punctuates Sam's and Mary's sudden embrace.

"Detroit." Sam has a three-week leave. His sublet tenant, Joe Scott, is a reporter. Sam visits Helen Swann, who says Eric is due to arrive Wednesday, April 18. Mary phones from Cleveland that she is coming to Detroit. Eric arrives, says Land deserted, and dines with Helen, Drake, and Mary. They find Land's wife, a drunken hooker, at the Paris Bar and Grill in a black section. She mutters that Land promised to leave the Navy once he joined "Black Israel." A skinny black shushes her. Next morning, Sam finds her in her apartment, her throat cut. The police rule the death suicide, which Sam disputes. A University of Michigan sociologist explains to Sam to the effect that Black Israel is an antimoderate, black-racist organization. Sam returns to the Paris Bar, sees the skinny fellow, chases but loses him; reports everything to an FBI agent named Hefler, who will investigate; telephones Mary, who has arrived, takes her to dinner; learns she is going to San Diego to work, and is invited to finish his leave with her there. Next morning Hefler phones Sam that Land was spotted crossing into "Tia Juana"; and Scott says that while reporting Bessie's death he read about Land's brother's death during Detroit's 1943 race riots, which turned Land violent.

"Transcontinental." Sam and Mary board a train in Chicago two days later. In the parlor car they chat and drink with Teddy Trask, Mrs. Tessinger and her daughter Rita, Anderson, and others. Teddy, a mind-reading "magician," explains he has a time code enabling a partner to signal names of objects by stopping patter after a certain number of precisely counted seconds. Rita, a teenage beauty, flirts with Teddy. Anderson, an oil executive, is with Miss Green. A dark, silent man eyes everyone. At Kansas City the train adds a Pullman. Private Rodney Hatcher, a combat soldier on his way to the West Coast, boards, drinks with Sam, and rambles about prewar merchant-service action in the Orient, seems to recognize Anderson, writes a letter and puts it in the train's mailbox, and returns with a bottle of bourbon. Drinking too much bourbon, Hatcher vomits in the men's room while Sam, having sipped a little, passes out on the Topeka platform. Sam is pulled from under the train. Major Wright, an army physician aboard, and the conductor find Hatcher dead, and alert the Shore Patrol. It is discovered that Hatcher's bottle had been poisoned with ether. Sam informs Mary, and they read through the mailbox glass Hatcher's envelope, addressed to Laura Eaton, Santa Barbara. Sam sleeps until noon; lunches with Wright, who says Hatcher's body was unloaded at Wichita; learns from a black porter named Edwards that Black Israel is a black-supremacy movement; and after dining with Mary, who says Sue was pro-Communist, accuses Anderson of knowing Hatcher in Shanghai and the dark man of eavesdropping. Edwards says the dark man, called Mr. Gordon, queried him about Black Israel. When questioned, Gordon snubs Sam. Sam sleeps with Mary, at last. In the morning, he asks Teddy if his code system could be used by radio. Yes.

Miss Green says Anderson and Gordon got off at Gallup. Arriving at Los Angeles, Sam infuriates Mary by insisting he must go to Santa Barbara to question Laura Eaton.

"The End of the Ride." Sam gets to Laura's home. He explains everything, including the letter coming from Hatcher, whom she says she knows. A man has just ransacked her house looking for the letter, which hasn't come yet. Gordon enters and identifies himself as an FBI agent, tracing Black Israel activities. When Sam tells him about a possible radio code from Honolulu to nearby Japanese submarines, Gordon leaves to alert Hawaiian offices. After napping a little, Sam intercepts Hatcher's letter in the morning's mail. It tells Laura that Anderson sold black-market rice in Nanking (1937). Gordon arrives, and he and Sam share information and agree to meet in San Diego. Sam flies from Burbank—where he meets Halford, who taunts him about Mary—to San Diego, where Mary awaits him at a hotel. She explains that she needed Halford's friendship to advance in radio work. Sam telephones Eric, on ship-repair duty in San Diego; Sam and Gordon go aboard. Gordon grills two shipmates of Land's and concludes from their comments on shipboard lotteries, run by Land and based on ships' numbers, that timed ticks on Honolulu radio broadcasts could relay those numbers. While collecting his luggage at the railroad station, Sam spots Miss Green, smelling of ether. She departs in a black car, which Sam gets a cab driver named Halloran to follow—into Tijuana and to a brothel. Sam dispatches Halloran with a note to Mary, enters, confronts Miss Green, but is knocked unconscious by her doorman. Reviving, he sees Anderson and his boss, called Baroness, reveals his knowledge of their spy system, and is driven by Anderson to a ranch house, where he is to be burned to death, and his body dressed like Anderson's. Anderson tells Land, who is there, that Sam killed Bessie. Sam convinces him that Anderson did so. They fight. Sam decks Anderson, whom Land kills before disappearing. Mary drives in, having received Halloran's message, pulls a gun on Sam, boasts of her long association with Anderson, and offers Sam either death at once or a nice life of crime with her. He stalls by encouraging her to spill everything. She hysterically shouts that she hated to have to kill Sue and Bessie. Land reappears, with Anderson's gun, kills Mary with its last bullet, fights Sam for Mary's gun, gets it, and kills himself.

Trouble Follows Me (retitled *Night Train* for a 1950 Lion paperback), was dedicated to Donald Ross Pearce,* Macdonald's friend. The complex plot is marred by monstrous coincidences. A good feature is Macdonald's sympathetic handling of racial tensions following the 1943 Detroit riots and his realistic portrayal of justifiably suspicious, nervous African Americans. The five chapters mainly on the train are cleverly paced by indications of towns and times. Over his sex scenes, Macdonald draws a verbal curtain, understandably translucent not transparent, given the publication date. One semi-idiotic sequence is notable: When a fatal shot makes "a nasty mess" of one of her breasts, Mary laments to Sam: "You liked it for a little while, didn't you, Sam?"

Bibliography: Nolan; Schopen.

TROY, DWIGHT. In *The Moving Target*, he is Fay Estabrook's husband. Morris Cramm calls Troy an "aging chorus boy," whereas he is really a gun-wielding sadist. Troy and Fay control the Wild Piano and smuggle illegal workers into California. Troy, with a big vocabulary and an icy manner, tortures Betty Fraley. Archer's report to Peter Colton of Troy's activities will lead to his arrest. In *The Way Some People Die*, Archer reminds Colton of Archer's part in Troy's capture.

TRUTTWELL, BETTY. In *The Goodbye Look*, she is John Truttwell's over-protected daughter, twenty-five. Her mother was killed in front of their Pacific Point house (July 3, 1945) by a hit-and-run driver. Truttwell discourages Betty's engagement to Nicholas Chalmers. Archer, hired to find Nicholas, who is suddenly missing, meets Betty, finds her charming though timid, and appreciates her steady cooperation.

TRUTTWELL, JOHN. In *The Goodbye Look*, he is a well-established Pacific Point attorney. His wife was killed (July 3, 1945) by a hit-and-run driver, who was never found, following which Truttwell overprotects their daughter, Betty. Truttwell has represented his neighbors, Lawrence and Irene Chalmers, for almost thirty years. Although Truttwell deplores Betty's relationship with Nicholas Chalmers, the Chalmerses' son, when Nicholas disappears, Truttwell hires Archer to find him. Truttwell buys from Louise Swain the incriminating family movies, which were taken in the summer of 1943 and crack the case. In *Sleeping Beauty*, when Captain Benjamin Somerville asks Archer to name someone who can vouch for him, Archer names John Truttwell of Pacific Point.

TRUTTWELL, MRS. JOHN. In *The Goodbye Look*, she was John Truttwell's wife, Betty Truttwell's mother, and Estelle Chalmers's friend. Mrs. Truttwell was killed in a hit-and-accident in front of her home (July 3, 1945).

TUBE, THE. In *The Dark Tunnel*, he is the proprietor of the brothel outside Arbana. His daughter, Florrie, works there. He came by his nickname because owing to throat cancer, he eats—and drinks whisky—through a tube.

TURNELL. In *The Galton Case*, he is the boss at the Luna Bay gas station where John Brown (Jr.) cleverly found temporary employment.

TURNER, ADMIRAL JOHNSTON. In "The Bearded Lady," he is Alice Turner's father and Sarah Turner's husband. He owns the painting stolen from the San Marcos museum, of which he is a trustee. Archer finds and returns the painting.

TURNER, ALICE ("ALLIE"). In "The Bearded Lady," she is Admiral Johnston Turner's daughter by his first wife, is Sarah Turner's stepdaughter, and is Hugh Western's fiancée. Outraged that Hugh likes Sarah, Alice kills him, then kills Hilary Todd. Alice felt neglected by her father after her mother's death.

TURNER, MRS. In "The Bearded Lady," she was Admiral Johnston Turner's first wife. Her father was in the French Embassy in Washington, D.C., and gave his daughter and the admiral the Chardin painting as a wedding gift.

TURNER, SARAH. In "The Bearded Lady," she is old Admiral Johnston Turner's second wife, over thirty and adulterous. She was a WAVE officer in Washington, D.C., during the war. She let Hugh Western draw her nude, consorts with Hilary Todd, and tries unsuccessfully to seduce Archer.

TYNDAL. In *The Far Side of the Dollar*, he is "a big shot in the government," according to his son, Frederick Tyndal.

TYNDAL, FREDERICK ("FRED"). In *The Far Side of the Dollar*, he is an unhappy student, smiling and hairy, at Laguna Perdida School, committed there for forging a check. Introducing himself as "Frederick Tyndal the Third," he tells Archer that Thomas Hillman told him that he, Hillman, had been adopted and planned to find "his true father."

u

THE UNDERGROUND MAN (1971). Novel. (Characters: Lew Archer, Roger Armistead, Fran Armistead, John Berry, Captain Leo Broadhurst, Elizabeth Broadhurst, Jean Broadhurst, Ronald Broadhurst, Stanley Broadhurst, Carlos, Lester Crandall, Martha Crandall, Susan Crandall, Elegant, Robert Falconer, Jr., Robert Driscoll Falconer, Harold, Dr. Jerome, Amos Johnstone, Joe Kelsey, Brian Kilpatrick, Ellen Kilpatrick, Jerry Kilpatrick, Willie Mackey, Mrs. Willie Mackey, Nickerson, Harvey Noble, Pedro, Vaughan Purvis, Rawlins, Mrs. Joy Rawlins, Reverend Lowell Riceyman, Captain Arnie Shipstad, Dr. W. Silcox, Snow, Frederick Snow, Mrs. Edna Snow, William Strome, Al Sweetner, Sheriff Tremaine, Laura Waller, Professor Bob Waller.)

One Saturday morning in September 1970, Archer is feeding jays some peanuts outside his apartment building in West Los Angeles. Ronald ("Ronny") Broadhurst, five or six, emerges from Professor Bob and Laura Waller's apartment. Ronny's pretty mother, Jean Broadhurst, appears. Stanley ("Stan") Broadhurst, her aggressive husband, drives up flourishing a cigarillo and preparing to take the reluctant Ronny to Elizabeth Broadhurst, Ronny's grandmother at Santa Teresa. An argument ensues. Jean asks if "that girl" is still in their home in Northridge. Stan drives off in his Ford convertible with Ronny and a busty blonde. When Archer sees Jean a little later, she tells him she called the Wallers at Tahoe last night asking to use their apartment and is now worried because the radio has just reported a forest fire in Santa Teresa; she phoned her mother-in-law there, but got no answer. Archer dials again. They learn that Stan and Ronny never appeared. Jean gripes that Stan brought that blonde home for dinner last night, and Jean ill-advisedly stormed out.

Jean hires Archer to drive her to find Stan and Ronny. On the way she explains: Stan's father abandoned his rich wife and their son, then about twelve; Jean and Stan met at the university; Stan works for a Northridge insurance company; he is neurotically bent on finding his father; the blonde, high on something, seemed about nineteen.

Archer suggests stopping at Stan and Jean's Northridge home first. They find the Mercedes the blonde drove last night, but no people. Jean says the blonde slept in Ronny's bed, beside which Archer finds and pockets a copy of William Henry Hudson's *Green Mansions*, with the names Ellen Strome and Jerry Kilpatrick on the flyleaf. Jean reveals more: Stan, twenty-seven, gathers and files information about his father, an infantry captain in the Pacific theater; Stan and Jean visited San Francisco last June to seek information; Sue, the blonde, last night told Ronny a story about a girl, whose parents were killed by monsters, being carried off by a condor.

A man calling himself Al and looking like an ex-cop drives up, warns Sue to tell Stan to give him $1,000 by tonight—or else—and says he can be reached at the Star Motel past Topanga Canyon. Archer checks the Mercedes, owned by a Roger Armistead of Santa Teresa, finds and phones his number, and tells his worried wife he is seeking a teenage blonde. Mrs. Armistead says the Mercedes is hers; she has a yacht, too, on which that blonde may have spent time Thursday; she'll pay Archer to return the car. Jean phones her mother-in-law and learns that Stan and Sue have gone to the family Mountain House near where the fire is.

Archer drives with Jean in the Mercedes through smoke-filled air to Elizabeth Broadhurst's canyon ranch house near Rattlesnake Creek. Appearing competent, cool, but strained, Elizabeth says Stan phoned last night asking for $1,500. Her gardener, Frederick ("Fritz") Snow, a timid man with a harelip, says he gave Stan the Mountain House key. Stan wanted Fritz to babysit Ronny, but Fritz refused. Elizabeth drives Archer in a pickup truck toward the Mountain House. They walk the rest of the way. In the Mountain House, deserted but with blood on one of the beds, Elizabeth suddenly has to rest. Archer sees Stan's car, approaches the fire-scorched woods, and encounters Joe Kelsey of the Forest Service. Kelsey has a half-burned cigarillo in an evidence case. He shows Archer a grave, with dead Stan in it. A spade and a bloody pickax are nearby. They put Stan under the ground again, retreat from the dangerous fire, stun Elizabeth with the news of her son's murder, and return with spade and pick to the ranch house and Jean.

Jean says Fritz cycled down to the home of his mother, Mrs. Edna Snow, who once worked for Elizabeth. Kelsey theorizes that Stan when killed dropped the cigarillo that started the fire. (Or did the killer start the fire to cover his tracks?) Kelsey and Archer drive to Mrs. Snow's, confront Fritz, semi-autistic and thirty, and learn this: Stan took the spade and pick ostensibly to dig for arrowheads; Sue and Ronny went along, returned without Stan, had sandwiches; Sue scared Ronny by talking about the bogey man, drove away with the boy in Fritz's '57 Chevy. Elizabeth has a heart attack and is taken by ambulance to Santa Teresa, with Jean driving behind. Kelsey radios the police Fritz's license number.

Archer delivers the Mercedes to Fran Armistead, at her fire-doomed home. Her servant says a blonde resembling Sue was with Fran's husband, Roger, on his sloop the *Ariadne*, climbed the mast crazily, and dived off. Carlos drives the Mercedes and Archer drives the Armisteads' Continental, with Fran, to the Armisteads' Santa Teresa beach house. On the way Fran says Roger's boat boy is Jerry Kilpatrick, son of the real-estate agent Brian Kilpatrick. Fran gives Archer $150 for delivering her Mercedes. Fran, who is the moneyed one, upbraids Roger, who is more youthful than she. She and Archer learn this from Roger: Sue is Susan Crandall; she is Jerry's girlfriend; she took the Mercedes at Jerry's insistance. Fran and Roger speak angrily, then soothingly, downstairs.

Archer finds the *Ariadne*. Jerry, skinny but wonderfully bearded, comes out, and talks with Archer. Jerry hates his father; the *Green Mansions* copy is his; when Sue is mentioned, he departs. Archer looks for Fritz's Chevy in the ghetto, has a hamburger, spots the car, and learns from a wino guarding it that Sue and Ron walked off toward the marina. Archer returns to the *Ariadne*. He finds Sue, lying stoned in a bunk, with Ronny, who has been terrified into wide-eyed silence, beside her. Jerry appears, flourishes a .38, and knocks Archer unconscious.

Coming to on the slip, Archer notes that the *Ariadne* is gone but his wallet is intact, gets to a phone, tries unsuccessfully to call the sheriff, leaves a message for Kelsey, finds Brian Kilpatrick's number, speaks with him, and is invited over. Arriving, Archer walks past a poolside brunette, attractive but "smashed," to Brian. In their conversation, this emerges: Jerry blamed Brian, his father, who drinks too much, when his mother, Ellen Kilpatrick (an uppity Stanford graduate), deserted them; Jerry, though bright, avoided college; Sue's father, Lester Crandall, called Brian just today to tell him that Sue left home Thursday; Crandall wants to hush everything up; Brian will phone his friend, Sheriff Tremaine, tonight but downplays the idea that Ronny has been kidnapped. When a man approaches and criticizes Brian for developing Canyon Estates and selling him a house now burned there, Brian waves him off with a revolver.

Archer takes a cab to his car, left at Stan's Northridge home. He sleeps on the way, arrives, and finds Stan's house broken into. Inside, stabbed to death, is Al, the man who demanded that repayment. He is wearing a wig and a false mustache. In some jimmied files, Archer finds this evidence: a want ad, with pictures of a man and a woman, that Stan placed in the San Francisco *Chronicle*; information suggesting that his father, Captain Leo Broadhurst, voyaged from San Francisco (1955); and a letter from Reverend Lowell Riceyman advising Stan to forget his father and remember his lovely wife, Jean. Archer alerts the Los Angeles police, which sends out his friend, Arnie Shipstad, a veteran Hollywood detective. Archer visits the Crandall home in Pacific Palisades, having phoned earlier. Mrs. Crandall is beautiful but chilly—and sorry they live here. Her husband, Lester Crandall, just back from looking for Sue to no avail along the youth-infested Sunset Strip, boasts of his string of coastal motels, the result of hard work. In denial, both parents laud their pristine Sue for playing tennis, diving, studying French, and being admitted to UCLA. Jerry, whom they met in Newport, visited Sue here last June, argued about American values with Crandall, and was invited to leave. Mrs. Crandall gives Archer a photograph of Sue and shows him Sue's room, jam-packed with things but lifeless, and with a directory open to an advertisement for the Star Motel (where dead Al stayed).

Archer drives there and finds Al's room. He is admitted by a drugged-out, abused girl who calls herself Elegant and hopes Al will return with $1,000. Archer says Al is dead. For $50 and an offer of herself (courteously declined), Elegant maunders thus: Sunday, she and Al, an orphan, drove from Sacramento in her Volkswagen; a woman in a three-story house, with a Great Dane seemingly lost, gave Al the clipping of an ad Stan had placed in the *Chronicle* with pictures (Archer takes the clipping); Al got money from Mrs. Snow for gas; they went to San Francisco to answer the ad; Sue, whose photo Archer shows, was at the Star two days ago; Elegant got her high to loosen her tongue for Al; Al planned to head for Mexico. Archer drives home to West Los Angeles; hears from Shipstad that Al was Al Sweetner, often arrested, first in Santa Teresa; has some whisky; sleeps and dreams.

Sunday morning. After breakfast, Archer visits Fran Armistead, who insists that Roger and Jerry were never homosexually involved. Archer finds both Roger and Brian at the marina. The *Ariadne* is still missing. Conversation produces this: Roger blames Brian for not warning him about Jerry; Brian sought Sheriff Tremaine but learned he is at the firefighters' camp on the Santa Teresa College campus; the .38 Jerry slugged Archer with is probably one Roger had on his sloop; Jerry used drugs; Jerry sailed in a race last summer, south off Ensenada. Brian in his Cadillac leads Archer and his Ford to the campus. Even though Archer alerts Tremaine to the facts, he won't divert a plane from the fire, now spreading south and east, to locate the *Ariadne*. He tells Archer to discuss Al Sweetner's murder with Kelsey and says rain is going to hit the charred hills and cause mudslides. Shown the clipping, Brian shamefacedly reveals this: Leo Broadhurst's companion is Ellen, Brian's ex-wife, whose maiden name was Ellen Strome; fifteen years ago she divorced Brian in Reno and presumably married Leo; Jerry blamed Brian; last June, Jerry saw the *Chronicle* photos and recognized his mother.

Archer bypasses the campus and goes to where Stan's body is being disinterred. Kelsey, Jean, and a deputy coroner are there. Stan was stabbed to death. Archer tells them Al was stabbed in Jean's Northridge home. Kelsey tells Archer he checked and learned this: Fritz when a teenager was convicted of statutory rape, was sentenced to forestry-service work in lieu of jail, got interested in firefighting, and fifteen years ago helped bulldoze a canyon trail. Archer tells Kelsey that Al got money from Mrs. Snow. Archer drives Jean to Elizabeth's home. It has been scorched; the nearby barn, burned down. Archer phones his San Francisco detective-friend Willie Mackey, who says he's busy making love and will call back. Meanwhile, Archer looks around; reads a saccharin memo Elizabeth wrote about her grandfather (a Civil War veteran who moved to California and married into a landholding family), and her adored father (a bird-shooting ornithologist); and finds unpaid bills and a pair of fine German pistols. Archer and Jean exchange information. He feels half in love with the young widow, who alternates between anger and grief. Her mother left her father, who ran a Reno sports shop. Her mother-in-law has money, knows Brian well, and supported Stan and her embarrassingly. When Mackey returns the call, Archer provides details from the clipping with the reward offer. Mackey recalls having a copy in his files. Archer asks Mackey to look for Ellen Kilpatrick, a Stanford graduate, perhaps with Brian Kilpatrick, perhaps living on the Peninsula in a three-story house, with a seemingly lost Great Dane nearby. Archer suggests that Jean stay put and scare up some cash, and leaves her alone, crying.

In conversation with the too-righteous Mrs. Snow, Archer learns this: Al Sweetner, a troubled teenager, was assigned to the Snows instead of the Preston Reformatory; Martha Nickerson, a fifteen-year-old cutey, got Al and Fritz to steal a car from a motel owner (Lester Crandall); Al, a repeat offender, went to Preston until he came of age (1955); Martha, impregnated by Fritz, married Crandall and gave birth to Susan (December 15, 1952) in Petroleum City; Martha sent Fritz a Christmas note from the Yucca Tree Inn there; Fritz, who is chronically deranged, got probation and forestry work; Elizabeth paid Fritz's medical bills; Ellen Kilpatrick, even though married, "net[ted]" Leo; little Stan was distressed when he heard the adulterous pair "squeaking" the Broadhurst couch when his mother was away; Stan also knew of the sinful pair's Mountain House assignations; Al showed Mrs. Snow the *Chronicle* clipping last week; she identified the photo of Leo Broadhurst, whom Fritz adored; Mrs. Snow gave Al money. Kelsey phones to report this: Roger's *Ariadne* is grounded at Dunes Bay; a coed saw Al yesterday near where the fire started. Reappearing, Fritz, despite his protective mother, tells Archer he buried "Mr. Broadhurst['s]" body. Dr. Jerome, arriving to examine Fritz, tells Archer he cared for both Stan, long emotionally disturbed, and Fritz, who confesses to offenses he has not committed. He adds that Stan's hands were blistered, as though he had been gravedigging.

Archer drives to the beach near the dismasted *Ariadne*. Witnesses tell him Jerry, with an injured arm, Sue, and Ronny were rescued and driven in a blue Chevy to the Yucca Tree. Archer goes there and talks with a clerk named Joy Rawlins. Crandall, whose daughter Sue she knows, owns the place; Joy phoned Crandall; he ordered her to hold Sue, but Sue left. Archer phones Mackey and learns that a Great Dane, reported missing, was found in Sausalito. Crandall arrives, is updated by Archer, learns of his Sausalito lead, offers to pay him, but is declined. Crandall's wife, Martha, with him, says she knew Al in school; Ellen Kilpatrick was one of their teachers; Ellen, as Ellen Storm, is now an artist in Sausalito; Martha knew Ellen was Jerry's mother and invited Jerry to their home. Crandall bridles at this; they argue; Martha tells him to go get a drink while she talks to Archer. Archer says Al went from Sacramento to Sausalito (for information from Ellen on Leo) and was murdered last night. Martha bought a painting from Ellen; last month, Martha took Sue to see Ellen. Asked whether Fritz is Sue's father, Martha won't answer. Fatigued, Crandall figures Archer will drive them to Sausalito. Joy tells Archer that Crandall fired her for not holding Sue there; Joy adds that she knows plenty about the Crandalls. Irate, Archer drives alone to Sausalito.

Getting to Ellen's address, provided by Mackey, now nearby, Archer is allowed in. Ellen, a lonely, mystically inclined, schizoid painter of no great talent but considerable grace, reveals this: She fell in love with Leo; left Brian, who threatened her if she tried to include Jerry; got a Reno divorce but was stood up by Leo, a shallow loverboy after all, whose whereabouts she doesn't know; hasn't seen Jerry in fifteen years; gave Al, who came by last week, the *Chronicle* clipping, thinking Elizabeth was offering the reward and knowing Al could use cash. Suddenly the Crandalls drive up. Jerry also appears, sees the crowd, and warns Sue to "split." Mackey grabs Jerry. Archer drives after Sue's station wagon. The police, alerted by Mackey's radioed warning, stop her at the Golden Gate Bridge. Archer grabs Ronny. Sue threatens to jump from the bridge, but Archer talks her down.

While driving her back, Archer learns this from Sue, often evidently hallucinating: Sue when three saw someone shoot a man who was with her mother; Al raped Sue in the Mountain House loft; she bled on a bed; Sue and Stan got to the Mountain House; Stan was digging for a red car; a hairy, black-bearded man axed him. Archer delivers Sue to her parents and tells Crandall to grow up. Archer briefs and questions Martha, learning this: Al visited them at the Yucca Tree fifteen years ago; Crandall was so mean that Martha left with Al and Sue; Martha and Leo were making love in the cabin when someone shot him from behind; Martha ran away but returned, retrieved Sue, and went back to the Yucca; she "think[s]" Leo is Sue's father; yes, Martha will level with Sue at long last. Everyone leaves except Ellen, her son Jerry, Ronny, and Archer. Archer warns obstreperous Jerry to shape up; Jerry goes to bed; Archer and Ellen get

Ronny to sleep. Archer phones Jean that Ronny and Sue are safe. Ellen tells Archer this: Leo, stationed at Santa Teresa early in the war, married Elizabeth, a rich socialite but a frigid "daddy's girl"; Elizabeth found out when Leo turned to sexy Martha and threatened them; Brian forced Elizabeth into the Canyon Estates land deal, which made him money; Jerry overheard the two arguing this summer. Although Ellen offers to share her bed, Archer gently declines, gets a sleeping bag from his car, and beds down by Ronny's door.

Archer drives with Ronny to Palo Alto for breakfast, stops at the Yucca, learns that Crandall rehired Joy, and phones Kelsey to meet him at Elizabeth's at noon. Ronny tells Archer he saw a person with black hair and a black beard with Stan. Archer delivers the boy to Jean at Elizabeth's house and tells her that Sue, all distraught, should be forgiven since, when she was three, she saw Leo murdered and yesterday she saw Stan killed by someone disguised in black. Jean says that Elizabeth is recovering in the hospital, and that Brian phoned asking to come see her but she said no. Archer warns her to return to the Wallers's apartment. Kelsey enters and says the fire seems under control. Archer gets him to find a bulldozer. They return to the scene of Stan's burial, plow the region, and find Leo buried in his red Porsche. Poor Stan had been digging for his father.

Archer calls at the Snow house. Fritz, there alone, says Al ordered him to bury Leo and his car (1955). But they didn't kill Leo. Fritz told his mother about the event only yesterday. She drives up with groceries, rebukes Archer for meddling, but with great reluctance reveals that she was babysitting Stan at the Broadhurst home fifteen years ago and heard Elizabeth and Leo in "a nasty quarrel" about her frigidity and his determination to sail to Hawaii, not with Ellen Kilpatrick, but with Martha and Sue. When he angrily left in his sports car, Elizabeth followed, Stan sneaked after them, and later said he heard a shot. Mrs. Snow noted that a German .22 pistol was missing. Covering up to protect one's "own flesh and blood," Mrs. Snow told Stan his father was in Australia.

Through pouring rain, Archer drives to the Santa Teresa hospital and talks with Elizabeth, who is much better. She thanks him for saving Ronny. When Archer says Leo's body was just dug up, she insists she didn't kill him and wonders what Sue's involvement was. When Archer says Stan may have seen Leo shot, Elizabeth offers Archer some of the little money she has left. He counters by saying Brian has been taking her money. The coroner tells Archer that Leo's skull was creased by a .22 but he was killed by a butcher knife from the front.

Archer rushes to the Broadhurst house, finds Brian arguing with Jean, and keeps him from seizing Elizabeth's pistols and her legal papers. Archer takes the evidence from him, tells him his extortion plans are now foiled, and gets him to admit he told Elizabeth his wife, Ellen, and Leo were planning to desert their spouses together and sail away together. Threatening Archer with legal action, Brian storms out. Archer tells Jean to pack up, get Ronny, and let him take them to Los Angeles. He phones Shipstad and reels off and describes his list of suspects: Brian, Crandall, Ellen, and Fritz. When he mentions Fritz's harelip, Shipstad says they checked wig and supply shops, and learned that last month a man answering Fritz's description bought disguise material including a mustache to hide a lip scar. Ronny tardily reveals that he saw Fritz in the barn a while ago, disguised and perusing a magazine full of nude photos.

After dropping Jean and Ronny at a restaurant, Archer dashes through flooded streets to Mrs. Snow's house. Fritz admits he bought the disguise to hide his mouth and "chase the chicks on Sunset Strip"—just once. He adds this: He killed no one; his mother stole his wig and things; she told him to fasten any blame on Al, who phoned Saturday night. Archer turns to Mrs. Snow. She admits killing the head-wounded Leo, "a cheat and a fornicator" who impregnated Martha and let Fritz be blamed. She had Fritz dig a big grave with his bulldozer. Al knew the location. As Archer is phoning the police, she ineffectively rushes at him with a butcher knife. He follows the authorities, who have arrested Mrs. Snow and Fritz, to the police station, dictates a statement, learns from Brian's girlfriend that Brian has just committed suicide, and takes Jean and her son to safety.

For *The Underground Man* Macdonald rejected the following titles: "The Bogey Man," "The Burial Party," "Digger," "The Dissolving Man," "The Dying Animal," "Rattlesnake," "The Warm Body," "Where the Body Was Buried," and "Wildfire." A good title might have been "Fifteen Years," which phrase is repeated mantra-like dozens of times, to remind the reader that fifteen years (1955–1970) have passed between the first murder and the last ones. Macdonald's title may reflect that of *Notes from the Underground* by Fyodor Dostoevsky, one of Macdonald's favorite authors. A personal influence was Macdonald's close-hand observation of the 1964 Coyote Canyon fire that nearly destroyed his Santa Barbara home. The following coups helped the popular and critical success for *The Underground Man*: Eudora Welty, the brilliant Southern writer, whom Macdonald knew and esteemed, wrote a laudatory front-page review in the *New York Times Book Review* (February 14, 1971); and *Newsweek* featured a cover story by Raymond Sokolov on Macdonald (March 22, 1971). *The Underground Man* became Macdonald's biggest bestseller. Prepublication printings of 35,000 copies quickly sold out; four more printings in hardcover were required the first year. Almost 100,000 copies were sold in six months. Alfred A. Knopf* was more than justified in paying Macdonald a $7,500 advance. A condensed version appeared in *Cosmopolitan* (February 1971). A large-type edition appeared (Boston: G.K. Hall, 1971). It was issued in London (Book Club Associates, 1972; Odhams, 1972). A third of a million Bantam paperbacks were printed (beginning February 1972), in addition to British paperbacks (Fontana/ Collins, beginning 1973). In 1972, Bantam paid Macdonald more than $40,000 in royalties. Marty Ransohoff of Filmways was so enamored of Macdonald in general, and *The Underground Man* in particular, that in 1971 he tentatively offered $1.35 million to film it and six other Macdonald novels, and to obtain movie and television rights to "Lew Archer" for twenty years. The only result was NBC's 1974 TV version of *The Underground Man* starring Peter Graves, Jack Klugman, and Celeste Holm.

Bibliography: Bruccoli; Susan Runholt Busch, "Ross Macdonald and the Chronicles of Southern California," *South Dakota Review* 24 (Spring 1986): 111–120; Leonard W. Engel, "Locked Up: A Close Look at the Claustrophobic Imagery in Ross Macdonald's *The Underground Man*," *The Armchair Detective* 20 (Spring 1987): 183–185; G.A. Finch, "The Case of *The Underground Man*: Evolution or Devolution," *The Armchair Detective* 6 (August 1973): 210–212; Nolan; Elmer R. Pry, "Ross Macdonald's Violent California: Imagery Patterns in *The Underground Man*," *Western American Literature* 9 (Fall 1974): 197–203; Speir.

"THE UNDERSIDE OF THE WEAVE." *See The Far Side of the Dollar*.

V

VALLON. In *The Dark Tunnel*, he teaches Romance languages at Midwestern University and is a member of its War Board. Slim and elegant, Vallon is descended from "a Rochellois Protestant" who migrated to America early in the eighteenth century.

VALMY. In *The Drowning Pool*, he and his family live in the fashionable Staffordshire Estates.

VAN. In *The Ivory Grin*, he is a Detroit operative who informs Maxfield Heiss about Leo Durano and his sister Una Durano. Van says Leo had been living with Bess Wionowski (*see* Benning, Elizabeth).

VAN HORN, WALTER. In *The Ferguson Affair*, his name, among others, appears in the clipping in Larry Gaines's wallet.

VERA. In *The Barbarous Coast*, she mans Archer's answering service and reports that George Wall is hospitalized in Las Vegas.

VERA. In *Black Money*, she is old Peter Jamieson's domineering housekeeper—and perhaps more than that with him.

VERNON. In *The Far Side of the Dollar*, he owns the Pacific Palisades building where Harold Harley worked as a photographer after the war, until competition forced him to quit.

VIOLET. In *The Way Some People Die*, she is black Simmie's black girlfriend. She warns Simmie not to talk to Archer about Herman Speed.

VLATHEK, LUDWIG. In *The Dark Tunnel. See* Schneider, Peter.

VON AUW, IVAN (1903–1991). Literary agent. During his decades-long career with Harold Ober* Associates (1938–1973), von Auw represented, among others, the following writers: Pearl Buck, James M. Cain, Agatha Christie, John Gunther, Langston Hughes, and T.H. White, and both Macdonald and Margaret Millar.* When von Auw retired, he maintained one home in Portugal and another in San Juan, Puerto Rico, where he died.

When Macdonald sent *The Dark Tunnel* to Ober, von Auw placed it with Dodd, Mead, which published it (1944). Von Auw placed Margaret Millar's fine novel, *The Iron Gates* (1945), with Random House. Macdonald asked von Auw to send *Blue City* to Dodd, Mead, hoping it would be rejected, thus freeing him to go elsewhere. Alfred A. Knopf* accepted it (1946), on condition that minor changes were made. Von Auw continued placing Macdonald's works advantageously, including condensed versions of several novels in well-paying periodicals. When Macdonald was disgruntled over Knopf's financial, promotional, reprint, and movie-rights strategies, von Auw mediated helpfully. *Find a Victim* (1954) is dedicated to "Ivan von Auw, Jr." The two corresponded when Macdonald had personal problems or writing hangups. Macdonald sat with von Auw, among others, at the Edgar Allan Poe Awards ceremony, held at New York's Hotel Astor (April 30, 1965). During the evening, Macdonald saw to it that von Auw met with Victor Gollancz, Margaret Millar's British publisher. Later that year, von Auw vacationed in North Africa and Macdonald had to deal directly with Knopf, which he had begun to dislike doing. Macdonald wrote von Auw (April 27, 1966), prohibiting Ober's firm from sharing any more of his movie and television income. Von Auw attended a cocktail party Knopf threw in his New York City apartment in Macdonald's honor (May 18, 1971). Another guest was Eudora Welty, who relished Macdonald's novels and had just reviewed his *The Underground Man* (*New York Times Book Review*, February 14, 1971). Von Auw's and Macdonald's correspondence is deposited at Princeton University.

Bibliography: Nolan.

VON ESCH. In *The Drowning Pool*, he and his family reside in the posh Staffordshire Estates.

VON ESCH, CAPTAIN CARL. In *The Dark Tunnel*, he is a homosexual, transvestite German army officer. A rabid Nazi, he slugged Robert Branch in the eye in Munich (1937), was a prisoner of war held at Kirkland Lake, Canada, but escaped. He and Peter Schneider captured Carl's sister, Ruth Esch, in Canada, threw her down a mine shaft, and left her for dead. Carl, disguised as Ruth, and Peter make their way to Peter's father, Dr. Herman Schneider. Seeing the pair dueling with sabres and then kissing disgusts him. They kill Dr. Schneider. The FBI, led by Chester Gordon, traces von Esch to Chicago.

W

WADLEY, MISS. In *The Chill*, Mrs. Bradshaw says Miss Wadley was her summer "nurse-companion." Mrs. Bradshaw lies to Archer that she dictated letters to her son, Dean Roy Bradshaw, and Miss Wadley sent them to him in Europe.

WALES, FREDERICK. In *Blue City*, he is Floraine Weather's father, of Ventura, California.

WALES, MRS. FREDERICK. In *Blue City*, she is Floraine Weather's mother, of Ventura, California.

WALL, GEORGE. In *The Barbarous Coast*, he is a Toronto sportswriter. He married Hester Campbell (*see* Wall, Hester), who deserted him but phoned him from Los Angeles in danger. Flying there, he hires Archer to assist. George's semi-idiotic actions get him hurt by Lance Leonard, Simon Graff, and Carl Stern. When Wall is hospitalized in Las Vegas, Archer finds him, reassures him, promises to bill him, and never sees him again. Meanwhile, Hester has been murdered.

WALL, HESTER. In *The Barbarous Coast*, she is the beautiful daughter of Teeny Campbell and the late Raymond Campbell, Rina Campbell's younger sister, George Wall's wife, and a friend of Channel Club manager Clarence Bassett. Hester fell in with bad company in Los Angeles and was involved in a blackmail scheme with many criminals. Simon Graff, the movie magnate, establishes Hester in her old family mansion. Isobel Graff, Simon's wife and already a murderess, regards Hester as one of Simon's paid sex partners and brains her with a poker. Archer forces

Leroy Frost, a Graff thug, to lead Archer to Hester's corpse, flown to Las Vegas and incinerated.

WALLACE, DR. In *The Wycherly Woman*, Helen Trevor names him as her husband Carl's physician.

WALLER, LAURA. In *The Underground Man*, she and her husband, Professor Bob Waller, live in an apartment in the building where Archer also lives. The Wallers, at Tahoe, let Jean Broadhurst use their apartment.

WALLER, PROFESSOR BOB. In *The Underground Man*, he is Laura Waller's husband. They live near Archer, who meets Jean Broadhurst when she is using their apartment.

WALLINGFORD, GEORGE. In *The Barbarous Coast*, Teeny Campbell tells Archer that George Wallingford, a Canadian, married her daughter Hester, died, and left her wealthy with uranium holdings. Hester fabricated the story. *See* Wall, Hester; and Wall, George.

WALTERS, ARNIE. In *The Zebra-Striped Hearse*, he runs a Reno detective agency with his wife Phyllis. Archer, who knows them, asks them to trace Burke Damis (*see* Campion, Bruce). Arnie helps Archer look for clues at Colonel Mark Blackwell's Tahoe lodge. In *The Chill*, Archer asks Arnie Walters to check on Sally Burke and her brother, Judson Foley, around Reno. Arnie learns that Foley helped Helen Haggerty try to blackmail Dean Roy Bradshaw. In *The Far Side of the Dollar*, Arnie helps Archer check on Harold Harley and Mike Harley, who are brothers. Arnie visits their parents in Pocatello. Arnie Walters is partly based on Armand Girola, the Reno detective who, with his wife, Thelma Girola, found Macdonald's daughter, Linda Millar,* when she was a runway (1959).

Bibliography: Nolan.

WALTERS, PHYLLIS. In *The Zebra-Striped Hearse*, she is Arnie Walters's wife and with him runs a Reno detective agency. Archer notes that, though an "ex-policewoman," she cannot hide an "exuberant femininity." In *The Chill*, Phyllis, called an ex-Pinkerton, enables Archer to meet Sally Burke. In *The Far Side of the Dollar*, Phyllis relays messages to Archer. Phyllis Walters is partly patterned after Thelma Girola, the wife of Armand Girola. The two, a husband-and-wife detective team in Reno, found Macdonald's missing daughter, Linda Millar* (1959).

WALTHER, CARL. In *The Barbarous Coast*, Simon Graff boasts that Carl Walther, a famous German gunsmith, made Graff's .22.

WANGER, FRAU. In *The Dark Tunnel*, she was the hostess at a Munich tea party Robert Branch and Ruth Esch attended (1937). Described as "a political widow" when she left her Nazi husband, she lived with her daughter and tutored foreigners in German.

WANLESS, DR. SIMEON. In *Trouble Follows Me*, he is the University of Michigan sociologist who tells Sam Drake about Black Israel.

"THE WARM BODY." *See The Underground Man*.

WARREN, LIEUTENANT SAMUEL. In *The Three Roads*, he was the policeman in charge of Lorraine Taylor's murder scene.

WATKINS. In *Meet Me at the Morgue*, he owns the mortuary near Pacific Point's courthouse. People meet there to view corpses.

WATKINS, MRS. In *The Wycherly Woman*, she is a nurse in Dr. Sherrill's mental asylum near Palo Alto. She takes care of Phoebe Wycherly.

THE WAY SOME PEOPLE DIE **(1951).** Novel. (Characters: Lew Archer, George Barron, Marjorie Barron, Blaney, Callahan, Ciro, Peter Colton, Keith Dalling, Danny Dowser, Fenton, Sergeant Fern, Lieutenant Gary, George, George, Gino, Audrey Graham, Jane Starr Hammond, Irene, Judas, Dr. Samuel Lawrence, Galley Lawrence, Mrs. Samuel Lawrence, Dr. McCutcheon, Mosquito, Raisch, Rassi, Ronnie, Runceyvale, Ruth, Sandra, Chief Schreiber, Joshua Severn, Simmie, Mrs. Kingsley Soper, Herman Speed, Mrs. Caroline Standish, Sullivan, Joseph Tarantine, Mario Tarantine, Mrs. Sylvia Tarantine, Sergeant Tolliver, Torres, Trick Curley, Trim, Violet, Westmore, Zizi.)

On an early January Monday in Santa Monica, Mrs. Samuel Lawrence, hires Lew Archer to find her missing daughter, Galatea ("Galley") Lawrence, a gorgeous nurse, twenty-four. She took care of Herman Speed, a gunshot gangster. Archer takes Galley's photograph and begins.

Archer drives to the Pacific Point hospital and learns this from Audrey Graham, another nurse; Audrey and Galley shared an Acacia Court apartment; Galley was sexually provocative; Speed was an Arena wrestling promoter; Galley knew a fellow named "Turpentine" or "Tarantula." Archer drives to the Acacia, sees Raisch, its owner-operator, and learns this: Raisch was sorry ever to see Galley with Joseph Tarantine, "one of these pretty-boy wops"; two "poolroom cowboys" are seeking Tarantine.

At Point Arena, Archer finds the black janitor, Simmie, training to box, and Violet, his girlfriend. Archer learns that Joe Tarantine has a beautiful girl or wife and is not in trouble with pinball collections. Archer locates a "Sylvia Tarantine" and learns from her neighbor that she is visiting her hospitalized son, Mario, who has a boat, the *Aztec Queen*. Mario, badly roughed up, tells Archer that his brother, Joe, left Mario holding the bag, skipped town with Galley, and lives at the Casa Loma near Sunset Boulevard. After dinner in Hollywood, Archer goes there, notes that Keith Dalling lives next to Joe's apartment, which he enters. Unoccupied, it has been ransacked. A gunman named Blaney and a cohort appear, disarm Archer, and take him to their boss, Danny Dowser. He has a gated bungalow between Santa Monica and Pacific Palisades. Dowser is a short, courteous, dangerous criminal. His girlfriend, Irene, interrupts their conversation about Archer's admitted mission to say that a friend told her Galley is in Palm Springs. Archer ostensibly will find Galley and Joe and bring them to Dowser, for $1,000 and $5,000, respectively.

Archer checks several Palm Springs bars and at one finds a bartender who recognizes Galley from her photograph. The fellow quickly makes a phone call. The handsome Keith Dalling soon appears. He tells Archer he is a radio actor, has property in Oasis, a desert development, and has rented Galley and Joe a house there. Although a friend just told him about Joe's likely criminality, Keith will drive Archer there. When they arrive, Archer proceeds alone. Galley opens the door. Archer says her mother wants her, but he is knocked unconscious from the rear and his gun is stolen. Marjorie Fellows drives by and revives Archer. Pretending that Joe's house is his property, he looks around but remains clueless. Marjorie is looking for her husband, Colonel Henry Fellows; on their honeymoon, they rented a place from Keith. She drives Archer to the local inn. Henry emerges, all blustery and wondering where she has been.

Back at the Casa Loma before 8:00 A.M., Archer enters Keith's apartment, finds him shot dead, and looks around. A book is lovingly inscribed by Jane; a memo from Jane's Hollywood radio station indicates that she sent him money; his address book identifies Jane as Jane Starr Hammond and includes Galley's mother's name and Archer's. Archer finds Jane's office. She says that through Keith she knows Galley and Joe. When Archer fibs that Keith has said he has a friend working in radio interested in crime stories, she names Joshua Severn. Archer finds his office nearby. Severn says he knows Archer's reputation, is glad to meet him, and reluctantly fired Keith for drunkenness, which cost him Jane's love. Archer tells only the police, by a phone tip, about Keith's death. The police will be telling Jane.

Archer revisits Mrs. Lawrence, who confesses that she hired him to find Galley because a handsome plainclothes "policeman" told her to do so secretly and not mention that Galley's boyfriend was crooked. She says Galley visited her last night until a skinny man took her away. Archer thinks the cop was Keith, the thin fellow, Blaney.

On to Dowser, who says a woman phoned that Galley was with her mother. Since Blaney got her, Dowser won't pay Archer but locks him up with Galley to gain information on Joe. Behold Galley, somewhat roughed-up, and Archer together in a bedroom. He says her mother is concerned. She says she tried to stop Joe from knocking him unconscious; sensing Keith brought Archer to Oasis, Joe forced Galley to pack and leave. Joe stopped at Keith's apartment but said he was gone. She dropped Joe at the pier. She says she met Joe through Speed, her gunshot patient. He was Joe's boss and worked for Dowser, whose pinball-machine profits Joe skimmed. Attractive though Galley is, Archer, up since the previous morning, snoozes.

A couple of hours later, Dowser orders Blaney to take Galley to her mother. Archer and Dowser play snooker, eat, and talk. Dowser offers Archer a job. No. Dowser sends a thug named Sullivan to Ensenada to find Joe. Returning, Blaney reports that cops are now interviewing Galley. When Archer mentions that Keith has been murdered, Dowser seems ignorant of the name. Archer leaves, finds Mario back home, and tells him the *Aztec Queen* is gone. With Joe? They drive to the shore, see the *Queen* smashed on the rocks and deserted, and proceed to a waterfront bar for refreshments. Callahan, a deputy sheriff, is there. Mario, irate, suspects Joe of faking his own death by drowning. The authorities will notify Galley of her husband's demise, while Mario is suspected of foul play.

Archer drives Mario home. On the way, they see a crowd at the Arena. Mario chases Simmie and brass-knuckles him, but he escapes. A girl shouts to Mario that she knows something about Joe, but he ignores her. After Archer gets Mario to his mother, he follows the girl and her escort from an Arena wrestling show to a dingy motel bedroom, from which Ronnie, who is her pimp and the motel clerk, takes their male victim away to cash traveler's checks for their payoff. Archer queries the girl, who reveals this: Ruth is her name; she is an addict needing a fix from Joe; last night, while on Mackerel Beach, she saw a man rise from the sea with a bundle around his neck; Ronnie pushed drugs for Speed, whom he describes; Ronnie now sells for "Mosquito." Ronnie bursts in, but Archer knocks him down, orders Ruth out, and forces Ronnie to talk: Joe fingered Speed, and the mob hijacked his drugs and shot him. Joe used the *Queen* to transport drugs from Mexico. Mosquito is Gilbert Moreno, a drug pusher who frequents The Den, in Pacific Point.

At 11:05 P.M., Archer goes to the courthouse, where Callahan is interviewing Galley. Archer quietly tells her about Ruth seeing a man emerge from the sea. While Archer drives Galley home to her mother, she says this: Blaney probably shot Speed; Joe seemed all right when they married, but she found he sold heroin; Keith loved her but was going to marry someone else; Joe didn't shoot Keith. Archer drives to his house, between Hollywood and Los Angeles, but two police sergeants grab him. At police headquarters, Lieutenant Gary grills him. Admitting he has bungled, Archer dictates details about Joe, Dowser, and Keith, who was killed with Archer's gun, found near the Casa Loma parking lot.

Archer goes home and sleeps until noon. His answering service tells him Mrs. Fellows phoned. She persuades him to drive to Oasis for lunch and some business talk. Once there, he learns that her husband got a call from San Francisco, took $30,000 and a car from her, and decamped. After much exchange of information, including about her husband's war wound, Archer guesses her husband is Speed. She hires him to recover her money.

By midnight Archer is at The Den, seeking Mosquito. Archer bribes a drug-addicted pianist to name the hotel where Mosquito lives, goes there, pretends he needs a fix, and slaps the needle away when it is produced. Mosquito pulls a knife. Archer grabs it and knocks him out. Ruth creeps out of the bathroom. When Mosquito comes to, Archer forces him to lead him to Speed or face a drug arrest. Once at Speed's lonely cabin, Archer releases Mosquito and confronts Speed, threatens to expose him as Colonel Henry Fellows, declines to be bribed into taking Joe's heroin, and persuades the tired fellow to surrender it to Dowser and get lost. Otherwise, his days are numbered. Archer returns to Ruth, loads her into his car, drives six hours to Los Angeles, and delivers her to Peter Colton, his old friend in the D.A.'s office. Ruth identifies Keith's photograph as that of the man from the sea. So if Joe were killed in the boat, Keith did it. Ruth will get medical treatment. Archer startles Colton by reporting that he has Dowser's heroin.

Late that afternoon Archer reports to Dowser, tries but fails to learn what woman called to tell him that Galley was with her mother, says he has Dowser's $100,000 stash of heroin in his car, and accepts $15,000 for it. Blaney retrieves it, but also Mosquito's initialed knife. Dowser gloats that Mosquito has just been reported killed, figures Archer did it, takes his money back, and gloats that he can safely let Archer leave. Safely outside, Archer watches Colton lead a squad to arrest Dowser. At twilight, Archer goes to the morgue, where Mario and his mother identify Joe's body. Dining nearby, Archer queries Galley, also there, about her movements at Oasis. Archer says Joe fingered Speed to the mob and Keith was seen leaving Mario's *Queen*. Galley says Keith had her mother hire Archer to create trouble between Keith and Joe. Archer checks with the coroner: Joe drowned, was smothered, or—Archer's idea—was frozen. When Callahan says Mario was looking for Galley, Archer, alerted to danger, drives furiously to Oasis after them. Galley, her face bleeding, says this: Galley drove Joe to the pier, saw Keith's car there; Keith killed Joe; Galley killed Keith with Archer's gun. In reality, Mario just now brass-knuckled Galley, who wounded him in the Oasis garage. He crawls in; with her remaining bullets, she kills him and says Mario forced her to Oasis to retrieve the money Joe hid there. While the authorities, phoned by Archer, are approaching, he summarizes accurately: Galley learned about mob activity from Speed, poisoned Joe, who betrayed Speed, and with Keith's help put Joe in her freezer to die; Keith deposited him onto Mario's *Queen*; she drove Keith from the beach to his place and killed him there. The police arrest Galley.

Friday morning. Archer finds Marjorie still at Oasis. She says the police told her Speed parked her car on the Golden Gate Bridge and leaped into the water below. She introduces her husband, George Barron, here from Toledo and happy she is his again. By noon, Archer is at Galley's mother Mrs. Lawrence's home. Aware of Galley's arrest, she remains confident of her innocence. Mrs. Lawrence produces $30,000, left by Galley. She won't follow Archer's advice and have a lawyer broker a deal with it. The God-given money will aid her daughter in this perilous hour. Archer wearily acquiesces.

Reviewers praised *The Way Some People Die*. A second printing by Alfred A. Knopf* was necessary within months. The novel went into paperback (Pocket Books, New York, 1952, Canada, 1953; London, Pan, 1956) and was issued in London as a hardcover (Cassell, 1953). Archer labels rival Arena wrestlers as "Right" and "Wrong"; but, in his real world evil has attractive features, while good is often tainted. Of Macdonald's women here, only Ruth, the teenage drug waif, merits Archer's sympathy. The title of the novel can mean "Golly, the way some poor creatures die" or "Let me count the ways." The first paragraph is a brilliant overture, a medley of onrushing themes. In the last chapter, Archer, paralyzed by more than fatigue, says, "Now there were four men violently dead, five if I counted Mosquito."

Bibliography: Nolan; Speir.

WEATHER, FLORAINE. In *Blue City*, she is Roger Kerch's wife, formerly Floraine Wales, of Ventura, California, then Chicago. The two married in Portland, Oregon (May 14, 1931). She went to the "blue city" and evidently became a bigamist by marrying Jerry D. Weather shortly before he was murdered (1944). She inherited his property, including the Weather House, which she sold to Alonzo P. Sanford, and the Cathay Club, which she and Kerch are running as a nightclub cum upstairs brothel. Now about thirty-five and sensual, she is Kerch's thug Joseph Sault's lover. Floraine wouldn't mind seducing Jerry's son, John Weather. Floraine's "live, stirring body in that still room [in her redecorated Weather residence] was like a snake in a sealed tomb, fed by unhealthy meat." She persuades Sault to try to kill Kerch and take over his setup with her. Kerch discovers their intention, kills them both, and tries to blame her murder on Weather.

WEATHER, JERRY D. In *Blue City*, he was John Weather's philandering father. His disillusioned wife died (1941). Jerry was a corrupt but generous power behind city leaders including Alonzo P. Sanford, Roger Kerch, and Inspector Ralph Hanson. Jerry married Floraine Wales (*see* Weather, Floraine) and was soon murdered (April 3, 1944). John returns home (early 1946) determined to learn about his father, long a stranger to him.

WEATHER, JOHN ("JOHNNY"). In *Blue City*, of which he is the narrator, he is the son of Jerry D. Weather and his wife, who, discovering Jerry's infidelity when John was about twelve, threw Jerry out, poisoned John's mind against him, and died (1941). John joined the U.S. Army, was in England when his father was murdered, knew nothing of the event, fought in France and Germany, and was discharged (early 1946). Now twenty-two, John hitchhikes from near Chicago to the "blue city" of his youth to seek work. He learns of his father's second marriage—to Floraine Wales (*see* Weather, Floraine)—and of his murder (April 3, 1944). Determined to learn the truth, John encounters Alonzo P. Sanford, Inspector Ralph Hanson, Roger Kerch and his goons, Carla Kaufman, Freeman Allison, and others. Though battered by the police, John wins out and will marry Carla and clean up the city.

WEATHER, MRS. JERRY D. In *Blue City*, she was Jerry D. Weather's wife and John Weather's mother She discovered her husband's villainous nature, dismissed him from her life, poisoned John's mind against him, and died (1941).

WEBER. In *Blue City*, he is the owner of a poolroom Joseph Sault does not frequent.

WEIL, MRS. SONIA. In *Blue City*, she is a tenant in the apartment building where Carla Kaufman and Francesca Sontag also live.

WEINSTEIN, BELLE. In *The Ferguson Affair*, she is William Gunnarson's secretary, widowed, "fortyish, dark, and intense." Belle, Gunnarson's tactful "personal goad," helps him locate witnesses in Mountain Grove, stays with Gunnarson's pregnant wife, Sally, and gets her to the hospital in time to give birth.

WEINTRAUB, DR. ELIJAH ("WEINIE"). In *The Far Side of the Dollar*, he is a Los Angeles physician, a little older than Archer. During the war, he was a Navy surgeon serving with Ralph Hillman. Casualties at Midway were so horrifying that Weintraub had a nervous breakdown. He delivered Carol Harley's baby by Hillman (1945) and arranged for Hillman to adopt him. The son, called Thomas Hillman, when seventeen, forces Weintraub to name his parents, then slugs him.

WEISING, LIEUTENANT. In *The Three Roads*, he is on duty at the San Diego naval hospital where Bret Taylor is a patient.

WELLESLEY. In *The Galton Case*, he is Gordon Sable's partner in Wellesley and Sable, a Santa Teresa law firm.

WEST. In *The Three Roads*, he was Paula West's father, an alcoholic who never provided properly for his family.

WEST, PAULA. In *The Three Roads*, she worked for the *Free Press* in Detroit, moved to Hollywood as a script rewriter, married Jack Pangborn, a drunk, and divorced him (1940), and met Bret Taylor, a Navy lieutenant, in La Jolla (winter 1943). The two fell in love. He proved sexually timid. He returned (fall 1944), but the two argued and he married Lorraine Berger (*see* Taylor, Lorraine). Taylor and Paula went to Lorraine's Los Angeles home (May 1945), where she was found murdered. Taylor became an amnesiac. Paula, not quite thirty, tries to shield the truth from him so they may find love, not justice. When he remembers that truth—that he killed his wife—he and Paula settle for love.

WESTERN, HUGH. In "The Bearded Lady," he was a combat artist who served with Archer in the Philippines during the war. Archer drops in to visit Western in San Marcos, but Western is soon murdered. Could Macdonald have been playing with "Wystan Hugh," the first two names of his friend and mentor, W.H. Auden,* in creating the name Hugh Western?

WESTERN, MARY. In "The Bearded Lady," she is Hugh Western's sister, twelve years younger than he. She is a hospital x-ray technician. Once she trusts Archer, she cooperates with his investigation.

WESTMORE. In *The Way Some People Die*, Irene, Danny Dowser's girlfriend, says she will shop at Westmore's "for the works."

WESTMORE, MARION. In *Find a Victim*, Hilda Church names Marion as a friend. Marion's husband, Sam Westmore, is the Las Cruces D.A.

WESTMORE, SAM. In *Find a Victim*, he is from the Ivy League, has been in law practice in Las Cruces for fifteen years, is ambitious, and cooperates with Archer. Westmore wants to rush to judgment and convict Bozey, a criminal, of crimes he did not commit. Archer sets the record straight.

WHEELING, WILLIAM C. ("BILL"), JR. In *The Wycherly Woman*. *See* Archer, Lew.

"WHERE THE BODY WAS BURIED." *See The Underground Man*.

WHITE, DR. In *The Zebra-Striped Hearse*, he performs the autopsy on Quincy Ralph Simpson's body at Citrus Junction. He determines the cause of death to be an icepick puncture of the heart.

"THE WHITEHEADED BOY." *See The Zebra-Striped Hearse*.

WHITEY. In *Blue City*, he is an albino whom John Weather defeats at pool in Charlie's poolroom. Whitey tells Weather he can find Joseph Sault at F. Garland's place.

WHITMORE. In *The Chill*, he is or was the founder of Pacific Point's Whitmore Nursing Home, where Dr. James Godwin places Dolly McGee for treatment.

WHITMORE, JACOB ("JAKE"). In *The Blue Hammer*, he was an imitative painter. Archer, disputing the report of his death by heart attack and drowning, is responsible for the discovery that Whitmore was murdered in fresh water and dumped in the ocean. He left a girlfriend, Jessie Gable, with multiple so-so paintings.

WHITMORE, MRS. JACOB. In *The Blue Hammer*, she is a woman whose husband was stolen by Jessie Gable, Jacob's girlfriend. Or so Jessie tells Archer.

WHITTEMORE, SHERIFF. In *Sleeping Beauty*, he works with Captain Dolan. They show Archer Tony Lashman's murdered body.

WIENER, DR. In *The Dark Tunnel*, he was a Jewish physician in Munich when Robert Branch was there (1937). Branch and Ruth Esch saw Wiener after some Nazis attacked him. Despite their efforts to aid him, he is murdered by Nazi soldiers, including Captain Carl von Esch, Ruth's brother.

"WILD GOOSE CHASE" (1954, 1955). Short story. (Characters: Anne, Lew Archer, Glenway Cave, Ruth Cave, Rhea Harvey, Rod Harvey, Frank Kilpatrick, Janet Kilpatrick, Janie Kilpatrick.) Ruth Cave, who was wealthy, was murdered by Rhea Harvey, jealous that her husband, Rod Harvey, was attracted to Ruth. Glenway Cave won't testify that he was with Janet Kilpatrick during the murder hour. Rhea murders Janet, who is about to testify tardily, and is arrested. Frank Kilpatrick, Janet's ex-husband, gets custody of his daughter, Janie. Glenway inherits, buys a Ferrari, is killed in a car crash. Midway through this tangle, Janet hires Archer to observe Glenway's trial, to determine whether she ought to testify.

"WILDFIRE." *See The Underground Man.*

WILDING, HORACE. In *The Ivory Grin*, he is an affected painter who taught in the Arroyo Beach Prep School. Charles A. Singleton, Jr., was his student. They became neighbors in a canyon nearby. Wilding, telling Archer he heard the shot that wounded Charles, leads Archer to Charles's cabin.

WILKINSON, BILL. In *The Zebra-Striped Hearse*, he is Helen Wilkinson's husband, in his thirties. Married a couple of years, they live in Ajijic, Mexico. Bill's well-to-do parents cut him off for being a wastrel. He lives off his wife, is a heavy drinker, and drives a Porsche carelessly. When he starts to talk about Burke Damis (*see* Campion, Bruce), Helen shuts him up.

WILKINSON, HELEN. In *The Zebra-Striped Hearse*, she and Bill Wilkinson, wretchedly married, live in Ajijic on her money. She is almost twice his age. When Archer meets her, he recognizes her as Helen Holmes, a favorite old movie star. Bruce Campion, calling himself Burke Damis, a painter, sold her a picture. Her refusal to sell it back to him caused a falling out. Bill, who calls Helen a "sexoholic," talks too freely to Archer. Helen grabs a gun and fires it at Archer, who escapes.

WILLIAMS. In *The Goodbye Look*, he was Mrs. Florence Williams's deceased husband. They bought the Conchita Cabins, at Imperial Beach, from Conchita's estate.

WILLIAMS, MRS. DOROTHY. In *Blue City*, she is a neighbor in the apartment building where Francesca Sontag and Carla Kaufman live. Carla tells John Weather that Mrs. Williams drinks heavily, especially when the man supporting her is away.

WILLIAMS, MRS. FLORENCE. In *The Goodbye Look*, she and her late husband bought the Conchita Cabins, at Imperial Beach, from Conchita's estate thirty years ago. She tells Archer that Rita Shepherd (*see* Chalmers, Irene) and Eldon Swain shacked up there, and that Randolph Shepherd pursued them. Mrs. Williams can date these occurrences because she and her husband were listening at the time to radio reports concerning the Battle of Okinawa (April–June 1945).

WILLIE. In *The Galton Case. See* Brown, John (Jr.).

WILLS, DETECTIVE-LIEUTENANT HARVEY. In *The Ferguson Affair*, he investigates the Buenavista burglary ring and arrests Ella Barkin as a suspect. His investigation of the murders of Hector Broadman and Augustine Donato leads him to Larry Gaines. Gaines's relationship with Hilda Dotery is something William Gunnarson, Ella's lawyer, probes for Colonel Ian Ferguson, also Gunnarson's client. Gunnarson comes close to withholding evidence from Wills.

WILLS, DR. In *Black Money*, he is Montevista's deputy coroner. Archer disputes his opinion that Roy Fablon died of drowning in the ocean.

WILSON, COMMANDER. In *The Goodbye Look*, he was Dr. Ralph Smitheram's commanding officer of the *Sorrel Bay*, a U.S. Navy escort carrier in the Pacific. Lawrence Chalmers sent letters to his mother, Estelle Chalmers, containing plagiarized passages about Wilson from Smitheram's letters to his wife, Moira (1945). In them, Chalmers wrote about Wilson's Yale education, naval service, and death. This led to Chalmers's undoing when Archer shows Smitheram the evidence.

WINIOWSKI, MRS. In *The Three Roads*, she is a customer of Theodora Swanscott, who runs a lending library. Theodora telephones Mrs. Winiowski to tell her that *Forever Amber* [by Kathleen Winsor, 1946] has just become available.

WINKLER, JERRY. In *The Ferguson Affair*, he is an impoverished fellow living in a hotel next door to Manuel Donato's tamale shop. For $5, Winkler tells William Gunnarson about Augustine Donato's criminal activitivies.

WINOWSKY. In *The Drowning Pool*, he is the police photographer at the scene of Olivia Slocum's drowning.

WIONOWSKI, BESS. In *The Ivory Grin. See* Benning, Elizabeth.

WOLFE, DANIEL ("DANNY"). In *Meet Me at the Morgue*, he is Amy Miner's father. He runs a grocery store near San Diego. He tells Howard Cross about Amy's background. At Wolfe's store Howard Cross and Sam Dressen apprehend Amy.

WOLFSON, DR. In *The Barbarous Coast*, he is a Santa Monica physician Archer knows. After George Wall is battered by Lance Leonard, Archer takes him to Dr. Wolfson to be examined.

WOLSON, LIEUTENANT WILL. In *Trouble Follows Me*, he is the communications officer aboard the vessel on which Lieutenant Eric Swann also serves. Wolson tells Eric and Sam Drake about his suspicions concerning Hector Land, a black sailor on board.

WOOD. In *The Drowning Pool*, he and his family reside in the upscale Staffordshire Estates.

WOOD, MARGUERITE. In *The Ferguson Affair*, her name appears with other names in the clipping found in Larry Gaines's wallet.

WOOD, SHEILA. In *The Ferguson Affair*, her name is also in the clipping in Larry Gaines's wallet.

WRIGHT, COMMANDER. In *The Three Roads*, he is a medical officer in the San Diego naval hospital where Bret Taylor is a patient, suffering from amnesia. Wright and Dr. Theodore Klifter differ as to how best to treat patients. It is possible that Wright is so attracted to Paula West, Taylor's friend, that he may be slowing his treatment so she will visit the hospital often.

WRIGHT, MAJOR. In *Trouble Follows Me*, he is an Army physician, pompous but competent, aboard the Chicago–Los Angeles train, the passengers of which include Sam Drake and Private Rodney Hatcher. When Hatcher drinks ether-laced bourbon and dies, Wright examines him and advises Drake, who fortunately took only a few sips of the whisky.

"THE WRITER AS DETECTIVE HERO." *See On Crime Writing.*

"WRITING THE GALTON CASE." *See On Crime Writing.*

WYCHERLY. In *The Wycherly Woman*, he was Homer Wycherly's grandfather, who "made a farm out of semi-desert."

WYCHERLY. In *The Wycherly Woman*, he was Homer Wycherly's father, who struck oil on the family property outside San Francisco, founded a company, and started the Wycherly family fortune.

WYCHERLY, CATHERINE. In *The Wycherly Woman*, she was Homer Wycherly's ex-wife, thirty-nine or forty. She was a secretary and fancied herself a painter. Just before Catherine, eighteen, married Homer, twenty-one or -two years earlier, she had an affair with Carl Trevor, who was and still is married to Homer's sister Helen. Catherine gave birth to Carl's daughter, whom she and Homer, ignorant of the facts, called their daughter and named Phoebe. Catherine, already unfaithful to Homer with other men, and Carl, whose wife turned frigid after losing a child of her own, resumed their sexual relationship in the Conquistador, an apartment where she called herself Mrs. Smith. She divorced Homer, bought a house in Atherton, drank, and turned vulgar. Carl murdered her there. Carl called Catherine "Kitty."

WYCHERLY, HOMER. In *The Wycherly Woman*, he is the grandson and son of San Francisco men more successful than he. When well into his thirties, he married Catherine (*see* Wycherly, Catherine), then eighteen. Homer thinks the daughter that Catherine and Carl Trevor, Homer's sister Helen Trevor's husband, produced is his. The Wycherlys name her Phoebe Wycherly and live just outside San Francisco. Homer is the nominal head of his oil and land company, but Carl runs it. Homer took a two-month cruise aboard the *President Jackson*, on returning (January 7) learned that Phoebe was missing, and hires Archer the next day to investigate. It has been suggested that Homer Wycherly, vain, old, and feeble, resembles Alfred A. Knopf* in appearance and behavior.

Bibliography: Nolan.

WYCHERLY, PHOEBE. In *The Wycherly Woman*, she is nominally the daughter, twenty-one, of Homer and Catherine Wycherly. Phoebe is really Catherine's and Carl Trevor's child. When her "parents" argued, Phoebe blamed herself. She got pregnant by Robert Doncaster, transferred from Stanford to Boulder Beach College, where he is a student, and roomed with Dorothea S. Lang in the house of Mrs. Doncaster, Robert's mother. Phoebe and Robert drove to San Francisco to get married. But after seeing Homer off on a cruise, Catherine and Phoebe lived as Mrs. Smith and Miss Smith at the Conquistador. After Catherine was murdered, Phoebe pretends she is her mother and lives as Mrs. Smith in the Champion Hotel, then the Hacienda Inn. At the Hacienda bar, Phoebe fools Archer, hired by Homer to find Phoebe. Robert gets Phoebe to a motel where they register as Mr. and Mrs. Smith. Robert and Archer return her to Dr. Sherrill, her Palo Alto psychiatrist. Archer persuades the expectant lovers that life is worth living.

THE WYCHERLY WOMAN (1961). Novel. (Characters: Lew Archer, Dr. Broch, John Burns, Deputy Carstairs, Clement, Consuela, Jerry Dingman, Doncaster, Robert Doncaster, Mrs. Doncaster, Jessie Drake, Fillmore, Nick Gallorini, Jack Gayley, Mrs. Gayley, Sam Gayley, Alec Girston, Mrs. Alec Girston, Mrs. Sammy Green, Sammy Green, Dr. Grundle, Dr. Herman Grupp, Harry, Sheriff Herman, Sheriff Hooper, Dorothea S. Lang, William Mackey, Captain Theodore Mandeville, Lieutenant Mandeville, Mrs. Man-

deville, McEachern, Ben Merriman, Sally Merriman, Puddler Stanley Quil-
lan, Captain Lamar Royal, Dr. Sherrill, Mrs. Silvado, Deputy Snider, Mrs.
Spurling, Dr. Ambrose Sylvan, Thorne, Sam Todd, Tonia, Carl Trevor,
Helen Trevor, Dr. Wallace, Mrs. Watkins, Wycherly, Wycherly, Catherine
Wycherly, Homer Wycherly, Phoebe Wycherly.)

January 8. Archer drives from Los Angeles past oil derricks to Meadow
Farms, outside San Francisco, to Homer Wycherly's house, partly deco-
rated with his ex-wife Catherine Wycherly's paintings. Hired by Wycherly,
Archer learns this: Wycherly was seen off on a cruise aboard the *President
Jackson* to the South Seas (November 2), by Catherine Wycherly and
Phoebe, their daughter, twenty-one, a Boulder Beach College senior; the
Jackson returned to San Francisco (January 7); Homer learned that
Phoebe is missing. Archer, given a $500 retainer, must find her.

While Archer drives to Boulder Beach, Homer tells him that he nominally heads his rich family's oil company, but it is run by Carl Trevor,
Homer's sister Helen's husband, suffering after a coronary. Phoebe's ex-
landlady calls Phoebe "a spoiled rich brat" and feels she never intended
to return to school. Archer learns this from Dorothea S. ("Dolly") Lang,
Phoebe's ex-roommate: Phoebe met Robert ("Bobby") Doncaster, the
landlady's red-haired son, at the beach last summer; Bobby liked Phoebe;
Phoebe mentioned anonymous poison-pen letters arriving at the Wycherly house criticizing Catherine for adultery, was elated and depressed,
talked about suicide; when leaving, she said she would soon return. Archer notes Dorothea's typed class paper has a distorted "e."

Archer finds Bobby working in the basement, looks with him through
Phoebe's stored things, and learns this: Bobby and Phoebe met last August at the beach (he never told mamma); he suggested that Phoebe
transfer to Boulder Beach, got her a room in mamma's house, hoped to
marry her, noted her moodiness, helped her select a used Volkswagen;
she drove to San Francisco Friday, November 2, 1958. Archer tries to
force him to admit he accompanied her for the weekend. Bobby's domineering mother storms in, makes him deny everything, and threatens to
sue Archer.

Over lunch, Homer tells Archer this: Phoebe was upset by those hate
letters; Homer hired William Mackey, a San Francisco detective, to investigate, fired him, and destroyed the letters; the *Jackson* sailed a day late;
Homer wants Archer not to interview Catherine.

Archer gets Phoebe's VW license-plate number, drives to San Francisco,
boards the *Jackson*, and learns this from the purser and the master-at-
arms: Catherine and Phoebe boarded to see Homer off (November 2);
Catherine, drunk and obscene, argued with him; a taxi driver nicknamed
"Garibaldi" took the women to the St. Francis Hotel; Homer's steward
was black Sammy Green, of East Palo Alto. At the St. Francis, Archer finds
neither Phoebe's car nor Garibaldi. He phones Mackey's office, but he is

away. Archer finds and dials Catherine's number, which is disconnected. He drives to her home in Atherton. It is empty, and November newspapers are in the yard; a man with a bow tie draws "a nasty little gun," and waves him off. On to Palo Alto. Sammy's "handsome Negro" wife says he is visiting his parents.

At Woodside, beyond Stanford, is lush Leafy Acres, the home of childless Helen and Carl Trevor. Aloof Helen says this: She regrets not seeing Phoebe during Christmas vacation; Catherine despicably spoiled Phoebe's goodbye to Homer, as well as Carl's, aboard the *Jackson*; Catherine bought Captain Theodore Mandeville's house in Atherton. Carl, amiable, forceful, but ill, reveals this: Phoebe, like a daughter to him, was caught between quarreling parents; there was tension between Helen and Phoebe at the beach last August, where they casually saw Bobby. Carl gives Archer photographs of Phoebe and will ask local authorities to investigate Phoebe's disappearance, discreetly.

Ben Merriman's real-estate sign was at Catherine's house; so Archer goes to Ben's Camino Real office. His sexy, tipsy wife Sally is there. Archer professes interest in buying Catherine's house. A goateed roughneck with bruised knuckles enters, warns Ben's wife to keep Ben away from "Jessie," and leaves. When Sally says Archer might bribe new buyers into selling the Mandeville house, he takes Merriman's blotter with his photo, revisits the house, enters through the open door, and finds the man with the bow tie beaten to death. His driver's license names him as Ben Merriman, and his little gun is missing. Archer phones the police anonymously, returns to the gin-redolent Sally, and watches as she gets a phone call announcing Ben's death. She tells Archer that crazy Mandeville thought Ben cheated him during the resale, threatened him with a gun, and must have killed him.

Archer finds Mandeville's hotel address, goes there, and is courteously admitted. Mandeville, a retired Navy man, says this: Mrs. Mandeville died last spring, and he sold their memory-laden house for $50,000 to Ben Merriman; Ben resold it for $75,000 to Catherine Wycherly; she now lives in Sacramento's Champion Hotel. Mandeville's lawyer plans to sue Ben for fraud. When Archer says Merriman was murdered and the police will be questioning Mandeville soon, the old fellow, bridling, asks him to leave.

At the slummy Champion, Archer pretends to be looking for his wife, Catherine Wycherly. She left an hour ago. He rents a room. For $20, Jerry Dingman, the bellhop, reveals this: Catherine (really Phoebe) stayed about two weeks, mostly drinking; Mandeville (described by Archer) tried unsuccessfully to talk with her; Ben (identified from his picture) visited her last night, slapped her around; no girl resembling Phoebe in the photo visited Catherine; Catherine drove off with a big man (really Carl) not resembling Homer (according to Jerry's description), headed for the

Hacienda. Sneaking into her untidy room, Archer sees a Sacramento paper with the arrival of the *Jackson* checked.

On to the Hacienda, in Sacramento's fashionable outskirts. Archer joins the woman called Catherine at the bar, where she is drunk. Her sloppy talk reveals self-destructive sorrow and guilt. When she sees his holstered gun, she thinks he is a gangster. They go to her bungalow. She wants him to kill a man who gave her these black eyes. She turns seductive, suddenly retches, and passes out. He revives her and tells her that she wanted Ben dead, but that Ben is dead, and that Homer hired Archer to find Phoebe. Catherine insists she last saw Phoebe leaving their taxi in San Francisco November 2. Archer taunts her, opens her front door to leave, but is knocked unconscious by a masked man (Carl) wielding a tire iron.

Archer comes to and drives back to the Champion. Jerry calls Dr. Broch, who stitches Archer's head wound and says Catherine was so depressed that she ate great quantities of food in her room several days. Enough for two? (Phoebe was fattening up to resemble her mother.) The next morning Jerry brings Archer breakfast, after which he shows a maid Phoebe's picture. The maid says she may have seen her here. The hotel manager, Fillmore, tells Archer that Catherine was melancholy, had him cash a $3,000 alimony check New Year's Day, then stayed in her room for four or five days.

Back in San Francisco, Archer asks the taxi dispatcher to tell "Garibaldi" he wants to see him. Conferring with Carl, Archer reveals his suspicion that Ben, whose death he mentions, may have been blackmailing Catherine, who is capable of killing Phoebe for the insurance policy Carl says the Wycherlys bought when she was born. They phone Homer, still at Boulder Beach College and considering suing the trustees for improperly handling Phoebe's disappearance. Homer won't let Archer hire Mackey to find and follow Catherine while he continues to look for Phoebe. Carl reluctantly engages Archer, despite Carl's saying Homer dislikes him.

Archer lunches with Mackey, and over martinis and steaks learns this: Homer got the sheriff to confiscate evidence Mackey developed; Mackey won't pursue Catherine but does have "Thermofaxed" copies of one letter Homer wrote him and copies of the two letters calling Catherine an adulteress. When Mackey gives them to Archer, he notes a distorted "e."

On the street, Archer is approached by "Garibaldi" (real name: Nick Gallorini), who, when prompted and paid, reveals much: Catherine and Phoebe argued during their taxi ride from the *Jackson*; ten days later Gallorini saw Phoebe disheveled in the rain, gave her a free lift; Phoebe said she couldn't go to Woodside and an aunt (Helen) there who hated her; Gallorini drove her to the Conquistador near San Mateo, helped her into her upstairs corner apartment; a mean-talking "blondie guy . . . [with] a little chin beard" barged in and told him to get lost. Gallorini leads Archer, who follows in his own car, to the Conquistador. Pretending interest in renting, Archer learns from Mrs. Alec Girston, the manager's wife, that "Mrs. Smith" and her daughter—probably Catherine and Phoebe—rented rooms last fall, furnished them, departed, left their furniture. Archer cases the empty apartment, finds an initialed painting in it by Catherine, notes a possible bullet hole, goes next door to check, and is admitted by a talkative airhead named Jessie Drake. He learns and observes this: Jessie has a boyfriend named Stanley Quillan, with a record shop near San Carlos; sound equipment is scattered about; a drilled hole is in a wall baseboard. Ergo, Catherine's apartment was bugged. Archer drives ahead, with Gallorini following, to Stanley's shop. Gallorini identifies Stanley as the guy with Phoebe. Paying the taxi driver, Archer enters, recognizes Stanley as the goateed roughneck from Ben's office, shows him Phoebe's picture, and reminds him that he lived next door to Phoebe at the Conquistador a week or so in November. Stanley admits he knew her; but when Archer accuses him of bugging her place, Stanley pulls a gun. Archer leaves.

When Stanley drives off, Archer follows him to a house in Menlo Park with a Merriman real-estate sign wired to the gate. He plants a contact microphone on a window, listens, and learns this: Stanley and Sally Merriman, who is inside, are siblings; Ben lost money gambling in Las Vegas and Reno; Stanley and Ben planned the profitable resale of Mandeville's house; according to Jessie, who was the object of Ben's affections, he had $50,000 with him when he was murdered; neither sibling killed him, and the money is gone; Ben's safe contains a tape worth blackmail money; Stanley asks Sally to go get it, but she says she won't.

Archer parks near Stanley's shop, has a hamburger, and, when Stanley fails to appear, goes to the Conquistador. For $20, Alec Girston reveals this: Ben, a trickster, got Mrs. Smith (Catherine) the apartment; she said she painted; her daughter left with Ben in November; Ben planned to find a new house for Catherine; in March or April, she complained that Stanley was spying on her. Archer visits Jessie, who says Ben showed her lots of money, wanted to go to Mexico with her. Stanley phones. Jessie must do certain things for him, then meet him. Archer leaves, tails her cab ride to the International Airport, and spies on her there as she waits ninety minutes—for nothing. Night has fallen. Archer goads Jessie that Stanley has ditched her, drives her to Stanley's shop, and finds him shot dead with loose currency scattered about.

Captain Lamar Royal of the Redwood City police arrests Jessie, since she has old narcotics and prostitution charges pending, and wants to arrest Archer too, on suspicion that both killed Stanley. Archer is allowed one phone call. When it is to Carl Trevor, Royal becomes cooperative. Carl says Phoebe's VW may have been located, and Archer must drive him to Medicine Stone, where Carl has a summer place.

Archer picks up Carl, sick but determined, and, over his henpecking wife Helen's objections, drives him a hundred miles to Medicine Stone. On the way, Archer says Catherine could have killed both Ben and Stanley, who cheated her in the house sale. At the beach, Archer and Carl find several men, including a diver named Sam Gayley and his father, Jack, trying to raise the VW, stuck in rocks and filled with sand. Carl identifies the corpse already retrieved as Phoebe's, falls stricken by another coronary, and is rushed to the Terranova hospital. Archer talks with the Gayleys and is told this: A red-haired lad was at the beach last August; a car resembling Phoebe's was seen on November 2 driven fast toward the beach; Phoebe's corpse was in the back seat of the submerged car. This doesn't square with accounts by Gallorini, Girston, and Stanley of seeing Phoebe later. Archer visits the hospital, calls to tell Helen that Carl had another coronary but is resting, and is rebuked.

Archer gets to Boulder Beach, finds Bobby's mother, who admits Bobby could have been gone on November 2, received a phone call on Dolly's line, and driven away. Archer visits Dolly and tells her Phoebe is dead. Dolly says Bobby's call was from Palo Alto, but she didn't hear from whom. He checks her typewriter, and her typing matches the hate letters Mackey showed him. Dolly says the typewriter belonged to Phoebe, who left it behind. Archer gets the Palo Alto telephone number from the operator by saying he is Robert Doncaster, rings the number, but no one answers.

Lugging the typewriter along, Archer registers at the Boulder Beach Inn, where Homer Wycherly is staying. At 8:00 A.M., he stops by Homer's bungalow, gets him to identify the typewriter as Catherine's, and tells him the hate letters were typed on it and perhaps by Catherine. Only then does Archer say that his daughter Phoebe is dead and Carl keeled over upon viewing her body. Going on, Archer theorizes that so-called Mrs. Smith's daughter might be a girl posing as Phoebe after November 2.

Archer learns that Bobby phoned from a nearby gas station, goes there, learns from the attendant that a plump blonde used the phone, walked to the Fiesta motel nearby, and was followed by a man looking like a doctor. Archer finds Bobby's car at the motel and waits for him. He reluctantly admits much.

They go to Dr. Sherrill, Phoebe's psychiatrist, to whose Palo Alto sanitarium she has just returned. The following emerges: Bobby impregnated Phoebe last summer; they drove in her VW to San Francisco to marry; she saw Catherine and changed her mind; Phoebe evidently killed Catherine at her Atherton house; Ben walked in, helped load her body in the VW, which Bobby drove to the cliff and shoved over; Ben forced Phoebe to gain weight, impersonate her mother, give him Homer's alimony checks and the house-scam money; Phoebe entered the sanitarium yesterday, escaped to the Fiesta, returned with Sherrill. Sherrill theorizes that through guilt over her parents' divorce Phoebe, who may have written those hate letters, insanely fancies she killed Catherine. When Sherrill says Phoebe imagines she hired a gunman two nights ago to kill Ben, Archer says he was that man and Ben was already dead.

Letting Bobby wait, Sherrill takes Archer to see Phoebe. Her highly disordered words amount to this: Phoebe saw her mother and Carl smooching in a taxi, told Helen, who wrote the hate letters; Catherine, dying, told Phoebe "her father" (Catherine meant Carl, not Homer) killed her; to protect Homer, Phoebe told Bobby, then Ben, that she did the killing; later she told Ben about Homer; Ben planned blackmail, blackened her eyes when she wouldn't make love with him; through guilt, she ate and drank too much; Carl visited her at the Champion, initially thought she was embraceable Catherine; Phoebe told him Homer killed Catherine; Carl took her to the Hacienda, then to Sherrill.

Archer visits two people and learns this: Sammy Green, the *Jackson* steward, says Homer lacked time that first evening to get to Atherton and back on board. Next, Archer outfoxes sexy Sally Merriman into revealing that she retrieved a tape Ben said was worth money. Played, it was what Stanley recorded when he bugged Catherine, was Carl's and Catherine's pillow-talk, and reveals this: Catherine is alarmed that Phoebe saw her smooching with Carl; Carl is Phoebe's father and wants to tell her so; Catherine prefers the financially advantageous status quo. Resisting Sally's voluptuousness, Archer gives her $250 and leaves with the tape.

Archer visits Carl in the hospital, confronts him with the truth, forces him to write out a confession in return for handing him a bottle of enough digitalis pills to kill him, and sits waiting in the silent darkness.

The Wycherly Woman dramatizes the consequences when family members place money ahead of affection. Carl Trevor says, "Security. The great American substitute for love." To Dolly's psychobabble about assigning blame to others, Archer replies, "People should take a close look at themselves. Blaming is the opposite of doing that." *The Wycherly Woman* is unusually bookish. It contains references and allusions to Joseph Addison, Joseph Conrad, Dante, F. Scott Fitzgerald, and Ernest Hemingway. Moreover, Captain Mandeville's name may derive from Sir John Mandeville's; Phoebe, named after the classical huntress, is bagged by Archer; and Archer says that perhaps Sally ought to leave Camino Real for Ephesus.

Alfred A. Knopf* paid a $2,500 advance for *The Wycherly Woman*. It was originally titled "The Basilisk Look" and for a $5,000 fee was condensed in *Cosmopolitan* (April 1961) as "Take My Daughter Home." The novel was republished in London (Collins, 1962). Bantam began reprinting it in 1963. The back cover of one such Bantam paperback reads "The Wycherly Woman Was Twenty-one, rich and beautiful, But her body was in San Francisco Bay." This is one of the stupidest, most misleading climax-wreckers in publishing history. Not until chapter 21 of the 28-chapter novel does the reader learn that Phoebe is alive; in addition, she was not rich.

Bibliography: Nolan; Elmer R. Pry Jr., "Lew Archer's 'Moral Landscape,' " *Armchair Detective* 8 (February 1975): 104–107; Speir.

Y

YOGAN, SAM. In *The Doomsters*, he is a Japanese gardener working for Jerry and Zinnie Hallman. When Duane Ostervelt, the sheriff, harshly questions Yogan about Jerry's murder, he remains courteous but minimally informative. To throw investigators off the track, Dr. J. Charles Grantland tries unsuccessfully to implicate Yogan.

"YOU'LL FIND OUT ON JUDGMENT DAY." *See The Far Side of the Dollar*.

Z

ZANELLA, CLAIRE. In *The Ferguson Affair*, his name is in the clipping in Larry Gaines's wallet, as are other names.

***THE ZEBRA-STRIPED HEARSE* (1962).** Novel (Characters: Ada, Lew Archer, Sue Archer, Colonel Mark Blackwell, Harriet Blackwell, Isobel Blackwell, Mrs. Blackwell, Mrs. Sloan Buzzell, Ray Buzzell, Bill Campbell, Campion, Bruce Campion, Dolly Stone Campion, Jack Campion, Annie Castle, Peter Colton, Cruttworth, Dr. Edmund Burke Damis, Mrs. Damis, Miss Ditmar, Drake, Miss Letty Flavin, Detective Sergeant Sam Garlick, Miss Gomez, Haley, Jim Hanna, Keith Hatchen, Pauline Hatchen, Ronald Jaimet, Johnson, Evelyn Jurgensen, Thor Jurgensen, Thor Jurgensen, Jr., Nelson Karp, King, Fawn King, Kito, Mrs. Wesley Leonard, Sergeant Wesley Leonard, Marie, Mr. Merritt, Manny Meyer, Michelangelo, Deputy Patrick Mungan, Norton, José Perez, Chauncey Reynolds, Gladys Reynolds, Jim Rowland, Captain Lamar Royal, Henry Sholto, Molly Sholto, Quincy Ralph Simpson, Vicky Simpson, Claude Stacy, Elizabeth Stone, Jack Stone, Mona Sutherland, Todd, Arnie Walters, Phyllis Walters, Dr. White, Bill Wilkinson, Helen Wilkinson.)

Monday, January 17, 1961. In his Sunset Boulevard office, Archer interviews Isobel Blackwell, then her husband, Colonel Mark Blackwell. These facts emerge: Blackwell's first wife, Pauline, is the mother of their daughter, Harriet Blackwell, twenty-four, soon to inherit $500,000 from a deceased aunt. Divorced and remarried, Pauline lives in Ajijic, by Lake Chapala, near Mexico City, with her new husband (soon identified as Keith Hatchen). Blackwell has discouraged early love affairs of Harriet, who, now with her mother, has met an artist named Burke Damis in Mexico and wants to marry him. Blackwell asks Archer to determine whether Damis is a fortune hunter. Isobel Blackwell, Blackwell's pert, young second wife, doesn't get along well with Harriet and wants her to have her freedom.

Alone with Archer, Blackwell reveals this: Harriet and Damis flew from Mexico last week and dined with the Blackwells. Blackwell caught Damis looking through his wardrobe, to see "how the other half lives," he said. The two men argued. Earlier, Harriet wheedled Blackwell into letting Damis use their beach house near Malibu as a studio. Driving there, Archer finds the muscular fellow, about thirty, painting an abstract. Pretending he wants to rent the place, Archer is let in to look around. Harriet, tall and bony-faced, says she and her fiancé may soon depart, and kisses Damis, who is unresponsive and seems sad. Following Archer out, Harriet says she eavesdopped when daddy phoned to hire him. Archer's replies that she should help him, because her father would only hire a worse replacement detective. She reveals that Damis, an orphan, avoids discussing his background, is nonmaterialistic, met her in Mexico some weeks ago, and wants to marry her and live abroad simply.

While having some beer at a nearby shrimp diner, Archer sees a zebra-striped hearse disgorge six surfers—four lads and two girls—and then sees Harriet drive by, with Damis, toward Los Angeles. Archer follows, loses them, and reports to Blackwell's Bel Air residence. Damis is already there. Blackwell waves him off with a shotgun. Archer disarms Blackwell. Isobel comes out; then Harriet, all packed for travel. Announcing their imminent marriage, she and Damis drive away. Blackwell, discouraged, retires. Urging Archer to remain on the case, Isobel says she was married before, has known the Blackwells since Harriet's childhood, and married Blackwell just last fall.

Archer returns to the empty beach house and finds burned papers but also an airline envelope wedged in a sliding door to prevent it from rattling. It reveals that Q.R. Simpson flew on Mexicana Airlines from Guadalajara to Los Angeles (July 10). After photographing Damis's unfinished, wet painting, Archer proceeds to the airport. A clerk tells him that Simpson and Harriet landed July 10, but no one named Damis did. Archer learns from his friend Peter Colton of the D.A.'s office that Quincy Ralph Simpson was recently reported missing in San Mateo by his wife.

Archer flies to San Francisco, obtains Ralph Simpson's address, and taxis to it, near Luna Bay. Simpson's wife, Vicky, lets him in and reveals this: Ralph had a juvenile record, painted her portrait, gambled in Reno, claimed he did undercover work for the police, took his birth certificate when he left for Nevada two months ago, but does not resemble Archer's description of Damis. Vicky suddenly gets a phone call from the Citrus County police: The body of Simpson, about two months deceased, has just surfaced at a freeway construction project near Los Angeles. Archer and Vicky fly there, and at the mortuary she identifies Ralph's mangled remains. Death was caused by an icepick to the heart. With Vicky cared for overnight by Sergeant Wesley Leonard and his wife, Archer can drive home for some rest.

Tuesday. Archer checks with Miss Gomez, a Mexicana Airlines stewardess. She recalls that on July 10 Harriet and an unpleasant man, whose name she cannot remember, flew from Guadalajara to Los Angeles. Archer phones Blackwell, who authorizes him to fly to Guadalajara. During the flight, Miss Gomez says she checked the earlier seating chart, which named Q.R. Simpson as Harriet's companion. When he lands at Mazatlán, Archer must be vaccinated, queries the nice nurse, describes Damis, and ascertains that a Simpson was vaccinated there (May 10).

On to Mexico City. Archer takes a cab to Ajijic, gets a *posada* cottage, and learns from the night clerk, Claude Stacy, where Harriet's mother, Pauline Hatchen, is now living with her new husband. Late though it is, Archer taxis there, is invited in for a drink, and learns the following from an affected, rambling Pauline: Harriet so favored her father that Pauline deserted them, got a Reno divorce, met Keith Hatchen, a retired dentist also divorcing there, married him; they have retired to Mexico; Harriet came to visit about a month ago, seemed to want something of Pauline, quarreled, moved out, picked up good-looking, "arty" Burke Damis at the nearby *Cantina*, and was smitten by his attentiveness. Archer says Harriet intends to marry Damis. Does the name Q.R. Simpson mean anything to her? No. Archer adds this: Damis used Simpson's name while traveling; Simpson was murdered two months ago; he suspects Damis.

At the *Cantina*, Archer talks with the owner, a painter named Chauncey Reynolds. Introducing himself as a detective seeking Burke Damis, he learns this: Damis's closest male friend, Bill Wilkinson, drinks at The Place, no longer at the *Cantina*, ever since Reynolds argued over art with Helen Wilkinson, Bill's wife; Damis's girlfriend used to be Annie Castle, an "artsy-craftsy shop" owner; "Miss Blackstone," a tall, naive girl, came along and threw herself at Damis, who dumped Annie. Archer finds "Annie's Native Crafts," and rouses Annie. Attractive and sensitive, Annie says José Perez, the *Cantina* bartender, warned her that Archer was seeking Damis. Annie admits this: Damis needed a studio; she rented him a room, soon slept with him, partly financed him; Damis met Harriet Blackwell through the Wilkinsons, sold them a portrait he painted of a singular woman; argued with Helen when she wouldn't sell it back, hinted to Annie he had strangled a woman; Harriet boasted of her father's money and Lake Tahoe house. Annie gives him a self-portrait Damis painted for her.

Annie drives Archer to the Wilkinsons. Helen, a faded film star named Helen Holmes, lets him in, hints over drinks at Stacy's homosexuality, and says her young husband Bill quarreled with Damis and burned his painting. She won't discuss whom the portrait depicted, knows no Simpson, won't discuss Harriet. Forced out, Archer walks to the *posada*, rouses Stacy, identifies himself as a detective, and learns this while Stacy drinks: Helen's money supports Bill, wild and disinherited by his rich Texas family; Damis asked Helen to invite Harriet to a party; Bill soon got annoyed, threatened to tell the authorities rumors had it that Damis had killed his wife. Stacy drives Archer back to the Wilkinsons. Bill, returning from Guadalajara and drunk, says this: He and Helen were in San Francisco last May; while there, they saw a newspaper murder story which included a photograph of the strangled woman; Damis later partied at their house; when he painted a woman's portrait from memory, Bill recognized it as that of the murder victim and avoided Damis thereafter. Suddenly reappearing, Helen orders him to shut up. When Bill counters that she planned to blackmail Damis, she shoots at Archer and he flees.

Wednesday. Stacy drives Archer to the airport. Back in Los Angeles, he calls to tell Blackwell that Harriet and Damis could be at Tahoe, and phones a Reno detective named Arnie Walters to seek and detain Damis, whose actions and appearance he describes. He goes to Manny Meyer, a UCLA art critic, and shows him Damis's self-portrait and photos of his Bel Air painting. Meyer identifies the artist as Bruce Campion of San Francisco, praises his work, but says he is wanted for murdering his wife.

Archer drives to Blackwell's home and reports on Campion. Blackwell faints, comes to, and permits Archer to phone Captain Royal of the San Mateo police homicide division from Isobel's room. Royal says Campion's wife, Dolly Stone Campion, had their baby. Blackwell eavesdrops; when he hears Archer speak critically about him and his love-struck daughter, he fires him and leaves to get money to pay him. Isobel drives up, learns details, and rehires Archer with a cash advance.

Archer flies to Reno, is met by Arnie, and they drive to Blackwell's Tahoe lodge. Archer finds Harriet's bloody hat and veil in the water nearby. An area caretaker named Henry Sholto tells them Ralph Simpson helped Blackwell open the lodge early to show Isobel; Ralph gambled and stole something—according to a houseboy, now gone—and was fired; Ralph had a girlfriend named Fawn King, now at nearby State Line's Solitaire Club.

Dropped by Sholto at the club, Archer asks around, rents a car, and drives to Fawn's motel. The pretty girl, a shill to entice gamblers, explains: Fawn knew Ralph from school days in San Francisco; Ralph and Campion were friends from Army days in Korea; Campion, often sad, got his girlfriend Dolly to pose nude; Dolly became pregnant; Ralph played detective a week at Blackwell's lodge, said he learned something there, said the police withheld evidence after Dolly's murder; Campion had access to a lakeside cabin. While driving Fawn there, Archer tells her Ralph was murdered, perhaps by Campion. She is sad. She waits outside the cabin; inside, Archer finds the cabin owner, Dr. Edmund Burke

Damis, a Berkeley art department professor, abroad until last week. He knows Campion, admires his painting, dislikes his womanizing, lent him his cabin last August and September, was disgusted at finding it messy. Edmund is shocked when Archer says Campion is calling himself Burke Damis and perhaps murdered his wife, Dolly. Campion appeared here this morning, forced Edmund to lend him his Chevy convertible, and may be at the home of Campion's sister, Mrs. Thor Jurgensen of Menlo Park.

Leaving Fawn at the club, Archer phones Arnie and learns that the cops briefly spotted the elusive Campion at a Salina City motel. Archer goes there, quizzes the clerk, learns that Campion looked at the May 5th register, tried to get the clerk to remember if he saw him there. Is Campion trying to phony an alibi? Archer phones the Jurgensen house. No answer. Arriving there at 1:00 A.M., Archer sees Edmund's Chevy, observes Campion asleep in the house, lures him outside by a car-horn honk, knocks him unconscious, and tells the astonished neighbors to phone the Redwood City police.

Royal and Archer interview Campion, who is recovering in the hospital. The surly fellow denies involvement in his wife's murder. When his sister, Evelyn Jurgensen, and her husband rush in—they were in San Francisco overnight—Campion orders them away. Royal is convinced of Campion's guilt. When Archer expresses doubts, Royal invites him to go check "evidential details," which Deputy Patrick Mungan holds at the nearby Luna Bay substation. After a nightmare-haunted sleep in a Camino Real motel, Archer does so. He and Mungan, who are old friends, consider Campion's possible innocence. Campion was friendly with Ralph, who found Campion and Dolly a shack and paid the doctor when Dolly's baby was born last March. Dolly did not struggle when strangled. The baby, parked that May 5th night in a neighbor's car, had a leather button in his hand.

Thursday. Failing to find Ralph's wife, Vicky, Archer returns his car and flies from San Francisco to Los Angeles and locates Dolly's mother, Elizabeth Stone, at Citrus Junction. She expresses joy that Campion, Dolly's murderer, is caught. She lets Archer see Dolly's baby son, says Campion hinted he wasn't the father, mentions Fawn as Dolly's friend, adds that Dolly knew Ralph, and hints that Dolly associated with a married man once. Through Sergeant Leonard, Archer learns that Vicky is in a local hotel. She admits Ralph knew Campion and Dolly, adds that Dolly flourished money, doubts Ralph was Dolly's baby's father, says Campion gave his birth certificate to Ralph, who went to Nevada. Vicky says Ralph returned from Tahoe with a tweed coat missing a button. Archer suddenly remembers: A girl at the zebra-striped hearse had such a coat.

Archer drives to Malibu, learns from a highway patrolman that Ray Buzzell owns the striped hearse, and finds Ray's drunken mother, who says Ray and his surfing cronies are at Zuma beach. Archer drives there. Ray's girl is wearing the tweed coat, which they say washed ashore near the shrimp diner, on May 19. They determine this date by tide charts. They release the coat to Archer, who proceeds to the Blackwell residence. The maid says Blackwell is at Tahoe with the authorities, and Isobel has taken some sleeping pills and is resting. Archer's answering service reports two calls—one from Pauline, Harriet's mother, now at the Santa Monica Inn; the other, from Leonard. Pauline is out; Leonard, at home, wants to see Archer. Leonard lends Archer a silver-handled icepick, just found where Simpson's body was unearthed and already traced as purchased by Mrs. Stone. Archer goes with it to her home. The following emerges: Mrs. Jaimet, their lovely neighbor, was devoted to Dolly; when widowed Mrs. Jaimet sold her house to the Rowlands and moved to Santa Barbara three-plus years ago; the Rowlands' house was demolished during highway construction; Mrs. Jaimet remarried; Mrs. Stone sent the icepick, with matching corkscrew, as a wedding present. When Mrs. Stone praises Isobel Jaimet, Archer asks if her new name is Blackwell. Yes.

Archer returns to Leonard, gives him the coat, and is shown a cleaner's initials in it that can be identified. On to the Blackwell house. Pauline, there from the inn by taxi, shows Archer a letter received from Harriet successfully begging for a $5,000 loan because she and "Burke" want to wed. Archer says Burke is Campion, in jail. Pauline says Blackwell ruined Harriet by smother-loving her, precisely as his mother treated him.

Back to Isobel. Archer mentions the icepick, Ralph's death, Dolly's murder, his suspicions, and Ronald Jaimet, Isobel's first husband. Isobel says Dolly, whom she tried to educate informally, was overactive sexually and "made a play for Ronald." Archer theorizes: Blackwell, who she says was Ronald's cousin, may have killed him during a hike long ago, and perhaps Dolly, Ralph, and even Harriet too; Dolly's killer went to a nearby car with her baby, whose fist held a tweed-coat button. While Isobel rushes off to vomit, Archer finds a coat in Blackwell's closet with a cleaner's numbers identical to those in the tweed coat. Archer phones Arnie, says Campion asserts his innocence, learns Blackwell is not at Tahoe, and asks Arnie to have the cops find Harriet's car and hold Blackwell if possible. Isobel, freshened, returns; Archer, attracted to her, theorizes that Blackwell impregnated Dolly last summer and Ralph found the coat, confronted him with it; Isobel says Blackwell took the icepick. Arnie phones Archer, who says Blackwell probably killed Dolly and Ralph and is told that Harriet's car has been spotted near the Malibu shrimp diner.

Friday. Archer drives there before dawn, goes to Blackwell's beach house, and finds blood all over. Stunned, Blackwell confesses or half-admits this: Ronald hated Blackwell's attentions to Dolly; while hiking, Blackwell may have shoved Ronald; Dolly willingly had sex with Blackwell but when pregnant threatened to tell Harriet and demanded money from him; so he strangled Dolly, let Campion be blamed, killed Ralph for threatening him with the coat, slit Harriet's throat when she appeared here, and hid her corpse. Then Blackwell whips out a gun and kills himself.

Returning to Isobel, Archer explains: Blackwell told Harriet he got Dolly pregnant; Harriet told Isobel; Campion located Harriet in Mexico; psychologically deranged, Harriet attached herself to him, Dolly's widower; Campion was willing, so as to return home, clear his name through Blackwell; Campion told Harriet his motive; they argued; he hit her, thought he killed her; she escaped to daddy at Malibu, and to her death. Archer sees Campion in jail, gets him to reveal this: Campion married pregnant Dolly, met Harriet through her, pretended he and Harriet had first met in Mexico, was lured back north because of her money, resisted her demand that he divorce Dolly for her, finally concluded that Blackwell had impregnated Dolly.

About to fly from San Francisco to Los Angeles, Archer sees Annie Castle, up from Mexico to stand by Campion, whose arrest she read about. Archer tells her Campion is innocent, should soon be freed, illegally called himself Q.R. Simpson, partly caused Harriet's death. Annie stuns Archer by saying Harriet is alive in Guadalajara. Next Monday Archer flies there, finds her, tells her Blackwell shot himself. Harriet confesses that she was jealous of Dolly big-time, icepicked Ralph, buried him near Isobel's old house maybe with a purpose, threw the coat into the ocean, strangled Dolly, took her money, saved her baby, fought with Campion, drove to the beach house, cut her wrists, was saved by daddy, let daddy put her on the plane to Mexico. Archer persuades Harriet to waive extradition and return with him.

To prepare to write *The Zebra-Striped Hearse*, Macdonald visited Lake Tahoe briefly and, for ten days, an expatriate artists' hangout in Ajijic, Mexico. Discarded titles include "The Blackwell Imbroglio," "The Blackwell Tragedy," "The Living Eye," "Murder Country," "The People Watcher," and "The Whiteheaded Boy." For $5,000, Macdonald and Margaret Millar* prepared a 25,000-word condensation, which was published as "The Zebra-Striped Hearse" in *Cosmopolitan* (September 1962), before its November appearance in book form. The novel was issued in London (Cassell, 1963), then began to appear in paperback (Bantam, 1964; Collins/Fontana, 1965). Although reviews ranged from complimentary to rave in nature, sales were not substantial and nothing came of nibbles from Hollywood independent producers for movie options. A Czech edition appeared in 1968. The twin themes of *The Zebra-Striped Hearse* are the ruined family, and the sin of denial and escapism. The moral: Imitate splendid Annie Castle, who loves and helps others.

Bibliography: Nolan; Schopen; Speir.

ZIZI. In *The Way Some People Die*, he is the goofy, drunk pianist at The Den. Pretending he needs a fix, Archer bribes Zizi to say where he can find Mosquito, a drug source. Zizi, who calls Archer "boy friend," is probably homosexual.

General Bibliography

Allen, Dick, and David Chacko. *Detective Fiction: Crime and Compromise*. New York: Harcourt Brace Jovanovich, 1974.

Browne, Ray B. "Ross Macdonald: Revolutionary Author; or The Need for the Oath of Macdonald," *Journal of Popular Culture* 24 (Winter 1990): 101–111.

Bruccoli, Matthew J. *Ross Macdonald*. New York: Harcourt Brace Jovanovich, 1984.

———. *Ross Macdonald/Kenneth Millar: A Descriptive Bibliography*. Pittsburgh: University of Pittsburgh Press, 1983.

Carroll, Jon. "Ross Macdonald in Raw California," *Esquire*, June 1972, pp. 148–149, 188.

Evans, T. Jeff. "A Cultural Confluence: Ross Macdonald and F. Scott Fitzgerald." *Clues* 13 (Spring–Summer 1992): 21–43.

Grella, George. "Evil Plots." *New Republic*, July 26, 1975, pp. 24–26.

Holton, Judith, and Orley I. Holton. "The Time-Space Dimension in the Lew Archer Detective Novels." *North Dakota Quarterly* 40 (Autumn 1972): 30–41.

Lee, L. L. "The Art of Ross Macdonald." *South Dakota Review* 24 (Spring 1986): 55–67.

Macdonald, Ross. "Writing the Galton Case." In *On Crime Writing*. Santa Barbara, Calif.: Capra Press, 1963.

McCann, Sean. *Gumshoe America: Hard-Boiled Crime Fiction and the Rise and Fall of New Deal Liberalism*. Durham, N.C., and London: Duke University Press, 2000.

Margolies, Edward. *"Which Way Did He Go: The Private Eye in Dashiell Hammett, Raymond Chandler, Chester Himes, and Ross Macdonald*. New York and London: Holmes & Meier Publishers, 1982.

Nolan, Tom. *Ross Macdonald: A Biography*. New York: Scribner, 1999.

Roth, Marty. *Four & Fair Play: Reading Genre in Classic Detective Fiction*. Athens: University of Georgia Press, 1995.

Schopen, Bernard A. *Ross Macdonald*. Boston: Twayne, 1990.

Sipper, Ralph B., ed. *Inward Journey: Ross Macdonald*. New York: Mysterious Press, 1984.

Skenazy, Paul. "Bringing It All Back Home: Ross Macdonald's California." *South Dakota Review* 24 (Spring 1986): 68–110.

Skinner, Robert. *The Hard-boiled Explicator: A Guide to the Study of Dashiell Hammett, Raymond Chandler, and Ross Macdonald*. Metuchen, N.J.: Scarecrow Press, 1985.

Sokolov, Raymond A. "The Art of Murder." *Newsweek*, (March 22, 1971): 101–108.

Speir, Jerry. *Ross Macdonald*. New York: Frederick Ungar, 1978.

———. "The Ultimate Seacoast: Ross Macdonald's California," in *Los Angeles in Fiction: A Collection of Original Essays*, ed. David Fine, pp. 133–144. Albuquerque: University of New Mexico Press, 1984.

Steiner, T. R. "The Mind of the Hardboiled: Ross Macdonald and the Roles of Criticism." *South Dakota Review* 24 (Spring 1986): 29–54.

Symons, Julian. *Bloody Murder: From the Detective Story to the Crime Novel*. 3rd rev. ed. New York: Mysterious Press, 1992.

Warner, Nicholas O. "City of Illusion: The Role of Hollywood in California Detective Fiction," *Armchair Detective* 16 (1983): 22–25.

Wolfe, Peter. *Dreamers Who Live Their Dreams: The World of Ross Macdonald's Novels*. Bowling Green, Ohio: Bowling Green University Popular Press, 1976.

Index

Note: Peripheral and incidental references, including nonsubstantive references to titles of works that did not evidently influence Macdonald, are omitted. Nicknames, alternate names, and subtitles are also omitted. Page references to main entries are in **boldfaced type**.

Stone, Elizabeth (*The Zebra-Striped Hearse*), **268**

Stone, Jack (*The Zebra-Striped Hearse*), **268**

Strang, Mrs. (*The Drowning Pool*), **268**

Strome (*Black Money*), **268**

Strome, Ella (*Black Money*), **268**

Strome, William (*The Underground Man*), **268**

Stump, Alvin, **269**

Sturm, Margaret Ellis (wife), 226. *See also* Millar, Margaret

"The Suicide," 6, 191-92, 219, **269**

"The Suicide Room," 139

Sullivan (*The Way Some People Die*), **269**

Summer, Jo (*Find a Victim*), **269–70**

Sunderland, Dr. (*The Instant Enemy*), **270**

Sunderland, Eddie (*The Goodbye Look*), **270**

Sunderland, Laura (*The Chill*), **270**

Sunderland, Mona (*The Zebra-Striped Hearse*), **270**

Swain, Eldon (*The Goodbye Look*), **270**

Swain, Louise (*The Goodbye Look*), **270–71**

Swainie (*Blue City*), **271**

Swann, Helen (*Trouble Follows Me*), **271**

Swann, Lieutenant Eric (*Trouble Follows Me*), **271**

Swanscutt, Franklin (*The Three Roads*), **271**

Swanscutt, Theodora (*The Three Roads*), **271–72**

Sweetner, Al (*The Underground Man*), **272**

Swift (*The Moving Target*), **272**

Swift, Lefty (*The Three Roads*), **272**

Swift, Ronald (*Blue City*), **272**

Swift, Sammy (*The Barbarous Coast*), 218, **272**

Sylvan, Dr. Ambrose (*The Wycherly Woman*), **272**

Sylvester, Audrey (*Black Money*), **272**

Sylvester, Dr. George (*Black Money*), **273**

Sylvester, Joe (*The Far Side of the Dollar*), **273**

Sylvie (*The Dark Tunnel*), **273**

Symons, Julian, **273–74**

Taggert, Alan (*The Drowning Pool*), 216, **275**

"Take My Daughter Home," 324

Tappinger (daughter) (*Black Money*), **275**

Tappinger (son) (*Black Money*), **275**

Tappinger, Bess (*Black Money*), **275**

Tappinger, Taps (*Black Money*), **275–76**

Tappinger, Teddy (*Black Money*), **276**

Tappingham (*The Drowning Pool*), **276**

Tarantine, Joseph (*The Way Some People Die*), **276**

Tarantine, Mario (*The Way Some People Die*), **276**

Tarantine, Mrs. Joseph (*The Way Some People Die*), **276**

"The Tarantula Hawk," 37

Tarko, Hairless (*Find a Victim*), **276**

"A Taste of Fire," 104

Taylor, Bret (*The Three Roads*), **277**

Taylor, George Watt (*The Three Roads*), **277**

Taylor, Lorraine (*The Three Roads*), **277**

Teagarden (*Blue City*), **277**

Terhune, Terry (*Blue City*), **277**

Tessinger, Mrs. (*Trouble Follows Me*), **277**

Tessinger, Rita (*Trouble Follows Me*), **278**

Thatcher, Simmie (*Meet Me at the Morgue*), **278**

Theo (*The Chill*), **278**

The Theory of the Leisure Class (Veblen), 29

Theuriet, Paul (*The Ivory Grin*), **278**

Thomas (*The Dark Tunnel*), **278**

Thompson (*The Chill*), **278**

About the Author

ROBERT L. GALE is Professor Emeritus of English at the University of Pittsburgh. His previous books include *A Dashiell Hammett Companion* (2000), *An Ambrose Bierce Companion* (2001), and *A Lafcadio Hearn Companion* (2002), all available from Greenwood Press.